THE MODERN LIBRARY

OF THE WORLD'S BEST BOOKS

AN ANTHOLOGY OF IRISH LITERATURE

THE MODERN LIBRARY

OF THE WORLD'S BEST BOOKS

AN ANTHOLOGY

OF IRISH

LITERATURE

The publishers will be pleased to send, upon request, an illustrated folder setting forth the purpose and scope of THE MODERN LIBRARY, *and listing each volume in the series. Every reader of books will find titles he has been looking for, handsomely printed, in definitive editions, and at an unusually low price.*

AN ANTHOLOGY OF IRISH LITERATURE

EDITED, WITH AN INTRODUCTION, BY

David H. Greene, NEW YORK UNIVERSITY

THE MODERN LIBRARY · NEW YORK

Library of Congress Catalog Card Number: 54-6896

Random House IS THE PUBLISHER OF *The Modern Library*

BENNETT A. CERF · DONALD S. KLOPFER · ROBERT K. HAAS

Manufactured in the United States of America by H. Wolff

CONTENTS

INTRODUCTION

I

IRELAND today is an independent republic with little but her independence to compensate her for centuries of agitation. She is dollar poor. Her population is shrinking because of emigration and the lowest marriage rate in Europe. The only influence she wields in the society of nations is through the millions of Irishmen who are citizens of other countries. But she helps feed other nations with her beef and potatoes, clothe them with her homespuns and make them happy with Jameson's Irish whiskey and Guinness' beer. She also continues to produce writers who display an attitude to their craft which can only be explained by the fact that an ancient poetic tradition is still alive.

The Celtic poet of old practiced his art according to rules which had been formulated as early as the eighth century and continued to be enunciated as late as the sixteenth century. His people considered him a vital part of their society and awarded him a privileged position, which he managed to retain among the country people at least until modern times. His power for satire made him so formidable a foe that nobody dare cross him. He once became the center of a fierce controversy in which he was accused of having too much power and threatened with banishment, but one of the greatest of Irish saints (St. Columkille) intervened in his behalf. Like the priest he eventually became the target of oppressive legislation directed at him by the English who conquered his people. Even today the title of poet has a meaning in Celtic countries which it does not have anywhere else in western Europe.

The modern Irish poet cannot fail to be aware of this. Neither exile—the customary fate of Irish writers—nor the fact that he writes in English, which his ancient predecessors considered the language of a foreign enemy, makes him any less conscious of the heritage. The greatest of modern Irish poets, who knew scarcely a word of Gaelic, wrote at the very threshold of his career, "Can we not build up . . . a national literature which shall be none the less Irish in spirit from being English in language?" Yeats knew that a literary movement taking its inspiration from the Gaelic past as the Irish Literary Revival did must avoid mere antiquarianism. "Can we not keep the continuity of the nation's life," he wrote, "by translating or retelling in English which shall have an indefinable Irish quality of rhythm and style, all that is best of the ancient literature? Can we not write and persuade others to write histories and romances of the great Gaelic men of the past, from the son of Nessa to Owen Roe, until there has been made a golden bridge between the old and the new?" The golden bridge between the old and the new was to be built by listening to the country people upon whose lips the tales of the Fiana were still alive, and who spoke English with that "indefinable Irish quality of rhythm and style." Irish writers, Synge wrote in the preface to one of his plays, "start with a chance that is not given to writers in places where the springtime of the local life has been forgotten, and the harvest is a memory only, and the straw has been turned into bricks."

II

LOOKING back to the earliest point in history where the tradition can be observed, we find that the poet of ancient Ireland, called a *fili,* was a professional who had gone through many years of training so that he could discharge the official duties of composing in verse the laws and genealogies, and listing the kings, festivals and traditions of his people. Much of what he wrote should probably be described as state papers, put into verse because they could more easily be memorized and recited by the bards, who were strictly performers, not composers, and who came to be the walking repositories of the national traditions. Many of the Irish manuscripts which have survived—there are, for example, more than thirteen hundred in the Royal Irish Academy alone—are treatises on ecclesiastical, historical and learned subjects having only a subsidiary interest for the student of imaginative literature. But the body of narrative tales and poems of warfare, romance and adventure —of deities or mortals, or of both—is impressive in bulk and imaginative power and is probably older than the vernacular literature of any other western European people.

The story of how this literature of the ancient Celt has come down to us largely centers about the scribe, that consummate artist who copied, illustrated and annotated the great stories of his people and treasured up the lifeblood of long-dead master spirits in great folio vellum manuscripts—each one of them a whole library in itself. *The Book of the Dun Cow,* the work of a scribe who died in 1106, gives us many of the Ulster sagas and some Fenian pieces. *The Book of Leinster,* written before 1160, gives us history, genealogy, imaginative stories of place names, poetry and some of the same stories found in *The Book of the Dun Cow. The Great Book of Lecan, The Book of Hy Many, The Book of Ballymote, The Speckled Book of MacEgan, The Book of Lismore* and *The Book of Fermoy,* all written in the fourteenth and fifteenth centuries, are some of the other important manuscripts.

Since none of these compilations was made before the twelfth century, the language of the tales they give us is largely Middle Irish. The stories themselves, however, are not of the Middle Irish period but are for the most part Old Irish texts modernized by the scribe, who altered the language so as to bring it into some agreement with that of his own day. It has been possible to determine on the basis of the Old Irish word forms and inflectional marks which still remain in a twelfth-century text that the story it tells has gone through several such modernizations since it was first committed to writing some three or four hundred years earlier.

For our knowledge of Old Irish we are chiefly indebted not to the scribe who compiled the great Middle Irish vellums of the twelfth and succeeding centuries but to his predecessor of the ninth century, particularly the scribe in the Irish monasteries on the continent who in transcribing a text of St. Paul or Priscian was given to providing his reader with marginal paraphrases or amplifications of the text, not in Latin but in his native language. It was these Old Irish glosses which supplied modern philologists with the key to the language of ancient Ireland. In addition to glossing his text—and this appears to have been characteristic of only Irish scribes at this time—the Irish scribe also used the margins for recording personal observations, prayers to his favorite saint and snatches of poetry from his native land. Thus we find in a manuscript of Priscian in the monastery of St. Gall, Switzerland, a short poem on the enjoyment a scribe has working in the open air after a long winter indoors ("The Scribe," p. 10) and a quatrain commenting on the fact that although bad weather is uncomfortable it discourages Viking raids ("The Viking Terror," p. 3). In a codex of St. Paul in the monastery of St. Paul in Carinthia, Austria, we find a poem in praise of a Leinster chieftain named Aed ("In Praise of Aed," p. 9) and the celebrated poem about a scholar and his favorite cat ("Pangur Ban," p. 11).

These brief lyrics—originally the work of hermit poet and *fili* of the seventh, eighth and ninth centuries—are the earliest examples we have in manuscript of the imaginative literature of the medieval Celt. Not all of them are preserved in continental manuscripts. For example, *The Martyrology of Angus the Culdee*, from which a charming poem about St. Ita (p. 13) who nurses the baby Jesus in a vision is taken, is a ninth- or tenth-century festology or calendar of saints' days, composed in Ireland by a monk named Angus. (*Culdee* in Old Irish means *fellow of God* and was apparently used to describe an ascetic monk.) Angus was patriotic. In recording the festivals of saints he was partial to Irish saints, particularly if they also had some claim to literary eminence. His glosses and notes are extensive. They give us, for example, a personal description of St. Columkille and tell a story about the subject of the poem "On a Dead Scholar" (p. 14) who was "master in theology, in history, in Brehon law and in poetry" and who greedily hid his books so that St. Columkille, who was visiting him, could not borrow them. "So Columkille left a curse on the books," writes Angus. " 'May that which thou grudgest be useless after thee,' said he. And so it was, for the books abide still, but no man can read them."

Turning from these glosses to the longer pieces preserved in the great vellum manuscripts of the Middle Irish period, we find the bulk of early Irish imaginative literature classified into types. The most famous group of stories is the Ulster cycle. Cuchulain, about whom Yeats wrote no fewer than five plays, is the central hero. The stories deal with the ancient kingdom of Ulster, its king Conchubor MacNessa and the warriors of the Red Branch House. Modern scholarship and tradition agree in assigning a date of the first century before Christ to the heroes and events. But the stories did not assume literary form until the seventh century, and they have come down to us in recensions made no earlier than the eighth century.

The Cattle Raid of Cooley, the great epic of the Ulster cycle, which tells the story of how Maeve, queen of Connaught, stole a prize bull and fought a war over it with Cuchulain and the men of Ulster, is preserved in *The Book of the Dun Cow* and also in *The Book of Leinster*. Cuchulain had to fight Maeve's army single-handed because the men of Ulster were all stricken with birth pangs as the result of an ancient curse levelled against them for an indignity they once administered to a pregnant goddess. Among Cuchulain's feats was the defeat of Ferdiad, his boyhood friend and sworn brother, who with other Ulster warriors had gone over to the enemy after the betrayal of the sons of Usnech by Conchubor, the king of Ulster. The lamentation (p. 66) which the hero utters over the body of his friend is one of the most moving passages in Irish literature.

"The Tragic Death of Connla" (p. 61), preserved in *The Yellow Book of Lecan*, is an Irish equivalent of the story of Sohrab and Rustum. When Cuchulain was in Scotland he defeated and seduced an amazon named Aife, who gave birth to his son. When the boy Connla came to Ireland he was forced into a fight to the death with his own father because he had been instructed never to refuse combat and never to divulge his identity on demand. Such injunctions, by which many Irish heroes, including Cuchulain, were bound, were called geasa. Modern readers are familiar with the story through Yeats's poem "Cuchulain's Fight With the Sea" (p. 428) and his play *On Baile's Strand*, in which the hero is deluded by a Druid's spell into taking his anger out on the waves of the sea, a modern addition to the story.

But heroes must die, and the story of Cuchulain's death is told in "The Death of Cuchulain" (p. 68), from *The Book of Leinster*. The story has survived in a fragment, however, and we must go to later versions to learn that Cuchulain's old enemy Maeve assembles another army, supplemented this time by the sons of men whom Cuchulain had killed. She once more times her attack so that he has to fight singlehanded, this time knowing that he is doomed because he has violated one of his *geasa*. Help from the men of Ulster does not arrive until Cuchulain has died against a stone pillar to which he had lashed himself with his belt so that he might meet death on his feet.

The most famous single story from the Ulster cycle, however, does not deal with Cuchulain but with Deirdre. "The Story of Deirdre" (p. 76), from *The Book of Leinster*, has furnished many modern Irish writers, including Yeats, Synge (p. 451), AE and James Stephens, with a theme for tragedy, epic or romance. In its essentials—the destruction of Deirdre and her lover Naisi by Deirdre's betrothed, Conchubor—it resembles the story of Tristan and Iseult and also the great romance of the Fenian cycle, "The Pursuit of Diarmait and Grania."

The next great collection of stories is the Fenian cycle, which deals with bands of semi-nomadic warriors known as the *fiana*. The most important of the leaders of the *fiana* was Finn MacCumail, whose *fian*, it appears, was composed of two clans, one commanded by himself, the other by Goll MacMorna, who had slain Finn's father at the battle of Cnucha. Though Finn is at first reconciled to Goll, warfare ultimately breaks out between the two clans and Goll is destroyed. Other heroes associated with Finn are his son Oisin, Oscar son of Oisin, Cailte son of Ronan and Diarmait, who elopes with Grania, Finn's betrothed. In modern times Oisin's fame eclipsed his father's when the eighteenth-century Scottish poet James Macpherson published "An Ancient Epic Poem in Six Books" purporting to be a translation of a third-century Fenian poem written by

Oisin. Macpherson's *Fingal* took the public by storm, and before the fraud was exposed the Fenian hero had become famous throughout Europe, then in the grip of the romantic movement, as an example of "the noble savage."

Finn and his companions are generally believed to have lived in the third century, three hundred years later than Cuchulain. There are other differences between the two cycles. The action of the Ulster cycle is located mainly in Connaught and Ulster, the north of Ireland, the texts are mostly of the Old Irish or early Middle Irish periods and the tales are heroic in temper. They give the impression of having been the property of an aristocratic people who were preserving the record of their own past. The action of the Fenian cycle is confined mainly to Leinster and Munster, the south of Ireland, the texts are mostly of the late Middle Irish period and the tales and poems are romantic in temper, their most characteristic form being the ballad. They give the impression of having been the property of a subject race. Finally the *Fiana*, with their strange initiation rites, are a feature of the Fenian tradition for which there is no parallel in the older cycle. The warrior had to pass prescribed physical ordeals, excel in the twelve traditional forms of poetry and renounce family life within the tribe for a life outside it ("The Fianna," p. 95).

"The Colloquy of the Old Men" (p. 81), preserved in two fifteenth-century manuscripts and in a manuscript of the seventeenth century, is a formless compilation of Fenian stories from many sources, some of them clearly inconsistent with others. The narrative tells how a handful of warriors, including Oisin and Cailte, not only survived the disastrous defeat of Finn and his *fian* at the Battle of Ventry but also managed to live for a century and a half after the battle so that they could meet St. Patrick and regale him with stories of the heroic past. After visiting Finn's old governess, who has also defied the ravages of time, Oisin disappears forever into a fairy mound, but Cailte and his companions go south to Tara. The meeting with St. Patrick results in the conversion of the Fenians to Christianity. The stories which Cailte tells of the mighty Finn enthrall the saint and his clerics so much that

Patrick has a guilty conscience. Finally his two guardian angels assure him that it is not only proper for him to listen to pagan tales but necessary so that he might be the agent of the preservation for posterity. The pleasant synthesis of Fenian paganism and Patrician Christianity contrasts sharply with a later ballad on the same theme in which St. Patrick denounces the Fenians as sinful pagans and is defiantly told that it is better to be in Hell with Finn than in heaven with flimsy angels.

"The Colloquy of the Old Men" bears an obvious relationship to "Oisin in the Land of Youth" (p. 105), a poem written by an eighteenth-century poet named Michael Comyn, in which Oisin's longevity is explained by his having been in *Tir na n-Og*, a kind of Celtic Shangrila. Comyn's poem is one of the great achievements of later Gaelic poetry. Published with translation for the first time in 1859 in *The Transactions of the Ossianic Society*, it provided Yeats with the material for his narrative poem "The Wanderings of Oisin."

The other great collection of Fenian stories is "The Poem Book of Finn," a seventeenth-century manuscript with an interesting history of its own. Characteristic of the stories in this collection are "The Headless Phantoms" (p. 96), in which Finn and his companions fight a desperate hand-to-hand encounter in a darkened house with headless apparitions; "The Bathing of Oisin's Head" (p. 100), in which the aged warrior on his deathbed laments the passing of "the fair hair that all men saw on my head; it has left me for good and all, till I am a disease-smitten grey-face"; and "Goll's Parting With His Wife" (p. 103), in which Finn's rival, cornered by his enemy on a crag, urges his wife to leave him before he is slain.

Not all, or necessarily the best, of early Irish literature belongs to these two heroic cycles. The mythological cycle, for example, which is made up of tales dealing with exploits of supernatural beings from the Celtic pantheon, contains some of the best stories in Irish literature. "The Dream of Oenghus" (p. 39), which gave Yeats the material for one of his poems, tells the story of Angus Og the master of love, who pined for a girl he had seen in a dream only to discover when he found her in the flesh, after long searching, that it was swan's flesh.

How he became a swan in order to "paddle in the cold companionable streams or climb the air" with her provides an interesting contrast to the classical myth in which Zeus became a swan in order to effect a union with a mortal.

The ancient Celt was apparently fond of tall tales and adventures, if one can judge by the texts which have come down to us. The early scribes distinguished between a Voyage (*Imram*), which was merely a traveller's tale, and an Adventure (*Echtrae*), which was an account of a visit to the other world. Only three Voyages have survived, the most interesting being "The Voyage of Maelduin," which apparently influenced the author of the famous medieval story of the voyage of St. Brendan the Navigator. *The Voyage of Bran* (p. 131) is perhaps the best known of the Adventures. It is preserved in seven different manuscripts, the oldest of which, from *The Book of the Dun Cow*, is unfortunately a fragment. Kuno Meyer, who published an edition of the text in 1895, was able to reconstruct the entire poem from later copies belonging to the fourteenth, fifteenth and sixteenth centuries.

The Frenzy of Suibhne ("Mad Sweeney" p. 143), a Middle Irish romance, belongs to the Historical cycle, or the "Cycles of the Kings" as these tales are frequently referred to. Although the action in these stories, unlike that in the Ulster, Fenian or Mythological cycles, the Adventures or the Voyages, revolves around historical personages, the blending of history and legend is frequently so complete as to make it impossible for the modern reader to distinguish fact from fiction. Certainly the author of *The Frenzy of Suibhne* found the historical framework of his story no deterrent in utilizing legendary material or in exercising his imagination. The madness which came upon Sweeney, ruler of a petty kingdom in southern Antrim and County Down, was the result of a curse laid upon him by St. Ronan. Sweeney had interrupted the saint in the act of pacing off boundaries for a new church by throwing the saint's psalter into the lake and laying hands on him. The saint was saved by the arrival of a messenger summoning Sweeney to the battle of Mag Rath, an actual battle fought in 637 between the king of Ireland and the king of Dal Riada, an Irish kingdom in Scotland which included a small part of Ulster. Sweeney's wits went astray at the height of the battle, and he fled thenceforth to wander naked through Ireland, flitting from tree to tree like a bird. Whether or not the remarkable poetry which Sweeney utters was part of the metamorphosis which the saint prophesied is not made clear. But Sweeney mad achieved a fame which Sweeney sane could only have envied. George Moore believed that the story of Sweeney's madness was one of the world's great stories. Flann O'Brien is indebted to it for the motif—and large parts of the text—of his satire *At Swim-Two-Birds*. William Saroyan is indebted to it for the title of his play *Sweeney in the Trees*. Although *The Frenzy of Suibhne* survives in three relatively late manuscripts, the most important having been written between 1671 and 1674 in County Sligo, the story is older than the twelfth century. In fact a poem called "The Ivy Crest" (p. 19) is attributed to Sweeney the Mad in a ninth-century manuscript.

III

After the Norman invasion of Ireland in 1170 the rule of the *fili*, who composed poetry, blended with that of the bard, who recited it. The word *bard* is Celtic and during the Middle Irish period, between the twelfth and seventeenth centuries, was applied to a professional poet attached to the household of a chieftain whose achievements he recorded and recited in verse. The bardic poet belonged to a privileged, hereditary class and practiced a profession in which membership was carefully restricted on a family basis. The poetry he wrote was dominated by formal conventions. The tricks of the trade were passed on only to those who were eligible and willing to study for six or seven years in a school presided over by a master bard.

A trustworthy account of life in the Irish bardic schools, written before 1722 in Tipperary where the tradition lingered, tells us that the neophyte attended regular classes during a school term which ran from November to March, lived in a cubicle and did homework which consisted of composing a poem on an assigned theme while he lay in darkness upon his bed. In the morning he recited his poem to the teacher who criticized it. Although the core of the curriculum was obviously metrics—bardic poetry was written in complicated meters and was characterized by an elaborate system of rhyme, assonance, consonance and alliteration—the student had also to acquire a knowledge of the legends and history of his people and become an educated man generally.

Edmund Spenser was almost certainly describing bardic poems of the formal kind when he wrote in *A View of the Present State of Ireland*,

> I have caused divers of them to be translated unto me, that I might understand them; and surely they savoured of sweet wit and good invention, but skilled not of the goodly ornaments of poetry; yet were they sprinkled with some pretty flowers of their natural device which gave good grace and comeliness unto them, the which it is great pity to see so abused, to the gracing of wickedness and vice, which with good usage would serve to adorn and beautify virtue. This evil custom therefore needeth reformation.

It hardly needs to be pointed out that Spenser was an enemy and that he held an altogether different view of the nature and function of poetry. His judgment upon this "evil custom" was prompted more by political than aesthetic considerations, for the Irish bardic poet exercised a political influence which made him dangerous. Had not The Statute of Kilkenny in the fourteenth century forbade under penalty of heavy fine the harboring or encouraging of Irish minstrels, rhymers or taletellers?

The influence of the bard was not entirely secular. There is evidence which indicates that bardic schools were sometimes affiliated with monastic schools so that the training of both bard and cleric could be mutually enriched. We have a large body of religious poetry written within the bardic tradition. But mostly the bard depended for his existence upon a society composed of powerful clans and ruled over by affluent chieftains. After the Williamite War of the seventeenth century, when the Gaelic order had been destroyed and the last of the chieftains had fled to the continent, the bard fell on evil days.

Looking through the volumes of bardic poetry which have

been published by the Irish Texts Society, one wonders why Irish poetry allowed itself to get sidetracked for nearly four hundred years. The bard was a professional and seldom put his pen to any use for which he was not paid. And since he was paid chiefly to compose only formal verse which glorified his patron we can thank him for little of the personal or popular poetry written in Ireland during the period. With few exceptions, therefore, the bardic poems do not appeal to modern taste any more than they did to Spenser's. In fact the only good one can see in a system which left the writing of personal verse largely to amateurs, discouraged originality of thought or expression, and made writing poetry a mystery into which only the elite could be initiated was that it helped to save the language, preserved the tradition and gave Irish writers of a later period the historical sense so indispensable, as T. S. Eliot says, to a literature that would achieve maturity.

The most famous of the court poets would appear to have been Tadhg Dall O'Huiginn. Of the forty poems ascribed to him which survive in manuscript copies none are in the author's hand and only two could have been copied in his lifetime. According to the popular traditions about him which flourished as late as the eighteenth century, he was born about 1550 and brought up in Donegal, was attached to the household of the chieftain O'Connor Sligo, was blind for all or most of his life—his middle name means *blind*—and was murdered in 1593 by members of the O'Hara clan whom he had satirized in one of his poems. Tradition has apparently been more faithful in preserving biographical facts about him than it has the texts of his poems, for his editor Eleanor Knott believes that the surviving poems represent only a small part of his entire work.

Six years after their defeat at Kinsale in 1601, the earls of Tyrone (Hugh O'Neill) and Tyrconnell (Rory O'Donnell, the brother of Red Hugh O'Donnell) fled to the continent with the surviving members of their clans. What remained of the Gaelic aristocracy was either destroyed or driven into exile during the Williamite War of 1690-91. The bardic poet was then left high and dry, without patron or audience and surrounded by a people who, even if they had a taste for his formalized and sophisticated verse, had not the means to subsidize it. Complains one poet,

> Her chiefs are gone. There's none to bear
> Her cross or lift her from despair;
> The grieving lords take ship. With these
> Our very souls pass overseas. (p. 199)

And another,

> Ask but a lodging for the night
> And all men turn you from the door. (p. 197)

The bardic poet who achieved the greatest influence, though not because of his verse, was Geoffrey Keating, the Irish Herodotus, who was born about 1570 in Tipperary of Anglo-Norman stock. Keating is the bridge between ancient and modern Ireland, for his *History of Ireland* marks the beginning of modern Irish literature and at the same time is one of our most important sources of information about medieval Ireland. It was Keating who during the darkest days kept alive in the people a feeling for their own past. Educated for the priesthood on the continent, he returned to Tipperary about 1610 and lived the life of a parish priest until he was forced to take to the hills as a fugitive because an influential woman parishioner whom he had publicly reprimanded for loose morals brought the soldiers of the crown after him. The *History of Ireland* was apparently written before 1640, during the years when he was either hiding in the glens or, as tradition has it, travelling in disguise throughout the country. Eventually he was able to come out of hiding and return to his parish, where he died about 1650. The *History of Ireland* seems to have been the most popular book ever written in Irish. Literally hundreds of transcripts of it were made and continued to be made over one hundred years after it had been printed in an English translation in 1723. In fact it was probably the last important book in western Europe to circulate in manuscript.

IV

NATURALLY not all Irish poetry written between the twelfth and the seventeenth centuries was the work of professional poets. Gifted amateurs like Gerald Fitzgerald, the Earl of Desmond, in the fourteenth century, Manus O'Donnell in the sixteenth century, or semi-professionals like Pierce Ferriter in the seventeenth century were writing lyric poetry that was more popular than the set pieces which were the bardic poet's stock in trade. A collection of love lyrics written during this period has been edited by T. F. O'Rahilly (*Danta Gradha*, Cork, 1926) and a good many of them have been translated by Robin Flower, Frank O'Connor and the Earl of Longford. Flower claimed that the Irish love lyric developed out of a French original imported from Europe by the Normans but that it took "a very different form, extremely characteristic of the Irish situation." In translation, however, most of these lyrics are little different in either theme or manner from the English love lyric of the same period. Desmond's "Against Blame of Women" (p. 219) and Pierce Ferriter's "He Charges Her to Lay Aside Her Weapons" (p. 235), for example, could easily have been written by English poets. One novel adaptation of the form which was distinctly Irish, however, may be seen in the kind of poem of which "Dark Rosaleen" (p. 226) is the most celebrated example—the love lyric in praise of a woman who is Ireland. The usual explanation of this phenomenon is that the singing of patriotic songs was illegal, like the wearing of the green, and patriotic verse had to assume an erotic disguise.

Readers of Daniel Corkery's *The Hidden Ireland* know that Gaelic poetry of distinction was written throughout the darkest days of the eighteenth century. In fact three poems written in this period—Michael Comyn's "Oisin in the Land of Youth" (p. 105), Eileen O'Leary's "The Lament for Art O'Leary" (p. 241), and Brian Merriman's "The Midnight Court" (p. 252) —are as remarkable as anything in Irish literature. Eileen O'Leary was the aunt of Daniel O'Connell, the great nineteenth-century patriot. When her husband was murdered in

1773 by soldiers in the employ of an enemy she composed a lament modelled upon a traditional kind of utterance called a keen. The practice of keening, which Edmund Spenser described as "lamentations at their burials with dispairful outcries and immoderate wailings," is a primitive custom which had the significance of ritual in the early history of the race. The custom was peculiar to Ireland to the extent only that it survived almost to our own day. J. M. Synge saw women keening in the Aran Islands as recently as 1898 and described the scene in a notable passage. "Each old woman, as she took her turn in the leading recitative, seemed possessed for the moment with a profound ecstasy of grief swaying to and fro, and bending her forehead to the stone before her, while she called out to the dead with a perpetually recurring chant of sobs."

Out of this primitive custom developed a form of literary composition which F. B. Gummere, who saw keening in the Isle of Man, described as "never-ending, intricate, genealogical verses." A nineteenth-century collector named Thomas Crofton Croker translated and published a number of these compositions in *The Keen of the South of Ireland* (London, 1844). "The Lament for Art O'Leary," which its translator Frank O'Connor describes as "first and foremost a ritual over the dead, with its dramatised characters, its story-telling, its chorus of cloaked weepers who keep up a continuous humming and break in at some moment of excitement with shrill cries," is not so far removed from the "dispairful outcries and immoderate wailings" which Spenser described. When one considers the associations with the racial past which such a poem suggests it does not seem so strange that it should exist only in two modern texts both of which had to be assembled entirely from oral sources.

Not much is known about the author or the composition of "The Midnight Court," that strange masterpiece of Gaelic mockery. Brian Merriman's brief obituary in a Limerick newspaper gives us the only solid facts we have about him—that he was a teacher of mathematics and that he died in that city on July 27, 1805. If one can conclude anything from the evidence of the poem, he was a native of Clare, well-educated and a Protestant—though it has been argued from the same evidence that he was a Roman Catholic. "The Midnight Court" is a vision poem and to that extent belongs to a native *genre*. But it is written in the idiom of Merriman's own day and not in the formal language of the bardic schools. Moreover, as Frank O'Connor points out, the poem is classical in temper and has a closer kinship with English poetry of Merriman's day than with native literary tradition. Whatever the major influences on Merriman may have been, one thing is clear. His poem deals with an Irish problem which is even more acute today than it was in Merriman's day—the lack of enthusiasm which Irishmen demonstrate for matrimony. According to the census figures of 1946 more than 80 percent of the men between twenty-five and thirty years of age, and 63 percent of the men between thirty and thirty-five, are unmarried. Many writers have called attention to these figures, and some have even seen in the population decline which is obviously explained by it the eventual disappearance of the Irish people. Is it any wonder that the young girl in Merriman's poem should complain,

> For here I am at the place I started,
> And this is the cause of all my tears,
> I am fast in the rope of the rushing years
> With age and want in lessening span
> And death at the end and no hopes of a man.

V

THE READER who finds it a paradox that so much of Ireland's literature should be written in English, some of it indeed at a time when Irish was still spoken by a majority of the people who lived there, need only think of the ironic fact that Ireland was a colony and at the same time a mother country. Up to the time of Elizabeth I, when a new wave of English conquest and colonization began, Ireland had been able to absorb and even Hibernicize her invaders. But the colonists who flocked into Ireland in 1586 with the plantation of Munster—they included Sir Walter Raleigh and Edmund Spenser—were not to be absorbed as their Anglo-Norman predecessors had been. They settled down on their newly acquired lands, survived the rebellion led by Hugh O'Neill and Hugh O'Donnell at the end of the sixteenth century, the Ulster rebellion of 1641 and the Cromwellian and Williamite wars of the seventeenth century. During these two troublous centuries they maintained their link with the crown, their language, their religion and their culture. By the beginning of the eighteenth century the country was in their hands and the native Gael was groaning under the infamous penal laws which were designed to subdue him by destroying his culture, his language and his priests.

One need only turn to Lecky's *History of Ireland in the Eighteenth Century*, to the accounts of European travellers in Ireland, or to Swift's great satire "A Modest Proposal" (p. 299), for an indication of how life in the hovel differed from life in the big house. "It is a melancholy object to those who walk through this great town [Dublin] or travel in the country when they see the streets, the roads and cabin doors crowded with beggars of the female sex, followed by three, four, or six children, all in rags and importuning every passenger for an alms."

Needless to say the penal laws did not wholly succeed. The priest and the schoolmaster took to the hills and the hedges, the old traditions survived—even if it seemed that the people would not—and throughout the eighteenth century at least native poets continued to compose in Gaelic for the people outside the cities and the Pale who could still understand and appreciate them.

But if the period which began with the Treaty of Limerick in 1691 saw the complete ascendancy of the Anglo-Irish, it also witnessed the gradual rift between the Anglo-Irish and the crown. It is one of the ironies of Irish history that the descendants of those Elizabethan, Stuart, Cromwellians and Williamite settlers who had resisted absorption by the native Irish, now began to resist domination by the crown. No longer in fact English but Anglo-Irish, they had begun to erect the big houses, develop a distinctive culture of their own and build up industries which placed them into direct competition with England. It was no longer the impoverished and disfranchised Celts who provided rich pickings for the royal treasury but the landowning Anglo-Irish capitalists who were building breweries, manufacturing silk, glass and pottery, and establishing a linen and a cotton industry. When the mother country systematically destroyed their industries and by the Act of Union in 1800 abolished their parliament, the gap between English and Anglo-Irish was nearly as great as that between Irish and Anglo-Irish. It was not a Celt but an Anglo-Irishman who wrote in *The Drapier's Letters,* "Am I a freeman in England, and do I become a slave in six hours by crossing the Channel?" Henceforth the great rebel leaders for a whole century from Wolfe Tone to Parnell were to be, with few exceptions, Anglo-Irishmen. One final irony is to be seen in the fact that when at the end of the nineteenth century Ireland began to reconstruct a picture of her ancient past, the chief figures in the movement known as the Irish Literary Revival were, at first, men whose ancestors were not Celts but Saxons. Today the Anglo-Irish, who are mostly Episcopalians and members of the Church of Ireland, comprise only 6 percent of the population of the Republic of Ireland. Unlike the Scottish Presbyterians on the other side of the border in northeast Ulster, they have lost their political influence, seen their big houses go up in flames during the troubles or be taken over by a Free State government and even yielded their leadership in the arts.

One might then ask how many of Ireland's writers who wrote in English had any awareness of Gaelic Ireland. Or to put it more directly, how many of the writers represented in Part V of this book had any knowledge of the literature represented in Parts I through IV. With few exceptions the literature in English written before the nineteenth century—while the Gaelic tradition was still intact—was the work of Anglo-Irish, Protestant writers. Of the first four selections in Part V, the only one which can with certainty be ascribed to an author resident in Ireland complains about fraternization and the evil that will result if the garrison continues to adopt native customs.

and speak the language of the natives ("An Anglo-Irishman's Complaint," p. 298). With the next two selections we jump over a vast territory but a bleak one to the eighteenth century and to Swift and Goldsmith, who were born and educated in Ireland but are better known for their contributions to the literature of England.

For the nineteenth century the story is the same. Of the nine writers represented who predate the Literary Revival—which began in the nineties—six were educated at Trinity College, the fountainhead of Ascendancy culture (Moore, Lever, Ferguson, DeVere, Todhunter and Larminie). Only one of the nine came from Irish peasant stock and had heard Gaelic spoken in his youth (Carleton). One was a serious student of Gaelic antiquity (Ferguson). One is credited with being successful in capturing an authentic note in his adaptations of Gaelic poems, though he knew no Gaelic and was forced to work from English translations (Mangan). Thomas Moore, the most famous of the nine and known throughout the English-speaking world as the national poet of Ireland, has been treated harshly by some Irish writers of the twentieth century and described as "an old shopkeeper who had dealt in the marrowbone of his neighbors"[1] and as "a Firbolg in the borrowed cloak of a Milesian."[2]

By 1890, the picture begins to change. The story of the Irish Literary Revival which produced Synge, O'Casey, Yeats and Joyce, to mention only the Titans, is well known and does not need repeating here. Yeats, Lady Gregory, George Moore and Synge founded their movement upon the rediscovery of Gaelic Ireland and the common people, whom AE once described as the descendants of Oscar and Cuchulain. Lady Gregory retold the ancient stories of the heroic past, Yeats wrote

---

[1] Patrick Kavanagh, "A Wreath for Tom Moore's Statue," *A Soul for Sale* (London, 1947), p. 29.

[2] James Joyce, *A Portrait of the Artist as a Young Man* (New York, The Modern Library), p. 209. The Firbolgs were one of the pre-Gaelic peoples of Ireland, described in the legends as small, dark and evil. The Milesians were the last invaders of ancient Ireland and the legendary founders of the Celtic aristocracy.

"The Wanderings of Oisin" and "Cathleen Ni Houlihan," and Synge went to the Aran Islands to study the peasant and, in Yeats's words, "to express a life that has never found expression." But the fact is that the native Celt had never really lost the ability to express his own life. He needed only the new Ireland, with its language revival, its national theatre, and its new burst of revolutionary zeal to give him his opportunity. Yeats, Lady Gregory, George Moore and Synge gave him his new models. Only twenty-five years separate Synge's visit to Aran and the arrival upon the literary scene of one of those Aran peasants—Liam O'Flaherty.

Perhaps these facts explain why the literature of modern Ireland, unlike the literature of ancient Ireland, is largely in English. The term Anglo-Irish cannot accurately be applied to all the literature in English any more than the term Irish can be exclusively reserved for the literature in Gaelic. It would be just as absurd to assume that all the literature in English was written by Anglo-Irishmen as it would be to claim that all Irishmen write in Gaelic. The fact is that the literature of the last two centuries and a half is bilingual, and one is forced to describe all of it as Irish.

DAVID H. GREENE

ACKNOWLEDGMENTS

I am indebted to the following people for their suggestions, criticism, and help on textual matters: Russell Alspach, John Fisher, Devin Garrity, John Kelleher, David McDowell, Vivian Mercier, Frank O'Connor, Karl Pfeiffer, Horace Reynolds, my wife Catherine Greene and my editors Leonore Crary and Jess Stein.

Acknowledgments are also due to the following publishers and individuals who have granted permission for the inclusion of material in this book:

George Allen & Unwin Ltd. and Random House, Inc., for the excerpt from *Deirdre of the Sorrows* by J. M. Synge. Copyright renewed 1937, by the executors of the estate of John M. Synge.

Ernest Benn Ltd.:

For "The Brow of Nephin," "My Grief on the Sea," "Ringletted Youth of My Love," and "I Shall Not Die for Thee," from Douglas Hyde's *Love Songs of Connaught*. By permission also of Dr. Hyde's executors, The Royal Bank of Ireland.

For "The Croppy Boy" from Donagh MacDonagh's *Literature in Ireland*.

For "Cuchulain's Lament for Ferdiad" from George Sigerson's *Bards of the Gael and the Gall*.

Daniel Binchy and R. J. Best, as executors of the estate of Osborn Bergin, for "On the Breaking-Up of a School," translated by Osborn Bergin.

The Henry Bradshaw Society for the version of "The Vision of Ita" by Whitley Stokes.

Cambridge University Press, for "Cokaygne," "The Irish Dancer," "A Rhyme-beginning Fragment," and "An Anglo-Irishman's Complaint" from St. John Seymour's *Anglo-Irish Literature*.

Simon Campbell, for the following poems by Joseph Campbell: "The Old Age Pensioner," "The Unfrocked Priest," "I Am the Mountainy Singer," "I Am the Gilly of Christ," "As I Came Over the Grey, Grey Hills," "The Herb Leech," and "I Will Go with My Father A-Ploughing."

The Clarendon Press, Oxford, and Dr. Robin Flower, for the following poems from *The Irish Tradition*: "Pangur Ban," "In Praise of Aed," "The Ivy Crest," "On a Dead Scholar," "He That Never Read a Line,"

"A Storm at Sea," "Death's Warning to Beauty," "Of Women No More Evil," "No Sufferer for her Love," "He Praises His Wife When She Has Left Him," "The Good Tradition," "On the Flight of the Earls," and "Were Not the Gael Fallen."

Constable & Co. Ltd., for the following translations from Kuno Meyer's *Selections from Ancient Irish Poetry*: "The Deer's Cry," "To Crinog," "A Song of Winter," "St. Columcille the Scribe," "The Scribe," "The Blackbird," "The Pilgrim at Rome," "The Church Bell in the Night."

The Devin-Adair Company:

For "A Drover" and "A Poor Scholar of the 'Forties" by Padraic Colum.

For "Night and Morning," "Tenebrae," and "The Straying Student" by Austin Clarke.

For "The Crab Tree," "Ringsend," "Exorcism," "To the Liffey with the Swans," "Per Iter Tenebricosum," "Verse," "To the Maids not to Walk in the Wind," "To W. B. Yeats, who says that his Castle of Ballylee is his Monument," and "Leda and the Swan" by Oliver St. John Gogarty.

Doubleday and Company, Inc., for "A Difficult Question" from *The Land of Spices* by Kate O'Brien. Copyright 1941 by Kate O'Brien. Reprinted by permission of Doubleday & Company, Inc.

John Farquharson, London, for "Poisson d'Avril" from *Further Experiences of an Irish R.M.* by E. Œ. Somerville and Martin Ross.

Farrar, Straus and Young, Inc., for "Lent," "Christ Walking on the Water," "The Net," and "Spring" from *Europa and the Bull*, Copyright 1952 by W. R. Rodgers, Farrar, Straus and Young, Inc., publishers.

M. H. Gill & Son Ltd., for "Dark Rosaleen," "The Woman of Three Cows," "Lamentation of Mac Liag for Kincora," "The Geraldine's Daughter," "A Vision of Connaught in the Thirteenth Century," and "To My Native Land" from *Poems* by James Clarence Mangan.

Harcourt, Brace and Company, Inc. and Martin Secker & Warburg Ltd., for "The Raider" from *Awake! and Other Wartime Poems* by W. R. Rodgers. Reprinted by permission of Harcourt, Brace and Company, Inc.

Harvard University Press and Routledge and Kegan Paul Ltd.:

For "The Story of Deirdre," "The Dream of Oenghus," "Reconciliation," "Do Not Torment Me, Woman," "Winter has Come," "The Praises of God," "Civil Irish and Wild Irish," "Egan

O'Rahilly and the Minister," "Who Will Buy a Poem," "St. Columba's Island Heritage," "The Wish of Manchin of Liath," "I Should Like to Have a Great Pool of Ale" from Kenneth Jackson, *A Celtic Miscellany*; and "The Convict of Clonmel" from Geoffrey Taylor, editor, *Irish Poets of the 19th Century* (The Muses' Library). Cambridge, Mass.: Harvard University Press, 1951.

Hodges, Figgis & Co. Ltd. and the Earl of Longford, for "Against Blame of Women," "He Praises Her Hair," and "He Charges Her to Lay Aside Her Weapons," from *Poems from the Irish*; and "The First Vision" and "The Second Vision" from *Dove in the Castle*.

The Irish Texts Society, for "The Headless Phantoms," "The Bathing of Oisin's Head," "Goll's Parting With His Wife," from *Duanaire Finn*; "Maelmora MacSweeney" from *The Bardic Poems of Tadhg Dall O'Huiginn*; "Sweeney the Mad" from *The Adventures of Suibhne Geilt*; and all the selections from *The History of Ireland by Geoffrey Keating*.

The Irish Times, Dublin, for "If Ever You Go To Dublin Town," by Patrick Kavanagh.

The Macmillan Company:

For "Cuchulain's Fight with the Sea," "The Folly of Being Comforted," "To a Shade," "In Memory of Robert Gregory," "Sailing to Byzantium," "Leda and the Swan," "Among School Children," "The Wild Old Wicked Man," and "The Statues" from *The Collected Poems of W. B. Yeats*, Copyright 1951 by The Macmillan Company and used with their permission and that of The Macmillan Co. of Canada, A. P. Watt & Son, and Mrs. W. B. Yeats.

For "The Wind," "The College of Surgeons," "The Crest Jewel," and "Check" from *Collected Poems* by James Stephens, Copyright 1944 by The Macmillan Company and used with their permission and that of Macmillan and Co., Ltd. And for "I Am Raftery" and "The County Mayo" from *Reincarnations* by James Stephens, Copyright 1944 by The Macmillan Company.

For "The Raid" from *Inishfallen, Fare Thee Well* by Sean O'Casey, Copyright 1949 by Sean O'Casey and used with the permission of The Macmillan Company and of Macmillan and Co., Ltd.

For "Song for the Clatter-Bones" from *The Gap of Brightness* by

F. R. Higgins, Copyright 1940 by The Macmillan Company and used with their permission.

Macmillan and Co., Ltd.:

For "Truth," "The Twilight of Earth," "A Prisoner," "On Behalf of Some Irishmen Not Followers of Tradition" from *Collected Poems* by AE, by permission of the publishers and Mr. Diarmuid Russell.

For "Father Mat" and "A Christmas Childhood" from *A Soul for Sale* by Patrick Kavanagh. By permission also of the St. Martin's Press, Inc., New York.

C. D. Medley, Esq., for "The Murrigan" from *A Story-Teller's Holiday* by George Moore.

Frank O'Connor and the office of Harold Matson:

For the translations "The Drowning of Conaing," "The Old Woman of Beare," "May," "The Student," "Hugh Maguire," "The Harper," "The Reverie," "A Sleepless Night," "A Grey Eye Weeping," "Lament for Art O'Leary," and "The Midnight Court"; and for the story "In the Train" from *Bones of Contention.*

A. D. Peters, for "The Wild Sow" from *The Short Stories of Liam O'Flaherty.*

The Public Trustee, London, and The Society of Authors, for the selection from the preface to "John Bull's Other Island," by George Bernard Shaw, Copyright, 1907, 1930, by G. Bernard Shaw.

G. P. Putnam's Sons for "The Rising of the Moon" from *Seven Short Plays* by Augusta, Lady Gregory.

Random House, Inc.:

For the excerpt from *Deirdre of the Sorrows* by J. M. Synge. Copyright renewed 1937, by the executors of the estate of John M. Synge.

For "Valediction," "Carrickfergus," "Autumn Journal," from *Poems 1925-1940* by Louis MacNeice. Copyright 1940 by Louis MacNeice.

Professor Fred N. Robinson, for his translation "The Viking Terror."

Routledge and Kegan Paul Ltd., for "Aghadoe" by John Todhunter.

The Royal Irish Academy, Dublin, for "The Tragic Death of Aife's Only Son," translated by Kuno Meyer in *Eriu*, Vol. 1.

The Talbot Press Limited, for "Tara is Grass" from *The Collected Works of P. H. Pearse.*

The University of Chicago Press, for "The Son of the King of Moy," "The Wife of Aed mac Ainmirech," "A Miserly Patron," "A Love Song," and "A Pet Crane" from *Early Irish Literature* by Myles Dillon.

The Viking Press, Inc., New York:

For "Starry Sky," "Penitentes," "The Desire for Hermitage," "At Saint Patrick's Purgatory," "Summer is Gone," "Fand Yields Cuchulain to Emer" from *The Silver Branch* by Sean O'Faolain. Copyright 1938 by The Viking Press, Inc. Reprinted by permission of The Viking Press, Inc.

For the selection from *Bird Alone* by Sean O'Faolain. Copyright 1936 by The Viking Press, Inc. Reprinted by permission of The Viking Press, Inc.

For "Ivy Day in the Committee Room" from *Dubliners*, included in *The Portable James Joyce*. Copyright 1936, 1947, by The Viking Press, Inc. Reprinted by permission of The Viking Press, Inc.

Williams and Norgate Limited, for "The Colloquy of the Old Men" and "The Fianna" translated by Standish Hayes O'Grady in the *Silva Gadelica*.

AN ANTHOLOGY
OF IRISH
LITERATURE

PART I

Early Irish Lyrics

TRANSLATIONS FROM THE GAELIC

The Viking Terror

Fierce is the wind tonight.
It ploughs up the white hair of the sea.
I have no fear that the Viking hosts
Will come over the water to me.

7TH OR 8TH CENTURY.
Translator F. N. Robinson.

A Pet Crane

My dear little crane
Is the glory of my goodly home.
I have not found so good a friend.
Though he is a servant he is a gentleman.

7TH OR 8TH CENTURY.
Translator Myles Dillon.

The Son of the King of Moy

The son of the king of Moy in midsummer
Found a girl in the greenwood.
She gave him black fruit from thornbushes.
She gave an armful of strawberries on rushes.

7TH OR 8TH CENTURY.
Translator Myles Dillon.

The Wife of Aed mac Ainmirech, King of Ireland, Laments Her Husband

Dear to me were the three sides
Which I hope not to visit again:
The side of Tara,[1] the side of Teltown[2]
And the side of Aed son of Ainmire.

7TH OR 8TH CENTURY.
Translator Myles Dillon.

---

[1] A dwelling place of the ancient High Kings of Ireland.
[2] Teltown (in County Meath) is the anglicized form of Tailltiu, dwelling place of a number of ancient High Kings of Ireland.

A Love Song

He is a heart,
An acorn from the oakwood.
He is young.
A kiss for him!

7TH OR 8TH CENTURY.
Translator Myles Dillon.

The Drowning of Conaing

The shining waters rise and swell
And break across the shining strand,
And Conaing gazes at the land,
Swung high in his frail coracle.

Then she with the white hair of foam,
The blinding hair that Conaing grips,
Rises, to turn triumphant lips,
On all the gods that guard his home.

8TH CENTURY.
Translator Frank O'Connor.

The Deer's Cry[1]

I arise to-day
Through a mighty strength, the invocation of the Trinity,
Through belief in the threeness,
Through confession of the oneness
Of the Creator of Creation.

I arise to-day
Through the strength of Christ's birth with His baptism,
Through the strength of His crucifixion with His burial,
Through the strength of His resurrection with His ascension,
Through the strength of His descent for the judgement of
Doom.

I arise to-day
Through the strength of the love of Cherubim,
In obedience of angels,
In the service of archangels,
In hope of resurrection to meet with reward,
In prayers of patriarchs,
In predictions of prophets,
In preachings of apostles,
In faiths of confessors,
In innocence of holy virgins,
In deeds of righteous men.

---

[1] Saint Patrick is supposed to have composed this hymn and sung it to deceive assassins, lying in wait for him, into thinking that he and his companions were a herd of deer passing.

I arise to-day
Through the strength of heaven:
Light of sun,
Radiance of moon,
Splendor of fire,
Speed of lightning,
Swiftness of wind,
Depth of sea,
Stability of earth,
Firmness of rock.

I arise to-day
Through God's strength to pilot me:
God's might to uphold me,
God's wisdom to guide me,
God's eye to look before me,
God's ear to hear me,
God's word to speak for me,
God's hand to guard me,
God's way to lie before me,
God's shield to protect me,
God's host to save me
From snares of devils,
From temptations of vices,
From every one who shall wish me ill,
Afar and anear,
Alone and in multitude.

I summon to-day all these powers between me and those evils,
Against every cruel merciless power that may oppose my body
and soul,
Against incantations of false prophets,
Against black laws of pagandom,
Against false laws of heretics,
Against craft of idolatry,
Against spells of women and smiths and wizards,
Against every knowledge that corrupts man's body and soul.

Christ to shield me to-day
Against poison, against burning,
Against drowning, against wounding,
So that there may come to me abundance of reward.
Christ with me, Christ before me, Christ behind me,
Christ in me, Christ beneath me, Christ above me,
Christ on my right, Christ on my left,
Christ when I lie down, Christ when I sit down,
Christ when I arise.
Christ in the heart of every man who thinks of me,
Christ in the mouth of every one who speaks of me,
Christ in every eye that sees me,
Christ in every ear that hears me.

I arise to-day
Through a mighty strength, the invocation of the Trinity,
Through belief in the threeness,
Through confession of the oneness
Of the Creator of Creation.

8TH CENTURY.
Translators Whitley Stokes, John Strachan, and Kuno Meyer.

In Praise of Aed[1]

Kindler of glory's embers,
Aed, goodly hand of giving;
Comeliest that song remembers
By pastoral Roeriu living.

A mighty shaft and loyal
Whom glory overarches;
Of all men else most royal
In grassy Maistiu's marches.

My love—if such his pleasure—
To Dermot's son I bring it;
My song—more worth than treasure—
To his high praise I sing it.

Dear name! renowned in story,
Aed! no man may decry him;
Where Liffey flows in glory
Fame's voice shall ne'er bely him.

Grandchild of that fierce fighter
Muireach, a cliff of splendours,
Honour—no fame is brighter—
To his race Cualu renders.

A stately tree, a glowing
Jewel whom strife embolden;
A silver sapling growing
From soil of princes olden.

---

[1] A chief of north Leinster.

Songs at the alefeast ringing,
Scales climbed of comely measures,
Bards with their heady singing
Acclaim Aed and his pleasures.

8TH CENTURY.
Translator Robin Flower.

The Scribe

A hedge of trees surrounds me.
A blackbird's lay sings to me.
Above my lined booklet
The trilling birds chant to me.

In a grey mantle from the top of bushes
The cuckoo sings.
Verily—may the Lord shield me!—
Well do I write under the greenwood.

8TH OR 9TH CENTURY.
Translator Kuno Meyer.

A Miserly Patron

I have heard
He does not bestow horses for poems;
He gives what fits his kind,
A cow!

9TH CENTURY.
Translator Myles Dillon.

Pangur Ban

I and Pangur Ban my cat,
'Tis a like task we are at:
Hunting mice is his delight,
Hunting words I sit all night.

Better far than praise of men
'Tis to sit with book and pen;
Pangur bears me no ill will,
He too plies his simple skill.

'Tis a merry thing to see
At our tasks how glad are we,
When at home we sit and find
Entertainment to our mind.

Oftentimes a mouse will stray
In the hero Pangur's way;
Oftentimes my keen thought set
Takes a meaning in its net.

'Gainst the wall he sets his eye
Full and fierce and sharp and sly;
'Gainst the wall of knowledge I
All my little wisdom try.

When a mouse darts from its den
O how glad is Pangur then!
O what gladness do I prove
When I solve the doubts I love!

So in peace our tasks we ply,
Pangur Ban, my cat and I;
In our arts we find our bliss,
I have mine and he has his.

Practice every day has made
Pangur perfect in his trade;
I get wisdom day and night
Turning darkness into light.

9TH CENTURY.
Translator Robin Flower.

The Vision of Ita

Jesukin, nursed by me in my little hermitage!
Though it be a cleric with treasures—
All is a lie save Jesukin.
The nursing that I do in my house
Is not the nursing of a base clown.
It is Jesus with the men of Heaven
Near my heart every night.

Young Jesukin, my eternal good!
For heed of Him he is not slack—
The King who controls all things.
Not to beseech Him will cause repentance.
It is Jesu, noble, angelic, not a boorish cleric
Who is fostered by me in my little hermitage
Jesus, son of the Hebrew woman.

Though sons of princes, sons of kings,
Should come into my country,
Not from them do I expect profit.
More likely from Jesukin.
Sing ye a chorus, O maidens, to Him who has a right
To your tribute. Who sits in His place above,
Though as Jesukin he sits at my breast.

9TH CENTURY.
Translator Whitley Stokes.

He That Never Read A Line

'Tis sad to see the sons of learning
In everlasting Hellfire burning
While he that never read a line
Doth in eternal glory shine.

9TH CENTURY.
Translator Robin Flower.

On A Dead Scholar

LONGARAD WHITEFOOT: a master in theology, in history, in the Brehon law and in poetry was he. To him came Columcille to be his guest and Lon hid his books from him. So Columcille left a curse on the books: "May that which thou grudgest be useless after thee," said he. And so it was, for the books abide still, but no man can read them. Now when Longarad died the men of learning say that all the book-satchels of Ireland fell down that night. Or rather it was the book-satchels in Columcille's oratory that fell, and Columcille and all they that were with him there fell silent at the noise of the falling of the books. Then said Columcille: "Longarad is dead in Ossory to-day, the master of every art." "May it be long ere that come true!" said Baothin. "Unfaith on the man that takes thy office after thee for that!" says Columcille.

Et dixit Columcille:

Lon's away,
Cill Garad[1] is sad today;
Many-familied Eire weeps,
Learning sleeps and finds no stay.

[1] A place name, Kilgarrow.

Lon's no more,
Cill Garad is weeping sore;
Learning lies bereft and poor
All along the Irish shore.

9TH CENTURY.
Translator Robin Flower.

The Church Bell in the Night

Sweet little bell
That is struck in the windy night,
I liefer go to a tryst with thee
Than to a tryst with a foolish woman.

9TH CENTURY.
Translator Kuno Meyer.

Starry Sky

O King of the starry sky,
Lest Thou from me withdraw Thy light—
Whether my house be dark or bright,
My door shall close on none tonight.

9TH CENTURY.
Translator Sean O'Faolain.

The Desire for Hermitage

Ah! To be all alone in a little cell
With nobody near me;
Beloved that pilgrimage
Before the last pilgrimage to Death.

To be cleansing my flesh with good habits,
Trampling it down like a man;
To be weeping wearily,
Paying for my passions.

A cold bed of fear—
The lying down of a doomed man;
A short sleep, waking to danger;
Tears from early morning.

Dry bread portioned out
A good thing to hollow the face;
An end to gossip; no more fables;
The knees constantly bent.

That will be an end to evil
When I am alone
In a lovely little corner among tombs
Far from the houses of the great.

Ah! To be all alone in a little cell,
To be alone, all alone,
Alone as I came into the world—
And as I shall go from it.

8TH-9TH CENTURY.
Translator Sean O'Faolain.

The Wish of Manchín of Liath

I wish, O son of the Living God, ancient eternal King, for a secret hut in the wilderness that it may be my dwelling.

A very blue shallow well to be beside it, a clear pool for washing away sins through the grace of the Holy Ghost.

A beautiful wood close by around it on every side, for the nurture of many-voiced birds, to shelter and hide it.

Facing the south for warmth, a little stream across its enclosure, a choice ground with abundant bounties which would be good for every plant.

A few sage disciples—I will tell their number—humble and obedient, to pray to the King.

Four threes, three fours, ready for every need, two sixes in the church, both south and north.

Six couples in addition to me myself, praying through the long ages to the King who moves the sun.

A lovely church decked with linen, a dwelling for God of Heaven; then, bright candles over the holy white Scriptures.

One room to go to for the care of the body, without ribaldry, without boasting, without meditation of evil.

This is the housekeeping I would get. I would choose it without concealing. Fragrant fresh leeks, hens, salmon, trou' bees.

My fill of clothing and of food from the King of good fame, and for me to be sitting for a while praying to God in every place.

9TH CENTURY.
Translator Kenneth Jackson.

The Pilgrim at Rome

To go to Rome
Is much of trouble, little of profit:
The King whom thou seekest here,
Unless thou bring Him with thee, thou wilt not find.

9TH CENTURY.
Translator Kuno Meyer.

Winter Has Come

Winter has come with scarcity,
Lakes have flooded on all sides,
Frosts crumble the leaves,
The merry wave mutters.

9TH CENTURY.
Translator Kenneth Jackson.

The Ivy Crest

In Tuaim Inbhir here I find
No great house such as mortals build,
A hermitage that fits my mind
With sun and moon and starlight filled.

'Twas Gobbán[1] shaped it cunningly
—This is a tale that lacks not proof—
And my heart's darling in the sky,
Christ, was the thatcher of its roof.

Over my house rain never falls,
There comes no terror of the spear;
It is a garden without walls
And everlasting light shines here.

9TH CENTURY.
Translator Robin Flower.

---

[1] The great artificer of Celtic mythology.

Summer Is Gone

I have but one story—
The stags are moaning,
The sky is snowing,
Summer is gone.

Quickly the low sun
Goes drifting down
Behind the rollers,
Lifting and long.

The wild geese cry
Down the storm;
The ferns have fallen,
Russet and torn.

The wings of the birds
Are clotted with ice.
I have but one story—
Summer is gone.

9TH CENTURY.
Translator Sean O'Faolain.

May

May's the merriest time of all,
Life comes back to everything,
While a ray of light remains
The never weary blackbirds sing.

That's the cuckoo's strident voice,
"Welcome summer great and good!"
All the fierceness of the storm
Lost in tangles of the wood.

Summer stems the languid stream,
Galloping horses rush the pool,
Bracken bristles everywhere,
White bog cotton is in bloom.

Scant of breath the burdened bees
Carry home the flowery spoil,
To the mountains go the cows,
The ant is glutted with his meal.

The woodland harp plays all day long,
The sail falls and the world's at rest,
A mist of heat upon the hills
And the water full of mist.

The corncrake drones, a mighty bard,
The cold cascade that leaps the rock
Sings of the snugness of the pool,
Their season come, the rushes talk.

The man grows strong, the virgin blooms
In all her glory, firm and light,
Bright the far and fertile plain,
Bright the wood from floor to height.

And here among the meadowlands
An eager flock of birds descends,
There a stream runs white and fast
Where the murmuring meadow bends.

And you long to race your horse
Wildly through the parted crowd,
The sun has scarcely touched the land
Yet the waterflags are gold.

Frightened, foolish, frail, a bird
Sings of it with throbbing breast,
The lark that flings its praise abroad,
May the brightest and the best.

9TH-10TH CENTURY.
Translator Frank O'Connor.

A Song of Winter

Cold, cold!
Cold to-night is broad Moylurg,
Higher the snow than the mountain-range,
The deer cannot get at their food.

Cold till Doom!
The storm has spread over all:
A river is each furrow upon the slope,
Each ford a full pool.

A great tidal sea is each loch,
A full loch is each pool:
Horses cannot get over the ford of Ross,
No more can two feet get there.

The fish of Ireland are a-roaming,
There is no strand which the wave does not pound,
Not a town there is in the land,
Not a bell is heard, no crane talks.

The wolves of Cuan-wood get
Neither rest nor sleep in their lair,
The little wren cannot find
Shelter in her nest on the slope of Lon.

Keen wind and cold ice
Has burst upon the little company of birds,
The blackbird cannot get a lee to her liking,
Shelter for its side in Cuan-wood.

Cozy our pot on its hook,
Crazy the hut on the slope of Lon:
The snow has crushed the wood here,
Toilsome to climb up Ben-bo.

Glenn Rye's ancient bird
From the bitter wind gets grief;
Great her misery and her pain,
The ice will get into her mouth.

From flock and from down to rise—
Take it to heart!—were folly for thee:
Ice in heaps on every ford—
That is why I say "cold"!

10TH CENTURY.
Translator Kuno Meyer.

To Crinog[1]

Crinog, melodious is your song.
Though young no more you are still bashful.
We two grew up together in Niall's northern land,
When we used to sleep together in tranquil slumber.

That was my age when you slept with me,
O peerless lady of pleasant wisdom:
A pure-hearted youth, lovely without a flaw,
A gentle boy of seven sweet years.

We lived in the great world of Banva[2]
Without sullying soul or body,
My flashing eye full of love for you,
Like a poor innocent untempted by evil.

Your just counsel is ever ready,
Wherever we are we seek it:
To love your penetrating wisdom is better
Than glib discourse with a king.

Since then you have slept with four men after me,
Without folly or falling away:
I know, I hear it on all sides,
You are pure, without sin from man.

---

[1] "Crinog was evidently what is known in the literature of early Christianity as ἀγαπητή, *virgo subintroducta* (συνεισάκτος) or *conhospita,* i.e., a nun who lived with a priest, monk, or hermit like a sister or 'spiritual wife' (*uxor spiritualis*). This practice, which was early suppressed or abandoned everywhere else, seems to have survived in the Irish Church till the tenth century." (Translator)

[2] A name for Ireland.

At last, after weary wanderings,
You have come to me again,
Darkness of age has settled on your face:
Sinless your life draws near its end.

You are still dear to me, faultless one,
You shall have welcome from me without stint;
You will not let us be drowned in torment:
We will earnestly practise devotion with you.

The lasting world is full of your fame,
Far and wide you have wandered on every track:
If every day we followed your ways,
We should come safe into the presence of dread God.

You leave an example and a bequest
To every one in this world,
You have taught us by your life:
Earnest prayer to God is no fallacy.

Then may God grant us peace and happiness!
May the countenance of the King
Shine brightly upon us
When we leave behind us our withered bodies.

10TH CENTURY.
Translator Kuno Meyer.

The Old Woman of Beare[1]

I the old woman of Beare
Once a shining shift would wear,
Now and since my beauty's fall
I have scarce a shift at all.

Plump no more, I sigh for these
Bones bare beyond belief;
Ebbtide is all my grief,
I am ebbing like the seas.

It is pay
And not men ye love today,
But when we were young, ah then
We gave all our hearts to men.

Men most dear,
Horseman, huntsman, charioteer;
We gave them love with all our will
But the measure did not fill.

When today they ask so fine,
And small good they get of it,
They are wornout in their prime
By the little that they get.

[1] The Old Woman of Beare still figures in Irish legend as a hag or witch of fabulous age. She had seven periods of youth and fifty foster children.

And long since the foaming steed
And the chariot with its speed
And the charioteer went by—
God be with them all, say.

Luck has left me, I go late
To the dark house where they wait;
When the Son of God thinks fit
Let Him call me home to it.

For my hands as you may see
Are but bony wasted things,
Hands that once would grasp the hand,
Clasp the haughty neck of kings.

O my hands as may be seen
Are so scraggy and so thin
That a boy might start in dread
Feeling them about his head.

Girls are gay
When the year draws on to May,
But for me, so poor am I,
Sun will scarcely light the day.

Though I care
Nothing now to deck my hair,
I had headgear bright enough
When the kings for love went bare.

'Tis not age that makes my pain
But the eye that sees so plain
How when all it loves decays,
Femon's ways are gold again.

Femon, Bregon, sacring stone,
Sacring stone and Ronan's throne,
Storms have sacked so long that now
Tomb and sacring stone are one.

Winter overwhelms the land,
The waves are noisy on the strand,
So I may not hope today
Faramuid will come my way.

Where are they? Ah, well I know
Old and toiling bones that row
Alma's flood or by its deep
Sleep in cold that slept not so.

Welladay!
Every child outlives its play,
Year on year has worn my flesh
Since my fresh sweet strength went grey.

And, O God,
Once again for ill or good
Spring will come and I shall see
Everything but me renewed.

Summer sun and autumn sun,
These I knew and they are gone,
And the winter time of men
Comes and they come not again.

And "Amen" I cry and "Woe!"
That the boughs are shaken bare
And that candlelight and feast
Leave me to the dark and prayer.

I that had my day with kings
And drank deep of mead and wine,
Drink whey-water with old hags
Sitting in their rags and pine.

"That my cups be cups of whey!
That Thy will be done," I pray,
But the prayer, O Living God,
Stirs up madness in my blood.

And I cry "Your locks are grey"
At the mantle that I stroke,
Then I grieve and murmur "Nay,
I am grey and not my cloak."

And of eyes that loved the sun
Age, my grief, has taken one,
And the other too will take
Soon for good proportion's sake.

Floodtide!
Flood or ebb upon the strand?
What floodtide brings to you,
Ebbtide carries from your hand.

Floodtide
And the swifter tides that fall,
All have reached me, ebb and flow,
Ay, and now I know them all.

Floodtide!
Not a man answers my call
Nor in darkness seeks my side,
A cold hand lies on them all.

Happy island of the main,
To you the tide will come again,
But to me it comes no more
Over the blank deserted shore.

Seeing it, I can scarcely say
"Here is such a place" today,
What was water far and wide
Changes with the ebbing tide.

10TH CENTURY.
Translator Frank O'Connor.

I Should Like to Have a Great Pool of Ale[1]

I should like to have a great pool of ale for the King of Kings; I should like the Heavenly Host to be drinking it for all eternity.

I should like to have the fruit of Faith, of pure devotion; I should like to have the couches of Holiness in my house.

I should like to have the men of Heaven in my own dwelling; I should like the vats of Long-Suffering to be at their disposal.

I should like to have the vessels of Charity to dispense; I should like to have the pitchers of Mercy for their company.

I should like there to be cheerfulness for their sake; I should like Jesus to be there too.

I should like to have the Three Marys of glorious renown; I should like to have the people of Heaven from every side.

I should like to be vassal to the Lord; if I should suffer distress he would grant me a good blessing.

10TH CENTURY.
Translator Kenneth Jackson.

---

[1] This poem is generally attributed to Brigid, the great saint of the fifth century.

St. Columcille the Scribe

My hand is weary with writing,
My sharp quill is not steady,
My slender-beaked pen juts forth
A black draught of shining dark-blue ink.

A stream of wisdom of blessed God
Springs from my fair-brown shapely hand:
On the page it squirts its draught
Of ink of the green-skinned holly.

My little dripping pen travels
Across the plain of shining books,
Without ceasing for the wealth of the great—
Whence my hand is weary with writing.

11TH CENTURY.
Translator Kuno Meyer.

A Storm at Sea

Tempest on the great seaborders!
Hear my tale, ye viking sworders:
Winter smites us, wild winds crying
Set the salty billows flying,
Wind and winter, fierce marauders.

Ler's[1] vast host of shouting water
Comes against us charged with slaughter;
None can tell the dread and wonder
Speaking in the ocean thunder
And the tempest, thunder's daughter.

With the wind of east at morning
All the waves' wild hearts are yearning
Westward over wastes of ocean
Till they stay their eager motion
Where the setting sun is burning.

When the northern wind comes flying,
All the press of dark waves crying
Southward surge and clamour, driven
To the shining southern heaven,
Wave to wave in song replying.

When the western wind is blowing
O'er the currents wildly flowing,
Eastward sets its mighty longing
And the waves go eastward, thronging
Far to find the sun-tree growing.

---

[1] Manannan macLir was god of the sea in Celtic mythology.

When the southern wind comes raining
Over shielded Saxons straining
Waves round Skiddy isle go pouring,
On Caladnet's beaches roaring,
In grey Shannon's mouth complaining.

Full the sea and fierce the surges,
Lovely are the ocean verges,
On the showery waters whirling
Sandy winds are swiftly swirling,
Rudders cleave the surf that urges.

Hard round Eire's cliffs and nesses,
Hard the strife, not soft the stresses,
Like swan-feathers softly sifting
Snow o'er Mile's folk[2] is drifting,
Manann's wife shakes angry tresses.

At the mouth of each dark river
Breaking waters surge and shiver,
Wind and winter met together
Trouble Alba[3] with wild weather,
Countless falls on Dremon quiver.

Son of God, great Lord of wonder,
Save me from the ravening thunder!
By the feast before Thy dying
Save me from the tempest crying
And from Hell tempestuous under!

11TH CENTURY.
Translator Robin Flower.

---

[2] I.e. the Irish people. Mil was the father of the sixth and last race to invade Ireland.

[3] England.

The Praises of God

It is folly for any man in the world
To cease from praising Him,
When the bird does not cease
And it without a soul but wind.

11TH CENTURY.
Translator Kenneth Jackson.

The Blackbird

Ah, blackbird, thou art satisfied
Where thy nest is in the bush.
Hermit that clinkest no bell,
Sweet, soft, peaceful is thy note.

11TH-12TH CENTURY.
Translator Kuno Meyer.

St. Columcille's Island Hermitage

Delightful I think it to be in the bosom of an isle, on the peak of a rock, that I might often see there the calm of the sea.

That I might see its heavy waves over the glittering ocean, as they chant a melody to their Father on their eternal course.

That I might see its smooth strand of clear headlands, no gloomy thing; that I might hear the voice of the wondrous birds, a joyful course.

That I might hear the sound of the shallow waves against the rocks; that I might hear the cry by the graveyard, the noise of the sea.

That I might see its splendid flocks of birds over the full-watered ocean; that I might see its mighty whales, greatest of wonders.

That I might see its ebb and its flood-tide in their flow; that this may be my name, a secret I tell, "He who turned his back on Ireland."

That contrition of heart should come upon me as I watch it; that I might bewail my many sins, difficult to declare.

That I might bless the Lord who has power over all, Heaven with its pure host of angels, earth, ebb, flood-tide.

That I might pore on one of my books, good for my soul; a while kneeling for beloved Heaven, a while at psalms.

A while gathering dulse from the rock, a while fishing, a while giving good to the poor, a while in my cell.

A while meditating upon the Kingdom of Heaven, holy is the redemption; a while at labour not too heavy; it would be delightful!

12TH CENTURY.
Translator Kenneth Jackson.

PART II

Myth, Saga, and Romance

TRANSLATIONS FROM THE GAELIC

The Dream of Oenghus[1]

OENGHUS was asleep one night, when he saw a girl coming towards him as he lay on his bed. She was the loveliest that had ever been in Ireland. Oenghus went to take her hand, to bring her to him in his bed. As he looked, she sprang suddenly away from him; he could not tell where she had gone. He stayed there till morning, and he was sick at heart. The apparition which he had seen, and had not talked with, made him fall ill. No food passed his lips. She was there again the next night. He saw a lute in her hand, the sweetest that ever was; she played a tune to him, and he fell asleep at it. He remained there till morning, and that day he was unable to eat.

He passed a whole year while she visited him in this way, so that he fell into a wasting sickness. He spoke of it to no one.

[1] Oenghus Mac Oc (Angus Og), the master of love in Celtic mythology, was the son of the Dagda, chieftain of the Tuatha De Danann—one of the ancient peoples who invaded Ireland—and Boann, a river goddess who gave her name to the Boyne river.

So he fell into wasting sickness, and no one knew what was wrong with him. The physicians of Ireland were brought together; they did not know what was wrong with him in the end. They went to Fínghen, Conchobhar's[2] physician, and he came to him. He would tell from a man's face what his illness was, and would tell from the smoke which came from the house how many people were ill in it.

He spoke to him aside. "Ah, unhappy plight!" said Fínghen, "you have fallen in love in absence." "You have diagnosed my illness," said Oenghus. "You have fallen into a wretched state, and have not dared to tell it to anyone," said Fínghen. "You are right," said Oenghus; "a beautiful girl came to me, of the loveliest figure in Ireland, and of surpassing form. She had a lute in her hand, and played it to me every night." "No matter," said Fínghen, "it is fated for you to make a match with her. Send someone to Boann, your mother, that she should come to speak with you."

They went to her, and Boann came then. "I am attending this man," said Fínghen, "a serious illness has fallen upon him." They told his story to Boann. "Let his mother take care of him," said Fínghen; "a serious illness has fallen on him. Have the whole of Ireland scoured to see if you find a girl of this figure which your son has seen."

They spent a year at this. Nothing like her was found. Then Fínghen was called to them again. "No help has been found in this matter," said Boann. Said Fínghen, "Send to the Daghdhae, that he should come to speak with his son." They went to the Daghdhae, and he came back with them. "Why have I been summoned?" "To advise your son," said Boann; "it is as well for you to help him, for it is sad that he is perishing. He is wasting away. He has fallen in love in absence, and no help is to be found for him." "What is the use of talking to me?" said the Daghdhae, "I know no more than you do." "More indeed," said Fínghen, "you are the king of the fairy folk

[2] Conchubor (Conor), the son of Nessa, was king of Ulster and one of the central figures in the Ulster cycle of tales. See Introduction, p. xiii.

of Ireland. Send someone to Bodhbh, king of the fairies of Munster; his knowledge is noised throughout Ireland."

They went to him. He welcomed them. "Welcome to you, men of the Daghdhae," said Bodhbh. "That is what we have come for." "Have you news?" said Bodhbh. "We have; Oenghus the son of the Daghdhae has been wasting away for two years." "What is the matter with him?" said Bodhbh. "He has seen a girl in his sleep. We do not know where in Ireland is the girl whom he has seen and loved. The Daghdhae bids you seek throughout Ireland for a girl of that figure and form." "She shall be sought," said Bodhbh, "and let me have a year's delay to find out the facts of the case."

They came back at the end of the year to Bodhbh's house at the Fairy Hill beyond Feimhen. "I went round the whole of Ireland until I found the girl at Loch Bél Dragon, at Crotta Cliach,"[1] said Bodhbh. They went to the Daghdhae, and they were made welcome. "Have you news?" said the Daghdhae. "Good news; the girl of that figure which you described has been found. Bodhbh bids you let Oenghus come away with us to him, to know whether he recognises the girl when he sees her."

Oenghus was taken in a chariot to the Fairy Hill beyond Feimhen. The king had a great feast ready for them, and he was made welcome. They were three days and three nights at the feast. "Come away now," said Bodhbh, "to know whether you recognise the girl when you see her. Even if you do recognise her, I have no power to give her to you, and you may only see her."

They came then to the lake. They saw three times fifty grown girls, and the girl herself among them. The girls did not reach above her shoulder. There was a chain of silver between each couple; and a necklet of silver round her own throat, and a chain of refined gold. Then Bodhbh said, "Do you recognise that girl?" "I do indeed," said Oenghus. "I can do no more for you," said Bodhbh. "That is no matter, then," said Oenghus,

[1] The Galtee mountains.

"since it is she that I saw; I cannot take her this time. Who is this girl, Bodhbh?" said Oenghus. "I know, truly," said Bodhbh, "she is Caer Ibhormheith, daughter of Ethal Anbhuail from the fairy hill of Uamhan in the land of Connaught."

Then Oenghus and his people set off for their own country. Bodhbh went with him, and talked with the Daghdhae and Boann at Bruigh Maic ind Óaig.[1] They told them their news, and told how she seemed, in figure and form, just as they had seen; and they told her name and the name of her father and grandfather. "We feel it to be discourteous that we cannot content you," said the Daghdhae. "What you should do, Daghdhae," said Bodhbh, "is to go to Ailill and Medhbh,[2] for they have the girl in their province."

The Daghdhae went till he reached the lands of Connaught, with three score chariots in his company. The king and queen made them welcome. They spent a full week banqueting round the ale after that. "What has brought you?" said the king. "You have a girl in your country," said the Daghdhae, "and my son has fallen in love with her, and has become sick. I have come to you to find out whether you would give her to the lad." "Who?" said Ailill. "The daughter of Ethal Anbhuail." "We have no power over her," said Ailill and Medhbh, "if we had she should be given him." "This would be good—let the king of the fairy hill be summoned to you," said the Daghdhae.

Ailill's steward went to him. "You have been ordered by Ailill and Medhbh to go to speak with them." "I will not go," said he, "I will not give my daughter to the son of the Daghdhae." That is told to Ailill; "He cannot be made to come, but he knows why he is summoned." "No matter," said Ailill, "he shall come, and the heads of his warriors shall be brought with him." At that, Ailill's household troops and the men of the Daghdhae rose up against the fairy hill, and overran the whole hill. They brought out three score heads, and the king, so that he was in captivity at Cruachu.

---

[1] New Grange mound, on the Boyne.

[2] Ailill and Medhbh (Maeve) were king and queen respectively of Connaught and traditional enemies of Ulster.

Then Ailill said to Ethal Anbhuail, "Give your daughter to the son of the Daghdhae." "I cannot," said he, "her magic power is greater than mine." "What is this great magic power she has?" said Ailill. "Easily told; she is in the shape of a bird every other year, and in human shape the other years." "What year is she in the shape of a bird?" said Ailill. "It is not for me to betray her," said her father. "Off with your head, unless you tell us!" said Ailill. "I will not hold out any longer," said he; "I will tell you," said he, "since you are so persistent about her. Next All Hallows she will be at Loch Bél Dragon in the shape of a bird, and wonderful birds will be seen with her there, there will be three times fifty swans around her; and I have made preparations for them." "I do not care, then," said the Daghdhae; "since you know her nature, do you bring her."

Then a treaty was made between them, between Ailill and Ethal and the Daghdhae, and Ethal was let go. The Daghdhae bade them farewell and came to his house and told his news to his son. "Go next All Hallows to Loch Bél Dragon, and call her to you from the lake." The Mac Óag[1] went to Loch Bél Dragon. He saw three times fifty white birds with their silver chains, and curls of gold about their heads. Oenghus was in human shape on the brink of the lake. He called the girl to him. "Come to speak to me, Caer!" "Who calls me?" said Caer. "Oenghus calls you." "I will go, if you will undertake on your honour that I may come back to the lake again." "I pledge your protection," said he.

She went to him. He cast his arms about her. They fell asleep in the form of two swans, and went round the lake three times, so that his promise might not be broken. They went away in the form of two white birds till they came to Bruigh Maic ind Óaig, and sang a choral song so that they put the people to sleep for three days and three nights. The girl stayed with him after that.

8TH CENTURY.
Translator Kenneth Jackson.

[1] I.e. Oenghus.

The Boyhood Deeds of Cuchulain[1]

"THIS BOY," said Fergus, "was reared in his father's and his mother's house, by the seaside northwards in the plain of Muirthemne, where someone gave him an account of the *macrad* or 'boy-corps' of Emain Macha;[2] how that Conchobar divides his day into three parts: the first being devoted to watching the boy-corps at their sport, especially that of hurling; the second to the playing of chess and draughts; the third to pleasurable consuming of meat and drink until drowsiness sets in, which then is promoted by the exertions of minstrels and musicians to induce favorable placidity of mind and disposition. And, for all that we are banished from him," continued Fergus, "by my word I swear that neither in Ireland nor in Scotland is there a warrior his (*i.e.*, Conchobar's) counterpart. The little lad, then, as aforesaid, having heard of all this, one day told his mother that he was bent on a visit to Emain Macha to test the boy-corps at their own sports. She objected that he was immature, and ought to wait until some grown warrior or other, or some confidential of Conchobar's should, in order to insure his safety, bind over the boy-corps to keep the peace toward him. He told his mother that that was too long an outlook, that he could not wait, and that all she had to do was to set him a course for Emain Macha, since he did not know in which direction it lay.

---

[1] The Achilles of the Ulster cycle was the son of Dechtire, sister of King Conchubor, by Lug, a prince of the Tuatha De Danann, or by Sualtach, an Ulster chieftain. His name Setanta was changed to Cuchulain (lit. the hound of Culann) when, at the age of seven, he destroyed the famous hound of Culann the smith. This story of Cuchulain's youth is taken from *The Cattle Raid of Cooley*, the great epic of the Ulster cycle and is told to Ailill and Maeve by several of the Ulster exiles serving in Maeve's army. See Introduction, p. xiii.

[2] The capital of Ulster near Armagh.

" 'It is a weary way from here,' said the mother, 'for between thee and it lies Sliab Fuait.'

" 'Give me the bearings,' said he; and she did so.

"Away he went then, taking with him his hurly of brass, his ball of silver, his throwing javelin, and his toy spear; with which equipment he fell to shortening the way for himself. He did it thus: with his hurly he would strike the ball and drive it a great distance; then he pelted the hurly after it, and drove it just as far again; then he threw his javelin, lastly the spear. Which done, he would make a playful rush after them all, pick up the hurly, the ball and the javelin, while, before the spear's tip could touch the earth, he had caught the missile by the other end.

"In due course Cu Chulainn reached Emain Macha, where he found the boy-corps, thrice fifty in number, hurling on the green and practising martial exercises with Conchobar's son Follamain at their head. The lad dived right in among them and took a hand in the game. He got the ball between his legs and held it there, not suffering it to travel higher up than his knees or lower down than his ankle-joints, and so making it impossible for them to get in a stroke or in any other way to touch it. In this manner he brought it along and sent it home over the goal. In utter amazement the whole corps looked on; but Follamain mac Conchobar cried: 'Good now, boys, all together meet this youngster as he deserves, and kill him; because it is taboo to have such a one join himself to you and interfere in your game, without first having had the civility to procure your guarantee that his life should be respected. Together then and at once attack him and avenge violation of your taboo; for we know that he is the son of some petty Ulster warrior, such as without safe-conduct is not accustomed to intrude into your play.'

"The whole of them assailed Cu Chulainn, and simultaneously sent their hurlies at his head; he, however, parried all the hundred and fifty and was unharmed. The same with the balls, which he fended off with fists, fore-arms, and palms alone.

Their thrice fifty toy spears he received in his little shield, and still was unhurt. In turn now, Cu Chulainn went among them, and laid low fifty of the best: five more of them," said Fergus, "came past the spot where myself and Conchobar sat at chess-play, with the young lad close in their wake.

" 'Hold, my little fellow,' said Conchobar, 'I see this is no gentle game thou playest with the boy-corps.'

" 'And good cause I have too,' cried Cu Chulainn: 'after coming out of a far land to them, I have not had a guest's reception.'

" 'How now, little one,' said the king, 'knowest thou not the boy-corps' conditions: that a newcomer must have them bound by their honor to respect his life?'

" 'I knew it not,' said the boy, 'otherwise I had conformed, and taken measures beforehand.'

" ' 'Tis well,' said the king: 'take it now upon yourselves to let the boy go safe.'

" 'We do,' the boy-corps answered.

"They resumed play; Cu Chulainn did as he would with them, and again laid out fifty of them on the ground. Their fathers deemed they could not but be dead. No such thing, however; it was merely that with his blows and pushes and repeated charges, he so terrified them that they took to the grass.

" 'What on earth is he at with them now?' asked Conchobar.

" 'I swear by my gods,' said Cu Chulainn, 'that until they in their turn come under my protection and guarantee, I will not lighten my hand from off them.'

"This they did at once. Now," said Fergus in conclusion, "I submit, that a youngster who did all this when he was just five years old, needs not to excite our wonder because, now being turned of seventeen years, he in this Cattle-Raid of Cooley cut a four-pronged pole and the rest, and that he should have killed a man, or two, or three men, or even, as indeed he has done, four."

Conchobar's son Cormac Conlonges spoke now, saying, "In the year after that, the same little boy did another deed."

"And what was that?" Ailill asked.

"Well," continued Cormac, "in Ulster there was a good smith and artificer, by name Culann. He prepared a banquet for Conchobar, and traveled to Emain Macha to bid him to it. He begged Conchobar to bring with him only a moderate number of warriors, because neither land nor domain had he, but merely the product of his hammer, of his anvil, and of his tongs. Conchobar promised that he would bring no more than a small company. Culann returned home to make his last preparations, Conchobar remaining in Emain Macha until the meeting broke up and the day came to a close. Then the king put on his light convenient travelling garb, and betook him to the green in order to bid the boy-corps farewell before he started. There, however, he saw a curious sight. One hundred and fifty youths at one end of the green, and at the other, a single one and he taking the goal against the crowd of them. Again, when they played the hole-game, and it was their turn to aim at the hole, it being his to defend it, he stopped all thrice fifty balls just at the edge of the hole, so that not one went in; when the defence was theirs and it was his turn to shoot, he would hole the entire set without missing one. When the game was to tear one another's clothes off, he would have the mantles off them all, while the full number could not even pull out his brooch. When it was to upset each other, he would knock over the hundred and fifty and they could not stretch him on the ground. All which when Conchobar had witnessed, he said: 'I congratulate the land into which the little boy has come; were his full-grown deeds to prove consonant with his boyish exploits, he would indeed be of some solid use.'

"To this doubtful expression Fergus objected, saying to Conchobar, 'That is not justly said; for according as the little boy grows, so also will his deeds increase with him.'

" 'Have the child called to us,' said the king, 'that he may come with us to share the banquet.'

" 'I cannot go thither just now,' said the boy.

" 'How so?' asked Conchobar.

" 'The boy-corps have not yet had enough of play.'

" 'It would be too long for us to wait until they had,' said the king.

" 'Wait not at all; I will follow after you.'

" 'But, young one, knowest thou the way?'

" 'I will follow the trail of the company, of the horses, and the chariots' tracks.'

"Thereupon Conchobar started; eventually he reached Culann's house, was received in becoming fashion, fresh rushes were laid, and they fell to the banquet. Presently the smith said to Conchobar, 'Good now, O king, has any one promised that this night he would follow thee to this dwelling?'

" 'No, not one,' answered Conchobar (quite forgetting the little boy); 'but wherefore do you ask?'

" ' It is only that I have an excellent ban-dog, from which when his chain is taken off no one may dare to be near him; for saving myself he knows not any man, and in him resides the strength of an hundred.'

"Conchobar said, 'Loose him then, and let him guard this place.'

"So Culann did; the dog made the circuit of his country, then took up his usual position whence to watch the house, and there he couched with his head on his paws. Surely an extraordinary, cruel, fierce and savage dog was he.

"As for the boy-corps, until it was time to separate, they continued in Emain Macha; then they dispersed, each one to his parent's house, or to his nurse's, or to his guardian's. But the little fellow, trusting to the trail, as aforesaid, struck out for Culann's house. With his club and his ball he shortened the way for himself as he went. So soon as ever he came to the green of Culann's fort, the ban-dog became aware of him and gave tongue in such a way as to be heard throughout all the countryside; not was it to carve the boy decently as for a feast that he was minded, but at one gulp to swallow him down. The child was without all reasonable means of defence; therefore as the dog charged at him open-jawed he threw his playing ball down his throat with great force, which mortally punished the creature's inwards. Cu Chulainn seized him by the hind legs and banged him against a rock to such purpose that he strewed all the ground in broken fragments.

"The whole company within had heard the ban-dog's challenge, at the sound of which Conchobar said, ' 'Tis no good luck has brought us on our present trip.'

" 'Your meaning?' asked the others.

" 'I mean that the little boy, my sister Dechtire's son, Setanta mac Sualtach, had promised to come after me; and he even now must be killed by the ban-dog.'

"To a man the heroes rose; and though the fort's doors were thrown open, out they stormed over the ramparts to seek him. Speedy as they were, yet did Fergus outstrip them; he picked up the boy, hoisted him on his shoulder, and carried him to Conchobar. Culann himself had come out, and there he saw his ban-dog lie in scraps and pieces; which was a heart's vexation to him. He went back indoors and said, 'Thy father and thy mother are welcome both, but most unwelcome thou.'

" 'Why, what hast thou against the little fellow?' asked Conchobar.

" 'It was no good luck that inspired me to make my feast for thee, O Conchobar: my dog now being gone, my substance is but substance wasted; my livelihood, a means of living set all astray. Little boy,' he continued, 'that was a good member of my family thou tookest from me: a safeguard of raiment, of flocks, and of herds.'

" 'Be not angered thereat,' said the child; 'for in this matter myself will pronounce a just award.'

" 'And what might that be?' inquired Conchobar.

"The little boy replied, 'If in all Ireland there be a whelp of that dog's breed, by me he shall be nurtured till he be fit for action as was his sire. In the meantime I, O Culann, myself will do thee a ban-dog's service, in guarding of thy cattle and substance and stronghold.'

" 'Well hast thou made the award,' said Conchobar; and Cathbad the druid, chiming in, declared that not in his own person could he have done it better, and that henceforth the boy must bear the name *Cu Chulainn*, 'Culann's Hound.' The youngster, however, objected; 'I like my own name better: Setanta mac Sualtach.'

" 'Say not so,' Cathbad remonstrated; 'for all men in the world shall have their mouths full of that name.'

"The boy answered that on those terms the name would be well pleasing to him, and in this way it came to pass that it stuck to him. Now the little fellow," continued Cormac Conlonges the narrator of all this, "who when just touching six years of age slew the dog which even a great company did not dare to approach, it were not reasonable to be astonished though the same at seventeen should come to the border of the province, and kill a man, or two, or three, or four, on the Cattle-Raid of Cooley."

Another exiled Ulsterman, Fiacha mac Firaba, taking up the recital, said that in the very year following that adventure of the dog, the little boy had performed a third exploit.

"And what was that?" Ailill asked.

"Why, it was Cathbad the druid," continued Fiacha, "who to the north-east of Emain Macha taught his pupils, there being with him eight from among the students of his art. When one of them questioned him as to what purpose that day was more especially favorable, Cathbad told him that any stripling who on that day should for the first time assume arms and armor, the name of such an one forever would surpass those of all Ireland's youths besides. His life, however, must be fleeting, short. The boy was some distance away on the south side of Emain Macha; nevertheless he heard Cathbad's speech. He put off his playing suit and laid aside his implements of sport; then he entered Conchobar's sleeping house and said, 'All good be thine, O king.'

"Conchobar answered, 'Little boy, what is thy request?'

" 'I desire to take arms.'

" 'And who prompted thee to that?'

" 'Cathbad the druid,' answered the boy.

" 'Thou shalt not be denied,' said the king, and forthwith gave him two spears with sword and shield. The boy suppled and brandished the weapons and in the process broke them all to shivers and splinters. In short, whereas in Emain Macha Conchobar had seventeen weapon-equipments ready for the boy-corps' service—since whenever one of them took arms, Conchobar it was who invested him with the outfit and brought him luck in the using of it—the boy made fragments of them all. Which done, he said, 'O my master, O Conchobar, these arms are not good; they suffice me not.' Thereupon the king gave him his own two spears, his own sword, and his own shield. In every possible way the boy tested them; he even bent them point to hilt and head to butt, yet never broke them: they endured him. 'These arms are good,' said he, 'and worthy of me. Fair fall the land and the region which for its king has him whose arms and armor are these.'

"Just then it was that Cathbad the druid came into the house and wondering asked, 'Is the little boy assuming arms?'

" 'Ay, indeed,' said the king.

" 'It is not his mother's son we would care to see assume them on this day,' said the druid.

" 'How now,' said the king, 'was it not thyself that prompted him?'

" 'Not I, of a surety.'

" 'Brat,' cried the king, 'what meanest thou by telling me that it was so, wherein thou hast lied to me?'

" 'O king, be not wroth,' the boy pleaded; 'for he it was that prompted me when he instructed his other pupils. For when they asked him what special virtue lay in this day, he told them that the name of whatsoever youth should therein for the first time take arms, would top the fame of all other Erin's men; nor thereby should he suffer resulting disadvantage, save that his life must be fleeting, short.'

" 'And it is true for me,' said Cathbad; 'noble and famous indeed thou shalt be, but transitory, soon gone.'

" 'Little care I,' said Cu Chulainn, 'nor though I were but one day or one night in being, so long as after me the history of myself and doings may endure.'

"Then said Cathbad again, 'Well then, get into a chariot, boy, and proceed to test in thine own person whether mine utterance be truth.'

"So Cu Chulainn mounted a chariot; in divers ways he tried

its strength, and reduced it to fragments. He mounted a second, with the same result. In brief, whereas in Emain Macha for the boy-corps' service Conchobar had seventeen chariots, in like wise the little fellow smashed them all; then he said, 'These chariots of thine, O Conchobar, are no good at all, nor worthy of me.'

" 'Where is Iubar mac Riangabra?'[1] cried Conchobar.

" 'Here I am,' he answered.

" 'Prepare my own chariot and harness my own horses for him there.'

"The driver did his will, Cu Chulainn mounted, tested the chariot, and it endured him. 'This chariot is good,' he said, 'and my worthy match.'

" 'Good now, little boy,' said Iubar, 'let the horses be turned out to grass.'

" 'Too early for that yet, Iubar; drive on and round Emain Macha.'

" 'Let the horses go out to graze.'

" 'Too early yet, Iubar; drive ahead, that the boy-corps may give me salutation on this the first day of my taking arms.'

"They came to the place where the boy-corps was, and the cry of them resounded, 'These are arms that thou hast taken.'

" 'The very thing indeed,' he said.

"They wished him success in spoil-winning and in first-slaying, but expressed regret that he was weaned away from them and their sports. Cu Chulainn assured them that it was not so, but that it was something in the nature of a charm that had caused him to take arms on this day of all others. Again Iubar pressed him to have the horses taken out, and again the boy refused. He questioned the driver, 'Whither leads this great road here running by us?' Iubar answered that it ran to Ath an Foraire (the Lookout Ford) in Sliab Fuait. In answer to further questions with which he plied the charioteer, Cu Chulainn learned that the ford had that name from the fact that daily

---

[1] Conchubor's charioteer. His brother Loeg became Cuchulain's charioteer.

there some prime warrior of the Ulstermen kept watch and ward to see that no foreign champion came to molest them, it being his duty to do single combat on behalf of his whole province. Should poets and musicians be coming away from Ulster dissatisfied with their treatment, it was his duty, acting for the whole province, to solace them with gold and other gifts. On the other hand, did poets and musicians enter his province, his duty was to see that they had safe-conduct up to Conchobar's bed-side. This sentinel's praise then would be the theme of the first pieces, in divers forms of verse, the poets would rehearse upon arriving in Emain Macha.

"Cu Chulainn inquired whether Iubar knew who it was that on this particular day mounted guard. 'I know it well,' the charioteer replied; 'it is Conall mac Amergin, surnamed Cernach (the Victorious), Ireland's pre-eminent warrior.'

" 'Onward to that ford, then, driver!" cried the boy.

"Sure enough at the water's edge they came upon Conall, who received them with, 'And is it arms that you have taken today, little boy?'

" 'It is indeed,' Iubar answered for him.

" 'May his arms bring him triumph and victory and drawing of first blood,' said Conall. 'The only thing is that in my judgment thou hast prematurely assumed them, seeing that as yet thou art not fit for exploits.'

"For all answer the boy said, 'And what dost thou here, Conall?'

" 'On behalf of the province I keep watch and ward.'

" 'Come,' said the youngster, 'for this day let me take the duty.'

" 'Never say it,' replied Conall, 'for as yet thou art not up to coping with a real fighting man.'

" 'Then will I go down to the shallows of Loch Echtra, to see whether I may draw blood on either friend or foe.'

" 'And I,' said Conall, 'will go to protect thee and to safeguard, so that thou wilt not run into dangers on the border.'

" 'Nay,' said Cu Chulainn, 'come not.'

" 'I will so,' Conall insisted, 'for were I to permit thee all alone to frequent the border, the Ulstermen would avenge it on me.'

"Conall had his chariot made ready and his horses harnessed; he started on his errand of protection, and soon overtook Cu Chulainn, who had cut the matter short and had gone on before. They now being abreast, the boy deemed that, in event of opportunity to do some deed of mortal daring, Conall would never allow him to execute it. From the ground therefore he picked up a stone about the size of his fist, and took very careful aim at Conall's chariot-yoke. He broke it in two, the vehicle came down, and Conall was hurled prone, so falling that his mouth was brought over one shoulder.

" 'What's all this, boy?'

" 'It was I: in order to see whether my marksmanship was good and whether there was in me the material of a good warrior.'

" 'Poison take both thy shot and thyself as well; and though thy head should fall as a prize to some foe over yonder, yet never a foot further will I budge to save thee!'

" 'The very thing I crave of thee,' said the boy; 'and I do this in this particular manner because to you Ulstermen it is taboo to persist after violence is done to you.' With that Conall went back to his post at the ford.

"As for the little boy, southwards he went his way to the shallows of Loch Echtra, and until the day's end abode there. Then spoke Iubar: 'If to thee we might venture to say so much, little one, I should be more than rejoiced that we made instant return to Emain Macha. For already for some time the carving has been going on there; and whereas there thou hast thine appointed place kept till thou come—between Conchobar's knees—I on the contrary can do nothing but join the messengers and jesters of his house, to fit in where I may; for which reason I judge it now fitting that I were back in time to scramble with them.'

"Cu Chulainn ordered him to harness the chariot; which being done, they drove off, and Cu Chulainn inquired the name of a mountain that he saw. He learned that it was Sliab Morne, and further asked the meaning of a white cairn which appeared on a summit. It was Finnchairn; the boy thought it inviting, and ordered the driver to take him thither. Iubar expressed great reluctance and Cu Chulainn said, 'Thou art a lazy loon, considering that this is my first adventure-quest, and this is thy first trip with me.'

" 'And if it is,' said Iubar, 'and if I ever reach Emain Macha, for ever and for ever may it be my last!'

" 'Good now, driver,' said the boy when they were on the top of the hillock; 'in all directions point out to me the topography of Ulster, a country in which I know not my way about.' The charioteer from that position pointed out the hills and the plain lands and the strongholds of the province.

" ' 'Tis well, O driver; and what now is yon well-defined glen-seamed plain before us to the southward?'

" 'That is the plain of Bray (Mag Breg).'

" 'Proceed then and instruct me concerning the strongholds and forts of that plain.' Then Iubar pointed out to him Tara and Tailltiu, Cletty and Knowth and the brug of Angus mac Oc on the Boyne, and the stronghold of Nechtan Sceine's sons.

" 'Are they those sons of Nechtan of whom it is said, that the number of Ulstermen now alive exceeds not the number of them fallen by their hands?'

" 'The same,' said Iubar.

" 'Away with us then to the stronghold of Nechtan's sons.'

" 'Woe waits on such a speech; and whosoever he be that goes there, I will not be the one.'

"Cu Chulainn said, 'Alive or dead, thither shalt thou go, however.'

" 'Alive I go then, and dead I shall be left there.'

"They made their way to the stronghold, and the little boy dismounted upon the green, a green with this particular feature: in its center stood a pillar stone, encircled with an iron collar, test of heroic accomplishment; for it bore graven writing to the effect that any man (if only he were one that carried arms) who should enter on this green, must hold it taboo to him to depart from it without challenging to single combat some of the dwellers in the stronghold. The little boy read the Ogam,[1] threw his arms around the stone to start it, and eventually pitched it, collar and all, into the water close at hand.

"'In my poor opinion,' ventured Iubar, 'it is no better so than it was before; and I well know that this time at all events thou wilt find the object of thy search: a prompt and violent death.'

"'Good, good, O driver, spread me now the chariot-coverings that I may sleep a little while.'

"'Alas that one should speak so; for a land of foemen and not of friends is this.'

"Iubar obeyed, and on the green at once the little fellow fell asleep. Just then it was that Foill mac Nechtain issued forth, and, at the sight of the chariot, called out, 'Driver, do not unharness those horses!' Iubar made answer that he still held the reins in his hand—a sign that he was not about to unharness them.

"'What horses are these?'

"'Conchobar's two piebalds.'

"'Even such at sight I took them to be,' said Foill; 'and who has brought them into these borders?'

"'A young bit of a little boy; one who for luck has taken arms to-day, and for the purpose of showing off his form and fashion has come into the borders.'

"'Never let it thrive with him,' said Foill; 'were it sure that he is capable of action, it is dead in place of alive that he would go back to Emain Macha.'

"'Indeed he is not capable, nor could it be rightly imputed to him; this is but the seventh year since his birth.' Here the little one lifted his face from the ground; not only that but his whole body to his feet, blushed deep at the affront which he had overheard, and said, 'Ay, I am fit for action!'

"But Foill rejoined, 'I rather would incline to hold that thou art not.'

[1] An alphabet of twenty characters used by the ancient British and Irish. NED.

"'Thou shalt know what to hold in this matter, only let us repair to the ford; but first, go fetch thy weapons; in cowardly guise thou art come hither, for nor drivers nor messengers nor folk unarmed slay I.' Foill rushed headlong for his weapons, and Iubar advised the boy that he must be careful with him. Cu Chulainn asked the reason, and was told that the man was Foill mac Nechtain Sceine, invulnerable to either point or edge of any kind.

"'Not to me should such a thing be spoken,' he replied, 'for I will take in hand my special feat: the tempered and refined iron ball, which shall land in his forehead's midst and backwards through his skull shall carry out his brain, so leaving his head traversed with a fair conduit for the air.' With that, out came Foill mac Nechtain again; the little lad grasped his ball, hurled it with the exact effect foretold, and he took Foill's head.

"Out of the stronghold now the second son emerged on the green, whose name was Tuachall mac Nechtain, and he said, 'Belike thou art inclined to boast of that much.' Cu Chulainn replied that the fall of a single warrior was for him no matter of boast, and Tuachall told him that in that case he should not boast at all, because straightway he would perish by his hand. 'Then make haste for thy weapons,' said the boy, 'for in cowardly guise thou comest hither.'

"Away went Tuachall; Iubar repeated his admonitions. 'Who is that?' asked the boy. He was told not only that he was a son of Nechtan but also that he must be slain by the first stroke or shot or other attempt of whatsoever sort, or not at all; and this because of the extraordinary activity and skill which in front of weapons' points he displayed to avoid them. Again Cu Chulainn objected that such language ought not to be addressed to him. Said he, 'I will take in my hand Conchobar's great spear, the Venomous; it shall pierce the shield over his breast and, after holing the heart within him, shall break three ribs in his side that is the farthest from me.' This also the boy performed, and took the victim's head before his body touched the ground.

"Now came out the youngest of the sons, Fainnle mac

Nechtain, and said, 'But simpletons they were with whom thou hast had to do.' Cu Chulainn asked him what he meant, and Fainnle invited him to come away down and out upon the water where his foot would not touch bottom, himself on the instant darting to the ford. Still Iubar warned the boy to be on his guard. 'How is that then?' said Cu Chulainn.

" 'Because that is Fainnle mac Nechtain; and the reason why he bears that name is that as it were a *fáinnle* (swallow) or a weasel, even so for swiftness he travels on the water's surface, nor can the whole world's swimmers attempt to cope with him.'

" 'Not to me ought such a thing to be said,' objected the boy again; 'for thou knowest the river which we have in Emain Macha, the Callan: well, when the boy-corps break off from their sports and plunge into it to swim, on either shoulder I take a lad of them, on either palm another, nor in the transit across that water ever wet as much as my ankles.'

"Then he and Fainnle entered the ford and there wrestled. The youngster clasped his arms around him and got him just flush with the water; then he dealt him a stroke with Conchobar's sword and took his head, letting the body go with the current. To finish up, Cu Chulainn entered the stronghold and harried it; then he and Iubar fired it and left it burning brightly, then turned about to retrace their steps through Sliab Fuait, not forgetting to carry with them the heads of Nechtan Sceine's sons.

"Soon they saw in front of them a herd of deer, and the boy sought to know what were those numerous and restless cattle. Iubar explained that they were not cattle, but a herd of wild deer that kept in the dark glens of Sliab Fuait. He being urged to goad the horses in their direction, did so; but the king's fat horses could not attain to join company with the hard-conditioned deer. Cu Chulainn dismounted therefore and by sheer running and mere speed captured in the moor two stags of the greatest bulk, which he made fast to the chariot with thongs. Still they held a course for Emain Macha, and by-and-by, when nearing it, perceived a certain flock of whitest swans. The boy asked were they pet birds or wild, and learned that they were wild swans which used to congregate from rocks and islands of the sea, and for feeding's sake, infest the country. Cu Chulainn questioned further, and wished to know which was the rarer thing: to bring some of them back to Emain Macha alive, or to bring them dead. Iubar did not hesitate to say that bringing them back living would be the more creditable by far; 'for,' said he, 'you may find plenty to bring them in dead; perhaps not one to bring them in living.'

"Into his sling Cu Chulainn laid a little stone, and with it at a cast brought down eight swans of the number. Again he loaded, this time with a larger stone, and now brought down sixteen. 'Driver, bring along the birds,' he said.

"But Iubar hesitated. 'I hardly can do that.'

" 'And why not?' said the boy.

" 'Because if I quit my present position, the horses' speed and the action being what they are, the chariot wheels will cut me into pieces; or else the stags' antlers will pierce and otherwise wound me.'

" 'No true warrior art thou, Iubar; but come, the horses I will gaze upon with such a look that they shall not break their regulation pace; as for the gaze that I will bend upon the stags, they will stoop their heads for awe.'

"At this Iubar ventured down and retrieved the swans, which with more of the thongs and ropes he secured to the chariot. In this manner they covered the rest of the way to Emain Macha.

"Leborcham, daughter of Aed and messenger to the king, perceived them now and cried, 'A solitary chariot-fighter draws near to thee now, O Conchobar, and terribly he comes! The chariot is graced with the bleeding heads of his enemies; beautiful white birds he has which in the chariot bear him company, and wild unbroken stags bound and tethered to the same. Indeed if measures be not taken to receive him prudently, the best of the Ulstermen must fall by his hand.'

" 'I know that little chariot-fighter,' Conchobar said: 'the little boy, my sister's son, who this very day went to the border. Surely he will have reddened his hand; and should his fury not be timely met, all Emain Macha's young men will perish by him.'

"At last they hit upon a method to abate his manly rage (the result of having shed blood), and it was this: Emain Macha's women all (six score and ten in number) bared their bosoms, and without subterfuge of any kind trooped out to meet him (their manoeuver being based on Cu Chulainn's well-known modesty, which, like all his other qualities, was excessive). The little fellow leaned his head against the rail of the chariot and shut them from his sight. Then was the desired moment; all unawares he was seized, and soused in a vat of cold water ready for the purpose. In this first vessel the heat generated by his immersion was such that the staves and hoops flew asunder instantly. In a second vat the water escaped (by boiling over); in yet a third the water still was hotter than one could bear. By this time, however, the little boy's fury had died down in him; from crown to sole he blushed a beautiful pink red all over, and they clad him in his festive clothes. Thus his natural form and feature were restored to him.

"A beautiful boy indeed was that: seven toes to each foot he had, and to either hand as many fingers; his eyes were bright with seven pupils apiece, each one of which glittered with seven gem-like sparkles. On either cheek he had four moles: a blue, a crimson, a green, and a yellow one. Between one ear and the other he had fifty clear-yellow long tresses that were as the yellow wax of bees, or like a brooch of white gold as it glints in the sun unobscured. He wore a green mantle silver-clasped upon his breast, a gold-thread shirt. The small boy took his place between Conchobar's knees, and the king began to stroke his hair. Now the stripling who by the time seven years were completed since his birth, had done such deeds: had destroyed the champions by whom two-thirds of the Ulstermen had fallen unavenged,—I hold," said Fiacha mac Firaba, the narrator, "that there is scant room for wonder though at seventeen he comes to the border, and kills a man, ay, two or three, or four, all in the Cattle-Raid of Cooley."

9TH CENTURY.
Translator Standish Hayes O'Grady.

The Tragic Death of Connla[1]

WHAT WAS the cause for which Cu Chulainn slew his son?

Not hard to tell. Cu Chulainn went to be taught craft of arms by Scathach, daughter of Ardgeimm, in Letha,[2] until he attained mastership of feats with her. And Aife, a neighboring princess, went to him, and he left her pregnant. And he said to her that she would bear a son. "Keep this golden thumb-ring," said he, "until it fits the boy. When it fits him, let him come to seek me in Ireland. Let no man put him off his road, let him not make himself known to any man, nor let him refuse combat to any."

That day seven years the boy went forth to seek his father. The men of Ulster were at a gathering by Tracht Eisi (Strand of the Track), when they saw the boy coming towards them across the sea, a skiff of bronze under him, and gilt oars in his hand. In the skiff he had a heap of stones. He would put a stone in his staff-sling, and launch a stunning shot at the sea-birds, so that he brought them down, and they alive. Then would he let them up into the air again. He would perform his palate-feat, between both hands, so that it was too quick for the eye to perceive. He would tune his voice for them, and bring them down for the second time. Then he revived them once more.

"Well, now," said Conchobar, "woe to the land into which yonder lad comes! If grown-up men of the island from which he comes were to come, they would grind us to dust, when a

[1] See Introduction, p. xvii.

[2] Brittany or the continent in general.

small boy makes that practice. Let some one go to meet him! Let him not allow the boy to come on land at all!"

"Who shall go to meet him?"

"Who should it be," said Conchobar, "but Condere son of Eochaid?"

"Why should Condere go?" said the others.

"Not hard to tell," said Conchobar. "If it is reason and eloquence he practises, then Condere is the proper person."

"I shall go to meet him," said Condere.

So Condere went just as the boy took the beach. "Thou hast come far enough, my good boy," said Condere, "for us to know whither thou goest and whence is thy race."

"I do not make myself known to any one man," said the lad, "nor do I avoid any man."

"Thou shalt not land," said Condere, "until thou hast made thyself known."

"I shall go whither I have set out," said the lad.

The boy turned away. Then said Condere: "Turn to me, my boy; Conchobar will protect thee. Turn to Conchobar, the valiant son of Nessa; to Sencha, the son of Coscra; to Cethern, the red-bladed son of Fintan, the fire that wounds battalions; to Amergin the poet; to Cumscraid of the great hosts. Welcome he whom Conall the Victorious protects."

"Thou hast met us well," said the lad. "Therefore shalt thou have thy answer. Turn back again!" said the lad. "For though thou hadst the strength of a hundred, thou art not able to check me."

"Well," said Condere, "let someone else go to speak to thee!" So Condere went to the men of Ulster and told them.

"It shall not be," said Conall the Victorious, "that the honor of Ulster be carried off while I am alive." Then he went towards the boy. "Thy play is pretty, my good boy," said Conall.

"It will not be less pretty against thee," said the lad. The lad put a stone in his sling. He sent it into the air, so that its noise and thunder as it went up reached Conall, and threw him on his back. Before he could rise, the lad put the strap of his shield upon his arms.

"Someone else against him!" said Conall. In that way the boy made mockery of the host of Ulster.

Cu Chulainn, however, was present at the time, going towards the boy, and the arm of Emer, Forgall's daughter, over his neck. "Do not go down!" said she. "It is a son of thine that is down there. Do not murder thy only son! It is not fair fight nor wise to rise up against thy son. Turn to me! Hear my voice! My advice is good. Let Cu Chulainn hear it! I know what name he will tell, if the boy down there is Connla, the only son of Aife," said Emer.

Then said Cu Chulainn: "Forbear, woman! Even though it were he who is there," said he, "I would kill him for the honor of Ulster."

Then he went down himself. "Delightful, my boy, is the play which thou makest," said he.

"*Your* play, though, is not so," said the little boy, "that two of you did not come, so that I may make myself known to them."

"It would have been necessary to bring a small boy along with me," said Cu Chulainn. "However, thou wilt die unless thou tellest thy name."

"Let it be so!" said the lad. The boy made for him. They exchanged blows. The lad, by a properly measured stroke with the sword, cropped off Cu Chulainn's hair. "The mockery has come to a head!" said Cu Chulainn. "Now let us wrestle!"

"I cannot reach thy belt," said the boy. He got upon two stones, and thrust Cu Chulainn thrice between two pillar-stones, while the boy did not move either of his feet from the stones until his feet went into the stones up to his ankles. The track of his feet is there still. Hence is the Strand of the Track (Tracht Eisi) in Ulster.

Then they went into the sea to drown each other, and twice the boy ducked him. Thereupon Cu Chulainn went at the boy from the water, and played him false with the *gae bulga*;[1] for to

[1] A mysterious weapon, probably some kind of spear (gae), given to Cuchulain by Scathach.

no man had Scathach ever taught the use of that weapon save to Cu Chulainn alone. He sent it at the boy through the water, so that his bowels fell about his feet.

"Now, this is what Scathach never taught me!" cried the boy. "Woe that thou has wounded me!"

"It is true," said Cu Chulainn. He took the boy between his arms, and carried him till he let him down before the men of Ulster. "Here is my son for you, men of Ulster," said he.

"Alas!" said the men; and "It is true," said the boy. "If I were among you to the end of five years, I should vanquish the men of the world before you on every side, and you would hold kingship as far as Rome. Since it is as it is, point out to me the famous men that are on the spot, that I may take leave of them!"

Thereupon he put his arms round the neck of one after another, bade farewell to his father, and forthwith died. Then his cry of lament was raised, his grave made, his stone set up, and to the end of three days no calf was let to their cows by the men of Ulster, to commemorate him.

9TH CENTURY.
Translator Kuno Meyer.

Fand Yields Cuchulain to Emer[1]

Emer, he is your man, now,
And well may you wear him.
When I can no longer hold him,
I must yield him.

Many a man has wanted me,
But I have kept my vows.
I have been an honest woman,
Under the roofs and boughs.

Pity the woman loves a man,
When no love invites her.
Better for her to fly from love
If unloved, love bites her.

9TH CENTURY.
Translator Sean O'Faolain.

---

[1] In this poem taken from *The Sick-Bed of Cuchulain,* a story preserved in *The Book of the Dun Cow,* Fand, a woman of the other world, yields to Emer, her earthly rival for the love of Cuchulain.

Cuchulain's Lament for Ferdiad[1]

Play was each, pleasure each,
Till Ferdiad faced the beach;
One had been our student life,
One in strife of school our place,
One our gentle teacher's grace
Loved o'er all and each.

Play was each, pleasure each,
Till Ferdiad faced the beach;
One had been our wonted ways,
One the praise for feat of fields,
Scathach gave two victor shields
Equal prize to each.

Play was each, pleasure each,
Till Ferdiad faced the beach;
Dear that pillar of pure gold
Who fell cold beside the ford.
Hosts of heroes felt his sword
First in battle's breach.

[1] In the war between Ulster and Connaught, which is the theme of *The Cattle Raid of Cooley*, Cuchulain vanquishes Ferdiad, his boyhood friend and sworn brother, who with other Ulster warriors had gone over to the enemy after the betrayal of the sons of Usnech by Conchubor king of Ulster.

Play was each, pleasure each,
Till Ferdiad faced the beach;
Lion fiery, fierce and bright,
Wave whose might no thing withstands,
Sweeping, with the shrinking sands,
  Horror o'er the beach.

Play was each, pleasure each,
Till Ferdiad faced the beach;
Loved Ferdiad, dear to me:
I shall dree his death for aye—
Yesterday a mountain he,
  A shade today.

9TH CENTURY.
Translator George Sigerson.

The Death of Cuchulain[1]

When Cu Chulainn's foes came for the last time against him, his land was filled with smoke and flame, the weapons fell from their racks, and the day of his death drew nigh. The evil tidings were brought to him, and the maiden Leborcham bade him arise, though he was worn out with fighting in defence of the plain of Muirthemne, and Niam, wife of Conall the Victorious, also spoke to him; so he sprang to his arms, and flung his mantle around him; but the brooch fell and pierced his foot, forewarning him. Then he took his shield and ordered his charioteer Loeg to harness his horse, the Gray of Macha.

"I swear by the gods by whom my people swear," said Loeg, "though the men of Conchobar's province were around the Gray of Macha, they could not bring him to the chariot. I never refused thee till today. If thou wilt, come thou, and speak with the Gray himself."

Cu Chulainn went to him. And thrice did the horse turn his left side to his master. On the night before, the Morrigu[2] had broken the chariot, for she liked not Cu Chulainn's going to the battle, for she knew that he would not come again to Emain Macha. Then Cu Chulainn reproached his horse, saying that he was not wont to deal thus with his master.

Thereat the Gray of Macha came and let his big round tears of blood fall on Cu Chulainn's feet. And then Cu Chulainn leaped into the chariot, and drove it suddenly southwards along the Road of Midluachar.

And Leborcham met him and besought him not to leave them; and the thrice fifty queens who were in Emain Macha and who loved him cried to him with a great cry. And when he turned his chariot to the right, they gave a scream of wailing and

[1] See Introduction, p. xviii.

[2] A female demon associated with battle and slaughter.

lamentation, and smote their hands, for they knew that he would not come to them again.

The house of his nurse that had fostered him was before him on the road. He used to go to it whenever he went driving past her southwards and from the south. And she kept for him always a vessel with drink therein. Now he drank a drink and fared forth, bidding his nurse farewell. Then he saw three Crones, blind of the left eye, before him on the road. They had cooked on spits of rowantree a dog with poisons and spells. And one of the things that Cu Chulainn was bound not to do, was going to a cooking-hearth and consuming the food.[1] And another of the things that he must not do, was eating his namesake's flesh.[2] He sped on and was about to pass them, for he knew that they were not there for his good.

Then said a Crone to him: "Visit us, O Cu Chulainn."

"I will not visit you in sooth," said Cu Chulainn.

"The food is only a hound," said she. "Were this a great cooking-hearth thou wouldst have visited us. But because what is here is little, thou comest not. Unseemly are the great who endure not the little and poor."

Then he drew nigh to her, and the Crone gave him the shoulder-blade of the hound out of her left hand. And then Cu Chulainn ate it out of his left hand, and put it under his left thigh. The hand that took it and the thigh under which he put it were seized from trunk to end, so that the normal strength abode not in them.

Then he drove along the Road of Midluachar around Sliab Fuait; and his enemy Erc son of Cairbre saw him in his chariot, with his sword shining redly in his hand, and the light of valor hovering over him, and his three-hued hair like strings of golden thread over the edge of the anvil of some cunning craftsman.

"That man is coming towards us, O men of Erin!" said Erc; "await him." So they made a fence of their linked shields, and

---

[1] Because of his *geasa* or taboos.

[2] Since his name was Cu (hound), he was forbidden to eat dog's flesh.

at each corner Erc made them place two of their bravest feigning to fight each other, and a satirist with each of these pairs, and he told the satirists to ask Cu Chulainn for his spear, for the sons of Calatin had prophesied of his spear that a king would be slain by it, unless it were given when demanded. And he made the men of Erin utter a great cry. And Cu Chulainn rushed against them in his chariot, performing his three thunder-feats; and he plied his spear and sword; so that the halves of their heads and skulls and hands and feet, and their red bones were scattered broadcast throughout the plain of Muirthemne, in number like to the sands of the sea and stars of heaven and dewdrops of May, flakes of snow, hailstones, leaves in the forest, buttercups on Mag Breg, and grass under the hoofs of herds on a day in summer. And gray was the field with their brains after that onslaught and plying of weapons which Cu Chulainn dealt unto them.

Then he saw one of the pairs of warriors contending together, and the satirist called on him to intervene, and Cu Chulainn leaped at them, and with two blows of his fist dashed out their brains.

"That spear to me!" said the satirist.

"I swear what my people swear," said Cu Chulainn, "thou dost not need it more than I do. The men of Erin are upon me here and I am attacking them."

"I will revile thee if thou givest it not," said the satirist.

"I have never yet been reviled because of my niggardliness or my churlishness."

With that Cu Chulainn flung the spear at him with its handle foremost, and it passed through his head and killed nine on the other side of him.

And Cu Chulainn drove through the host, but Lugaid son of Cu Roi got the spear.

"What will fall by this spear, O sons of Calatin?" asked Lugaid.

"A king will fall by that spear," said the sons of Calatin.

Then Lugaid flung the spear at Cu Chulainn's chariot, and it reached the charioteer, Loeg mac Riangabra, and all his bowels came forth on the cushion of the chariot.

Then said Loeg, "Bitterly have I been wounded," etc.

Thereafter Cu Chulainn drew out the spear, and Loeg bade him farewell. Then said Cu Chulainn: "Today I shall be warrior and I shall be charioteer also."

Then he saw the second pair contending, and one of them said it was a shame for him not to intervene. And Cu Chulainn sprang upon them and dashed them into pieces against a rock.

"That spear to me, O Cu Chulainn!" said the satirist.

"I swear what my people swear, thou dost not need the spear more than I do. On my hand and my valor and my weapons it rests today to sweep the four provinces of Erin today from the plain of Muirthemne."

"I will revile thee," said the satirist.

"I am not bound to grant more than one request this day, and, moreover, I have already paid for my honor."

"I will revile Ulster for thy default," said the satirist.

"Never yet has Ulster been reviled for my refusal nor for my churlishness. Though little of my life remains to me, Ulster shall not be reviled this day."

Then Cu Chulainn cast his spear at him by the handle and it went through his head and killed nine behind him, and Cu Chulainn drove through the host even as he had done before.

Then Erc son of Cairbre took the spear. "What shall fall by this spear, O sons of Calatin?" said Erc son of Cairbre.

"Not hard to say: a king falls by that spear," said the sons of Calatin.

"I heard you say that a king would fall by the spear which Lugaid long since cast."

"And that is true," said the sons of Calatin. "Thereby fell the king of the charioteers of Erin, namely Cu Chulainn's charioteer, Loeg mac Riangabra."

Now Erc cast the spear at Cu Chulainn, and it lighted on his horse, the Gray of Macha. Cu Chulainn snatched out the spear. And each of them bade the other farewell. Thereat the Gray of

Macha left him with half the yoke under his neck and went into the Gray's Linn in Sliab Fuait.

Thereupon Cu Chulainn again drove through the host and saw the third pair contending, and he intervened as he had done before, and the satirist demanded his spear and Cu Chulain at first refused it.

"I will revile thee," said the satirist.

"I have paid for my honor today. I am not bound to grant more than one request this day."

"I will revile Ulster for thy fault."

"I have paid for Ulster's honor," said Cu Chulainn.

"I will revile thy race," said the satirist.

"Tidings that I have been defamed shall never reach the land I have not reached. For little there is of my life remaining."

So Cu Chulainn flung the spear to him, handle foremost, and it went through his head and through thrice nine other men.

" 'Tis grace with wrath, O Cu Chulainn," said the satirist.

Then Cu Chulainn for the last time drove through the host, and Lugaid took the spear, and said:

"What will fall by this spear, O sons of Calatin?"

"I heard you say that a king would fall by the spear that Erc cast this morning."

"That is true," said they, "the king of the steeds of Erin fell by it, namely the Gray of Macha."

Then Lugaid flung the spear and struck Cu Chulainn, and his bowels came forth on the cushion of the chariot, and his only horse, the Black Sainglenn, fled away, with half the yoke hanging to him, and left the chariot and his master, the king of the heroes of Erin, dying alone on the plain.

Then said Cu Chulainn, "I would fain go as far as that loch to drink a drink thereout."

"We give thee leave," said they, "provided that thou come to us again."

"I will bid you come for me," said Cu Chulainn, "if I cannot come myself."

Then he gathered his bowels into his breast, and went forth to the loch.

And there he drank his drink, and washed himself, and came forth to die, calling on his foes to come to meet him.

Now a great mearing went westwards from the loch and his eye lit upon it, and he went to a pillar-stone which is in the plain, and he put his breast-girdle round it that he might not die seated nor lying down, but that he might die standing up. Then came the men all around him, but they durst not go to him, for they thought he was alive.

"It is a shame for you," said Erc son of Cairbre, "not to take that man's head in revenge for my father's head which was taken by him."

Then came the Gray of Macha to Cu Chulainn to protect him so long as his soul was in him and the "hero's light" out of his forehead remained. And the Gray of Macha wrought three red routs all around him. And fifty fell by his teeth and thirty by each of his hoofs. This is what he slew of the host. And hence is the saying, "Not keener were the victorious courses of the Gray of Macha after Cu Chulainn's slaughter."

And then came the battle goddess Morrigu and her sisters in the form of scald-crows and sat on his shoulder. "That pillar is not wont to be under birds," said Erc son of Cairbre.

Then Lugaid arranged Cu Chulainn's hair over his shoulder, and cut off his head. And then fell the sword from Cu Chulainn's hand, and smote off Lugaid's right hand, which fell on the ground. And Cu Chulainn's right hand was cut off in revenge for this. Lugaid and the hosts then marched away, carrying with them Cu Chulainn's head and his right hand, and they came to Tara, and there is the "Sick-bed" of his head and his right hand, and the full of the cover of his shield of mould.

From Tara they marched southwards to the river Liffey. But meanwhile the hosts of Ulster were hurrying to attack their foes, and Conall the Victorious, driving in front of them, met the Gray of Macha streaming with blood. Then Conall knew that Cu Chulainn had been slain. And he and the Gray of Macha sought Cu Chulainn's body. They saw Cu Chulainn at the pillar-stone. Then went the Gray of Macha and laid his head on Cu Chulainn's breast. And Conall said, "A heavy care to the Gray of Macha is that corpse."

And Conall followed the hosts meditating vengeance, for he was bound to avenge Cu Chulainn. For there was a comrades' covenant between Cu Chulainn and Conall the Victorious, namely, that whichever of them was first killed should be avenged by the other. "And if *I* be the first killed," Cu Chulainn had said, "how soon wilt thou avenge me?"

"The day on which thou shalt be slain," said Conall, "I will avenge thee before that evening. And if I be slain," said Conall, "how soon wilt thou avenge me?"

"Thy blood will not be cold on earth," said Cu Chulainn, "before I shall avenge thee." So Conall pursued Lugaid to the Liffey.

Then was Lugaid bathing. "Keep a lookout over the plain," said he to his charioteer, "that no one come to us without being seen."

The charioteer looked. "One horseman is here coming to us," said he, "and great are the speed and swiftness with which he comes. Thou wouldst deem that all the ravens of Erin were above him. Thou wouldst deem that flakes of snow were specking the plain before him."

"Unbeloved is the horseman that comes there," said Lugaid. "It is Conall the Victorious, mounted on the Dewy-Red. The birds thou sawest above him are the sods from that horse's hoofs. The snow-flakes thou sawest specking the plain before him are the foam from that horse's lips and from the curbs of his bridle. Look again," said Lugaid, "what road is he coming?"

"He is coming to the ford," said the charioteer, "the path that the hosts have taken."

"Let that horse pass us," said Lugaid. "We desire not to fight against him." But when Conall reached the middle of the ford he spied Lugaid and his charioteer and went to them.

"Welcome is a debtor's face!" said Conall. "He to whom he oweth debts demands them of him. I am thy creditor for the slaying of my comrade Cu Chulainn, and here I am suing thee for this."

They then agreed to fight on the plain of Argetros, and there Conall wounded Lugaid with his javelin. Thence they went to a place called Ferta Lugdach.

"I wish," said Lugaid, "to have the truth of men from thee."

"What is that?" asked Conall the Victorious.

"That thou shouldst use only one hand against me, for one hand only have I."

"Thou shalt have it," said Conall the Victorious.

So Conall's hand was bound to his side with ropes. There for the space between two of the watches of the day they fought, and neither of them prevailed over the other. When Conall found that he prevailed not, he saw his steed the Dewy-Red by Lugaid. And the steed came to Lugaid and tore a piece out of his side.

"Woe is me!" said Lugaid, "that is not the truth of men, O Conall."

"I gave it only on my own behalf," said Conall. "I gave it not on behalf of savage beasts and senseless things."

"I know now," said Lugaid, "that thou wilt not go till thou takest my head with thee, since we took Cu Chulainn's head from him. So take," said he, "my head in addition to thine own, and add my realm to thy realm, and my valor to thy valor. For I prefer that thou shouldst be the best hero in Erin."

Thereat Conall the Victorious cut off Lugaid's head. And Conall and his Ulstermen then returned to Emain Macha. That week they entered it not in triumph. But the soul of Cu Chulainn appeared there to the thrice fifty queens who had loved him, and they saw him floating in his phantom chariot over Emain Macha, and they heard him chant a mystic song of the coming of Christ and the Day of Doom.

8TH CENTURY.
Translator Whitley Stokes.

The Story of Deirdre

The men of Ulster were drinking in the house of Feidhlimidh son of Dall, Conchobhar's story-teller. Now Feidhlimidh's wife was waiting on the company, standing before them, and she was pregnant. Drinking-horns and servings of food went round, and the men raised a howl of drunkenness. When they were about to go to bed, the woman came to her couch. As she crossed the middle of the house the baby shrieked in her womb, so that it was heard throughout the courtyard. Everyone inside jumped up at each other at that screech, so that they were face to face in the house. Then Senchae son of Ailill restrained them. "Do not move," said he, "let the woman be brought to us so that the cause of this noise may be discovered." The woman was brought to them then . . . Then she ran to Cathbhadh, because he was a seer; . . . and Cathbhadh said:

"Under the cradle of your womb
cried a woman of curling yellow golden hair,
with slow grey-pupilled eyes.
Like the foxglove are her purple cheeks,
to the colour of snow we compare
the spotless treasure of her teeth.
Bright are her lips, of vermilion red.
A woman for whom there will be many slaughters
among the chariot-warriors of Ulster." . . .

Then Cathbhadh put his hand on the woman's belly, so that the baby stormed under his hand. "Truly," said he, "it is a girl there, and *Deirdriu* shall be her name, and evil will come of her." The girl was born after that. . . .

"Let the girl be killed," said the warriors. "Not so," said Conchobhar, "the girl shall be taken by me to-morrow," said Conchobhar, "and shall be brought up under my own control, and shall be the woman who will be in my company." And the Ulstermen did not dare correct him in this.

It was done, then. She was brought up by Conchobhar until she was the most wonderfully beautiful girl in Ireland. In a court apart she was reared, so that none of the Ulstermen might see her until the time when she should sleep with Conchobhar; and there was no one who might be allowed into that court but her foster-father and her foster-mother, and also Lebhorcham, for she could not be excluded because she was a satirist.

Now once upon a time the girl's foster-father was skinning a trespassing calf in the snow outside, in the winter, to cook it for her. She saw a raven drinking the blood on the snow. Then she said to Lebhorcham, "I should dearly love any man with those three colours, with hair like the raven and cheek like the blood and body like the snow." "Dignity and good luck be yours," said Lebhorcham, "it is not far from you. He is in the house beside you, Noísi the son of Uisliu." "I shall not be well, truly," said she, "until I see him." . . .

Now when he, this same Noísi, was alone outside, she stole away out to him as if to pass him by, and he did not recognise her. "Pretty is the heifer which passes by us," said he. "The heifers are bound to be well-grown," said she, "where there are no bulls." "You have the bull of the province, the king of Ulster," said he. "I would choose between you two," said she, "and I would take a young little bull like you." "Not so," said he, "because of Cathbhadh's prophecy." "Is it to reject me that you say that?" said she. "It is indeed," said he. At that she leaped at him and seized his ears on his head. "Two ears of shame and derision are these," she said, "unless you carry me off with you." "Away from me, woman," said he. "That will happen to you," she said. At this his bass call went up from him. When the Ulstermen beyond heard the call, every one of them fell upon the other. The sons of Uisliu came out to restrain their brother. "What is the matter with you?" they said, "do not let the Ulstermen kill each other because of your fault." Then he told them what had been done to him. "Evil will come of it," said the warriors. "Though it should, you shall not be in disgrace as long as we are alive. We will go with her into another land. There is not a king in Ireland who will not make us welcome." This was their conclusion. They went off that night, with a hundred and fifty warriors of theirs and a hundred and fifty women and a hundred and fifty hounds and a hundred and fifty servants, and Deirdriu along with the others with them.

They were in sanctuary for a long while throughout Ireland, so that their destruction was often attempted by the kings of Ireland through the plots and wiles of Conchobhar, round from Assaroe southwest to Howth again to the northeast. However the Ulstermen hounded them across to the land of Scotland, and they settled down in the wilds there. When the hunting of the mountain failed them they turned to taking the cattle of the men of Scotland for themselves. These went to destroy them in a single day, whereupon they went to the king of Scotland, and he admitted them into his household, and they took service with him; and they set up their huts on the green. Because of the girl the huts were made, so that no one with them should see her, for fear they would be killed for her sake.

Once upon a time then, the steward went early in the morning so that he went round their house. He saw the couple asleep. He went thereupon and woke the king. "I have not found a woman worthy of you until to-day," said he; "there is a woman worthy of the King of the Western World with Noísi son of Uisliu. Let Noísi be killed immediately, and let the woman sleep with you," said the steward. "No," said the king, "but you do go to woo her for me secretly every day." That was done. But what the steward used to say to her by day, she would tell her husband straightway the same night. Since nothing was got from her, the sons of Uisliu were ordered to go into risks and fights and difficulties, so that they might be killed. Nevertheless they were so brave in every slaughter that it was impossible to do anything to them in these attacks.

After taking counsel about it against her, the men of Scotland were mustered to kill them. She told Noísi. "Go away," said she, "for if you have not gone away by to-night you will be killed to-morrow." They went away that night, so that they were on an island of the sea. This was told to the Ulstermen. "It is sad, Conchobhar," said the Ulstermen, "that the sons of Uisliu should fall in a hostile land through the fault of a bad woman. It would be better to escort them and feed them, and not to kill them, and for them to come to their land, rather than to fall before their enemies." "Let them come, then," said Conchobhar, "and let sureties go for them." That was brought to them. "It is welcome to us," they said; "we shall go, and let Ferghus and Dubhthach and Cormac son of Conchobhar come as sureties for us." These went and escorted them from the sea.

Now, through the counsel of Conchobhar people rivalled each other to invite Ferghus to ale-feasts, for the sons of Uisliu declared that they would not eat food in Ireland except the food of Conchobhar first.[1] Then Fiachu son of Ferghus went with them, and Ferghus and Dubhthach stayed behind, and the sons of Uisliu came until they were on the green at Emhain. Then too Éoghan son of Durthacht, the king of Fernmhagh, came to make peace with Conchobhar, for he had been at war with him for a long time. It was he who was entrusted with killing the sons of Uisliu, with the soldiers of Conchobhar around him so that they might not come at him.

The sons of Uisliu were standing in the middle of the green, and the women were sitting on the rampart of Emhain. Then Éoghan went against them with his troop over the green, but the son of Ferghus came so that he was beside Noísi. Éoghan welcomed them with a thrusting blow of a great spear into Noísi, so that his back broke within him. At that the son of Ferghus threw himself and put his arms round Noísi and bore him under, so that he cast himself down on him. And so it is

[1] Conchubor's strategy was to separate the Sons of Uisliu from Fergus, their surety, who was under taboo not to refuse an invitation to an ale-feast. Conchubor also knew that the Sons of Uisliu, on the other hand, were obligated to refuse such an invitation since they had sworn, for their own protection, to partake only of his food according to the rule of hospitality.

that Noísi was struck from above, right through the son of Ferghus. They were killed then all over the green, so that none escaped but those who went by point of spear and edge of sword; and she was brought across to Conchobhar so that she was beside him, and her hands were bound behind her back.

Then this was told to Ferghus and Dubhthach and Cormac. They came and did great deeds straightway; that is to say, Dubhthach killed Maine son of Conchobhar, and Fiachna son of Feidhelm, daughter of Conchobhar, was slain by a single thrust, and Ferghus killed Traighthrén son of Traighlethan and his brother; and this was an outrage to Conchobhar. And a battle was fought between them after that on the same day, so that three hundred Ulstermen fell between them; and Dubhthach killed the girls of Ulster before morning and Ferghus burned Emhain. Then they went to Ailill and Medhbh, because they knew that couple would be able to support them; but it was no love-nest for the Ulstermen. Three thousand was the number of the exiles. Till the end of sixteen years, weeping and trembling never ceased in Ulster at their hands, but there was weeping and trembling at their hands every single night.

She was a year with Conchobhar, and during that time she did not smile, and did not take her fill of food or sleep, and did not raise her head from her knee . . . "What do you see that you most hate?" said Conchobhar. "Yourself, surely," said she, "and Éoghan son of Durthacht." "Then you shall be a year with Éoghan," said Conchobhar. He brought her then beside Éoghan. They went the next day to the assembly of Macha. She was behind Éoghan in a chariot. She had vowed that she would not see her two husbands together on earth. "Well, Deirdriu," said Conchobhar, "it is the eye of a ewe between two rams that you make between me and Éoghan." There was a great boulder of stone before her. She dashed her head on the stone so that she made fragments of her head, so that she died.

8TH OR 9TH CENTURY.
Translator Kenneth Jackson.

The Colloquy of the Old Men[1]

WHEN THE Battle of Comar, the Battle of Gabra, and the Battle of Ollarba had been fought, and after the fian[2] were for the most part extinguished, the residue of them had dispersed in small bands and in companies throughout all Ireland, until at the time which concerns us there remained of them two good warriors only: Oisin son of Finn, and Cailte son of Crunnchu son of Ronan (whose lusty vigor and power of spear-throwing were now dwindled down), and so many fighting men as with themselves made twice nine. These twice nine came out of the flowery-soiled and well-wooded borders of Sliab Fuait and into the Lugbarta Bana, at the present day called Lugmad, where at the falling of the evening clouds that night they were melancholy, dispirited.

Cailte said to Oisin then, "Good now, Oisin, before the day's end what path shall we take in quest of entertainment for the night?"

Oisin answered, "I know not, seeing that of the ancients of the fian, and of Finn's former people but three survive: I and thyself, Cailte, with Cama, the female-chief and female-custodian who, from the time he was a boy until the day he died, kept Finn mac Cumaill safe."

Cailte said, "We are entitled to this night's lodging and provision from her; for it is not possible to rehearse nor to show the quantity which Finn, captain of the fian, bestowed on her of precious things and of treasures, including the third best thing of price that Finn ever acquired, namely, the Anga-

---

[1] See Introduction, p. xix.

[2] A band of semi-nomadic guerrilla fighters, particularly that commanded by Finn. The modern English word *Fenian*, meaning follower of Finn, derives not from Finn's name but from *fian* (plu. *fianna*). See "The Fianna," p. 95.

lach or drinking horn which Moriath daughter of the king of Greece gave to Finn, and Finn to Cama."

With Cama, therefore, they got hospitality for the night; their names she inquired of them and at their sound wept vehement showers of tears; then she and they, each of the other, sought to have tidings. Next they entered into the bed-house disposed for them, and Cama the female chief prescribed their repast: that the freshest of all kinds of meats and the oldest of all sorts of drink be given them, for she knew in what fashion they used to be fed. She knew also how much it was that many a time before the present had constituted a sufficiency for Oisin and Cailte. Languidly and feebly she arose and held forth on the fian and on Finn mac Cumaill; of Oisin's son Oscar too she spoke, of Mac Lugach, of the Battle of Gabra with other matters; and by reason of this in the end a great silence settled on them all.

Then Cailte said, "Such matters we hold to be not more painful than the way in which the twice nine that we are of the remnant of that great and goodly fellowship must perforce part, and separate from each other."

Oisin answered, "Since they have departed, in me, by my word, there is no more fight and pith."

Valiant as were these warrior-men, here nevertheless with Cama they wept, in gloom, in sadness, and in dejection. Their adequate allowance of meat and drink was given them; they tarried there for three days and three nights, then bade Cama farewell, and Oisin said:

> Cama to-day is sorrowful: she is come to the point where she must swim; Cama without either son or grandson: it has befallen her to be old and blighted.

Forth from the enclosure they came now, and out upon the green; there they took a resolve, which was this: to separate, and this parting of theirs was a sundering of soul and body. Even so they did: for Oisin went to the fairy-mound of Uch Cletigh, where was his mother, Blai daughter of Derc Dianscothach; while Cailte took his way to Inber Bic Loingsigh which at present is called Mainister Droichid Atha (the monastery of Drogheda) from Beg Loigsech son of Arist that was drowned in it, that is, the king of the Romans' son, who came to invade Ireland; but a tidal wave drowned him there in his *inber* (river-mouth). He went on to Linn Feic (Fiace's Pool), on the bright-streaming Boyne; southwards over the Old Mag Breg, and to the rath (stronghold) of Drum Derg, where Patrick mac Calpuirn was.

Just then Patrick was chanting the Lord's order of the canon (i.e., Mass), and lauded the Creator, and pronounced a benediction on the rath where Finn mac Cumaill had been, the rath of Drum Derg. The clerics saw Cailte and his band draw near them; and fear fell upon them before the tall men with their huge wolf-dogs that accompanied them, for they were not people of one epoch or of one time with the clergy.

Then Heaven's distinguished one, that pillar of dignity and angel on earth, Calpurn's son Patrick, apostle of the Gael, rose and took the sprinkler to sprinkle holy water on the great men; floating over whom until that day there had been and were now a thousand legions of demons. Into the hills and brush wood, into the outer borders of the region and of the country, the demons departed forthwith in all directions; after which the enormous men sat down.

"Good now," said Patrick to Cailte, "what name hast thou?"

"I am Cailte son of Crunnchu son of Ronan."

For a long while the clergy marvelled greatly as they gazed upon them; for the largest man of them reached but to the waist, or else to the shoulder of any given one of the others, and they sitting.

Patrick said again, "Cailte, I wish to beg a favor of thee."

He answered, "If I have but that much strength or power, it shall be had; at all events, tell me what it is."

"To have in our vicinity here a well of pure water, from which we might baptize the tribes of Breg, of Meath, and of Usnech."

"Noble and righteous one," said Cailte, "that have I for thee," and they, crossing the rath's wall, came out; in his hand Cailte took Patrick's staff and in a little while right in front of them they saw a loch-well, sparkling and very clear. The size and thickness of the cress and of the brooklime that grew on it was a wonderment to them; then Cailte began to tell its fame and qualities, in doing of which he said:

> O Well of Traig Da Ban (Strand of the Two Women), beautiful thy cresses, luxurious-branching. Since thy produce is neglected on thee thy brooklime is not suffered to grow. Forth from thy banks thy trout are to be seen, thy wild swine in the neighboring wilderness; the deer of thy fair hunting cragland, thy dappled and red-chested fawns! Thy mast all hanging on the branches of thy trees; thy fish in estuaries of thy rivers; lovely the color of thy purling streams, O thou that thyself art azure-hued, and again green with reflection of surrounding copsewood! . . .

" 'Tis well," Patrick said; "hath our dinner and our provisions reached us yet?"

"It has so," answered the bishop Sechnall.

"Distribute it," said Patrick, "and one half give to yon nine tall warriors of the survivors of the fian." Then his bishops and his priests and his psalmodists arose and blessed the meat; and of both meat and liquor they consumed their full sufficiency, yet so as to serve their soul's welfare.

Patrick said then, "Was he not a good lord with whom ye were, that is, Finn mac Cumaill?"

Upon which Cailte uttered this little tribute of praise:

> Were but the brown leaf which the wood sheds from it gold—were but the white billows silver—Finn would have given it all away.

"Who or what was it that maintained you so in your life?" Patrick inquired; and Cailte answered, "Truth that was in our hearts, and strength in our arms, and fulfillment in our tongues."

"Good, Cailte," Patrick went on; "in the houses which

before our time thou didst frequent were there drinking-horns, or cups, or goblets of crystal and of pale gold?"

And Cailte answered, "The number of the horns that were in my lord's house was as follows:

> Twelve drinking-horns and three hundred made of gold
> Finn had; whenever they came to the pouring out, the quantity of liquor they held was immense.

"Were it not for us an impairing of the devout life, an occasion of neglecting prayer, and of deserting converse with God, we, as we talked with thee, would feel the time pass quickly, O warrior."

Then Cailte began to rehearse the drinking-horns, with the chiefs and lords whose they had been:

> Horns that were in Finn's house, their names I bear in mind.

. . . .

"Success and benediction attend thee, Cailte," Patrick said; "this is to me a lightening of spirit and of mind; and now tell us another tale."

"I will indeed; but say what story thou wouldst be pleased to have."

"In the fian had ye horses or cavalry?"

Cailte answered, "We had so; thrice fifty foals from one mare and a single sire."

"Whence were they procured?"

"I will tell thee the truth of the matter:

"A young man that served with Finn, Arthur son of Beine Brit, his company being thrice nine men. Finn set on foot the hunting of Benn Etair (which indeed turned out to be a bountiful and fruitful hunt). They slipped their hounds accordingly, while Finn took his seat on Carn an Feinneda (Cairn of the Fian) between Etar's top and the sea; there his spirit was gay within him when he listened to the maddened stags' bellowing as by the hounds of the fian they were rapidly killed.

"Where Arthur son of Beine Brit was stationed was between

the main body of the hunt and the sea in order that the deer should not take to the sea and elude them by swimming. But Arthur, being thus on the outside and close against the shore, marked three of Finn's hounds, Bran, Sceolaing, and Adnuall, and he resolved on a plan, which was: himself and his three nines to depart away across the sea, he carrying off with him into his own land those same three hounds. This plot was put into action then; for well I know that they, having with them those three hounds, crossed the sea's surface and at Inber Mara Gaimiach in Britainland took harbor and haven. They landed there, proceeded to the mountain of Lodan son of Lir, and hunted it.

"After this occurrence the fian made an end of their hunting and of their woodland slaughter, and camped on the eminence of Etgaeth's son Etar (Benn Etair), and as the custom was then, Finn's hounds were counted. Now his hounds were many in number, as the poet said:

> An enumerating of branches on the tree was that of Finn's full-grown hounds with his sleek melodious pack of youngsters; three hundred of the first there were, and puppy-hounds two hundred.

"Many men they must have been who owned those," said Patrick.

"True for you indeed," Cailte answered, "for the tale that used to be in Finn's house was this:

> They that dwelt in the house of Finn were three times fifty of joyous leaders of the fian; three hundred confidential servitors as well, and two hundred fosterlings that were worthy of their chiefs.

"But when the hounds were counted, a great shortcoming was discovered in them: Bran, Sceolaing, Adnuall were missing, and it was told to Finn. 'Have all three battalions of the fian searched out,' he said; yet though the search was made the hounds were not found.

"To Finn then was brought a long basin of pale gold; he washed his kingly face, put his thumb under his tooth of knowledge,[1] truth was revealed to him, and he said, 'The king of the Britons' son has deprived you of your hounds; pick ye therefore nine men to go in quest of them!' They were chosen, their names being these: Diarmuid O'Duibne, of the Erna of Munster in the south; Goll mac Morna—"

"Was Goll a chief's son, or a simple warrior's?" Patrick inquired.

"A chief's," answered Cailte:

> He was son of Teigue son of Morna of the Mag, that was son of Feradach son of Fiacha son of Art of the Mag son of Muiredach son of Eochaid.

"There was Cael Croda the hundred-slayer, grandson of Nemnann, a champion that Finn had, and endowed with a deadly property, that his arm never delivered a cast that missed its mark, and that never was his hand bloodied on a man but that the same would before a nine days' term were out be dead; there was Finn's son Oisin—he that, if only a man had a head to eat with and legs to go upon and carry off his largess, never refused any."

---

[1] According to a passage in a twelfth century text (*The Boyhood Deeds of Finn*) Finn, while still a young man, went to study the art of poetry under a master named Finneces, who for seven years had been engaged in fishing the river Boyne for the fabulous salmon of knowledge. When he finally caught the salmon he gave it to his pupil to cook with instructions not to eat any of it. "The youth brought him the salmon after cooking. 'Hast thou eaten any of the salmon, my lad?' said the poet. 'No,' said the youth, 'but I burned my thumb and put it into my mouth afterwards.' 'What is thy name, my lad?' said he. 'Demne,' said the youth. 'Finn is thy name, my lad,' said he; 'and to thee was the salmon given to be eaten, and indeed thou art Finn.' Thereupon the youth ate the salmon. It is that which gave the knowledge to Finn, so that whenever he put his thumb into his mouth and sang by means of chewing marrow whatever he had been ignorant of would be revealed to him."

"Cailte," said Patrick, "that is a great character."

"And though it be so is it a true one," Cailte answered, and said:

> In the matter of gold, of silver, or concerning meat, Oisin never denied any man; nor, though another's generosity were such as might fit a chief, did Oisin ever seek ought of him.

"There was Oisin's son Oscar, the chief's son that in all Ireland was best for spear-throwing and for vigorous activity; also Ferdoman son of Bodb Derg son of the Dagda; Finn's son Raigne Wide-eye; his son Caince the Crimson-red; Glas son of Enchard Bera mac Lugach; and myself. Now, saintly Patrick, we the aforesaid within ourselves were confident that from Taprobane in the east to the garden of the Hesperides in the world's westernmost part were no four hundred warriors but, on the battle-field and hand-to-hand, we were a match for them. We had not a head without a helmet, nor a shoulder without a whitened shield, nor a right fist that grasped not two great and lengthy spears. On this expedition we went our way then until we reached Lodan mac Lir's mountain in Britain, where we had been no long time before we heard talk of men that hunted in the field.

"As regards Beine Brit's son Arthur, he just then, with his people, sat on his hunting ground. Them we charged in lively fashion, and killed all Arthur's people; but round him Oscar knit both his arms, gave him quarter, and we brought off our three hounds. Here Goll mac Morna chancing to look about him saw an iron-grey horse, flecked with spots, and wearing a bridle fitted with wrought ornaments of gold. At another glance that he threw to his left he discerned a bay horse, one not easy to lay hold of, having a wrought bridle of twice-refined silver fitted with a golden bit. This second horse Goll also seized and put into the hand of Oisin, who passed him on to Diarmuid. After successful execution and due celebration of our slaughter we came away, bringing with us the heads of those thrice nine, our hounds, and the horses, too, with

Arthur himself a prisoner, and so back to where Finn was on Benn Etair. We reached his tent, and Cailte said, 'We have brought Arthur.' This latter entered into bonds with Finn, and thereafter, up to the day on which he died, was Finn's follower. The two horses we gave to Finn, horse and mare, of whose seed were all the horses of the fian, who hitherto had not used any such. The mare bred eight times, at every birth eight foals, which were made over to the various detachments and notables of the fian, and these afterwards had chariots made." . . .

"Success and benediction be thine, Cailte. All this is to us a recreation of spirit and of mind, were it only not a destruction of devotion and a dereliction of prayer."

There they were until the morrow's morning came, when Patrick robed himself and emerged upon the green; together with his three score priests, three score psalmodists, and holy bishops three score as well, that with him spread faith and piety throughout Ireland. Patrick's two guardian angels came to him now—Aibellan and Solusbretach, of whom he inquired whether in God's sight it were convenient for him to be listening to stories of the fian. With equal emphasis, and concordantly, the angels answered him, "Holy cleric, no more than a third part of their stories do those ancient warriors tell, by reason of forgetfulness and lack of memory; but by thee be it written on tables of poets, and in learned men's words; for to the companies and nobles of the later time to give ear to these stories will be a pastime." Which said, the angels departed.

From Patrick messengers were accordingly dispatched to fetch Cailte, and he, along with the nine that were in his company, were brought to the saint; whose names were Failbe son of Flann, Eogan the Red-weaponed the King of Ulster's son, Flann son of Fergus king of Kinelconnell, Conall the Slaughterer son of Angus king of Connacht, Scannlan son of Ailill king of Ossory, Baedan son of Garb king of Corkaguiney, Luamnech Linn son of the king of Dalaradia's sons out of the north, with Fulartach son of Fingin king of the peoples of Breg and of Meath.

Patrick said, "Know ye why ye are brought to confer with me?"

"In truth we do not," they answered.

"To the end you should conform to the gospel of Heaven's and of Earth's king, the most glorious God." Then and there the water of Christ's baptism was by Patrick sprinkled on them preparatory to the baptism and conversion of all Ireland.

Then with his right hand Cailte reached across him to the rim of his shield, and gave to Patrick a ridgy mass of gold in which there were three times fifty ounces; this as a fee for the baptism of the nine with him. He said, "That was Finn's, the chief's, last wage to me and, Patrick, take it for my soul's and for my chief's soul's weal." The extent to which this mass reached on Patrick was from his middle finger's tip to his shoulder's highest point, while in width and in thickness it measured a man's cubit. Now this gold was bestowed upon the Tailchenn's[1] canonical hand-bells, on psalters, and on missals.

Patrick said again, "It is well, Cailte. What was the best hunting that the fian ever had, whether in Ireland or in Scotland?"

"The hunting of Arran."

Patrick asked, "Where is that land?"

"Between Scotland and Pictland. On the first day of the Trogan-month (which is now called Lugnasad *i.e.*, Lammastide) we, to the number of the three battalions of the fian used to repair thither and there have our fill of hunting until such time as from the tree-tops the cuckoo would call in Ireland. More melodious than all music whatsoever it was to give ear to the voices of the birds as they rose from the billows and from the island's coast-line; thrice fifty separate flocks there were that encircled her, and they clad in gay brilliance of all colors, as blue and green and azure and yellow." Here Cailte uttered a lay:

---

[1] Literally "adze-head," an epithet applied to St. Patrick.

> Arran of the many stags—the sea impinges on her very shoulders! an island in which whole companies are fed—and with ridges among which blue spears are reddened! Skittish deer are on her pinnacles, soft blackberries on her waving heather; cool water there is in her rivers, and mast upon her russet oaks! Greyhounds there were in her, and beagles; berries and sloes of the dark blackthorn; dwellings with their backs set close against her woods, and the deer fed scattered by her oaken thickets! A crimson crop grew on her rocks, in all her glades a faultless grass; over her crags, affording friendly refuge, leaping went on and fawns were skipping! Smooth were her level spots—her wild swine, they were fat; cheerful her fields (this is a tale that may be credited), her nuts hung on her forest-hazels' boughs, and there was sailing of long galleys past her! Right pleasant their condition all when the fair weather sets in: under her rivers' brinks trout lie; the sea-gulls wheeling round her grand cliff answer one the other—at every fitting time delectable is Arran!

"Victory and blessing wait on thee, Cailte!" said Patrick; "for the future thy stories and thyself are dear to us."

Straightway now before him Patrick saw a stronghold, a fair dwelling, and, "Cailte," he said, "what is yon town?"

"That is the proudest place that ever I was in, in Ireland or in Scotland."

"Who lived there?"

"The three sons of Lugaid Menn son of Angus, that is, the king of Ireland's three sons: Ruide and Fiacha and Eochaid were their names."

"What procured them their great wealth?"

"It was once upon a time that they came to have speech of their father to Fert na Druad northwest of Tara. 'Whence come ye, young men?' he inquired. They made answer, 'From Echlais Banguba to the southward, out of our nurse's and our guardian's house.' 'My lads, what set you on your way?' 'To crave a heritage of you, a domain.' For a space the king was silent, and then said, 'No father it was that on me conferred either country or domain, but my own luck and bright achievement. Lands therefore I will not bestow on you, but win lands for yourselves.' Whereupon they, with the ready rising of one man, rose and took their way to the green of the Brug upon the Boyne[1] where, none other in their company, they sat down. Ruide said, 'What is your plan tonight?' His brothers answered, 'Our project is to fast on the Tuatha De Danann, aiming thus to win from them good fortune in the shape of a country, of a domain, of lands, and to have vast riches.' Nor had they been long there when they marked a cheery-looking young man of a peaceful demeanor that came towards them. He saluted the king of Ireland's sons, and they replied in like manner. 'Young man, whence art thou? Whence camest thou?' 'Out of yonder brug checkered with the many lights hard by you here.' 'What name wearest thou?' 'I am the Dagda's son Bodb Derg; and to the Tuatha De Danann it was revealed that you would come to fast here to-night for lands and for great fortune. But come with me.' Simultaneously they rose and entered into the brug; supper was served to them, but they ate it not. Bodb inquired of them why it was they took no meat. 'Because the king of Ireland, our father, denied us territory and lands. Now there are in Ireland but two tribes that are equal: the sons of Mil and the Tuatha De Danann; to the alternative one of which we have come now.'

"Then the Tuatha De Danann went into council, he that in such council was most noble in rank, and authoritative, being Mider Yellow-mane son of the Dagda, who said, 'Accommodate those yonder now with three wives, since it is from wives that either fortune or misfortune is derived.' Whereat were given to them Mider's three daughters, Doirenn and Aife and Ailbe. Said Mider, 'Tell us, Bodb, what gifts shall be given them?' Bodb said, 'I will tell you. Three times fifty sons of kings are in this fairy-mound; every king's son shall give them thrice

[1] A famous fairy dwelling, now a group of prehistoric mounds on the river Boyne in Leinster.

fifty ounces of red gold, while from me they shall have in addition thrice fifty suits of raiment various with all hues.' Aed son of Aeda Nabusach from Cnoc Ardmulla out in the sea, which to-day is called Rachrainn, a youth of the Tuatha De Danann, said, 'From me too a gift for them, viz. a horn and a vat; regarding which it needs but to fill the vat with pure water, and of this it will make mead both drinkable and having virtue to intoxicate; into the horn put bitter brine out of the deep, and on the instant it shall turn into wine.' 'A gift for them from me,' said Lir of the fairy-mound of Finnachad; 'three times fifty swords, and thrice fifty well-riveted spears of length.' 'A gift from me to them,' said the Dagda's son Angus Oc; 'a fort and stronghold, and a most excellent spacious town with lofty stockades, with light-admitting bowers, with houses of clear outlook and very roomy; all this in whatsoever place it shall please them between Rath Cobtaig and Tara.' 'A gift for them from me," said Aine daughter of Modarn; 'a she-cook that I have, to whom it is taboo to refuse meat to any; but according as she serves out, so too is her store replenished.' 'A gift from me to them,' said Bodb Derg; 'a good minstrel that I have (Fertuinne mac Trogain is his name), and though saws were being plied where there were women in sharpest pains of childbirth, and brave men that were wounded early in the day, nevertheless would they be put to sleep by the wistful melody that he makes. Yet to the dwelling in which for the time being he actually is he is not minstrel more effectively than to that whole country's inhabitants in general, for all they as well may hear him.' For three days and three night they abode in the fairy-mound.

"Angus told them to carry away out of Fid Omna three apple-trees; one in full bloom, another shedding its blossoms, and another covered with ripe fruit. Then they repaired to the stronghold given them by Angus, where they abode for three times fifty years, and until those kings disappeared; for in virtue of marriage alliance they returned again to the Tuatha De Danann and from that time forth have remained there. And that, Patrick, is the stronghold concerning which you inquired of me," said Cailte. And he sang this lay:

Three things in great plenty, and O great plenty of three things, that out of Ruide's high fort issued! a crowd of young men, a great troop of horses, the numerous greyhounds of Lugaid's three sons. Three sorts of music and O music of three kinds, that comely kings enjoyed! music of harps, melody of sweet timpans, humming of Trogan's son Fertuinne. A triple stronghold and a stronghold of three fold! sound of tramping ascending from the green of that stronghold, uproar of racing, boom of lowing kine. Three noises, and O noises three! sound of its swine, span-thick in fat and excellent, buzz of the crowd upon the palace lawn, hilarity of revellers with mead-begotten clamor. Fruit-crops in three stages, and O crops in stages three, that used to be there hanging on its boughs! a tree shedding, a tree in bloom, and yet another laden ripe. Three sons it was that Lugaid left (though their great deeds are passed away): Ruide, spacious Lugaid's son, Eochaid, and manly Fiacha. I will testify to Eochaid that never took a step in flight: never was he without his customary music, nor ever for any time without quaffing of ale. I will testify to Fiacha, though the fame of his depredations be obscured: never he uttered an expression that was excessive, and in his time was none that excelled more in valor. I will testify to Ruide, to whom those aforesaid three things (young men, horses, hounds) in great plenty flowed in: that never a thing he denied to any man, nor of a man sought anything at all. Thirty chieftains, thirty leaders, thirty champions that might befit a king: while the strength of his hundredfold host was hundreds thirtyfold thrice told.

12TH CENTURY.
Translator Standish Hayes O'Grady.

The Fianna

THIS IS the enumeration of Finn's people. Their strength was seven-score-and-ten officers, each man of these having thrice nine warriors, every one bound (as was the way with Cuchulain in the time when he was there) to certain conditions of service, namely that in satisfaction of a guarantee violated they must not accept material compensation in the matter of valuables or of meat, must not deny any guarantee, nor any single individual of them fly before nine warriors.

Not a man was taken into the Fianna nor admitted whether to the great Gathering of Usnach, to the Convention of Taillte, or to Tara's Feast, until both his paternal and his maternal correlatives, his *tuatha*[1] and kindreds, had given securities for him to the effect that though at the present instant he were slain, yet should not claim be urged in lieu of him, and this in order that to none other but to themselves alone should the Fianna look to avenge themselves. On the other hand, in case it were they that inflicted great mischiefs upon others, reprisals were not to be made upon their relatives.

Again not a man was taken until he was a prime poet versed in the twelve books of poetic composition. No man was taken till in the ground a large hole had been made (such as to reach the fold of his belt) and he put into it with his shield and a forearm's length of a hazel stick. Then must nine warriors, having nine spears, with a ten furrows width betwixt them and him, assail him and in concert let fly at him. If past that guard of his he were hurt then, he was not received into Fianship.

Not a man of them was taken till his hair had been interwoven into braids on him and he started at a run through Ireland's woods; while they, seeking to wound him, followed in his wake, there having been between him and them but one forest bough by way of interval at first. Should he be overtaken,

[1] People.

he was wounded and not received into the Fianna after. If his weapons had quivered in his hand, he was not taken. Should a branch in the wood have disturbed anything of his hair out of its braiding, neither was he taken. If he had cracked a dry stick under his foot as he ran he was not accepted. Unless that at full speed he had both jumped a stick level with his brow and stooped to pass under one even with his knee, he was not taken. Also, unless without slackening his pace he could with his nail extract a thorn from his foot, he was not taken into Fianship. But if he performed all this he was of Finn's people.

15TH OR 16TH CENTURY.
Translator Standish Hayes O'Grady.

The Headless Phantoms

This is a fair in Magh Eala of the king: the fair of Liffey with its brilliancy: happy for each one that goes thither, he is not like Guaire the Blind.

Guaire the Blind was not in truth my name when I used to be in the king's house, in the house of excellent Fearghus on the strand over Bearramhain.

The horses of the Fiana would come to the race, and the horses of the Munstermen of the great races: they once held three famous contests on the green of the sons of Muiridh.

A black horse belonging to Dil, son of Da Chreag, in each race that they held at the rock above Loch Goir, he won the three chief prizes of the fair.

Fiachra then besought the horse from the druid, his grand-father, gave him a hundred cattle of each kind, that he might give it in return.

"There is the fast black horse for thee," said Fiachra to the Fiana's chief: "here I give thee my sword of fame, and a horse for thy charioteer.

"Take my helmet equal to a hundred, take my shield from the lands of the Greeks, take my fierce spears and my silvern weapons.

"If it please thee better than to have nothing, chief of the Fiana, handsome king, thou shalt not go off without a gift, chief of the blade-blue Fiana."

Thereupon Fionn himself arose: he was thankful to Eoghan's son: they salute each other: not without stir was their rising together.

Fionn went before us on the way: we come with him three score hundred; to Cathair to Dún-over-Lake, 'tis there we went from the fair.

Three days and three nights in high honour we spent in Cathair's house, without lack of ale or food for Cumhall's son[1] from the great king.

Fifty rings Fionn gave him, fifty horses and fifty cows: Fionn gave the worth of his ale to Cathaoir son of Oilill.

Fionn went to try the black steed to the strand over Bearramhain; I and Caoilte follow in sportiveness, and we race right cunningly.

Even we were not slow, full swift were our bounds: one of us on his left, one on his right—there is no deer we could not have outrun.

When the king (Fionn) noticed this, he spurred his horse to Tráigh Lí, from Tráigh Lí over Tráigh Doimh Ghlais, over Fraochmhagh and over Fionn-ghlais.

Over Magh Fleisge, over Magh Cairn, over the Sean-umair of Druim Garbh, over the brink of the silvery Flesk, over the "Bedside" of the Cochrainn. Over Druim Eadair, over Druim Caoin, over Druim Dha Fhiach, over Formaoil.

When we had come to the hill, we were first by eight times: though it was we that got there first, the king's horse was nowise slow.

"This is night, the day is ended," said Fionn in good sooth- "folly it was that brought us here, let us go seek a hunting booth."

[1] I.e. Finn.

As the king glanced aside at the crag to his left, he saw a great house with a fire in the valley before him.

Then said Caoilte a stout saying that was no matter for boasting: "Till this night I have never seen a house in this valley though I know it well."

"Let us start off," quoth Caoilte, "and visit it; there are many things that I am in ignorance of:" a welcome, best of all things, was given to the son of Cumhall of Almhain.

After this we went in on a night's visit that was rued: we were met with screeching, wailing, and shouting, and a clamorous rabbly household.

Within stood a grey-haired churl in the midst: he quickly seizes Finn's horse: he takes down the door on this side from its iron hinges.

We sit down on the hard couch that has to rest us all at once: the log of elder that is on the hearth has all but quenched the fire.

The unmusical churl spoke a speech that did not greatly please us: "Rise up, ye folk that are within: sing a song for the king-feinnidh."[1]

Nine bodies rise out of the corner from the side next to us: nine heads from the other side on the iron couch.

They set up nine horrid screeches: though matched in loudness, they were not matched in harmony: the churl answered in turn, and the headless body answered.

Though each rough strain of theirs was bad, the headless body's strain was worse: there was no strain but was tolerable compared to the shriek of the one-eyed man.

The song they sang for us would have wakened dead men out of the clay: it well-nigh split the bones of our heads: it was not a melodious chorus.

After that the churl gets up and takes his firewood hatchet, comes and kills our horses, flays and cuts them up at one task.

---

[1] Literally member of the *fian*. Finn was called *rig-feinid*, king-Fenian.

Fifty spits that were pointed, the which were spits of rowan—on each in turn he puts two joints and sticks them round the fireplace.

No spit of them had to be taught, as he took them up from the fire; and he brought before Fionn his horse's flesh on spits of rowan.

"Thou churl, take off thy food: horse-flesh I have never eaten, and never yet will I eat, for the matter of going foodless for one mealtime."

"If for this my house has been visited, to refuse food," quoth the churl, "it will fall out pleasantly for you, Caoilte, Fionn and Oisin."

With that we started up to get our swords of temper: each man seized another's sword—it was an omen of fist-play.

The fire that was set is quenched, so that neither flame nor embers were visible: a dark and murky corner is narrowed round us three in one place.

When we were man to man, who should prove our stay but Fionn: slain outright were we, but for Fionn of the Fian.

Man against man we were in the house, the whole long night till morning, until the sun came in at rising time on the morrow.

When the sun rose, down fell each man eastward or westward: into each man's head a black mist came, till they lay lifeless in that hour.

Not long we were in our swoon: we rise up hale and sound: the house had vanished from us, and vanished from us are the inmates.

The party that had fought with us were the Nine Phantoms from Yewvalley, to avenge on us their sister whose name was Cuilleann broad of foot.

In this manner rose Fionn—his horse's reins in his hand: the horse was whole, head and foot: every injury had left him.

I am Caoilte the beloved, left behind the faultless heroes: greatly I miss it out and out that I no longer see the Fair.

17TH CENTURY.
Translator Eoin MacNeill.

The Bathing of Oisin's Head

Woman, bathe this head of mine: long since it parted with the Fian of Finn: this year and five, a long space, it has had no woman to bathe it.

This night sixteen years agone, happy was I with my fine head of hair: hard to know in it that head since it lost its wave-yellow torch-flame.

Ah, me! that is the poor head that hounds used to raise their hound-cry round: if it was the day on Leitir Lon, it would have women to bathe it.

Its outing to Leitir Lon—an outing on which great spoils used to be taken—when we killed brown stags above the brink of Loch Liathdroma.

An argument we had over there, I and light-footed Caoilte, when we divided the pleasant chase through quarrel and contention.

Darling Caoilte said—a man that was no shirker of combat, that excelled in bestowing cow and horse—that he was the greater champion.

I said he spoke untruly, the true prince,—it is no falsehood: though it fell out that I said so, dear Caoilte was indeed my friend.

Caoilte went to Ceann Con, I go to Leitir Lon: Caoilte with his fortunate folk, and I my lief alone.

Caoilte of the battles did not kill that day with his swift shooting—the man that often won fame—but one doe and one stag.

I vow to you, woman—it is no time for me to tell lies—that there came out with me over the plain thrice fifty fierce stags.

By thy hand, young woman, the cooking of Formaoil profited: thrice fifty stately stags in this place, with fifty pigs thrown in.

My shooting on Leitir Laoigh was not the tender shooting of a stripling: thrice fifty deer on the field, with the threescore wild pigs.

The hound I held in my active land—Gaillfheith, Fionn mac

Cumhaill's hound—there never touched the warm earth a hound that could win the day from Gaillfheith.

The small spear I had in my hand—seven rivets holding it—often had my hand been on its shaft, along the slope it was not unsteady.

A good spear was Fionn's spear: there was great venom in its steel-blue point: anyone whose blood it ever let never tasted food in his life again.

If it were that day, woman, to come to me above any man, thou wouldst wash my two hands, thou wouldst not avoid me.

It is a pity thou didst not do this for me, thou quiet, fair-haired girl, to lay my head on the cold pile of stone, and to wash for burial my poor bald pate.

Fine was the beauty of the fair hair that all men saw on my head: it has left me for good and all, till I am a disease-smitten grey-face.

Fine was the lustre of my hair, it was a fine setting for a body: never came through head's bone hair so good but the hair of Fionn.

Aye, and these teeth up here, away up in the old head, they were once on a time that they would crunch yellow-topt nuts.

They could gnaw a stag's haunch, hard and hungry and hound-like: they would not leave joint or jot of it but they would make mince-meat of.

Aye, and these eyes up here, away up in the old head, though they are roots of blood to-night, they were once thin pearly gems.

On a night of dark blind weather, they would not cause a stray step: to-night, though I should look out, I cannot see the fair.

Aye, and these legs below, nothing could have wearied them: to-night they are bowed and bent, pitiful, shrunken-sided.

Though they are without power or vigour—I cannot even turn them—they were swift on a time to follow the phantom of Fionnmhagh.

The phantom of Fionnmhagh or Magh Maoin, we got a turn of his ill-nature: on Sunday he was on the plain of Meath, when Cormac took . . . .

The Fiana ran towards him, sure they were that they would

overtake the phantom: they did not overtake him, though fierce their effort, except Oisin in Argadros.

The poor Oisin thou seest here, he encountered great harm and hardship, following the phantom southwards to cold Bearnan of edge-feats.

There he leapt a bold leap, highly, terribly, outlandishly, and he reached its arm with swiftness, up in the air he struck it.

I dealt a brave and hardy blow over its hideous clammy arm: I smote, without scarcity, on the eastward, the gold from its paw into the shield.

The little shield that was on my arm, over which I hewed the monster's paw, even had it desired the gold, it would have had it in its middle.

Ten rings in it of gold for Fionn, and ten for Croibhfinn, ten of them for Goll's daughter, and ten for the daughter of Iorgholl.

The reckoning of its gold from that out, besides gold that was hidden, even a seer does not know, for the greatness of its treasures.

I know ten hiding-places of Fionn's of treasures that I remember: pity they should be under the warm earth, each hiding-place having ten treasures.

His handsome drinking-horns are these, beside the pillar-stone of Carn Aodha: on the hillock hitherward from it he hid ten garments.

Beneath it are hunting spears wherewith red-headed stags were wounded: dear was the hero's hand that grasped them, meetly the stone of Almhain hath covered it.

Goblets that held the ale are there, beside the waterfall of Modhorn: let whoso seek them might and main, they shall not be found till the end of all.

These and the other treasures of Fionn, above all men might I reveal: I know no treasure of them all without its mounting of white bronze.

All we get in the lasting world, they would be numerous to recount: all that we laid in peopled earth will not be found till doom, woman.

I am left behind all these—it is right to thank the Lord for it—without vigour, without power while I live, at the back of Cionaodh's fortress.

Patrick's baptism is better for me than the deceitful bathing of women, protecting churches and peoples and habitations: if God permits it, do it, woman.

17TH CENTURY.
Translator Eoin MacNeill.

Goll's[1] Parting with his Wife

"Woman, take away my tunic: rise up and go from me: prepare to depart, clear one of rosy cheeks, the morn before my slaying."

"O Goll, what way shall I take? alas for those whose friends are few! rare is the woman that has grace. when she is left without head, without lord."

"Seek the camp of Fionn of the Fiana in its place on this westward side; wed there, gentle one of red lips, some good man worthy of thee."

"What man there might I wed, my great Goll that wast kind to me? where might I find west or east thy equal for a bedfellow?"

"Wilt thou have Oisin son of Fionn, or Aonghus son of Aodh Rinn, or muscular bloodstained Caireall, or the hundred-wounding Corr Chos-luath?"

"Conall of Cruachain is my father: I am fellow-fosterling[2] to Conn of the Hundred Battles: brother to me in the northern land is Ceidghein son of shaft-stout Conall.

[1] Although Goll Mac Morna opposed Finn at the battle of Cnucha and killed his father Cumall they were eventually reconciled when each commanded a clan in the same *fian*. But violence once more arose between them and Goll, after being cornered by his enemy on a narrow crag, was destroyed.

[2] The Celtic infant was not reared by his own parents but turned over to other parents to be brought up.

"It is the harder for me to leave thee, that thou art my gentle sweet first husband: seven years of bravery agone, thou broughtest me, husband, to thy couch.

"From that night until to-night, thou hast not shown me a harsh mind: from this night out I will not be light-minded, I will belong to no man on the surface of earth.

"Thirty days living without food scarcely was ever man before thee: a hundred heroes, Goll, by thy hand have fallen on the narrow crag."

"Wide is the sea around us, and I on the narrow of the crag: hunger for food is betraying me, and thirst is overmatching me.

"Though hunger for food is betraying me, though fierce is the warfare of the five battalions, still more it takes the beauty from my cheek, to have to drink bitter-strong brine.

"My own twenty-nine brothers if one man of the Fian had killed, it would make my peace with him (were he) to relieve me for one night from thirst."

"Goll son of Morna from Magh Maoin, eat those bodies at thy side: it will relieve thy thirst after [eating of] the men to drink the milk of my breasts."

"Daughter of Conall, I will not hide it—ah! it is pitiful how this thing has befallen—woman's bidding north or south I will not do and have never done."

"Ah! Goll, it is a woeful plight, five battalions or six against thee, and thou on the corner of a hard crag, a bare lofty chilly crag."

"That, O red mouth that wast musical, was my one fear on wave or land—Fionn and his Fian pressing on me and I without food in a narrow corner.

"I have stained my shafts right well in the bodies of the House of Tréanmhór: I have inflicted on them suffering and hardship, I have killed shaft-strong Cumhall.

"I brought the Munstermen to grief on the Tuesday in Magh Léana: I delivered battle bravely on the morn in Magh Eanaigh.

"Eochaidh Red-spot son of Mál, of Ulster's proud-faced over-king, I plunged into that hero my spear: I brought them to sorrow, woman."

17TH CENTURY.
Translator Eoin MacNeill.

Oisin in the Land of Youth

BY Michael Comyn[1]

PROLOGUE

Patrick. O noble Oisin, son of the king,
Whose deeds men sing this day in song!
Thy grief abate and to us relate
By what strange fate thou hast lived so long!

Oisin. O Patrick, here's the tale for thee,
Tho' sad to me its memories old—
'Twas after Gabra—I mind me well,
The field where fell my Oscar bold!

I. GOLDEN-HAIRED NIAMH

One day the generous Finn my sire
With olden fire led forth the chase—
But our band was small when gather'd all,
For past recall were the hosts of our race.

[1] Michael Comyn was a Gaelic poet who died in 1760. *Oisin in the Land of Youth* is based on the Fenian tradition of Oisin's visit to *Tir-na-n-Og*, the land of eternal youth in the otherworld, and his return to earth on a marvelous white steed from which he had been warned not to dismount.

'Twas a summer's morn and a mist hung o'er
The winding shore of sweet Loch Lein,
Where fragrant trees perfume the breeze
And birds e'er please with a joyous strain.

We soon awoke the woodland deer
That forced by fear fled far away—
Keenly our hounds with strenuous bounds
O'er moors and mounds pursued their prey.

When lo! into sight came a figure bright,
In a blaze of light from the west it rushed—
A lady fair of radiance rare
Whom a white steed bore to our band, now hush'd!

Amazed we halt, though hot the chase,
To gaze on the face of the fair young queen—
A marvel to Finn and his fian band,
Who ne'er in the land such beauty had seen!

A golden crown on her brow she bore,
A mantle she wore of silken sheen
All studded with stars of bright red gold—
Ample each fold fell on herbage green.

Her golden hair all fair to view
In golden curls on her shoulders fell—
Bright and pure were her eyes of blue
As drops of the dew in a blue harebell.

Ruddier far her cheek than the rose,
Her bosom more white than the swan's so free,
Sweeter the breath of her balmy mouth
Than spice of the south from over the sea.

Her milk-white steed was of worth untold
Nor bridle of gold did the charger lack—
A saddle all covered with purple and gold
Lay bright to behold on the steed's proud back.

Four shoes of gold his hoofs did guard,
Of gold unmarred by mixture base,
A silver wreath on his crest was shown—
Such steed was unknown on the earth's fair face.

To Finn's great presence drew the maid
Thus bright array'd and softly spake—
"O King of the fian host," she cried
"Far have I hied for sweet love's sake!"

"Who art thou, pray, O princess rare,
Of form most fair, of face divine?
Gently thy errand to us make known—
What land's thine own, what name is thine?"

"Niam the Golden-haired I'm named,
—O Finn far-famed for wisdom and truth!—
My praise harps ring, and bards e'er sing,
And my sire's the King of the Land of Youth!"

"Then tell us, most lovely lady now,
Why comest thou o'er seas so far?
Has heartless husband left thee to weep
With grief most deep, thy mind to mar!"

"No husband has left me, O lordly Finn,
—My heart within ne'er man did gain,
Till hero of Erin, thy famous son,
Its young love won, for aye to reign!"

"On which of my gallant sons, O maid,
Is thy heart's love laid, so frankly free?
Now hide not from us, O princess dear,
The causes clear of thy visit to me!"

"His name, O Finn, then I'll declare—
'Tis thy famed son, so fair, so brave,
Oisin the warrior, Erin's bard,
My fair reward for crossing the wave!"

"Then why hast thou hastened to give thy love,
O maiden above all maids most fair—
To Oisin my own beyond all known
Of princes high both rich and rare?"

"Good cause I ween for my course shall be seen,
O king of the Fian, when I tell thee truth:
Oisin's high deeds and noble name
Have won him fame in the Land of Youth.

"Full many a prince of high degree
Hath offered me both heart and hand;
But whoso appealed, I ne'er did yield
But my heart kept sealed for my hero grand!"

Oisin. O Patrick stern, how my soul did yearn
And with ardor burn for the peerless maid—
No shame to tell—each word was a spell,
That bound me well past mortal aid.

I took her gentle hand in mine
And with every sign of love I said,
"Welcome a hundred thousand times,
From fairy climes, O royal maid!

"Of women the rarest, fairest seen,
Thou art O queen, without compeer!
My soul, my life, my chosen wife,
Star of my way of ray most clear!"

II. THE DELIGHTS OF THE LAND OF YOUTH

"Request refused by no true knight
Who knoweth aright the knightly vogue,
I make of thee now—'tis hence to speed
With me on my steed to *Tír na n-Óg!*

"Delightful land beyond all dreams!
Beyond what seems to thee most fair—
Rich fruits abound the bright year round
And flowers are found of hues most rare.

"Unfailing there the honey and wine
And draughts divine of mead there be,
No ache nor ailing night or day—
Death or decay thou ne'er shalt see!

"The mirthful feast and joyous play
And music's sway all blest, benign—
Silver untold and store of gold
Undreamt by the old shall all be thine!

"A hundred swords of steel refined,
A hundred cloaks of kind full rare,
A hundred steeds of proudest breed,
A hundred hounds—thy meed when there!

"A hundred coats of mail shall be thine,
A hundred kine of sleekest skin,
A hundred sheep with fleece of gold,
And gems none hold these shores within.

"A hundred maidens young and fair
Of blithesome air shall tend on thee,
Of form most meet, as fairies fleet
And of song more sweet than the wild thrush free!

"A hundred knights in fights most bold
Of skill untold in all chivalry,
Full-armed, bedight in mail of gold
Shall in *Tír na n-Óg* thy comrades be.

"A corslet charmed for thee shall be made
And a matchless blade of magic power,
Worth a hundred blades in a hero's hands,
Most blest of brands in battle's hour!

"The royal crown of the King of Youth
Shall shine in sooth on thy brow most fair,
All brilliant with gems of luster bright
Whose worth aright none might declare.

"All things I've named thou shalt enjoy
And none shall cloy—to endless life—
Beauty and strength and power thou'lt see
And I'll e'er be thy own true wife!"

"Refusal of mine thou ne'er shalt hear,
O maid without peer, of the locks of gold!
My chosen wife for life I know
And gladly I'll go to *Tír na n-Óg!*"

III. THE DEPARTURE TO TIR-NA-N-OG

Forthwith the steed I then bestrode;
Before me rode my royal queen,
Who said, "O Oisin with caution ride
Till side of dividing sea we've seen!"

Then up rose that steed with a mighty bound,
Gave forth three sounding startling neighs,
His mane he shook, then with fiery look
His riders he took to the sea's known ways.

Now when from Finn and the fian host
The steed to the coast was coursing so,
There burst from the chief a cry of grief,
A wail of grief not brief nor low.

"Oh Oisin," cried Finn with faltering voice—
"My son most choice must I then lose,
With never a hope to see thee again?
—My heart in twain 'twill break and bruise!"

His noble features now clouded o'er
And tears did pour in showers free
Till breast and beard in tears were drowned—
"My grief! he e'er found this maid from the Sea!"

Oh Patrick, I grieve to tell thee the tale,
My words now fail to find their way—
How the father did part from the son of his heart,
My tears e'er start when I think of the day.

I drew up the steed for a moment's rest
And tenderly pressed on my sire a kiss,
Then bade farewell to the fian band,
Tho' the tears did stand in my eyes, I wis.

Full many a day great Finn and I
And our host all nigh in gay array
Held glorious feast where harps ne'er ceased
And highest and least had their choice alway.

Full oft our race held a royal chase
While at boldest pace ran our sweet-voiced
hounds—
Anon in battle our javelins rattle
And men like cattle fall in heaps and mounds!

Patrick. O vain old Oisin, dwell no more
On thy deeds of yore in the fian ranks,
How didst thou go to *Tír na n-Óg?*
Come let me know and I'll owe much thanks.

Oisin. We turned away as I truly said
And our horse's head we gave to the west,
When lo! the deep sea opened before
While behind us bore the billows that pressed.

Anon we saw in our path strange sights,
Cities on heights and castles fair,
Palaces brilliant with lights and flowers—
The brightest of bowers were gleaming there.

And then we saw a yellow young fawn
Leap over a lawn of softest green,
Chased by a graceful, snow-white hound
That with airy bound pressed on most keen.

We next beheld—I tell thee true,
A maid in view on a bright bay steed,
An apple of gold in her hand did she hold,
O'er the waves most bold she hied with speed.

And soon we saw another sight,
A youthful knight who a white steed rode,
The rider in purple and crimson array'd
Whilst a glittering blade in his hand he showed.

"Yon youthful pair both knight and maid—
Pray tell," I said, "who they may be—
The lady mild as a summer's morn
And knight high-born that fares so free."

"In all thy sight may light on here,
O Oisin dear, I say with truth,
There's nought of beauty, nought of strength,
Till we reach at length the Land of Youth!"

IV. FOMOR OF THE BLOWS

And now as we rode we came in sight
Of a palace bright, high-placed, and strong,
Shapely its hall and lofty its wall
Far beyond all e'er famed in song.

"What royal fort is yon, O queen,
That stands serene on yon hill-side,
Whose towers and columns so stately spring—
What prince or king doth there abide?"

"In yonder fort a sad queen dwells
Whom force compels her life to mourn—
Whom Fomor fierce of the Mighty Blows
Doth there enclose from friends' arms torn.

"But captive though to that pirate proud,
She yet hath vowed by taboos grave,
Never for life to be his wife
Till won in strife 'gainst champion brave!"

"Blessing and bliss be thine," I cried
"O maid bright eyed, for thy welcome word,
Tho' grieved that woman such fate should meet,
Music more sweet I ne'er have heard!

"For now we'll go to that high-placed fort
And help full soon that maid distressed;
A champion's steel shall Fomor feel
And 'neath my heel shall his neck be pressed!"

To Fomor's stronghold then we rode—
Unblest abode for a captive sweet!
At once the queen with joyous mien,
Came forth on the green with welcome meet.

In robe of rich-hued silk arrayed
Was this queenly maid with the brow of snow,
Her neck all fair could with swan's compare
Her cheeks did wear the rose's glow.

Of golden hue was her hair, 'tis true,
Of heavenly blue her bright eyes clear,
Her lips were red as berries on bough,
Shapely each brow with rare compeer!

To seat ourselves we then were told—
In a chair of gold each one sat down,
Most royal fare was set forth there
In royal ware of great renown.

Now when of food we had had our fill
And of wine as will might fancy e'en,
Thus spoke the queen, her face now pale,
"Now list my tale, with ears all keen!"

From first to last she told her tale
Her cheek all pale and wet with tears—
How kith and kin ne'er more she'd see
Whilst Fomor free provoked her fears.

"Then weep no more, O fair young queen,
Henceforth, I ween, thou needst not mourn,
Fomor shall pay with his life this day
In mortal fray for the wrongs thou'st borne!"

"Alas! no champion can be found
On earth's great round, I fear me much,
Could hand to hand such foe withstand
Or free me from this tyrant's clutch."

"I tell thee truly, lady fair,
  I'll boldly dare him to the field,
  Resolved to save thee or in strife
  Never while life doth last to yield!"

Ere cease my words, in savage trim
  The giant grim against us hies—
  In skins of beasts uncouthly clad,
  Whilst a club he had of monstrous size.

No salutation from him came,
  But his eyes aflame glared all around;
  Forthwith he challenged me to fight
  And I with delight took up my ground.

For full three nights and eke three days
  Our deadly fray's end seemed in doubt,
  Till at length his head with my sword I sped
  O'er the plain now red with the blood pour'd out!

Now when the two young maids beheld
  Fierce Fomor felled by my good sword,
  They gave three shouts of joy and glee
  Of joy for freedom now restored.

We then returned to the giant's fort,
  Where faint in swoon at last I fell,
  Faint from wounds and loss of blood
  That still in flood gushed like a well.

But now the maid from Fomor freed
  Ran up with speed, to help me fain—
  My wounds she washed, and bathed with balm,
  And health and calm I found again.

The giant grim we buried him
  Deep down in earth in widest grave—
  We raised a stone his grave to note
  And his name we wrote in Ogam-craev.

A merry feast we then did hold
  And stories told of olden days—
  And when night fell we rested well
  On couches such as poets praise.

When morning fair the sun did greet,
  From slumbers sweet we fresh awoke—
  "Dear friend, to my land now depart—"
  'Twas thus my lovely princess spoke.

We soon equipped us for our way,
  For longer stay was needed not,
  Sad, sorrowful the leave we took,
  And sad the maiden's look, I wot.

The further fate of that sweet maid,
  O Patrick staid, I could not tell,
  No word of her I've heard one say
  E'er since the day we said farewell.

V. IN THE LAND OF YOUTH

We turned once more upon our course,
And fleetly sped our horse along—
No wind that sweeps the mountain drift
Was half so swift or half so strong.

But now the sky began to lower,
The wind in power increased full fast—
Red lightning lights the mad sea-waves,
And madly raves the thunder past!

A while we cowered 'neath the storm,
—All nature's form in darkness dread—
When lo! the winds' fierce course was run,
And bright the sun appear'd o'erhead!

And now there spread before our sight
A land most bright, most rich, and fair,
With hill and plain and shady bower
And a royal tower of splendor rare.

And in this royal mansion fair
All colors were that eye hath seen—
The blue most bright, the purest white
With purple and yellow and softest green.

To left and right of this palace bright
Rose many a hall and sun-lit tower,
All built of brilliant gems and stones
By hands, one owns, of wondrous power.

"What lovely land is that we see?
  Pray answer me with maiden's truth—
  Is't penned in page that man may read,
  Or is it indeed the Land of Youth?"

"It is indeed the Land of Youth—
  And maiden's truth I've ever told—
  No joy or bliss I've promised thee
  But thou shalt see this land doth hold!"

And now there rode from the king's abode
  To meet us on the lawn of green
  Thrice fifty champions of might,
  In armor bright, of noble mien.

And then there came in hues arrayed
  A hundred maids in maiden vogue—
  In silken garments bright and brave
  Who welcome gave to *Tír na n-Óg*.

And next marched forth a chosen band
  Of the troops of that land, a lovely sight—
  A king at their head of kingly tread
  Of mighty name and fame in fight.

A yellow shirt of silken weft,
  A cloak most deftly broidered o'er
  On the king in folds hung freely down
  Whilst a glittering crown on his head he wore.

And close behind him there was seen
His youthful queen—a consort meet—
With fifty maidens in her train
Who sang a strain divinely sweet.

Then spoke the king in kindly voice,
"O friends, rejoice, for here you see
Oisin the famous son of Finn,
Who spouse of our Niam shall be!"

He takes me warmly by the hand,
Then as we stand he speaks anew—
"Welcome," he cries, "I give thee now,
A hundred thousand welcomes true!

"This kingdom which o'er seas and lands
Thou'st sought, now stands reveal'd to thee;
Long shalt thou live our race among
And ever young as thou shalt see.

"No pleasure e'er that entered mind
But here thou'lt find without alloy,
This is the land thy bards e'er sing,
And I am the King of this Land of Joy.

"Here is our gentle, fair young queen.
Mother of Niam the Golden-haired,
Who crossed for thee the stormy sea
And thine to be all dangers dared!"

I thanked the king with grateful heart,
To the queen apart I bowed me low—
We tarried no longer without the walls
But entered the halls of *Rí na n-Óg*.[1]

There came the nobles of all that land,
The great and grand to sing our praise—
And feast was held with all delights
For ten long nights and ten long days.

I then was wedded to Gold-haired Niam—
And there to leave the tale were well—
Thus did I go to *Tír na n-Óg*,
Though grief and woe 'tis now to tell.

Patrick. Come, finish the charming tale thou'st told,
O Oisin of gold, of the weapons of war—
Why from such land didst thou e'er return?
I fain would learn what the causes are.

And say whilst there thou didst abide
If thee thy bride any children bore,
Or wast thou for long in the Land of Youth?
—I long in truth to list such lore!

Oisin. I had by Niam of the Golden Hair
Three children fair as ever smiled,
Whose sweetness gave us daily joys—
Two gallant boys and a maiden mild.

[1] "King of [the Land of] the Young."

Patrick. O sweet-voiced Oisin, do not grieve,—
Where didst thou leave those children sweet?
Tell me the names of thy offspring fair,
And tell me where they mirthful meet.

Oisin. Those children three rich heirs would be
To kingdoms free and fair and great,
To royal scepter, crown of gold
And wealth untold, no tongue could state.

My gentle Niam on her boys bestowed
The names I owed most honor to—
Finn the bright of the hosts of might,
And Oscar who'd fight for the right and true.

And I my daughter fair did call
By a name which all fair names o'ershades—
In beauty's virtue and sweetness' power
By rightful dower—the Flower-of-Maids!

VI. THE RETURN FROM TIR-NA-N-OG

Long lived I there as now appears,
Tho' short the years seemed e'er to me,
Till a strong desire of my heart took hold
Finn and my friends of old to see.

One day of the king I asked for leave
And of loving Niam who grieved the while,
To visit dear Erin once again
My native plain, my native isle.

"I will not hinder thee," she cried,
"From crossing the tide for duty dear,
Tho' it bodes me ill and my heart doth fill
With doubts that chill and deadly fear!"

"Why shouldst thou fear, O queen my own,
When the way shall be shown by the magic
steed—
The steed that bore us o'er the sea—
And home to thee I'll safely speed?"

"Remember then what now I say—
If thou shouldst lay a foot to ground,
There's no return for thee e'ermore
To this fair shore when home thou'st found!

"I tell thee truly, vain's thy might
Shouldst thou alight from thy white steed,
For never again shouldst thou in truth
See Land of Youth or hither speed.

"A third time now I thee implore
And beg thee sore thy seat to hold,
Or else at once thy strength shall go,
And thou shalt grow both blind and old!

" 'Tis woe to me, Oisin, to see
How thou canst be so anxious-soul'd
About green Erin, changed for aye—
For past's the day of the fian bold.

"In Erin green there's now nought seen
But priests full lean and troops of saints—
Then Oisin, here's my kiss to thee,
Our last, may be—my heart now faints!"

I gazed into her soft sad eyes
Whilst the tears did rise and well in my own—
O saint severe, thou'dst weep a tear
To hear that dear wife's hopeless moan!

By solemn vow I then was bound,
To Erin's ground ne'er to descend,
And if to keep this vow I failed
No power availed or could befriend.

I pledged to keep my solemn vow
And do all now enjoined had been,
I mounted then my magic steed
And said farewell to king and queen.

I kissed once more my Gold-haired Niam,
—My heart doth grieve as I tell the tale—
I kissed my sons and daughter young,
Whose hearts were wrung and cheeks were pale.

I turned my steed at last to the strand
And passed from the Land of Lasting Youth—
Boldly my horse pursued his course
And the billows' force was nought in sooth.

O Patrick of the orders pure,
No lie, full sure, I've told but truth,
Thus have I tried my tale to weave
And thus did I leave the Land of Youth.

If of good bread I could get my fill
As Finn at will gave to each guest,
Each day I'd pray to the King of Grace
That Heaven might be thy place of rest.

Patrick. Those shalt of bread have quite thy fill
And drink at will, O ancient bard!
Dear to me thy pleasant tale!
It ne'er can fail to win regard.

Oisin. I need not tell each thing befell
Me and my spell-borne steed each day,
But at length green Erin's isle we reach,
And up the beach we bend our way.

When once I found my steed trod ground,
I looked around on every side,
Anxious for tidings small or great
Of Finn and his state, once Erin's pride.

Not long in doubt had I thus stayed
When a cavalcade came up the way—
Strange crowd, I thought, of women and men,
And past my ken their strange array.

Right gently they saluted me
But marvell'd much to see my size,
They marvell'd at my wondrous steed,
For on such breed they'd ne'er set eyes.

I asked—with fear my heart within—
If the noble Finn were yet alive,
Or if his hosts that kept the coasts
Of Erin safe, did yet survive.

"Of Finn," they said, "we oft have heard—
His name and fame are now world-wide,
But full three hundred years have passed
Since Finn and the last of the fian died.

"Many a book and many a tale
Have bards of the Gael that treat of Finn—
Of this strength and valor and wisdom bright,
Of his race of might and mighty kin.

"We've also heard of Finn's great son—
A youth of wondrous mien and mould,
That a lady came hither from over the sea
And with her went he to *Tír na n-Óg!*"

Now when those words fell on mine ear—
That Finn and his heroes were no more—
My heart was chilled—my soul was filled
With woe unwilled ne'er felt before.

I stopped no longer upon my course
 But swift my horse urged onward flew,
 Till Almu's hill o'er Leinster's plain
 Rose once again before my view.

What shock I felt none could report,
 To see the court of Finn of the steeds
 A ruin lone, all overgrown
 With nettles and thorns and rankest weeds!

I found alas, 'twas a vain pursuit,
 A bootless, fruitless, visit mine!
 Great Finn was dead and the hosts he led—
 For this I'd sped thro' ocean's brine!

But let me tell my story all—
 Tho' Almu's roofless hall I'd seen
 I still would see spots dear to me
 Where the fian free and Finn had been.

In passing through the Thrushes' Glen
 A crowd of men in straits I see;
 Full thrice five score and haply more
 At toil full sore awaited me.

Then forth there spoke a man of that herd,
 With suppliant word to me address'd—
 "Come to our help, O champion brave,
 Come quick to save us thus distress'd!"

I rode up briskly to the crowd
And found them bow'd beneath a weight—
A flag of marble great and long
Bore down the throng who moaned their fate.

Now all who tried to lift that stone
Did pant and groan most piteously—
Till some its crushing weight drove mad
And some fell dead, most sad to see!

Then cried a steward of that crowd,
And said aloud, "O haste and hie,
O gallant chief to our relief,
Or else 'tis brief ere all shall die!

"A shameful thing it is to say
—For such array of men these days—
They're powerless of blood and bone
Full easily that stone to raise!

"If Oscar, Oisin's valiant son
Laid hold upon that marble stone,
With right hand bare he'd hurl't in air,
Flinging it fair, with ne'er a groan!"

Asked thus for help, I did not lag
But 'neath the flag I placed one hand—
Full perches seven that stone I hurl
And scare each churl in all the band!

But scarce alas! that stone had passed
  With that fair cast when ah! the strain—
  The strain it broke the white steed's girth,—
  I fell to earth, doomed now to pain!

No sooner had I touched the ground
  Than with a bound my steed took fright—
  Away, away, to the west he rushed!
  Whilst all stood hush'd at such strange sight!

At once I lost the sight of my eyes,
  My youth's bloom died, lean age began,
  And I was left of strength bereft,
  A helpless, hopeless, blind old man!

O Patrick, now the tale thou hast,
  As each thing passed, indeed, in truth,
  My going away, my lengthened stay,
  And return for aye from the Land of Youth!

18TH CENTURY.
Translator Tomás O'Flannghaile.

The Voyage of Bran[1]

'TWAS FIFTY quatrains the woman from unknown lands sang on the floor of the house to Bran son of Febal, when the royal house was full of kings, who knew not whence the woman had come, since the ramparts were closed.

This is the beginning of the story. One day, in the neighborhood of his stronghold, Bran went about alone, when he heard music behind him. As often as he looked back, 'twas still behind him the music was. At last he fell asleep at the music, such was its sweetness. When he awoke from his sleep, he saw close by him a branch of silver with white blossoms, nor was it easy to distinguish its bloom from the branch. Then Bran took the branch in his hand to his royal house. When the hosts were in the royal house, they saw a woman in strange raiment therein. 'Twas then she sang the fifty[2] quatrains to Bran, while the host heard her, and all beheld the woman.

And she said:

A branch of the apple-tree from Emain
I bring, like those one knows;
Twigs of white silver are on it,
Crystal brows with blossoms.

There is a distant isle,
Around which sea-horses[3] glisten:
A fair course against the white-swelling surge,—
Four feet uphold it.[4]

---

[1] See Introduction, p. xxi.
[2] Only twenty-eight quatrains are given in the manuscripts.
[3] A kenning for "crested sea-waves."
[4] I.e. the island is supported by four pillars.

A delight of the eyes, a glorious range,
Is the plain on which the hosts hold games:
Coracle contends against chariot
In southern Mag Findargat[1]

Feet of white bronze under it
Glittering through beautiful ages.
Lovely land throughout the world's age,
On which the many blossoms drop.

An ancient tree there is with blossoms,
On which birds call to the Hours.[2]
'Tis in harmony it is their wont
To call together every Hour.

Splendors of every color glisten
Throughout the gentle-voiced plains.
Joy is known, ranked around music,
In southern Mag Argatnel[3]

Unknown is wailing or treachery
In the familiar cultivated land,
There is nothing rough or harsh,
But sweet music striking on the ear.

Without grief, without sorrow, without death,
Without any sickness, without debility,
That is the sign of Emain—
Uncommon is an equal marvel.

---

[1] Literally the "White-Silver Plain."
[2] I.e. the canonical hours.
[3] Literally "Silver-Cloud Plain."

A beauty of a wondrous land,
Whose aspects are lovely,
Whose view is a fair country,
Incomparable is its haze.

Then if Aircthech[1] is seen,
On which dragon-stones and crystals drop,
The sea washes the wave against the land,
Hair of crystal drops from its mane.

Wealth, treasures of every hue,
Are in Ciuin,[2] a beauty of freshness,
Listening to sweet music,
Drinking the best of wine.

Golden chariots in Mag Rein,[3]
Rising with the tide to the sun,
Chariots of silver in Mag Mon,[4]
And of bronze without blemish.

Yellow golden steeds are on the sward there,
Other steeds with crimson hue,
Others with wool upon their backs
Of the hue of heaven all-blue.

---

[1] Literally "Bountiful Land."
[2] Literally "Gentle Land."
[3] Literally "Plain of the Sea."
[4] Literally "Plain of Sports."

At sunrise there will come
A fair man illumining level lands;
He rides upon the fair sea-washed plain,
He stirs the ocean till it is blood.

A host will come across the clear sea,
To the land they show their rowing;
Then they row to the conspicuous stone,
From which arise a hundred strains.

It sings a strain unto the host
Through long ages, it is not sad,
Its music swells with choruses of hundreds—
They look for neither decay nor death.

Many-shaped Emne[1] by the sea,
Whether it be near, whether it be far,
In which are many thousands of motley women,
Which the clear sea encircles.

If he has heard the voice of the music,
The chorus of the little birds from Imchiuin,[2]
A small band of women will come from a height
To the plain of sport in which he is.

[1] Emne is the nominative of Emain.
[2] Literally "Very Gentle Land."

There will come happiness with health
To the land against which laughter peals,
Into Imchiuin at every season
Will come everlasting joy.

It is a day of lasting weather
That showers silver on the lands,
A pure-white cliff on the range of the sea,
Which from the sun receives its heat.

The host race along Mag Mon,
A beautiful game, not feeble,
In the variegated land over a mass of beauty.
They look for neither decay nor death.

Listening to music at night,
And going into Ildathach,[1]
A variegated land, splendor on a diadem of beauty,
Whence the white cloud glistens.

There are thrice fifty distant isles
In the ocean to the west of us;
Larger than Erin twice
Is each of them, or thrice.

A great birth[2] will come after ages,
That will not be in a lofty place,
The son of a woman whose mate will not be known,
He will seize the rule of the many thousands.

---

[1] Literally "Many-colored Land."
[2] I.e. Christ's.

A rule without beginning, without end,
He has created the world so that it is perfect,
Whose are earth and sea,
Woe to him that shall be under His unwill!

'Tis He that made the heavens,
Happy he that has a white heart,
He will purify hosts under pure water,
'Tis He that will heal your sicknesses.

Not to all of you is my speech,
Though its great marvel has been made known:
Let Bran hear from the crowd of the world
What of wisdom has been told to him.

Do not fall on a bed of sloth,
Let not thy intoxication overcome thee;
Begin a voyage across the clear sea,
If perchance thou mayst reach the land of women.

Thereupon the woman went from them, while they knew not whither she went. And she took her branch with her. The branch sprang from Bran's hand into the hand of the woman, nor was there strength in Bran's hand to hold the branch.

Then on the morrow Bran went upon the sea. The number of his men was three companies of nine. One of his foster-brothers and mates[1] was set over each of the three companies of nine. When he had been at sea two days and two nights, he saw a man in a chariot coming towards him over the sea. That man also sang thirty[2] other quatrains to him, and made himself known to him, and said that he was Manannan son of Lir,[3]

---

[1] Literally "men of the same age."
[2] Again only twenty-eight quatrains are given in the manuscripts.
[3] Manannan macLir was god of the sea in Celtic mythology.

and said that it was upon him to go to Ireland after long ages, and that a son would be born to him, Mongan son of Fiachna—that was the name which would be upon him.

So Manannan sang these thirty quatrains to Bran:

Bran deems it a marvellous beauty
In his coracle across the clear sea:
While to me in my chariot from afar
It is a flowery plain on which he rides about.

What is a clear sea
For the prowed skiff in which Bran is,
That is a happy plain with profusion of flowers
To me from the chariot of two wheels.

Bran sees
The number of waves beating across the clear sea:
I myself see in Mag Mon[1]
Red-headed flowers without fault.

Sea-horses glisten in summer
As far as Bran has stretched his glance:
Rivers pour forth a stream of honey
In the land of Manannan son of Lir.

The sheen of the main, on which thou art,
The white hue of the sea, on which thou rowest about,
Yellow and azure are spread out,
It is land, and is not rough.

Speckled salmon leap from the womb
Of the white sea, on which thou lookest:
They are calves, they are colored lambs
With friendliness, without mutual slaughter.

---

[1] Literally "Plain of Sports."

Though but one chariot-rider is seen
In Mag Mell[1] of many flowers,
There are many steeds on its surface,
Though them thou seest not.

The size of the plain, the number of the host,
Colors glisten with pure glory,
A fair stream of silver, cloths of gold,
Afford a welcome with all abundance.

A beautiful game, most delightful,
They play sitting at the luxurious wine,
Men and gentle women under a bush,
Without sin, without crime.

Along the top of a wood has swum
Thy coracle across ridges,
There is a wood of beautiful fruit
Under the prow of thy little skiff.

A wood with blossom and fruit,
On which is the vine's veritable fragrance,
A wood without decay, without defect,
On which are leaves of golden hue.

We are from the beginning of creation
Without old age, without consummation of earth,[2]
Hence we expect not that there should be frailty;
The sin has not come to us.

---

[1] Literally "Pleasant, or Happy Plain."
[2] I.e. of the grave.

An evil day when the Serpent went
To the father to his city![1]
She has perverted the times in this world,
So that there came decay which was not original.

By greed and lust he[2] has slain us,
Through which he has ruined his noble race:
The withered body has gone to the fold of torment,
And everlasting abode of torture.

It is a law of pride in this world
To believe in the creatures,[3] to forget God,
Overthrow by diseases, and old age,
Destruction of the soul through deception.

A noble salvation will come
From the King who has created us,
A white law will come over seas;
Besides being God, He will be man.

This shape, he on whom thou lookest,
Will come to thy parts;[4]
'Tis mine to journey to her house,[5]
To the woman in Line-Mag.

[1] I.e. to Adam in Paradise.
[2] I.e. Adam.
[3] I.e. to worship idols.
[4] I.e. to Ireland.
[5] I.e. to the wife of Fiachna, an Ulster king, whose royal seat was in Line-Mag (Moylinny), county Antrim.

For it is Manannan son of Lir,
From the chariot in the shape of a man;
Of his progeny will be a very short while
A fair man in a body of white clay.[1]

Manannan the descendant of Lir will be
A vigorous bed-fellow to Caintigern:[2]
He shall be called to his son in the beautiful world,
Fiachna will acknowledge him as his son.

He will delight the company of every fairy-knoll,
He will be the darling of every goodly land,
He will make known secrets—a course of wisdom—
In the world, without being feared.

He will be in the shape of every beast,
Both on the azure sea and on land,
He will be a dragon before hosts at the onset,
He will be a wolf of every great forest.

He will be a stag with horns of silver
In the land where chariots are driven,
He will be a speckled salmon in a full pool,
He will be a seal, he will be a fair-white swan.

[1] I.e. Mongan, fathered by Manannan upon Fiachna's wife.
[2] I.e. Fiachna's wife.

He will be throughout long ages
A hundred years in fair kingship,
He will cut down battalions,—a lasting grave—
He will redden fields, a wheel around the track.

It will be about kings with a champion
That he will be known as a valiant hero,
Into the strongholds of a land on a height
I shall send an appointed end from Islay.[1]

High shall I place him with princes,
He will be overcome by a son of error;[2]
Manannan the son of Lir
Will be his father, his tutor.

He will be—his time will be short—
Fifty years in this world:
A dragon-stone from the sea will kill him
In the fight at Senlabor.

He will ask a drink from Loch Lo,
While he looks at the stream of blood;
The white host[3] will take him under a wheel of clouds[4]
To the gathering where there is no sorrow.

Steadily then let Bran row,
Not far to the Land of Women,
Emne with many hues of hospitality
Thou wilt reach before the setting of the sun.

---

[1] The translation of this quatrain is uncertain because the Irish text is hopelessly corrupt in several places.
[2] Mongan was killed by Arthur, son of Bicor of Britain.
[3] I.e. the angels.
[4] I.e. in a chariot.

Thereupon Bran went from him. And he saw an island. He rowed round about it, and a large host was gaping and laughing. They were all looking at Bran and his people, but would not stay to converse with them. They continued to give forth gusts of laughter at them. Bran sent one of his people on the island. He ranged himself with the others, and was gaping at them like the other men of the island. Bran kept rowing round about the island. Whenever his man came past Bran, his comrades would address him. But he would not converse with them, but would only look at them and gape at them. The name of this island is the Island of Joy. Thereupon they left him there.

It was not long thereafter when they reached the Land of Women. They saw the leader of the women at the port. Said the chief of the women: "Come hither on land, O Bran son of Febal! Welcome is thy advent!" Bran did not venture to go on shore. The woman threw a ball of thread to Bran straight over his face. Bran put his hand on the ball, which adhered to his palm. The thread of the ball was in the woman's hand, and she pulled the coracle towards the port. Thereupon they went into a large house, in which was a bed for every couple, even thrice nine beds. The food that was put on every dish vanished not from them. It seemed a year to them that they were there,—it chanced to be many years. No savor was wanting to them.

Home-sickness seized one of them, even Nechtan son of Collbran. Bran's kindred kept praying him that he should go to Erin with them. The woman said to them their going would make them rue. However, they went, and the woman said that none of them should touch the land, and that they should visit and take with them the man whom they had left in the Island of Joy.

Then they went until they arrived at a gathering at Srub Brain on the coast of Erin. The men asked of them who it was came over the sea. Said Bran: "I am Bran the son of Febal."

One of the men said: "We do not know such a one, though the 'Voyage of Bran' is in our ancient stories."

The man[1] leaped from them out of the coracle. As soon as he touched the earth of Ireland, forthwith he was a heap of ashes, as though he had been in the earth for many hundred years. 'Twas then that Bran sang this quatrain:

For Collbran's son great was the folly
To lift his hand against age,
Without anyone casting a wave of pure water[2]
Over Nechtan, Collbran's son.

Thereupon, to the people of the gathering Bran told all his wanderings from the beginning until that time. And he wrote these quatrains in ogam, and then bade them farewell. And from that hour his wanderings are not known.

7TH OR 8TH CENTURY.
Translator Kuno Meyer.

Mad Sweeney[3]

FOR SEVEN whole years Sweeney wandered over Ireland from one point to another until one night he arrived at Glen Bolcain; for it is there stood his fortress and his dwelling-place, and more delightful was it to him to tarry and abide there than in any other place in Ireland; for thither would he go from every part of Ireland, nor would he leave it except through fear and terror. Sweeney dwelt there that night, and on the morrow morning Lynchehaun came seeking him. Some say that Lynchehaun was Sweeney's mother's son, others that he was a foster-brother, but, whichever he was, his concern for Sweeney was great, for he (Sweeney) went off three times in madness

[1] I.e. Nechtan, son of Collbran.
[2] I.e. holy water.
[3] See Introduction, p. xxi.

and thrice he brought him back. This time Lynchehaun was seeking him in the glen, and he found the track of his feet by the brink of the stream of which he was wont to eat the watercress. He found also the branches that used to break under his feet as he changed from the top of one tree to another. That day, however, he did not find the madman, so he went into a deserted house in the glen, and there he fell into deep sleep after the great labour of the pursuit of Sweeney whom he was seeking. Then Sweeney came upon his track so that he reached the house, and there he heard Lynchehaun's snore; whereupon he uttered this lay:

The man by the wall snores,
slumber like that I dare not;
for seven years from the Tuesday at Magh Rath[1]
I have not slept a wink.

O God of Heaven! would that I had not gone
to the fierce battle!
thereafter Sweeney Geilt[2] was my name,
alone in the top of the ivy.

Watercress of the well of Druim Cirb
is my meal at terce;
on my face may be recognized its hue,
'tis true I am Sweeney Geilt.

For certain am I Sweeney Geilt,
one who sleeps under shelter of a rag,
about Sliabh Liag if . . .
these men pursue me.

---

[1] I.e. the battle of Mag Rath (A.D. 637) at which Sweeney lost his wits.

[2] Mad.

When I was Sweeney the sage,
I used to dwell in a lonely shieling,[1]
on sedgy land, on a morass, on a mountain-side;
I have bartered my home for a far-off land.

I give thanks to the King above
with whom great harshness is not usual;
'tis the extent of my injustice
that has changed my guise.

Cold, cold for me is it
since my body lives not in the ivy-bushes,
much rain comes upon it
and much thunder.

Though I live from hill to hill
in the mountain above the yew glen;
in the place where Congal Claon[2] was left
alas that I was not left there on my back!

Frequent is my groan,
far from my churchyard is my gaping house;
I am no champion but a needy madman,
God has thrust me in rags, without sense.

'Tis great folly
for me to come out of Glen Bolcain,
there are many apple-trees in Glen Bolcain
for . . . of my head.

---

[1] A rude hut.
[2] One of the chief participants in the battle of Mag Rath.

Green watercress
and a draft of pure water,
I fare on them, I smile not,
not so the man by the wall.[1]

In summer amid the herons of Cooley,
among packs of wolves when winter comes,
at other times under the crown of a wood;
not so the man by the wall.

Happy Glen Bolcain, fronting the wind,
around which madmen of the glen call,
woe is me! I sleep not there;
more wretched am I than the man by the wall.

After that lay he came the next night to Lynchehaun's mill which was being watched over by one old woman, Lonnog, daughter of Dubh Dithribh, mother of Lynchehaun's wife. Sweeney went into the house to her and she gave him small morsels, and for a long time in that manner he kept visiting the mill. One day Lynchehaun set out after him, when he saw him by the mill-stream, and he went to speak to the old woman, that is, his wife's mother, Lonnog. "Has Sweeney come to the mill, woman?" said Lynchehaun. "He was last here last night," said the woman. Lynchehaun then put on the woman's garment and remained in the mill after her; that night Sweeney came to the mill and he recognised Lynchehaun. When he saw his eyes, he sprang away from him at once out through the skylight of the house, saying: "Pitiful is your pursuit of me, Lynchehaun, chasing me from my place and from each spot dearest to me in Ireland; and as Ronan[2] does not allow me to trust you,

[1] "The man by the wall" is a serf, whose place was farthest from the fire.

[2] Saint Ronan, whose curse upon Sweeney was responsible for Sweeney's madness.

it is tiresome and importunate of you to be following me"; and he made this lay:

O Lynchehaun, thou art irksome,
I have not leisure to speak with thee,
Ronan does not let me trust thee;
'tis he who has put me in a sorry plight

I made the luckless cast
from the midst of the battle at Ronan,
it pierced the precious bell
which was on the cleric's breast.

As I hurled the splendid cast
from the midst of the battle at Ronan,
said the fair cleric: "Thou hast leave
to go with the birds."

Thereafter I sprang up
into the air above;
in life I have never leaped
a single leap that was lighter.

Were it in the glorious morning,
on the Tuesday following the Monday,
none would be prouder than I am
by the side of a warrior of my folk.

A marvel to me is that which I see,
O Thou that hast shaped this day;
the woman's garment on the floor,
two piercing eyes of Lynchehaun.

"Sad is the disgrace you would fain put upon me, Lynchehaun," said he; "and do not continue annoying me further, but go to your house and I will go on to where Eorann is."

Now, Eorann at the time was dwelling with Guaire, son of Congal, son of Scannlan, for it was Eorann who was Sweeney's wife, for there were two kinsmen in the country, and they had equal title to the sovereignty which Sweeney had abandoned, viz.: Guaire, son of Congal, son of Scannlan, and Eochaidh, son of Condlo, son of Scannlan. Sweeney proceeded to the place in which Eorann was. Guaire had gone to the chase that day, and the route he took was to the pass of Sliabh Fuaid and by Sgirig Cinn Glinne and Ettan Tairbh. His camp was beside Glen Bolcain—which is called Glenn Chiach to-day—in the plain of Cinel Ainmirech. Then the madman sat down upon the lintel of the hut in which Eorann was, whereupon he said: "Do you remember, lady, the great love we gave to each other what time we were together? Easy and pleasant it is for you now, but not so for me"; whereupon Sweeney said, and Eorann answered him as follows:

Sweeney: At ease art thou, bright Eorann,
at the bedside with thy lover;
not so with me here,
long have I been restless.

Once thou didst utter, O great Eorann,
a saying pleasing and light,
that thou wouldst not survive
parted one day from Sweeney.

To-day, it is readily manifest,
thou thinkest little of thy old friend;
warm for thee on the down of a pleasant bed,
cold for me abroad till morn.

Eorann: Welcome to thee, thou guileless mad one!
thou art most welcome of the men of the earth;
though at ease am I, my body is wasted
since the day I heard of thy ruin.

Sweeney: More welcome to thee is the king's son
who takes thee to feast without sorrow;
he is thy chosen wooer;
you seek not your old friend.

Eorann: Though the king's son were to lead me
to blithe banqueting-halls,
I had liefer sleep in a tree's narrow hollow
beside thee, my husband, could I do so.

If my choice were given me
of the men of Erin and Alba,[1]
I had liefer bide sinless with thee
on water and on watercress.

Sweeney: No path for a beloved lady
is that of Sweeney here on the track of care;
cold are my beds at Ard Abhla,
my cold dwellings are not few.

---

[1] England.

More meet for thee to bestow love and affection
on the man with whom thou art alone
than on an uncouth and famished madman,
horrible, fearful, stark-naked.

Eorann: O toiling madman, 'tis my grief
that thou art uncomely and dejected;
I sorrow that thy skin has lost its colour,
briars and thorns rending thee.

Sweeney: I blame thee not for it,
thou gentle, radiant woman;
Christ, Son of Mary—great bondage—
He has caused my feebleness.

Eorann: I would fain that we were together,
and that feathers might grow on our bodies;
in light and darkness I would wander
with thee each day and night.

Sweeney: One night I was in pleasant Boirche,
I have reached lovely Tuath Inbhir,
I have wandered throughout Magh Fail,
I have happened on Cell Ui Suanaigh.

No sooner had he finished than the army swarmed into the camp from every quarter, whereupon he set off in his headlong flight, as he had often done. He halted not in his career until before the fall of night he arrived at Ros Bearaigh—the first church at which he tarried after the battle of Magh Rath—and he went into the yew-tree which was in the church.

Muireadach mac Earca was erenach[1] of the church at the time, and his wife happened to be going past the yew when

[1] A church official in charge of secular affairs and responsible for provisioning the establishment. He apparently farmed the church land.

she saw the madman in it; she recognized that it was Sweeney was there and said to him: "Come out of the yew, king of Dal Araidhe; there is but one woman before you here." She said so in order to seize the madman, and to deceive and beguile him. "I will not go indeed," said Sweeney, "lest Lynchehaun and his wife come to me, for there was a time when it would have been easier for you to recognize me than it is to-day"; whereupon he uttered these staves:

> O woman, who dost recognize me
> with the points of thy blue eyes,
> there was a time when my aspect was better
> in the assembly of Dal Araidhe.
>
> I have changed in shape and hue
> since the hour I came out of the battle;
> I was the slender Sweeney
> of whom the men of Erin had heard.
>
> Bide thou with thy husband and in thy house,
> I shall not tarry in Ros Bearaigh;
> until holy Judgment we shall not foregather,
> I and thou, O woman.

He emerged then from the tree lightly and nimbly, and went on his way until he reached the old tree at Ros Earcain. (For he had three dwellings in his own country in which he was wont to reside, viz.: Teach mic Ninnedha, Cluain Creamha, and Ros Earcain). Thereafter for a fortnight and a month he tarried in the yew-tree without being perceived; but at length his place and dwelling were discovered, and the nobles of Dal Araidhe took counsel as to who should go to seize him. Everyone said that it was Lynchehaun who should be sent. Lynchehaun undertook the task, and he went along until he came to the yew in which Sweeney was, whereupon he beheld the madman on the branch above him. "Sad is it, Sweeney," said he, "that your last plight should be thus, without food, without drink, without raiment, like any bird of the air, after having been in garments of silk and satin on splendid steeds from foreign lands with matchless bridles; with you were women gentle and comely, likewise many youths and hounds and goodly folk of every art; many hosts, many and diverse nobles and chiefs, and young lords, and landholders and hospitallers were at your command. Many cups and goblets and carved buffalo horns for pleasant-flavoured and enjoyable liquors were yours also. Sad is it for you to be in that wise like unto any miserable bird going from wilderness to wilderness." "Cease now, Lynchehaun," said Sweeney; "that is what was destined for us; but have you tidings for me of my country?" "I have in sooth," said Lynchehaun, "for your father is dead." "That has seized me," said he. "Your mother is also dead," said the young man. "Now all pity for me is at an end," said he. "Dead is your brother," said Lynchehaun. "Gaping is my side on that account," said Sweeney. "Dead is your daughter," said Lynchehaun. "The heart's needle is an only daughter," said Sweeney. "Dead is your son who used to call you 'daddy'," said Lynchehaun. "True," said he, "that is the drop which brings a man to the ground"; whereupon they, even Lynchehaun and Sweeney, uttered this lay between them:

Lynchehaun: O Sweeney from lofty Sliabh na nEach,
thou of the rough blade wert given to wounding;
for Christ's sake, who hath put thee in bondage,
grant converse with thy foster-brother.

Hearken to me if thou hearest me,
O splendid king, O great prince,
so that I may relate gently
to thee tidings of thy good land.

There is life for none in thy land after thee;
it is to tell of it that I have come;
dead is thy renowned brother there,
dead thy father and thy mother.

Sweeney: If my gentle mother be dead,
harder is it for me to go to my land;
'tis long since she has loved my body;
she has ceased to pity me.

Foolish the counsel of each wild youth
whose elders live not;
like unto a branch bowed under nuts;
whoso is brotherless has a gaping side.

Lynchehaun: There is another calamity there
which is bewailed by the men of Erin,
though uncouth be thy side and thy foot,
dead is thy fair wife of grief for thee.

Sweeney: For a household to be without a wife
is rowing a rudderless boat,
'tis a garb of feathers to the skin,
'tis kindling a single fire.

Lynchehaun: I have heard a fearful and loud tale
around which was a clear, fierce wail,
'tis a fist round smoke, however,
thou art without sister, O Sweeney.

Sweeney: A proverb this, bitter the . . . —
it has no delight for me—
the mild sun rests on every ditch,
a sister loves though she be not loved.

Lynchehaun: Calves are not let to cows
amongst us in cold Araidhe
since thy gentle daughter, who has loved thee, died,
likewise thy sister's son.

Sweeney: My sister's son and my hound,
they would not forsake me for wealth,
'tis adding loss to sorrow,
the heart's needle is an only daughter.

Lynchehaun: There is another famous story—
loth am I to tell it—
meetly are the men of the Arada
bewailing thy only son.

Sweeney: That is the renowned drop
which brings a man to the ground,
that his little son who used to say 'daddy'
should be without life.

It has called me to thee from the tree,
scarce have I caused enmity,
I cannot bear up against the blow
since I heard the tidings of my only son.

Lynchehaun: Since thou hast come, O splendid warrior,
within Lynchehaun's hands,
all thy folk are alive,
O scion of Eochu Salbuidhe.

Be still, let thy sense come,
in the east is thy house, not in the west,
far from thy land thou hast come hither,
this is the truth, O Sweeney.

More delightful deemest thou to be amongst deer
in woods and forests
than sleeping in thy stronghold in the east
on a bed of down.

Better deemest thou to be on a holly-branch
beside the swift mill's pond
than to be in choice company
with young fellows about thee.

If thou wert to sleep in the bosom of hills
to the soft strings of lutes,
more sweet wouldst thou deem under the oak-wood
the belling of the brown stag of the herd.

Thou art fleeter than the wind across the valley,
thou art the famous madman of Erin,
brilliant in thy beauty, come hither,
O Sweeney, thou wast a noble champion.

When Sweeney heard tidings of his only son, he fell from the yew, whereupon Lynchehaun closed his arms around him and put manacles on him. He then told him that all his people lived; and he took him to the place in which the nobles of Dal Araidhe were. They brought with them locks and fetters to put on Sweeney, and he was entrusted to Lynchehaun to take him with him for a fortnight and a month. He took Sweeney away, and the nobles of the province were coming and going during that time; and at the end of it his sense and memory came to him, likewise his own shape and guise. They took his bonds off him, and his kingship was manifest. Harvest-time came then, and one day Lynchehaun went with his people to reap. Sweeney was put in Lynchehaun's bed-room after his bonds were taken off him, and his sense had come back to him. The bed-room was shut on him and nobody was left with him but the mill-hag, and she was enjoined not to attempt to speak to him. Nevertheless she spoke to him, asking him to tell some of his adventures while he was in a state of madness. "A curse on your mouth, hag!" said Sweeney; "ill is what you say; God will not suffer me to go mad again." "I know well," said the hag, "that it was the outrage done to Ronan that drove you to madness." "O woman," said he, "it is hateful that you should be betraying and luring me." "It is not betrayal at all but truth"; and Sweeney said:

Sweeney: O hag of yonder mill,
why shouldst thou set me astray?
is it not deceitful of thee that, through women,
I should be betrayed and lured?

The Hag: 'Tis not I who betrayed thee,
O Sweeney, though fair thy fame,
but the miracles of Ronan from Heaven
which drove thee to madness among madmen.

Sweeney: Were it myself, and would it were I,
that were king of Dal Araidhe
it were a reason for a blow across a chin;
thou shalt not have a feast, O hag.

"O hag," said he, "great are the hardships I have encountered if you but knew; many a dreadful leap have I leaped from hill to hill, from fortress to fortress, from land to land, from valley to valley." "For God's sake," said the hag, "leap for us now one of the leaps you used to leap when you were mad." Thereupon he bounded over the bed-rail so that he reached the end of the bench. "My conscience!" said the hag, "I could leap that myself," and in the same manner she did so. He took another leap out through the skylight of the hostel. "I could leap that too," said the hag, and straightway she leaped. This, however, is a summary of it: Sweeney travelled through five cantreds of Dal Araidhe that day until he arrived at Glenn na nEachtach in Fiodh Gaibhle, and she followed him all that time. When Sweeney rested there on the summit of a tall ivy-branch, the hag rested on another tree beside him. It was then the end of harvest-time precisely. Thereupon Sweeney heard a hunting-call of a multitude in the verge of the wood. "This," said he, "is the cry of a great host, and they are the Ui Faelain coming to kill me to avenge Oilill Cedach, king of the Ui Faelain, whom I slew in the battle of Magh Rath." He heard the bellowing of the stag, and he made a lay wherein he eulogized aloud the trees of Ireland, and, recalling some of his own hardships and sorrows, he said:

O little stag, thou little bleating one,
O melodious little clamourer,
sweet to us is the music
thou makest in the glen.

Longing for my little home
has come on my senses—
the flocks in the plain,
the deer on the mountain.

Thou oak, bushy, leafy,
thou art high beyond trees;
O hazlet, little branching one,
O fragrance of hazel-nuts.

O alder, thou art not hostile,
delightful is thy hue,
thou art not rending and prickling
in the gap wherein thou art.

O little blackthorn, little thorny one;
O little black sloe-tree;
O watercress, little green-topped one,
from the brink of the ousel spring.

O *minen*[1] of the pathway,
thou art sweet beyond herbs,
O little green one, very green one,
O herb on which grows the strawberry.

---

[1] The name of some plant.

O apple-tree, little apple tree,
much art thou shaken;
O quicken, little berried one,
delightful is thy bloom.

O briar, little arched one,
thou grantest no fair terms,
thou ceasest not to tear me,
till thou hast thy fill of blood.

O yew-tree, little yew-tree,
in churchyards thou art conspicuous;
O ivy, little ivy,
thou art familiar in the dusky wood.

O holly, little sheltering one,
thou door against the wind;
O ash-tree, thou baleful one,
hand-weapon of a warrior.

O birch, smooth and blessed,
thou melodious, proud one,
delightful each entwining branch
in the top of thy crown.

The aspen a-trembling;
by turns I hear
its leaves a-racing—
meseems 'tis the foray!

My aversion in woods—
I conceal it not from anyone—
is the leafy stirk of an oak
swaying evermore.

Ill-hap by which I outraged
the honour of Ronan Finn,
his miracles have troubled me,
his little bells from the church.

Ill-omened I found
the armour of upright Congai,
his sheltering, bright tunic
with selvages of gold.

It was a saying of each one
of the valiant, active host:
"Let not escape from you through the narrow
  copse
the man of the goodly tunic.

"Wound, kill, slaughter,
let all of you take advantage of him;
put him, though it is great guilt,
on spit and on spike."

The horsemen pursuing me
across round Magh Cobha,
no cast from them reaches
me through my back.

Going through the ivy-trees—
I conceal it not, O warrior—
like good cast of a spear
I went with the wind.

O little fawn, O little long-legged one,
I was able to catch thee
riding upon thee
from one peak to another.

From Carn Cornan of the contests
to the summit of Sliabh Niadh,
from the summit of Sliabh Uillinne
I reach Crota Cliach.

From Crota Cliach of assemblies
to Carn Liffi of Leinster,
I arrive before eventide
in bitter Benn Gulbain.

My night before the battle of Congal,
I deemed it fortunate,
before I restlessly
wandered over the mountain-peaks.

Glen Bolcain, my constant abode,
'twas a boon to me,
many a night have I attempted
a stern race against the peak.

If I were to wander alone
the mountains of the brown world,
better would I deem the site of a single hut
in the Glen of mighty Bolcan.

Good its water pure-green,
good its clean, fierce wind,
good its cress-green watercress,
best its tall brooklime.

Good its enduring ivy-trees,
good its bright, cheerful sallow,
good its yewy yews,
best its melodious birch.

If thou shouldst come, O Lynchehaun,
to me in every guise,
each night to talk to me,
perchance I would not tarry for thee.

I would not have tarried to speak to thee
were it not for the tale which has wounded
me—
father, mother, daughter, son,
brother, strong wife dead.

If thou shouldst come to speak to me,
no better would I deem it;
I would wander before morn
the mountains of Boirche of peaks.

By the mill of the little floury one
thy folk has been ground,
O wretched one, O weary one,
O swift Lynchehaun.

O hag of this mill,
why dost thou take advantage of me?
I hear thee revile me
even when thou art out on the mountain.

O hag, O round-headed one,
wilt thou go on a steed?

The hag: I would go, O fool-head
if no one were to see me.

O Sweeney, if I go,
may my leap be successful.

Sweeney: If thou shouldst come, O hag,
mayst thou not dismount full of sense!

The hag: In sooth, not just is what thou sayest,
thou son of Colman Cas;
is not my riding better
without falling back?

Sweeney: Just, in sooth, is what I say,
O hag without sense;
a demon is ruining thee,
thou hast ruined thyself.

The Hag: Dost thou not deem my arts better,
thou noble, slender madman,
that I should be following thee
from the tops of the mountains?

Sweeney: A proud ivy-bush
which grows through a twisted tree—
if I were right on its summit,
I would fear to come out.

I flee before the skylarks—
'tis a stern, great race—
I leap over the stumps
on the tops of the mountains.

When the proud turtle-dove
rises for us,
quickly do I overtake it
since my feathers have grown.

The silly, foolish woodcock
when it rises for me
methinks 'tis a bitter foe,
the blackbird too that gives the cry of alarm.

Every time I would bound
till I was on the ground
so that I might see the little fox
below a-gnawing the bones.

Beyond every wolf among the ivy-trees
swiftly would he get the advantage of me,
so nimbly would I leap
till I was on the mountain-peak.

Little foxes yelping
to me and from me,
wolves at their rending,
I flee at their sound.

They have striven to reach me,
coming in their swift course,
so that I fled before them
to the tops of the mountains.

My transgression has come against me
whatsoever way I flee;
'tis manifest to me from the pity shown me
that I am a sheep without a fold.

The old tree of Cell Lughaidhe
wherein I sleep a sound sleep;
more delightful in the time of Congal
was the fair of plenteous Line.

There will come the starry frost
which will fall on every pool;
I am wretched, straying
exposed to it on the mountain-peak.

The herons a-calling
in chilly Glenn Aighle,
swift flocks of birds
coming and going.

I love not the merry prattle
that men and women make:
sweeter to me is the warbling
of the blackbirds in the quarter in which it is.

I love not the trumpeting
I hear at early morn:
sweeter to me the squeal
of the badgers in Benna Broc.

I love not the horn-blowing
so boldly I hear:
sweeter to me the belling of a stag
of twice twenty peaks.

There is the material of a plough-team
from glen to glen:
each stag at rest
on the summit of the peaks.

Though many are my stags
from glen to glen,
not often is a ploughman's hand
closing round their horns.

The stag of lofty Sliabh Eibhlinne,
the stag of sharp Sliabh Fuaid,
the stag of Ealla, the stag of Orrery,
the fierce stag of Loch Lein.

The stag of Seimhne, Larne's stag,
the stag of Line of the mantles,
the stag of Cooley, the stag of Conachail,
the stag of Bairenn of two peaks.

O mother of this herd,
thy coat has become grey,
there is no stag after thee
without two score antler-points.

Greater than the material for a little cloak
thy head has turned grey;
if I were on each little point,
there would be a pointlet on every point.

Thou stag that comest lowing
to me across the glen,
pleasant is the place for seats
on the top of thy antler-points.

I am Sweeney, a poor suppliant,
swiftly do I race across the glen;
that is not my lawful name,
rather is it Fer benn.

The springs I found best:
the well of Leithead Lan,
the well most beautiful and cool,
the fountain of Dun Mail.

Though many are my wanderings,
my raiment to-day is scanty;
I myself keep my watch
on the top of the mountains.

O tall, russet fern,
thy mantle has been made red;
there is no bed for an outlaw
in the branches of thy crests.

At ever-angelic Tech Moling,
at puissant Toidhen in the south,
'tis there my eternal rest-place will be,
I shall fall by a [spear]-point.

The curse of Ronan Finn
has thrown me in thy company,
O little stag, little bleating one,
O melodious little clamourer.

After that lay Sweeney came from Fiodh Gaibhle to Benn Boghaine, thence to Benn Faibhne, thence to Rath Murbuilg, but he found no refuge from the hag until he reached Dun Sobairce in Ulster. Sweeney leaped from the summit of the fort sheer down in front of the hag. She leaped quickly after him, but dropped on the cliff of Dun Sobairce, where she was broken to pieces, and fell into the sea. In that manner she found death in the wake of Sweeney.

12TH CENTURY.
Translator J. G. O'Keeffe.

PART III

The Bardic Tradition

COURT POETRY
TRANSLATED FROM THE GAELIC

Lamentation of Mac Liag for Kincora[1]

OH, WHERE, Kincora! is Brian the Great?
And where is the beauty that once was thine?
Oh, where are the princes and nobles that sate
At the feast in thy halls, and drank the red wine?
Where, oh, Kincora?

[1] Mac Liag, the bard of Brian Boru, laments the killing of his patron by the Vikings at the battle of Clontarf in 1014. Kincora was the site of Brian's palace in Clare.

Oh, where, Kincora! are thy valorous lords?
Oh, whither, thou Hospitable! are they gone?
Oh, where are the Dalcassians of the Golden Swords?
And where are the warriors Brian led on?
Where, oh, Kincora?

And where is Murrough, the descendant of kings—
The defeater of a hundred—the daringly brave—
Who set but slight store by jewels and rings—
Who swam down the torrent and laughed at its wave?
Where, oh, Kincora?

And where is Donogh, King Brian's worthy son?
And where is Conaing, the Beautiful Chief?
And Kian, and Corc? Alas! they are gone—
They have left me this night alone with my grief,
Left me, Kincora!

And where are the chiefs with whom Brian went forth,
The ne'er vanquished son of Erin the Brave,
The great King of Onaght, renowned for his worth,
And the hosts of Baskinn, from the western wave?
Where, oh, Kincora?

Oh, where is Duvlann of the swift-footed Steeds?
And where is Kian, who was son of Molloy?
And where is King Lonergan, the fame of whose deeds
In the red battle-field no time can destroy?
Where, oh, Kincora?

And where is that youth of majestic height,
The faith-keeping Prince of the Scots?—Even he,
As wide as his fame was, as great as was his might,
Was tributary, oh, Kincora, to thee!
Thee, oh, Kincora!

They are gone, those heroes of royal birth
Who plundered no churches, and broke no trust,
'Tis weary for me to be living on earth
When they, oh, Kincora, lie low in the dust!
Low, oh, Kincora!

Oh, never again will Princes appear,
To rival the Dalcassians of the Cleaving Swords!
I can never dream of meeting afar or anear,
In the east or the west, such heroes and lords!
Never, Kincora!

Oh, dear are the images my memory calls up
Of Brian Boru!—how he never would miss
To give me at the banquet the first bright cup!
Ah! why did he heap on me honour like this?
Why, oh, Kincora?

I am Mac Liag, and my home is on the Lake;
Thither often, to that palace whose beauty is fled
Came Brian to ask me, and I went for his sake.
Oh, my grief! that I should live, and Brian be dead!
Dead, oh, Kincora!

11TH CENTURY.
Translator James Clarence Mangan.

At Saint Patrick's Purgatory

BY Donnchadh mor O'Dala (d. 1244)

Pity me on my pilgrimage to Loch Derg!
O King of the churches and the bells—
Bewailing your sores and your wounds,
But not a tear can I squeeze from my eyes!

Not moisten an eye
After so much sin!
Pity me, O King! What shall I do
With a heart that seeks only its own ease?

Without sorrow or softening in my heart,
Bewailing my faults without repenting them!
Patrick the high priest never thought
That he would reach God in this way.

O lone son of Calpurn—since I name him—
O Virgin Mary, how sad is my lot!—
He was never seen as long as he was in this life
Without the track of tears from his eyes.

In a narrow, hard, stone-wall cell
I lie after all my sinful pride—
O woe, why cannot I weep a tear!—
And I buried alive in the grave.

On the day of Doom we shall weep heavily,
Both clergy and laity;
The tear that is not dropped in time,
None heeds in the world beyond.

I shall have you go naked, go unfed,
Body of mine, father of sin,
For if you are turned Hellwards
Little shall I reck your agony tonight.

O only begotten Son by whom all men were made,
Who shunned not the death by three wounds,
Pity me on my pilgrimage to Loch Derg
And I with a heart not softer than a stone!

Translator Sean O'Faolain.

The Dead at Clonmacnois

BY Angus O'Gillan

IN A quiet water'd land, a land of roses,
  Stands Saint Kieran's city fair:
And the warriors of Erin in their famous generations
  Slumber there.

There beneath the dewy hillside sleep the noblest
  Of the clan of Conn,
Each below his stone with name in branching Ogham
  And the sacred knot thereon.

There they laid to rest the seven Kings of Tara,
  There the sons of Cairbré sleep—
Battle-banners of the Gael, that in Kieran's plain of crosses
  Now their final hosting keep.

And in Clonmacnois they laid the men of Teffia,
  And right many a lord of Breagh;
Deep the sod above Clan Creidé and Clan Conaill,
  Kind in hall and fierce in fray.

Many and many a son of Conn, the Hundred-Fighter,
  In the red earth lies at rest;
Many a blue eye of Clan Colman the turf covers,
  Many a swan-white breast.

14TH CENTURY.
Translator T. W. Rolleston.

On the Breaking-Up of a School

BY Tadhg O'g O'Huiginn

Tonight the schools disperse,
Thereby are beds left widowed,
The folk of each bed will shed tears
At parting.

Many lay down, how sad,
Last night, in the home where I dwelt,
Although this eve they are more likely
To watch than to lie down.

The glory of the home I dwelt in,
O God, I see naught
So inglorious today;
It is a sermon to one who could understand.

The men of art had ever
A tryst against All Hallowtide:
Were but one man living
Their departure would be no dispersal.

O ye who were in his dwelling
In quest of art and residence,
Well might ye loathe to hear
The utterance of the cuckoos.

When the school dispersed
Each man of art went to his own homeland:
None cometh since then from his father's house
In quest of art.

Long seemed to me until dispersal of the school
That I saw by Ferghal's side:
Longer than the dispersal of the school
Is it to have lost my teacher's kindness.

It were easier for them to separate
Than to seek a teacher in his stead:
It is a doom of captivity, O God, to his pupil
If he be with a strange teacher.

For thirty years
Or longer, I bear witness,
I was full of my breath from pride
Until anguish came to cool me.

My prowess in his banqueting hall
Has been punished by draughts of sorrow:
If I have lived riotously, O God,
The punishment is sorer.

For my training he would not have
Me one night away from him,
Till he loosed me against the birds
I was ever in one hut with O'Huiginn.

A reproach against me, to my hurt,
Made in secret to my ollave,[1]
Little profit was it to anyone who should utter it—
He would not endure a breath against me.

From childhood he would share with me
(God reward O'Huiginn therefor)
Every eager design that he formed
Until it was time for us to part.

The teaching that I give today
To his pupils after the poet's death,
It was Ferghal Ruadh who made it:
O Lord that it were like his!

Dear is the mystic hut of poesy,
Which I recognize after his loss:
O empty hut before me
Thou wast not wont to have a neighbour.

---

[1] A chief poet.

That Aine's son lives not
Has robbed poesy of her gaiety:
As a plank goes out of the side of a cask
The wall of learning has broken.

16TH CENTURY.
Translator Osborn Bergin.

The Student

The student's life is pleasant
And pleasant is his labour,
Search all Ireland over,
You'll find no better neighbour.

Nor lords nor petty princes
Dispute the student's pleasure,
Nor chapter stints his purse
Nor stewardship his leisure.

None orders early rising,
Calf-rearing or cow-tending,
Nor nights of toilsome vigil,
His time is his for spending.

He takes a hand at draughts
And plucks a harp-string bravely,
And fills his nights with courting
Some golden-haired light lady.

And when spring-time is come
  The plough-shaft's there to follow—
A fistful of goosequills
  And a straight deep furrow!

17TH CENTURY.
Translator Frank O'Connor.

Hugh Maguire

BY Eochy O'Hussey

Too cold this night for Hugh Maguire,
I tremble at the pounding rain;
  Alas that venomous cold.
  Is my companion's lot.

It brings an anguish to my heart
To see the fiery torrents fall;
  He and the spiky frost—
  A horror to the mind!

The floodgates of the heavens yawn
Above the bosom of the clouds;
  And every pool a sea,
  And murder in the air.

One thinks of the hare that haunts the wood,
And of the salmon in the bay,
  Even the wild bird, one grieves
  To think they are abroad.

Then one remembers Hugh Maguire
Abroad in a strange land tonight
Under the lightning's glare
And clouds with fury filled.

He in West Munster braves his doom,
And without shelter strides between
The drenched and shivering grass
And the impetuous sky.

Cold on that tender blushing cheek
The fury of the springtime gales
That toss the stormy rays
Of stars about his head.

I can scarce bear to conjure up
The contour of his body crushed
This rough and gloomy night
In its cold iron suit.

The gentle and war-mastering hand
To the slim shaft of his cold spear
By icy weather pinned—
Cold is the night for Hugh.

The low banks of the swollen streams
Are covered where the soldiers pass;
The meadows stiff with ice,
The horses cannot feed.

And yet as though to bring him warmth
And call the brightness to his face
  Each wall that he attacks
  Sinks in a wave of fire,

The fury of the fire dissolves
The frost that sheaths the tranquil eye,
  And from his wrists the flame
  Thaws manacles of ice.

16TH CENTURY.
Translator Frank O'Connor.

Civil Irish and Wild Irish

BY Laoiseach Mac an Bhaird

Man who follow English ways, who cut short your curling hair, O slender hand of my choice, you are unlike the good son of Donnchadh!

If you were he, you would not give up your long hair (the best adornment in all the land of Ireland) for an affected English fashion, and your head would not be tonsured.

You think a shock of yellow hair unfashionable; *he* hates both the wearing of love-locks and being shaven-headed in the English manner—how unlike are your ways!

Eóghan *Bán*, the darling of noble women, is a man who never loved English customs; he has not set his heart on English ways, he has chosen the wild life rather.

Your ideas are nothing to Eóghan *Bán;* he would give breeches away for a trifle, a man who asked no cloak but a rag, who had no desire for doublet and hose.

He would hate to have at his ankle a jewelled spur on a boot, or stockings in the English manner; he will allow no love-locks on him.

A blunt rapier which could not kill a fly, the son of Donnchadh does not think it handsome; nor the weight of an awl sticking out behind his rear as he goes to the hill of the assembly.

Little he cares for gold-embroidered cloaks, or for a high well-furnished ruff, or for a gold ring which would only be vexatious, or for a satin scarf down to his heels.

He does not set his heart on a feather bed, he would prefer to lie upon rushes; to the good son of Donnchadh a house of rough wattles is more comfortable than the battlements of a castle.

A troop of horse at the mouth of a pass, a wild fight, a ding-dong fray of footsoldiers, these are some of the delights of Donnchadh's son—and seeking contest with the foreigners.

You are unlike Eóghan *Bán;* men laugh at you as you put your foot on the mounting-block; it is a pity that you yourself don't see your errors, O man who follow English ways.

16TH CENTURY.
Translator Kenneth Jackson.

Maelmora MacSweeny

BY Tadhg Dall O'Huiginn (1550-1593)[1]

One night I came to Eas Caoille, till the Day of Doom I shall remember it; when the fortress itself shall have perished there shall still remain forever the events of that night, the doings of all who were present. The like of the men whom I found in the polished bright-hued castle, on the shapely benches of the crimson fortress, eye never saw before. But few remain of the beloved company whom I found in the bright castle, the death of the four that were within was a grief from which Banbha[2] did not look to recover.

I found Maelmora MacSweeny on the central bench of the graceful mansion, a man of generous and pleasant manner, favorite pupil of the schools of Conn's land.[3] Dear as life to me was the man I found in that domed castle with its ivory-hilted swords; as I have experienced twice its value of misery from the loss of it, the honor I received from him is the worse from its greatness. Both pupil and fosterer to the poets of Banbha throughout his days was the chess-king of the Finn; the goal of our emulation, our ready gift, storehouse of the hearts of the learned. Our healing herb, our sleep charm, our fruitful branch, our house of treasure; a piece of steel, yet one who never denied any man, most precious offspring of the Grecian Gaels.

---

[1] See Introduction, p. xxiv.

[2] A name for Ireland.

[3] Ireland in the second century (A.D.) was divided into two kingdoms, one ruled over by Eogan Mor, the other by Conn of the Hundred Battles. Henceforward the northern kingdom became known as Conn's Half (or Land) and the southern kingdom as Eogan's Half.

I found beside the son of Maelmurray[1] many men of letters worthy of recompense, while the choicest of every craft in the world were also reclining beside the chief of Derg. Till the day of his death the poets of the host of the House of Trim were ever with the chief of Conn's tribe in a gathering large enough for battle or assembly.

At that time in particular there sat by the warrior of Loch Key—well did their scholarship become them—three of the poets of Té's Hill. There was the poet of the Earl of the Burkes, and also by his soft bosom was one of whom the very mention was a surety, the poet of the famous race of Niall. There was the poet of the chieftain of the Moy, Mac William Burke of just awards—discouraging in sooth are the changes of the world, that not one of these remains is in itself a sermon. Brian O'Donnellan, kindly countenance, poet to the lion of Loughrea; he with the schools as the moon above stars, peace to his gallant, noble form. Brian Macnamee, son of Angus, poet to the descendant of Nine-Hostaged Niall; a man whose attainment was the best of his time, he was fit to deliver wisdom's pledge. Conor, grandson of O'Huiginn, poet to the lord of Inishkea, almost equal to a prince was the poet, the head of his kindred in worth. The three poets that I found by the ruddy, fair-skinned hero—let a trio such as they be found in the land of Banbha!

With one accord they arise before me from beside the chieftain who was my chieftain; often I think of them in my heart, the utterances of the three drawing tears from my eyes. The soothing strains of harps, the sweetness of honey, the elation of ale—alas, that he of whom I had them no longer lives—these gave me pleasure.

For a while after my arrival they drank to me—gentlemen were their attendants—from cups of gold, from goblets of horn. When we had gone to our couches of rest to slumber, ere the coming of day, he who lay furthest from me would not admit that to be thus was not a sentence of bondage. I lay in

---

[1] I.e. MacSweeny, the host.

the midst of the four, the four forms that were most dear to me, the three comrades who have grieved my heart, and the champion of Magh Meann.

To the blossom of Tara and his three companions I relate a tale in return for reward; its dearness was a portent of fame for them, golden youth of the north. Four treasures endowed with virtue I take from them in payment for my story; that the like of the princely jewels may not be found—is not that enough to color one's tears? As the first award I was allowed I took the dappled steed from the hero of steed-abounding Slieve Gamph, him at whose death hospitality perished. The dappled steed that I took from Maelmora—woe is me that I took it—hardly is there its like in the world, a steed surpassing all the steeds of Bregian Banbha. From Brian son of Angus I took the choicest hound of Dá Thí's Plain; its excellence was such as to place it above all other hounds, it was one of the choice hounds of the world. It had been easier for Brian to renounce one by one all of the treasures of Ireland—wherefore should this not depress my spirit?—than his treasure of a noble handsome hound.

From Brian son of Owen, ere the fair, rosy, kindly fellow slept, I got as a reward for my story a precious book, a brimming spring of the genuine stream of knowledge. The "Cattle-raids," "Wooings," "Destructions" of all the world were in the gift I received, with descriptions of the battles and exploits thereof; it was the flower of the royal books of Ireland. Conor gave the magic harp, such a precious jewel as even a king would not bestow; long has that present been a sorrowful inheritance, it was no fitting gift from a poet. The harp of the poet of the Burkes will be ever an object of reverence; he from whom it was got is no more, but it remains in freshness to-day.

Alas for him by whom the givers of these were beloved, since it was destined that he should part from them; men never false in the house of election, men who loved to spread their fame. Alas for my beloved four, my bed-fellows, my confidants; four stems from a fruitful forest, trees fertile in gifts for us.

My reason wanders, restless is my mind after that shortlived company; alas for him who remains on earth without them, departing, they have left Brian's Banbha without fruits.

It is a heartbreak that the chief of the band which was within should be lacking to us; never before did poet lack the generous gift of his stout heart. May God requite Maelmora for the quantity of his wealth that I received; one who bestowed as much as any man gave, the benefactor of all. Suave in utterance, stern in resolve, ruthless in deeds, modest in speech; guardian of every man of his kindred, judge, soldier, poet, soothsayer. Treasure of contention of the race of Breóghan, winning of their game, defence of their pledge; satisfaction of the hearts of troublesome guests, love of melodious, merry, graceful women. Prudent preparation, generous disposition, a keeping of word, a breaking of peace; bright countenance from which the eyes could scarce wander, nursing knee of royal rule. Solving of problems, posing of counter-problems, Inisfail's[1] anvil of knowledge; hate of perpetual ease, love of conflict, surety for the peace and war of all. The son of Gormlaidh, a branch above the wood, keen in mind, gentle in response—where is his like for bestowing a troublesome award? Sternness and generosity he has in equal parts.

Though I have been in poverty since he fell, I should be above all the land of Fál in affluence if only Maelmora—lime-white skin, countenance of amber—remained. The remembrance of what I got from my friend will soon be but an omen of grief; I shall fear lest the greatness of my honor should come to me again in illusion.

Alas, not many of my comrades remain to me in their own shape; the world has cast me away, sending me travelling afar, in solitude. Pitiful it is to lack my three comrades, the race of Gormlaidh, from whom the day was short; Banbha, who looked for help from this clan, is now under a cloud of sorrow.

Translator Eleanor Knott.

---

[1] A name for Ireland (*Inis Fal*).

The First Vision

BY Tadhg Dall O'Huiginn

A Vision of a Queen of Fairyland
My soul to ravish came to me last night,
And never lady at my side did stand
To my undoing so unearthly bright.

Last night she came, a bright and lovely ghost,
And rose before me while I seemed to sleep,
And of that slumber where my soul was lost
My tongue shall tell while I my memory keep.

Fair was her face, her cheeks outblushed the rose;
There might you see the floods of crimson rise,
And dark unfaltering brows above disclose
The hyacinthine petals of her eyes.

Her pretty mouth more sweet than honeycomb
Would with red lips the budding rose excel,
And each soft whisper that from thence did come
Would charm the sick and make the dying well.

Between her lips like fallen rain of pearl
On scarlet cushions twain her teeth reposed;
How bright they shone, how sweetly spoke the girl;
Each languid word new loveliness disclosed.

Between her arms that taper to the hand
Are set twin glories, beautiful to see.
Two snowy mountains in her bosom stand,
Mid golden thickets of embroidery.

Gold-bordered slippers on her gentle feet
Do guard her steps wherever she may move;
You'd swear that maid so radiantly sweet
Had them a present from the God of Love.

Her purple mantle fringed with satin round,
Her golden shift with scarlet borders gay,
Her gilded bodice o'er her bosom bound
Did all her fairy loveliness display.

Then this fair lady spake in modest wise,
And gently did the amazéd dreamer greet,
And I when she had done did make replies
To that bright beauty with the visage sweet.

We spake awhile and then I made demand
That she should answer to my questioning:
"Fair lady, tell me of your native land!
Whence come you? From what country, or what king?"

'Run thro' two continents of earth or three!
'Tis easier so," said she to my appeal,
"But do not think to know my mystery,
For I have secrets I will ne'er reveal."

"I came to seek you: come away with me!"
Thus spake the lady, and her voice was low,
And in my ear she murmured secretly,
As softest notes from sweetest organs flow.

"I will not go!" I answered like a fool,
For love had brought me to distraction,
And as I spake that vision beautiful
Had vanished in the darkness and was gone.

And now my soul and body part in pain.
The queen with blushing cheek and brown-lashed eyes
Leaves me to pine and cometh not again,
Tho' she was kind and beautiful and wise.

To ruddy Connla long ago there came
A woman. Fodhla's[1] monarch to beguile,
And she I love is gentler, yet the same
As she that won his heart with many a wile.

A warrior father's noblest offspring he,
Brave Connla, son of Hundred-fighting Conn,
Thro' woman's guile he fled beyond the sea
And never vessel bore a braver one.

E'en such the woman who in mantle brown,
With branch of music from across the sea
Did visit Bran Mac Febal. ('Tis handed down,
A famous tale in Ireland's history.)[2]

The noblest sons of Desmond's land she bore
Across the sea, yea, even nine times nine,
Eighty with Bran to make the number more,
So by his flight perfecting her design.

---

[1] A name for Ireland.
[2] See page 131.

Connla deluded, Bran beguiled also,
By stranger woman ravished o'er the sea,
And I deceived by one I do not know!
Most strange of all the thing that's done to me!

The mound of Midhir with its rampart fair,
The fort of Sanbh, Abhartach's magic hill,
No lady in their castles can compare
With this sweet maid for whom I languish still.

Not in Emania of the apple-trees,
Nor halls of Aonghus of the golden sword,
The fairy dwells that hath such charms as these,
So soft a beauty or so kind a word.

But she is gone, and I would follow fast
To lands unknown, who languish in despair.
Would it were possible to find at last
That country and to dwell for ever there!

A little hour I loved her rosy cheek—
The ebb must follow ever on the flow—
The vision fled, the joy of love grew weak,
My spirit sank and I was left to woe.

Translator The Earl of Longford.

The Second Vision

BY Tadhg Dall O'Huiginn

Say, are you she that came to me last
Brought by enchantment in a vision?
My spirit ravished by the wondrous sight
Knows naught aright for deep distraction.

And if you be not she that came before
With slender body and soft fondling hand,
I'll ne'er believe that there are many more
So gently treading out of Fairyland.

Your kindling cheek, the azure of your eyes!
Could all the four great elements compose
Such coiling gold as o'er your shoulder lies,
A cheek so red, an eye to vie with those?

No tooth so white, no lip so crimson were,
No voice so soft to lull the brain to sleep,
No brow so dark as might with yours compare,
No wealth to match the treasure that you keep!

A throat more white than is the lily flower,
Long tapering hands, surpassing beautiful,
Soft flesh that robs the moonlight of its power,
And dims the foam and makes bright rivers dull.

White are your breasts as blossom, that do stand
High o'er the glorious slopes that gleam below,
Two gentle hills that rise from richest land,
Two wondrous mounds that Fairy people know.

Like flight of birds that sing not in the cold
About your body fall the rippling locks.
Oh, surely they are drenched in liquid gold,
As down they curve and glitter in their flocks!

Oh, trust me! You shall take no harm at all;
But tell if it was you that came last night,
To vex my heart, to trouble Inis Fail,[1]
Bright maid with eye so mild, with teeth so white!

Or was it you that came so long ago
To good King Arthur and his Table Round,
Sweet head whence radiant tresses softly flow?
For since that day no maid so fair was found.

Or was it you that came, for so 'twould seem,
Of old to Ughoine's son, the mighty Hugh,
From Slievenaman, of many a magic stream,
To Eire's people from the Fairy crew?

Or was it you, indeed I think 'twas you,
Who carried Murchadh across the sea,
The night you visited great Brian Boru,
Who lay encamped with all his soldiery?

---

[1] A name for Ireland.

Or was it you that came another day
The valiant Hound of Culann to beguile?
To lead the son of Deichtire astray
You left your bright and fruitful mound awhile.

Or was it you whose loveliness appealed,
O glorious vision with an angel's grace,
To Mahon O'Maille once on Banba's field,
Where many a war has marred the country's race.

Or was it you that came in days of old,
In ancient days when Conaire was King,
To craze the soul of warriors young and bold
At Tailteann Hill with valor mustering?

Or was it you, O maid of steadfast thought,
That bore young Bran away from Eire's strand?
The son of white-foot Febal once you brought
Across the Ocean to the Promised Land.

There came—Oh, were you there?—to Connacht's King
A glorious company of ladies fair,
On shores of Derg renowned, a wondrous thing,
As by the lake he lay. Oh, were you there?

Or was it you led Connla far away,
In spite of guarding spells of druidry,
From Fodhla's host, from cold, grey hills of Breagh,
O lovely face, not hateful unto me?

Or was it you that did myself beguile
A while ago, O vision of my joy.
And are you she that with her wizard wile
Doth still the men of Fodhla's land destroy?

Ah, yes! 'Tis she! I know that you must be
That very lady that before was here.
In leafy Banba there could never be
Another such; this beauty hath no peer.

O gentle maiden with the limbs of snow,
No fairy equals her I saw last night,
But you yourself. No magic castles show
By Boyne or waves of Cuan a form so bright.

For not the sea-washed mound of Assaroe,
Nor any fairy dwelling's warm recess,
Nor yet Rath Truim nor Youghal e'er did know
A maid of such unearthly loveliness.

For tho' last night I saw her beauty plain,
Another such I never shall discern
In dream or vision till she come again,
And all the wonder of that time return.

Twice hath she come. The maid with longing sore
Wasted my cheek and scarred my brow with care.
Twice hath she come and she will come once more.
And still I wait, for she is wondrous fair.

Translator The Earl of Longford

The Good Tradition

Ah! liberal-handed lady, though
Round Eire's shore the generous wave
Ebbs now, in thee 'tis still at flow;
No marvel that the bard's thy slave.

A lady passionate for song,
True friend of all the bardic kind,
Who cleaves to her can scarce go wrong;
Song to her loaned doth interest find.

The good tradition holds no more
Of open-handedness to art;
On later manners men set store
And close their purse-strings and their heart.

Now that the giving spirit's gone
And wealth and art are by the ears,
That poet's mad who labours on
And gives to song his wasted years.

In ancient Ulster as of old
Dwelt Liberality of right;
Now Ulster hearts are changed and cold,
From all that province she takes flight.

She's chased from Munster; Connacht too
Gives her no welcome as of yore;
The hapless hunger-stricken crew
Know Liberality no more.

She's known no more where the wide plain
Of Leinster spreads beneath the skies;
Unless another shape she's ta'en,
That hides her from the poet's eyes.

A mist has caught her from our sight,
A druid mist that hides her o'er;
Ask but a lodging for the night
And all men turn you from the door.

17TH CENTURY.
Translator Robin Flower.

The Flight of the Earls[1]

This night sees Eire desolate,
Her chiefs are cast out of their state;
Her men, her maidens weep to see
Her desolate that should peopled be.

How desolate is Connla's plain,
Though aliens swarm in her domain;
Her rich bright soil had joy in these
That now are scattered overseas.

---

[1] Six years after their defeat at Kinsale in 1601, the earls of Tyrone and Tyrconnell fled to the continent with the surviving members of their clans. What remained of the Gaelic aristocracy was either destroyed or driven into exile during the Williamite War (1690-2).

Man after man, day after day
Her noblest princes pass away
And leave to all the rabble rest
A land dispeopled of her best.

O'Donnell goes. In that stern strait
Sore-stricken Ulster mourns her fate,
And all the northern shore makes moan
To hear that Aodh of Annagh's gone.

Men smile at childhood's play no more,
Music and song, their day is o'er;
At wine, at Mass the kingdom's heirs
Are seen no more; changed hearts are theirs.

They feast no more, they gamble not,
All goodly pastime is forgot,
They barter not, they race no steeds,
They take no joy in stirring deeds.

No praise in builded song expressed
They hear, no tales before they rest;
None care for books and none take glee
To hear the long-traced pedigree.

The packs are silent, there's no sound
Of the old strain on Bregian ground.
A foreign flood holds all the shore,
And the great wolf-dog barks no more.

Woe to the Gael in this sore plight!
Hence forth they shall not know delight.
No tidings now their woe relieves,
Too close the gnawing sorrow cleaves.

These the examples of their woe:
Israel in Egypt long ago,
Troy that the Greek hosts set on flame,
And Babylon that to ruin came.

Sundered from hope, what friendly hand
Can save the sea-surrounded land?
The clan of Conn no Moses see
To lead them from captivity.

Her chiefs are gone. There's none to bear
Her cross or lift her from despair;
The grieving lords take ship. With these
Our very souls pass overseas.

17TH CENTURY.
Translator Robin Flower.

Were Not the Gael Fallen

BY Peadar O'Mulconry

Were not the Gael fallen from their high estate
And Fola's warrior kings cast down by fate
And learning mocked in Eire's evil day,
I were no servant, Edmond, in thy pay.

Ye shall not stay my toil, once held divine,
Thou and thy fleering harlots at their wine,
Till all the brave are dead and out of reach
Eireamhon's people of the golden speech.

Edmond, I give good counsel. Heed it thou!
Leave mocking at my holy labours now,
Or such a rain of venomed shafts I'll send
That never a man shall save thee nor defend.

A tale I've heard that well might tame thy mood.
A gamesome chief of Gascony's best blood
Refused a poet once. The satire sped
And the man withered, strengthless, leprous, dead.

17TH CENTURY.
Translator Robin Flower.

Who Will Buy a Poem?

BY Mahon O'Heffernan

I ask, who will buy a poem? Its meaning is the true learning of sages. Would anyone take, does anyone want, a noble poem which would make him immortal?

Though this is a poem of close-knit lore, I have walked all Munster with it, every market-place from cross to cross—and it has brought me no profit from last year to the present.

Though a groat would be small payment, no man nor any woman offered it; not a man spoke of the reason, but neither Irish nor English heeded me.

An art like this is no profit to me, though it is hard that it should die out; it would be more dignified to go and make combs—why should anyone take up poetry?

Corc of Cashel lives no more, nor Cian, who did not hoard up cattle nor the price of them, men who were generous in rewarding poets—alas, it is good-bye to the race of Éibhear.

The prize for generosity was never taken from them, until Cobhthach died, and Tál; I spare to mention the many kindreds for whom I might have continued to make poetry.

I am like a trading ship that has lost its freight, after the Fitz-Geralds who won renown. I hear no offers—how that torments me! It is a vain matter about which I ask.

17TH CENTURY.
Translator Kenneth Jackson.

Geoffrey Keating[1] (c.1570-c.1650)
FROM *The History of Ireland*

How Emain Macha[2] Got Its Name

Now the reason why it is called Eamhain Mhacha is this: three kings out of Ulster held the sovereignty of Ireland, namely, Aodh Ruadh son of Badharn, from whom is named Eas Ruaidh, and Diothorba son of Deaman of Uisneach in Meath, and Ciombaoth son of Fionntan from Fionnabhair; and it was with this Ciombaoth that Ughaine Mor son of Eochaidh Buadhach was brought up. And each of these kings reigned seven years in succession, until each had held the sovereignty of Ireland thrice. And the first of them to die was Aodh Ruadh; and he left no issue but one daughter named Macha. Macha demanded the sovereignty in her turn after her father's death; and Diothorba and his children said that they would not cede sovereignty to a woman; and a battle was fought between themselves and Macha; and Macha triumphed over them in that battle, and held the sovereignty of Ireland seven years; and Diothorba died and left five sons, namely, Baoth, Bedach, Bras, Uallach, and Borbchas. These demanded the sovereignty of Ireland for themselves, as it was held by their ancestors before them. Macha said she would only give them battle for the sovereignty. A battle was fought between them, and Macha defeated them. The children of Diothorba fled for safety to dark and intricate woods; and Macha took Ciombaoth son of Fionntan as her husband, and made him leader of her warriors, and went herself in pursuit of the sons of Diothorba in the guise of a leper, having rubbed her body with the dough of rye, and found them in an intricate forest in Burenn, cooking a wild boar. The sons of Diothorba asked news of her, and gave her a portion of the meat. She told them all the news she had.

[1] See Introduction, p. xxv.

[2] The capital of ancient Ulster.

And then one of the men said that the leper had a beautiful eye, and that he desired to lie with her. Thereupon he and Macha retired into the recesses of the wood, and Macha bound this man and left him there, and returned to the rest. And they questioned her, "Where didst thou leave the man who went with thee?" said they. "I know not," said she; "but I think he feels ashamed to come into your presence after embracing a leper." "It is not a shame," said they, "since we will do the same thing." Thus she went into the wood with each of them in turn; and she bound them all, and so took them bound together before the men of Ulster at Eamhain; and she asked the Ulster nobles what she should do with them. They all said with one accord that they should be put to death. "That is not just," said Macha, "for that would be contrary to law; but let them be made slaves of, and let the task be imposed on them of building a fort for me which shall be the capital of the province for ever." Thereupon Macha undid the gold bodkin that was in the mantle on her breast, and with it measured the site of the fort which the sons of Diothorba were obliged to build. Now, the fort is called Eamhain, eo being a word for "a bodkin," while *muin* means "the neck," and hence the fort is called Eamhain that is, eo *mhuin*. Or, it is called Eamhain from Eamhain Mhacha, that is, the wife of Cronn son of Adhnaman. Now this woman was forced against her will to run with the horses of Conchubhar, king of Ulster; and she, though pregnant, outran them; and at the end of the race she gave birth to a son and a daughter; and she cursed the men of Ulster, whence they were visited with the pangs of labour; and these pangs continued to afflict them during nine reigns, that is, from Conchubhar to the reign of Mal son of Rochruidhe. . . .

Loingseach's Horse Ears

We read of Labhraidh Loingseach[1] that his ears were like those of a horse; and hence he used to kill on the spot everyone who cut his hair, lest he or anyone else might be aware of this blemish. Now he was wont to have his hair cropped every year, that is, to have cut off the part of his hair that grew below his ears. It was necessary to cast lots to determine who should crop the king each year, since it was his wont to put to death everyone who cropped him. Now it happened that the lot fell on the only son of a widow who approached the close of her life, and who lived near the king's stronghold. And when she heard that the lot had fallen on her son, she came and besought the king not to put her only son to death, seeing he was her sole offspring. The king promised her that he would not put her son to death, provided he kept secret what he should see, and made it known to no one till death. And when the youth had cropped the king, the burden of that secret so oppressed his body that he was obliged to lie in the bed of sickness, and that no medicine availed him. When he had lain long in a wasting condition, a skilful druid came to visit him, and told his mother that the cause of his sickness was the burden of a secret, and that he would not be well till he revealed his secret to some thing; and he directed him, since he was bound not to tell his secret to a person, to go to a place where four roads met, and to turn to his right and to address the first tree he met, and to tell his secret to it. The first tree he met was a large willow, and he disclosed his secret to it. Thereupon the burden of pain that was on his body vanished; and he was healed instantly as he returned to his mother's house. Soon after this, however, it happened that Craiftine's harp got broken, and he went to seek the material for a harp, and came upon the very willow to which

[1] King of Leinster in the third century B.C.

the widow's son had revealed the secret, and from it he took the material for his harp; and when the harp was made and set to tune, as Craiftine played upon it all who listened imagined that it sang, "Da o phill ar Labhraidh Lorc," that is, Labraidh Loingseach, meaning, "Two horse's ears on Labhraidh Lorc"; and as often as he played on that harp, it was understood to sing the same thing. And when the king heard this story, he repented of having put so many people to death to conceal that deformity of his, and openly exhibited his ears to the household, and never afterwards concealed them. I think this part of the story is a romantic tale rather than history. . . .

The Death of Curaoi

There were three orders of champions in Ireland at the same time; and there lived neither before their time nor ever since a body of the sons of Milidh who were bigger, stronger, braver, more skilled, more intrepid on the field of battle, and in exercises of valour and bravery than they; for the Fian of Leinster were not to be compared with them. The first order of these were the champions of the Craobh Ruadh under Conchubhar; the second order the Gamhanruidh of Iorras Domhnonn under Oilill Fionn; and the third order clanna Deaghaidh under Curaoi son of Daire in west Munster.

It was thus that the death of Curaoi came about. The champions of the Craobh Ruadh went to pillage an island in the ocean near Alba[1] called Manainn, where there was much gold and silver and wealth of various kinds, and many precious valuables besides; and the lord of the island had a comely, marriageable daughter who surpassed the women of her time in form and beauty. Her name was Blanaid. And when Curaoi heard that the champions were setting out on that expedition, he put on a disguise by magic, and went with the party; and

[1] Scotland.

when they were about to plunder the island in the guise of jugglers, they apprehended great difficulty in seizing on the dun which was in the island in which was Blanaid, and all the precious valuables of the island, both on account of its strength and of the great skill in magic of those who were defending it. Then Curaoi, who was disguised as a man with a grey cloak, said that if he got his choice of the valuables in the dun he would capture it for them. Cuchulainn promised him this; and thereupon they attacked the dun with the man in the grey cloak at their head. He stopped the magic wheel that was in motion at the door of the fortress, and enabled all to enter; and they plundered the dun, and took from it Blanaid and all the precious valuables it contained. They thence set out for Ireland and reached Eamhain; and as they were dividing the valuables, the man in the grey cloak asked for the valuable he should choose as was promised to him. "Thou shalt have it," said Cuchulainn. "Well, then," said he, "Blanaid is my choice of the valuables." "Thou mayst have thy choice of the other valuables excepting only Blanaid." "I will not accept any but her," said the man of the grey coat. Thereupon Curaoi sought an opportunity of carrying off Blanaid, and, seizing her unperceived, he bore her off in an enchanted mask. When Cuchulainn noticed that the lady was missing, he concluded that it was Curaoi who carried her off, and he pursued them by direct route to Munster, and overtook them at Solchoid; and the champions grappled with one another and engaged in strong, valorous wrestling; and Cuchulainn was brought to the ground by Curaoi, who inflicted on him the binding of the five smalls, and left him there a bound captive, having cut off his hair with his sword; and, leaving Cuchulainn bound as we have said, he took Blanaid with him to west Munster. But after this Laogh son of Rian of Gabhra came and unbound Cuchulainn; and they proceeded thence to the north of Ulster, and settled down beside Beanna Boirche for a year without coming to a meeting of the men of Ulster until Cuchulainn's hair grew; and at the end of that year Cuchulainn happened to be on Beanna Boirche, and he saw a large flock of black birds coming southwards from the surface of the ocean; and when they reached land he pursued them, and slew with his sling, by the exercise called *taithbheim* or "return-stroke," a bird out of each county, till he killed the last black bird of them at Sruibh Broin in west Munster; and as he was returning eastwards, he found Blanaid alone beside the Fionnghlaise in Ciarraidhe, where Curaoi's dwelling-fortress stood at that time. A conversation then took place between them; and she made known to him that there was not on the face of the earth a man she loved more than him, and asked him to come on the following Samhain with a full host and carry her off by fraud or force; and that he might the more easily do this, she would bring about that Curaoi should at that time have but few warriors and attendants. Cuchulainn promised to come to fetch her at that time. Thereupon he bade her farewell, and proceeded to Ulster, and gave Conchubhar an account of the incident.

As to Blanaid, she told Curaoi that he ought to build a stone fortress for himself which would excel all the royal fortresses of Ireland, and that the way in which that could be done was to send the clanna Deaghaidh to collect and bring together all the large stones that were standing in Ireland for the purpose of making a stone fortress for himself. And Blanaid's object in this was that clanna Deaghaidh might be scattered through the distant regions of Ireland far from Curaoi where Cuchulainn should come to carry her off. Now when Cuchulainn heard that clanna Deaghaidh were thus dispersed throughout Ireland, he set out secretly from Ulster with an army, and no tidings are recorded of him till he reached the oak wood that lay beside Curaoi's fortress; and when he arrived there, he sent word privately to Blanaid that he was there with an army; and the sign she sent him was that she would steal Curaoi's sword, and would thereupon pour a vat of new milk that was in the lios into the stream which was flowing from the homestead through the wood in which Cuchulainn was. Not long after he was informed of this token he saw the stream become white from the milk; and with that they attacked the fortress and sprang upon Curaoi in the lios and slew him alone and unarmed as he was. And the river referred to was called Fionnghlaise, through its having become white from the milk.

Curaoi's poet, who was called Feircheirtne, went after Blanaid to Ulster in hope of getting an opportunity of slaying her to avenge Curaoi; and on reaching Ulster he found Conchubhar and Cuchulainn and Blanaid, with a large assembly round them, at Ceann Beara point; and when the poet saw Blanaid standing there on the brink of a precipice, he went towards her and twined his arms round her, and cast himself and herself suddenly down the precipice, and thus they were both killed. . . .

Mochua's Riches

Mochua and Columcille were contemporaries, and when Mochua or Mac Duach was a hermit in the desert the only cattle he had in the world were a cock and a mouse and a fly. The cock's service to him was to keep the matin time of midnight; and the mouse would let him sleep only five hours in the day-and-night, and when he desired to sleep longer, through being tired from making many crosses and genuflexions, the mouse would come and rub his ear, and thus waken him; and the service the fly did him was to keep walking on every line of the Psalter that he read, and when he rested from reciting his psalms the fly rested on the line he left off at till he resumed the reciting of his psalms. Soon after that these three precious ones died, and Mochua, after that event, wrote a letter to Columcille, who was in Iona, in Alba, and he complained of the death of his flock. Columcille wrote to him, and said thus: "O brother," said he, "thou must not be surprised at the death of the flock that thou hast lost, for misfortune exists only where there is wealth." From this banter of these real saints I gather that they set no store on worldly possessions, unlike many persons of the present time. . . .

St. Columkille

Columcille came to Ireland having a cerecloth over his eyes, so that he might not see the soil of Ireland. For he was forbidden to look at the soil of Ireland from the time that Molaise imposed as penance on him to go to Alba and not to see the land of Ireland till death, and it was for this reason that he kept the cerecloth over his eyes while he was in Ireland until his return to Alba; and it is to relate Columcille's fulfilment of this penance that Molaise composed this stanza:

> Though Colum came from the east
> In a bark across the great sea,
> He saw nothing in noble Ireland
> On his coming to the convention.

Now the reason why Molaise imposed on Columcille the penance of going to Alba was that Columcille caused three battles to be fought in Ireland, to wit, the Battle of Cuil Dreimhne, the Battle of Cuil Rathan, and the Battle of Cuil Feadha. The cause of the Battle of Cuil Dreimhne, according to the old book called Uidhir Chiarain, was this: Diarmaid, son of Fearghus Ceirrbheoil, king of Ireland, held a Feis of Tara, and a nobleman was slain at that feis by Cuarnan, son of Aodh, son of Eochaidh Tiormcharna; and the reason why Diarmaid slew this Cuarnan was that he had slain the nobleman at the feis in violation of the law and sanctuary of the feis. And before Cuarnan was slain he put himself under the protection of the two sons of Mac Earca, to wit, Fearghus and Domhnall, and they put him under the protection of Columcille, and Diarmaid slew him in violation of Columcille's protection for having transgressed the law of Tara, and the result of this was that Columcille assembled clanna Neill of the north (on account of his own protection and that of the children of Mac Earca having been violated), and the Battle of Cuil Dreimhne was fought against Diarmaid and the men of Connaught, and they were defeated through the prayer of Columcille.

The Black Book of Molaga gives another reason why the Battle of Cuil Dreimhne was fought, to wit, through the unjust judgment Diarmaid gave against Columcille, when he secretly copied the Gospel from Fionntain's book, and Fionntain claimed for his own the copy which was written from his own book. Accordingly, both sides chose Diarmaid as a judge between them; and the judgment Diarmaid gave was that to every cow belonged her calf and that to every book belonged a copy of it; and that was the second reason why the Battle of Cuil Dreimhne was fought.

The reason why Columcille caused the battle of Cuil Rathan to be fought against the Dal nAruidhe and the Ultonians was because a contention had arisen between Columcille and Comghall, when the Dal nAruidhe showed themselves partial in the contention.

The reason why Columcille had caused the Battle of Cuil Feadha to be fought against Colman, son of Diarmaid, was to avenge the affront given him in the murder of Baodan, son of Ninnidh, king of Ireland, at Leim an Eich by Coman, son of Colman, in violation of Colum's protection.

Now Colum, with his holy clerics, proceeded from Alba to Ireland, as we have said, and when he was approaching the convention the queen, Aodh's wife, told her son, Conall, not to show any reverence to the heron-cleric or to his company. And when Colum was informed of this before he arrived at the place he said: "It is my will that the queen and her handmaid, in the shape of two herons, be over that ford below until Doom." Here is a proof from the Amhra repeating the words of Colum in this stanza:

> Let her become a heron,
> Said the cleric in a great rage,
> And let her handmaid exactly be
> A heron in her company.

And the reason why he ordered that the handmaid become a heron together with the queen was that it was she who came with a message from the queen to Conall, telling him not to shew any reverence to the heron-cleric or to his company. And I hear from many people that ever since two herons are usually seen on the ford which is beside Drom Ceat.

As to Columcille, when he arrived at the convention the party of Conall, son of Aodh, son of Ainmire, was the nearest to him in the assembly, and when Conall saw the clerics he incited the rabble of his party against them, thrice nine their number, and they pelted them with clods of clay, and they bruised and hurt the clerics. And Colum asked who were thus beating them. Colum was told that it was Conall, son of Aodh, who was inciting them to do this deed, and he ordered that thrice nine bells be rung on the spot against Conall, whom he cursed and deprived of royalty, of authority, of senses, of memory, of his understanding. And from these bells that were rung against him he is called Conall Clogach.

After this Colum went to the party of Domhnall, son of Aodh, and Domhnall went to meet him and bade him welcome, and kissed his cheek and seated him in his own place. Colum gave his blessing to Domhnall, son of Aodh, and prayed God that he might attain the sovereignty of Ireland; and it happened ultimately that he held the sovereignty of Ireland for thirteen years before he died.

Colum, accompanied by Domhnall, proceeded thence to the king's party, and when he had come into the king's presence the latter welcomed him—the king dreaded him greatly on account of what he had done to Conall, to the queen, to her handmaid, as we have said. "My welcome is compliance with my wish," said Colum. "It shall be granted thee," said the king. "Then," said Colum, "what I wish is this: I make three requests of thee, namely, to keep the filés whom thou art banishing from Ireland, and to free Scannlan Mor, son of Ceannfaolaidh, king of Osruighe, from the bondage in which thou keepest him, and not to go to impose a tribute on the Dal Riada in Alba." "I do not wish to keep the filés," said the king, "so unjust are their demands and so numerous are they. For there are usually thirty in the train of an ollamh, and fifteen in that of an anroth, and so on for the other grades of the filé down to the lowest." Each of them used to have a separate train of attendants according to his degree, so that nearly the third of the men of Ireland followed the bardic profession.

Columcille said to the king that it was right to set aside many of the filés, as they were so numerous. But he advised him to maintain a filé as his own chief ollamh, after the example of the kings who went before him, and that each provincial king should have an ollamh, and, moreover, that each lord of a cantred or district in Ireland should have an ollamh, and Columcille proposed this plan and Aodh assented to it; and it was to celebrate this benefit which Columcille conferred on the filés that Maolsuthain composed this stanza:

> The filés were saved by this means
> Through Colum of the fair law;
> A filé for each district is no heavy charge.
> It is what Colum ordained.

From this regulation, which was made by Aodh, son of Ainmire, and Columcille, if followed that the king of Ireland and every provincial king and every lord of a cantred had a special ollamh, and that each of these ollamhs had free land from his own lord, and, moreover, the lands and worldly possessions of each of these ollamhs enjoyed general exemption and sanctuary from the men of Ireland. It was also ordained that a common estate should be set apart for the ollamhs where they could give public instruction after the manner of a University, such as Raith Cheannait and Masruidhe Mhuighe Sleacht, in Breithfne, where they gave free instruction in the sciences to the men of Ireland, as many as desired to become learned in seanchus and in the other sciences that were in vogue in Ireland at that time.

The ardollamh of Ireland at that time was Eochaidh Eigeas, son of Oilill, son of Earc, and it was he who was called Dallan Forgaill, and he sent out ollamhs and set them over the provinces of Ireland, namely, Aodh Eigeas over the district of Breagh and over Meath, Urmhaol chief eigeas over the two provinces of Munster, Sanchan, son of Cuairfheartach, over the province of Connaught, and Fear Firb, son of Muireadhach, son of Mongan, in the ollamhship of Ulster; and, moreover, an ollamh in every cantred in Ireland under these high ollamhs, and they were to have free land from their territorial chiefs, as well as sanctuary, as we have said; and each of them was to get certain rewards for their poems and compositions.

The second request Colum asked of Aodh was to set Scannlan Mor, king of Osruighe, free, and let him go to his own country. This the king refused. "I shall not press it further," said Colum, "if it be God's will may Scannlan untie my thongs or take off my shoes to-night when I am at matins."

"The third request I make of thee," said Columcille, "is to grant a respite to the Dal Raida and not to go to Alba to plunder them with a view of laying a tribute on them, for you have a right only to a head-rent from them and a levy of forces on land and sea." "I shall not grant them respite, but shall pay them a visit," said Aodh. "Then," said Colum, "they will have a respite from thee for ever," and so it was.

Thereupon Columcille, with his clerics, took leave of the king and of the convention, and the Book of Glendalough states that Aodhan, son of Gabhran, son of Domhanghurt, king of Alba, was at that convention, and that he took his leave of the king and of the assembly along with Columcille. The same book says that the convention of Drom Ceat sat for a year and a month instituting laws and regulating tributes and forming friendly alliances between the men of Ireland. . . .

Brian Boru[1]

When Brian Boraimhe was residing at Ceann Choradh without strife or discord he besought the king of Leinster, Maolmordha, son of Murchadh, to send him three masts of excellent wood from Fiodh Gaibhle. The king of Leinster had the masts cut down and went with them himself to Ceann Choradh where Brian then was; and he ordered the Ui Failghe to carry one of the masts and the Ui Faolain another and the Ui Muireadhaigh the third, and a war of words arose between them as they were going up Sliabh an Bhogaigh; and thereupon the king of Leinster himself put his shoulder under the mast assigned to the Ui Faolain, wearing a satin tunic which Brian had given him sometime before, and which had gold borders to it and a silver clasp. And so greatly did the king of Leinster exert himself in bearing up the mast that the clasp of his tunic snapped; and when they reached Ceann Choradh the king of Leinster took off his tunic and gave it to his sister Gormfhlaith, daughter of Murchadh (that is Brian's wife), to fix a clasp in it. The queen took the tunic and cast it into the fire that was in front of her, and proceeded to reproach her brother for being in slavery of subjection to anyone on earth, "a thing," said she, "which neither thy father nor thy grandfather brooked"; and she added, that Brian's son would make the same demand of his son. Now Maolmordha kept in mind the queen's remarks; and the next day Murchadh, son of Brian, and Conaing, son of Donn Cuan, happened to be playing chess, or according to others it was the comhorba of Caoimhghin of Gleann da Loch that was playing with Murchadh. Maolmordha, the king of Leinster, set to instruct Murchadh, and taught him a move

---

1 Patron of art, religion, and learning, Brian Boru was a Munster chieftain who made himself High King of Ireland by extorting tribute from all the other kings. He defeated the Danish king of Dublin at Clontarf in 1014 but was himself killed as Keating describes.

which caused the game to go against him. "It was thou who gavest advice to the Lochlonnaigh which caused them to be defeated at the Battle of Gleann Mama," said Murchadh. "If I gave them advice which caused them to be defeated there," said Maolmordha, "I will give them another advice through which they will defeat thee in turn." "I defy thee to do so," said Murchadh.

Maolmordha was enraged at this and he went to his sleeping apartment, and could not be got to come to the drinking hall that night, and he took his departure early the next morning without bidding farewell to Brian.

Now when Brian heard that the king of Leinster left the mansion without bidding him farewell, he sent a page of his household to detain him that he might give him wages and gifts. The place at which the page overtook him was at the end of the plank bridge of Cill Dalua on the east side of the Sionainn, as he was mounting his steed, and he delivered to him the message Brian had sent him. Maolmordha, the king of Leinster, turned on the page and gave him three blows with the yew wand he held in his hand, so that he broke the bones of his skull, and it was in a litter that he was carried to Brian's house. The page's name was Cogaran and from him are the Ui Cogarain of Munster.

A party of the household of Ceann Choradh desired to pursue the king of Leinster and not to allow him to go to Leinster until he had submitted to Brian. Brian, however, said that it would not be permitted to practise treachery against him in his own house. "But," added he, "it is from the door-post of his own house that justice will be required of him."

Maolmordha, king of Leinster, went into his own country, and summoned and brought together to him the Leinster nobles, and told them that himself and all his province had been dishonoured and treated to abusive speech at Ceann Choradh. Accordingly what they agreed on was that they themselves and a Lochlonnach force should go against Brian, so that the Battle of Cluain Tarbh was set on foot between them; and since Brian had not left in Ireland as many of the Lochlonnaigh as could fight a battle, having left only the party he suffered, on the excuse of trading, to remain in Ath Cliath, in Loch Garman, in Port Lairge, in Corcach and in Luimneach, for the purpose of attracting commerce from other countries to Ireland, what the king of Leinster and the Lochlonnaigh decided on was to send to the king of Lochloinn for a force with which to meet Brian in battle on Magh nEalta at Cluain Tarbh. And when the message reached the king of Lochloinn he sent his two sons Carolus Cnutus and Andreas with a host of twelve thousand Lochlonnaigh to help the king of Leinster to fight the Battle of Cluain Tarbh, and when they landed at Ath Cliath the king of Leinster sent word to Brian to give notice that he would give him battle at Cluain Tarbh. . . .

And when they came together to one place on Magh nEalta they prepared and arranged themselves for battle on either side, the king of Leinster and the Lochlonnaigh on one side, and two sons of the king of Lochloinn, to wit, Carolus Cnutus and Andreas being their leaders; Brian with the nobles of Munster, Connaught and Meath on the other side, with Murchadh, son of Brian, as their leader. Maoilseachlainn, however, did not wish to help them.

The battle was bravely fought between them, and the Lochlonnaigh and the Leinstermen were defeated; and the two sons of the king of Lochloinn and the nobles of the fleet who came with them fell there, together with six thousand and seven hundred Lochlonnaigh. There also fell the men of Ath Cliath and another company of the Lochlonnaigh of the fleet about four thousand. In like manner fell the king of Leinster and most of the nobles of Leinster together with three thousand one hundred Leinstermen.

Now on the other side fell Murchadh, son of Brian, the heir apparent to the throne of Ireland, and the majority of the Munster and Connaught nobles around him together with four thousand men. And a party of Lochlonnaigh who were fleeing into the country from the slaughter came upon Brian's tent, and some of them knew that it was Brian who was in it, and Bruadar, their leader, who was of the party, went towards Brian, and they slew him, but Brian's people slew Bruadar and his people. . . .

Translator Patrick S. Dineen

PART IV

Modern Irish Poetry

TRANSLATIONS FROM THE GAELIC

Against Blame of Women

BY Gerald, Earl of Desmond (c. 1398)

Speak not ill of womankind,
'Tis no wisdom if you do.
You that fault in women find,
I would not be praised of you.

Sweetly speaking, witty, clear,
Tribe most lovely to my mind,
Blame of such I hate to hear.
Speak not ill of womankind.

Bloody treason, murderous act,
Not by women were designed,
Bells o'erthrown nor churches sacked,
Speak not ill of womankind.

Bishop, King upon his throne,
Primate skilled to loose and bind,
Sprung of women every one!
Speak not ill of womankind.

For a brave young fellow long
Hearts of women oft have pined.
Who would dare their love to wrong?
Speak not ill of womankind.

Paunchy greybeards never more
Hope to please a woman's mind.
Poor young chieftains they adore!
Speak not ill of womankind.

Translator The Earl of Longford.

Do Not Torment Me, Woman

Do not torment me, woman, for your honour's sake do not pursue me; whether my life be long or short do not torment me through all eternity.

I entreat a boon of you, O bright face and fair hair, do not torment me any more wherever I may be.

I have not spent night nor day, whether I have been here long or no, but that you have been beside me—slow-pacing foot and bowed head!

O cheek like embers, do not come in dreams to seek me in my sleep; and when I wake, stately and sweet one, come not to drive me to distraction.

Though it is hard for me to tell you, let me see you no more, do not destroy me; since I cannot escape from death, come not between me and the love of God.

You, my one love of all creation, tender sapling whom God has taught, woe to you who have so slain me, and I never slew any man.

Let not my misery be your gain, O gentle bough, with crystal eye; if you were witless as I am I would not slay you like this ever.

I know not what to do, your mouth like red berries has consumed me; my blessing on you, but get you aside, and do not drive me from the bosom of God.

Sweet-smelling mouth and skin like flowers, many a man comes courting you; O woman, love of my soul, do not pursue me of all men.

15TH-16TH CENTURY.
Translator Kenneth Jackson.

Reconciliation

Do not torment me, woman, let us set our minds at one; you to be my mate in Ireland, and let us put our arms around each other.

Set your strawberry-coloured mouth against my mouth, O skin like foam; stretch your lime-white rounded arm about me, in spite of all our discord.

Slender graceful girl, be no longer inconstant to me; admit me, soft slender one, to your bed, let us stretch our bodies side by side.

As I have given up, O smooth side, every woman in Ireland for your sake, do you give up every man for me, if it is possible to do so.

As I have given to your white teeth passion which is beyond reckoning, so you should give to me your love in the like measure.

15TH-16TH CENTURY.
Translator Kenneth Jackson.

He Praises Her Hair

Lady, the meshes of your coiling hair
Hide like a mask my lovely one.
And thro' that veil I guess at things more rare
Than Absalom, King David's son.

A flight of cuckoos bursting from a curl
Do sing in every plaited tress,
Whose silent tune sets many hearts a-whirl,
O'erborne with so much loveliness.

The drooping ringlets of your long bright hair
Across your eyes their shadows fling,
Those eyes that flash and glow like crystal there,
Or precious jewels in a ring.

Like some strange beauty from an unknown land
In borrowed gems you ne'er were dressed.
I see no golden bracelets on your hand,
A hundred rings upon your breast.

Round your smooth neck the wreathéd floods of gold
Coil from your brows above,
And all your breast with jewelled chains enfold,
A breast for men to love.

15TH-16TH CENTURY.
Translator The Earl of Longford.

No Sufferer for Her Love

They lie who say that love must be
A sickness and a misery;
He that ne'er loved woman knows
Never anything but woes.

I too love a woman; yet
My clear eyes are never wet;
Death has claimed me for his own,
Yet I live by love alone.

Clad in flesh and blood I move,
Though a swan-white maid I love;
Though I love, I eat and sleep,
Music's service still I keep.

I'm no reed in water swaying,
My free thought goes lightly playing;
I'm no lover chill through all
The piled cloaks of Donegal.

I'm a man like others still,
Fires burn me, waters chill;
If the young and strong must die,
Ne'er so doomed a man as I.

Rope will bind me, this know I,
Like a sponge my mouth's ne'er dry,
Softer is my flesh than stone,
I can't drink the sea alone.

Though love within my bones doth play,
I know the night is not the day,
Black's black, white's white, a boat's a boat
And not a stately ship afloat.

I never call a horse a crow,
The sea's no hill, that much I know,
Small is less than great, I feel,
And a fly smaller than a seal.

Though I love her more than all
The sun-riped maids of Donegal,
Yet, by all the gods above!
I'm no sufferer for her love.

15TH-16TH CENTURY.
Translator Robin Flower.

Of Women No More Evil

Of women no more evil will I say,
The lightsome loves that help my heart to live
—The sun sees nothing sweeter on his way—
They pledge their faith and break it. I forgive,
All I forgive and scandal them no more.
I am their servant. Let the witless jeer.
Though their slain loves are numbered by the score,
I love them living and their ghosts are dear.
The cunning wits are loud in their dispraise,
And yet I know not. If their breed should fail,
What comfort were in all the world's wide ways?
A flowerless earth, a sea without a sail.
If these were gone that make earth Heaven for men,
Love them or hate, 'twere little matter then.

15TH-16TH CENTURY.
Translator Robin Flower.

He Praises His Wife When She Has Left Him

White hands of languorous grace,
Fair feet of stately pace
And snowy-shining knees—
My love was made of these.

Stars glimmered in her hair,
Slim was she, satin-fair;
The straight line of her brows
Shadowed her cheek's fresh rose.

What words can match her ways,
That beauty past all praise,
That courteous, stately air,
Winsome and shy and fair.

To have known all this and be
Tortured with memory—
Curse on this waking breath—
Makes me in love with death.

Better to sleep than see
This house now dark to me
A lonely shell in place
Of that unrivalled grace.

15TH-16TH CENTURY.
Translator Robin Flower.

Dark Rosaleen[1]

O, my Dark Rosaleen,
  Do not sigh, do not weep!
The priests are on the ocean green,
  They march along the Deep.
There's wine . . . from the royal Pope,
  Upon the ocean green;
And Spanish ale shall give you hope,
  My Dark Rosaleen!
  My own Rosaleen!
Shall glad your heart, shall give you hope,

[1] The author of "Dark Rosaleen" is unknown, but tradition has associated the poem with Hugh O'Donnell, Earl of Tyrconnell (c. 1572-1602), who depended on Papal and Spanish assistance to help him and Hugh O'Neill, Earl of Tyrone, repel the English at Kinsale in 1602. Rosaleen is Ireland.

Shall give you health, and help, and hope,
  My Dark Rosaleen!

Over hills, and through dales,
  Have I roamed for your sake;
All yesterday I sailed with sails
  On river and on lake.
The Erne . . . at its highest flood,
  I dashed across unseen,
For there was lightning in my blood,
  My Dark Rosaleen!
  My own Rosaleen!
Oh! there was lightning in my blood,
Red lightning lightened through my blood,
  My Dark Rosaleen!

All day long, in unrest,
  To and fro do I move.
The very soul within my breast
  Is wasted for you, love!
The heart . . . in my bosom faints
To think of you, my Queen,
My life of life, my saint of saints,
  My Dark Rosaleen!
  My own Rosaleen!
To hear your sweet and sad complaints,
My life, my love, my saint of saints,
  My Dark Rosaleen!

Woe and pain, pain and woe,
  Are my lot night and noon,
To see your bright face clouded so,
  Like to the mournful moon.
But yet . . . will I rear your throne
  Again in golden sheen;
'Tis you shall reign, shall reign alone,
  My Dark Rosaleen!
  My own Rosaleen!
'Tis you shall have the golden throne,
'Tis you shall reign, and reign alone,
  My Dark Rosaleen!

Over dews, over sands,
  Will I fly, for your weal;
Your holy delicate white hands
  Shall girdle me with steel
At home . . . in your emerald bowers,
  From morning's dawn till e'en,
You'll pray for me, my flower of flowers,
  My Dark Rosaleen!
  My fond Rosaleen!
You'll think of me through Daylight's hours,
My virgin flower, my flower of flowers,
  My Dark Rosaleen!

I could scale the blue air,
I could plough the high hills,
Oh, I could kneel all night in prayer,
To heal your many ills!
And one . . . beamy smile from you
Would float like light between
My toils and me, my own, my true,
My Dark Rosaleen!
My fond Rosaleen!
Would give me life and soul anew,
A second life, a soul anew,
My dark Rosaleen!

O! the Erne shall run red
With redundance of blood,
The earth shall rock beneath our tread,
And flames wrap hill and wood,
And gun-peal, and slogan cry,
Wake many a glen serene.
Ere you shall fade, ere you shall die,
My Dark Rosaleen!
My own Rosaleen!
The Judgment Hour must first be nigh,
Ere you can fade, ere you can die,
My Dark Rosaleen!

16TH CENTURY.
Translator James Clarence Mangan.

Death's Warning to Beauty

Lovely lady, rein thy will,
Let my words a warning be,
Bid thy longing heart be still.
Wed no man. Remember me.

If my counsel like thee not,
Winsome beauty, bright of blee,[1]
Thou knows't not what deeds I've wrought.
Wed no man. Remember me.

If thou knows't not they are clay:
That slim form eyes may not see,
That round breast silk hides away.
Wed no man. Remember me.

Keep my counsel lest thou slip.
If love or hate men offer thee,
Hide thy heart and hoard thy lip.
Wed no man. Remember me.

17TH CENTURY.
Translator Robin Flower.

[1] hue. NED.

He Charges Her To Lay Aside Her Weapons

BY Pierce Ferriter (c. 1653)

I charge you, lady young and fair,
  Straightway to lay your arms aside.
Lay by your armour, would you dare
  To spread the slaughter far and wide?

O lady, lay your armour by,
  Conceal your curling hair also,
For never was a man could fly
  The coils that o'er your bosom flow.

And if you answer, lady fair,
  That north or south you ne'er took life,
Your very eyes, your glance, your air
  Can murder without axe or knife.

And oh! If you but bare your knee,
  If you your soft hand's palm advance,
You'll slaughter many a company.
  What more is done with shield and lance?

Oh, hide your bosom limey white,
  Your naked side conceal from me.
Ah, show them not in all men's sight,
  Your breasts more bright than flowering tree.

And if in you there's shame or fear
For all the murders you have done,
Let those bright eyes no more appear,
Those shining teeth be seen of none.

Lady, we tremble far and near!
Be with these conquests satisfied,
And lest I perish, lady dear,
Oh, lay those arms of yours aside.

Translator The Earl of Longford.

The Harper

Master of discords John
Makes harmony seem wrong;
His treble sings to his bass
Like a sow consoling her young.

If he played with his shoulder blades
He'd make a pleasanter tone;
He reaches out for a chord
As a dog snaps at a bone.

Playing away to himself,
Nobody knows what tune,
Even the man who made it
Cannot recall his own.

A wonder, the way he works,
He never keeps tune or time;
With skill and care he goes wrong,
Mountains of error climb.

Give him the simplest catch
And at once you're in at the kill;
He mangles it patiently
Like an old loud derelict mill.

Copper scratched with a knife,
Brass cut with a rasp,
His nails scrape at the strings
Till all shudder and gasp.

God help you, gentle harp,
Pounded and plagued bv his fist,
There isn't a chord in your breast
Without a sprain or twist.

17TH CENTURY. Author unknown.
Translator Frank O'Connor.

The Woman of Three Cows

O Woman of Three Cows, *agra!* don't let your tongue thus rattle!
Oh, don't be saucy, don't be stiff, because you may have cattle.
I have seen—and, here's my hand to you, I only say what's true—
A many a one with twice your stock not half so proud as you.

Good luck to you, don't scorn the poor, and don't be their despiser;
For worldly wealth soon melts away, and cheats the very miser;
And death soon strips the proudest wreath from haughty human brows—
Then don't be stiff, and don't be proud, good Woman of Three Cows!

See where Mononia's heroes lie, proud Owen Mór's descendants.
'Tis they that won the glorious name, and had the grand attendants!
If *they* were forced to bow to Fate, as every mortal bows,
Can *you* be proud, can *you* be stiff, my Woman of Three Cows?

The brave sons of the Lord of Clare, they left the land to mourning;
Mavrone! for they were banished, with no hope of their returning.
Who knows in what abodes of want those youths were driven to house?
Yet *you* can give yourself these airs, O Woman of Three Cows.

Oh, think of Donnell of the Ships, the Chief whom nothing daunted,
See how he fell in distant Spain unchronicled, unchanted!
He sleeps, the great O'Sullivan, where thunder cannot rouse—
Then ask yourself, should *you* be proud, good Woman of Three Cows?

O'Ruark, Maguire, those souls of fire, whose names are shrined in story—
Think how their high achievements once made Erin's greatest glory.
Yet now their bones lie mouldering under weeds and cypress boughs,
And so, for all your pride, will yours, O Woman of Three Cows.

The O'Carrolls, also, famed when fame was only for the boldest,
Rest in forgotten sepulchres with Erin's best and oldest;
Yet who so great as they of yore in battle or carouse?
Just think of that, and hide *your* head, good Woman of Three Cows.

Your neighbour's poor; and you, it seems, are big with vain
ideas,
Because, inagh,[1] you've got three cows—one more, I see, than
she has;
That tongue of yours wags more at times than charity allows;
But if you're strong, be merciful—great Woman of Three
Cows.

Avran[2]

Now, there you go! You still, of course, keep up your scornful
bearing,
And I'm too poor to hinder you; but, by the cloak I'm wearing,
If I had but four cows myself, even though you were my spouse,
I'd thwack you well to cure your pride, my Woman of Three
Cows!

17TH CENTURY.
Translator James Clarence Mangan.

The Reverie

BY Egan O'Rahilly (1670-1726)

ONE morning before Titan thought of stirring his feet
I climbed alone to a hill where the air was kind,
And saw a throng of magical girls go by
That had lived to the north in Croghan time out of mind.

All over the land from Galway to Cork of the ships,
It seemed that a bright enchanted mist came down,
Acorns on oaks and clear cold honey on stones,
Fruit upon every tree from root to crown.

[1] Forsooth.
[2] Summing Up.

They lit three candles that shone in the mist like stars
On a high hilltop in Connello and then were gone,
But I followed through Thomond the track of the hooded queens
And asked them the cause of the zeal of their office at dawn.

The tall queen, Eevul, so bright of countenance, said
"The reason we light three candles on every strand
Is to guide the king that will come to us over the sea
And make us happy and reign in a fortunate land."

And then, so suddenly did I start from my sleep,
They seemed to be true, the words that had been so sweet—
It was just that my soul was sick and spent with grief
One morning before Titan thought of stirring his feet.

Translator Frank O'Connor.

The Geraldine's Daughter

BY Egan O'Rahilly

A beauty all stainless, a pearl of a maiden,
Has plunged me in trouble, and wounded my heart.
With sorrow and gloom are my soul overladen;
An anguish is there that will never depart.
I could voyage to Egypt across the deep water,
Nor care about bidding dear Eire farewell,
So I only might gaze on the Geraldine's daughter,
And sit by her side in some green, pleasant dell!

Her curling locks wave round her figure of lightness,
 All dazzling and long, like the purest of gold;
Her blue eyes resemble twin stars in their brightness,
 And her brow is like marble or wax to behold!
The radiance of heaven illumines her features
 Where the snows and the rose have erected their throne;
It would seem that the sun had forgotten all creatures,
 To shine on the Geraldine's daughter alone!

Her bosom is swan-white, her waist smooth and slender;
 Her speech is like music, so sweet and so fair;
The feelings that glow in her noble heart lend her
 A mien and a majesty lovely to see.
Her lips, red as berries, but riper than any,
 Would kiss away even a sorrow like mine!
No wonder such heroes and noblemen many
 Should cross the blue ocean to kneel at her shrine.

She is sprung from the Geraldine race, the great Grecians,
 Niece of Mileadh's sons of the Valorous Bands,
Those heroes, the seed of the olden Phenicians,
 Though now trodden down, without fame, without lands;
Of her ancestors flourished the Barrys and Powers,
 To the Lords of Bunratty she too is allied;
And not a proud noble near Cashel's high towers
 But is kin to this maiden—the Geraldine's Pride!

Of Saxon or Gael there are none to excel in
 Her wisdom, her features, her figure, this fair;
In all she surpasses the far-famous Helen,
 Whose beauty drove thousands to death and despair.
Whoe'er could but gaze on her aspect so noble
 Would feel from thenceforward all anguish depart,
Yet for me 'tis, alas! my worst woe and my trouble,
 That her image must always abide in my heart!

Translator James Clarence Mangan.

A Sleepless Night

BY Egan O'Rahilly

I have thought long this wild wet night that brought no rest
Though I have no gold to watch or horned kine or sheep,
A storm that made the wave cry out has stirred my breast—
Neither dogfish nor periwinkle was once my meat.

Ah, if the men that knew me were but here tonight
With their proud company that held me up secure,
Captains of Munster before their great defeat,
Not long would Corkaguiney see my children poor.

MacCarthy stern and fearless, that most upright man,
MacCarthy of the Lee whose hearth is dark and cold,
MacCarthy of Kanturk and all his kindred gone—
The heart within me breaks to think their tale is told.

The heart within my breast this night is wild with grief
Because of all the haughty men who ruled this place
From Cashel and through Thomond to the wave beneath
None lives, and where they lived lives now an alien race.

Ah, famous wave, you sang the livelong night below
And drove my senses crazy with your bellowing—
I swear if help could ever come to Ireland now
I'd strangle in your raucous throat that song you sing!

Translator Frank O'Connor.

A Grey Eye Weeping

BY Egan O'Rahilly.

That my old bitter heart was pierced in this black doom,
That foreign devils have made our land a tomb,
That the sun that was Munster's glory has gone down
Has made me a beggar before you, Valentine Brown.

That royal Cashel is bare of house and guest,
That Brian's turreted home is the otter's nest,
That the kings of the land have neither land nor crown
Has made me a beggar before you, Valentine Brown.

Garnish away in the west and her master banned,
Hamburg the refuge of him that has lost his land,
An old grey eye, weeping for lost renown,
Has made me a beggar before you, Valentine Brown.

Translator Frank O'Connor.

Egan O'Rahilly and the Minister

There was a splendid green-boughed tree of great value growing for many years close by a church which the wicked Cromwell had plundered, above a spring overflowing with bright cold water, in a field of green turf which a thieving minister had extorted from an Irish gentleman; one who had been exiled across the wild seas through treachery, and not through the edge of the sword. This stinking lout of a damned minister wanted to cut a long green bough of the tree to make household gear of it. None of the carpenters or workmen would touch the beautiful bough, for its shade was most lovely, sheltering them as they lamented brokenly and bitterly for the bright champions who were stretched beneath the sod. "I will cut it," said a bandy barelegged gallows-bird of a son of that portly minister, "and get me an axe at once." The dull-witted oaf went up into the tree like a scared cat fleeing a pack of hounds, until he came upon two branches growing one across the other. He tried to put them apart by the strength of his arms, but they sprang from his hands in the twinkling of an eye across each other again, and gripped his gullet, hanging him high between air and Hell. It was then the accursed Sassenach was wriggling his legs in the hangman's dance, and he standing on nothing, and his black tongue out the length of a yard, mocking at his father. The minister screamed and bawled like a pig in a sack or a goose caught under a gate, and no wonder, while the workmen were getting a ladder to cut him down.

Egan O'Rahilly from Sliabh Luachra of the Heroes was there, watching the gallows-bird of the noose, and he recited this verse:—

Good is your fruit, tree;
may the bounty of this your fruit be on every branch!
Alas, that the trees of Ireland
are not covered with your fruit every day!

"*What is the poor wild Irish devil saying?*"[1] said the minister. "*He is lamenting your darling son,*"[1] said an idler who was beside him. "*Here is twopence for you to buy tobacco with,*"[1] said the fat badger of a minister. "*Thankee,*[1] minister of the son of curses," i.e. the Devil, said Egan; and he recited a verse:—

---

[1] In English.

Hurroo, minister who gave me your twopence
for lamenting your child!
May the fate of that child befall the rest of them
down to the last of them.

18TH CENTURY.
Translator Kenneth Jackson.

The Lament for Art O'Leary[1]

BY Eileen O'Leary

My love and my delight,
The day I saw you first
Beside the market-house
I had eyes for nothing else,
And love for none but you.

I left my father's house,
Fled far away with you,
And that was no bad choice,
You gave me everything.
Parlours whitened for me,
Rooms painted for me,
Ovens reddened for me,
Loaves baked for me,
Roast spitted for me,
Beds made for me,
I took my ease on flock
Until the milking time
And later if I pleased.

---

[1] See Introduction, p. xxvii.

My mind remembers
That bright spring day,
How your hat with its band
Of gold became you,
Your silver-hilted sword,
Your manly right hand,
Your horse on his mettle,
The foes around you
Cowed by your air;
For when you rode by
On your white-nosed mare
The English bowed
The head before you,
Not out of love for you
But only fear,
For, sweetheart of my soul,
The English killed you.

My love and my calf
Of the race of the earls of Antrim
And the Barrys of Eemokilly,
A sword became you,
A hat with a band,
A slender foreign shoe,
And a suit of yarn
Woven over the water.

My love and my darling,
When I go home
The little lad, Conor,
And Fiach the baby
Will ask me surely
Where I left their father;
I shall say with anguish
'Twas in Kilnamartyr.
They will call the father
That will never answer.

My love and my darling
That I never thought dead
Till your horse came to me
With bridle trailing,
All blood from forehead
To polished saddle
Where you should be,
Sitting or standing;
I gave one leap to the threshold,
A second to the gate,
A third upon her back.

I clapped my hands,
And off at a gallop,
I did not linger
Till I found you lying
By a little furze-bush
Without pope or bishop
Or priest or cleric
One prayer to whisper
But an old, old woman

And her cloak about you,
And your blood in torrents,
Art O'Leary,
I did not wipe it,
I dipped my hands in it.

My love and my delight,
Rise up now beside me,
And let me lead you home
Until I make a feast,
And I will roast your meat
And send for company
And call the harpers in,
And I will make your bed
Of soft and snowy sheets
And blankets dark and rough
To warm the beloved limbs
An autumn blast has chilled.

(*His sister*)

My little love, my calf,
This is the picture
That last night brought me,
In Cork all lonely
On my bed sleeping,
That the white courtyard
And the great mansion
That we two played in
As children had fallen;
Ballingeary withered,
And your hounds were silent,
Your birds were songless,
The time they found you
On the open mountain

Without priest or cleric
But an old, old woman
And her coat about you,
When the earth caught you,
Art O'Leary,
And your life's blood stiffened
The white shirt on you.

My love and my treasure,
Where is the woman
From Cork of the white sails
To the Bridge of Tomey
With her dowry gathered
And cows at pasture
Would sleep alone
The night they waked you?

(*His wife*)

My darling, do not believe
One word she is saying!
It is a falsehood
That I slept when others
Sat up and waked you—
'Twas no sleep that took me
But the children crying;
They would not rest
Without me beside them.

O people, do not believe
Any lying story!
There is no woman in Ireland
That had slept beside him
And borne him three children
But would cry out

After Art O'Leary
That lies dead before me
Since yesterday morning.

Grief on you, Morris!
Heart's blood and bowels' blood!
May your eyes go blind
And your knees be broken!
You killed my darling
And no man in Ireland
Will fire the shot at you.

Grief and destruction,
Morris, the traitor!
That brought death to my husband,
Father of three children,
Two on the hearth,
One in the womb
I shall not bring forth.

It is my sorrow
That I was not near
When they fired the shot
To catch it in my dress,
Or in my heart, what harm
If you but reached the hills,
Rider of the ready hands.

My love and my fortune,
'Tis an evil portion
To lay for a giant
A shroud and a coffin,
For a big-hearted hero
Who fished in the hill-streams
And drank in bright halls
With white-breasted women.

My comfort and my friend,
Master of the bright sword,
Rise, I say, from your sleep;
Yonder hangs your whip,
Your horse is at the door,
Follow the lane to the east
V[illegible] every bush will bend
And every stream dry up
And man and woman bow
If things have manners yet
That have them not, I fear.

My love and my sweetness,
'Tis not the death of my people,
Donal Mor O'Connell,[1]
Conal[2] that died by drowning,
Nor the girl of six and twenty[3]
That went across the water
To be a king's companion,
'Tis not all these I speak of

And call on with voice broken,
But noble Art O'Leary,
Art of hair so golden,
Art of wit and courage,
Art the brown mare's master,
Swept last night to nothing,
Here in Carriganimma—
Perish it, name and people!

My love and my treasure,
Though I bring with me
No throng of mourners,

---

[1] Eileen O'Leary's father.
[2] Her brother.
[3] Her sister, who married an Irish officer in the Austrian army, became an intimate of Empress Maria Theresa and died of smallpox.

'Tis no shame for me,
For my kinsmen are wrapped in
A sleep beyond waking,
In narrow coffins
Walled up in stone.

Though but for the smallpox
And the black death
And the spotted fever
That host of riders
With bridles shaking
Would rouse the echoes
Coming to the wakehouse,
Art of the white breast.

Could my calls but wake my kindred,
In Derrynane across the mountains
And Capling of the yellow apples
Many a proud and stately rider
Many a girl with spotless kerchief
Would be here before tomorrow,
Shedding tears about your body,
Art O'Leary once so merry.

My love and my secret,
Your corn is stacked,
Your cows are milking,
On me is the grief
There's no cure for in Munster.
Till Art O'Leary rise
This grief will never yield
That's bruising all my heart
Yet shut up fast in it,
As 'twere in a locked trunk
With the key gone astray
And rust grown on the wards.

My love and my calf,
Noble Art O'Leary,
Son of Conor, son of Cady,
Son of Louis O'Leary,
West of the Valley,
And east of Greenan
(Where berries grow thickly
And nuts crowd on branches
And apples in heaps fall
In their own season),
What wonder to any
If Iveleary lighted
And Ballingeary
And Gougane of the saints
For the smooth-palmed rider,
The unwearying huntsman
That I would see spurring
From Grenagh without halting
When quick hounds had faltered?
O rider of the bright eyes,
What happened you yesterday?
I thought in my heart
When I bought you your fine clothes
You were one the world could not slay.

'Tis known to Jesus Christ,
Nor cap upon my head,
Nor shift against my back,
Nor shoe upon my foot,
Nor gear in all my house,
Nor bridle for the mare
But I will spend at law,
And I'll go oversea
To plead before the king,
And if the king be deaf
I shall come back alone

To the black-blooded rogue
That killed my man on me.

O rider of the white palms,
Go in to Baldwin,
And face the schemer,
The bandy-legged monster—
May he rot and his children!
(Wishing no harm to Maire,
Yet of no love for her
But that my mother's body
Was a bed to her for three seasons
And to me beside her.)

Take my heart's love,
Dark women of the Mill,
For the sharp rhymes ye shed
On the rider of the brown mare.

But cease your weeping now,
Women of the soft, wet eyes
Till Art O'Leary drink
Ere he go to the dark school,[1]
Not to learn music or song
But to prop the earth and the stone.

Translator Frank O'Connor.

[1] I.e. before he is buried in Kilcrea Abbey.

Tara Is Grass

The world hath conquered, the wind hath scattered like dust
Alexander, Caesar, and all that shared their sway:
Tara is grass, and behold how Troy lieth low—
And even the English, perchance their hour will come.

18TH CENTURY.
Translator Padraic Pearse.

The Convict of Clonmel

How hard is my fortune,
  And vain my repining!
The strong rope of fate
  For this young neck is twining!
My strength is departed,
  My cheeks sunk and sallow,
While I languish in chains
  In the jail of Clonmala.

No boy of the village
  Was ever yet milder;
I'd play with a child
  And my sport would be wilder;
I'd dance without tiring
  From morning till even,
And the goal-ball I'd strike
  To the lightning of heaven.

At my bed-foot decaying,
My hurl-bat is lying;
Through the boys of the village
My goal-ball is flying;
My horse 'mong the neighbors
Neglected may fallow,
While I pine in my chains
In the jail of Clonmala.

Next Sunday the patron
At home will be keeping,
And the young active hurlers
The field will be sweeping;
With the dance of fair maidens
The evening they'll hallow,
While this heart once so gay
Shall be cold in Clonmala.

18TH CENTURY.
Translator J. J. Callanan.

The Midnight Court[1]

BY Brian Merriman (c. 1750-1805)

'Twas my pleasure to walk in the river meadows
In the thick of the dew and the morning shadows,
At the edge of the woods in a deep defile,
At peace with myself in the first sunshine.
When I looked at Lough Graney my heart grew bright,
Ploughed lands and green in the morning light,
Mountains in ranks with crimson borders
Peering above their neighbours' shoulders.
The heart that never had known relief

1 See Inroduction, p. xxvii.

In a lonesome old man distraught with grief
Without money or home or friends or ease
Would quicken to glimpse beyond the trees
The ducks sail by on a mistless bay
And a swan before them leads away,
A speckled trout that in their tracks
Splashed in the air with arching back,
The grey of the lake and the waves around
That foamed at its edge with a hollow sound.
Birds in the trees sang merry and loud,
A fawn flashed out of the shadowy wood,
Lowing horn and huntsman's cry,
Belling hounds and fox slipped by.

Yesterday morning the sky was clear,
The sun fell hot on river and mere,
Her horses fresh and with gamesome eye
Harnessed again to assail the sky;
The leaves were thick upon every bough
And ferns and grass as thick below,
Sheltering bowers of herbs and flowers
That would comfort a man in his dreariest hours.
A longing for sleep bore down my head,
And in the grass I scooped a bed
With a hollow behind to house my back,
A place for my head and my legs stretched slack.
What more could I ask? I covered my face
To keep off the flies as I slept for a space
But my mind in dream was filled with grief
And I tossed and groaned as I sought relief.

I had only dozed when I felt a shock
And all the landscape seemed to rock,
A north wind made my senses tingle
And thunder crackled along the shingle,

And as I looked up, as I thought, awake
I seemed to see at the edge of the lake
As ugly a brute as a man could see
In the shape of a woman approaching me,
For if I calculated right
She must have been twenty feet in height
With several yards of a hairy cloak
Trailing behind her in the muck.
I never beheld such a freak of nature;
She hadn't a single presentable feature,
And her grinning jaws with the fangs stuck out
Would be cause sufficient to start a rout,
And in a hand like a weaver's beam
She raised a staff that it might be seen
She was coming to me on a legal errand
For pinned to the staff was a bailiff's warrant.

And she cried in a voice with a brassy ring
"Get up out of this, you lazy thing!
That a man of your age can think 'tis fitting
To sleep in a ditch while the court is sitting!
An honester court than ever you knew
And far too good for the likes of you;
Justice and Mercy, hand in hand,
Sit in the courts of Fairyland.
Let Ireland think, when her troubles are ended
Of those by whom she was befriended.
In Moy Graney palace twelve days and nights
They've sat, discussing your wrongs and rights,
And it saddened the heart of the fairy king
And his lords and influential men
When they studied the cause of each disaster
That happened your people, man and master;
Old stock uprooted on every hand,
Without claim to their rent or laws or land;
The country waste and nothing behind

Where the flowers were plucked but the weeds and wild;
The best of your breed in foreign places,

And upstart rogues with impudent faces
Planning with all their guile and spleen
To pick the bones of the Irish clean.
But the worst of all these bad reports
Was that truth was darkened in their courts,
And nothing to back a poor man's case
But whispers, intrigue and the lust for place;
The lawyer's craft and the rich man's might,
Cozening, favour, greed and spite;
Maddened with jobs and bribes and malice,
Anarchy loose on cot and palace.

"Twas all discussed, and along with the rest
There were women in scores who came to attest
A plea that concerns yourself as well,
That the youth of the country's gone to hell,
And the population in decline
As only happened within your time;
Nothing but weeds for the want of tillage
Since famine and war have struck the village
And a flighty king and the emigration—
And what have you done to restore the nation?
Shame on you there without chick nor child
And women in thousands running wild;
The blossoming tree and the young green shoot,
The strap that would sleep with any old root,
The little white saint at the altar rail
And the proud cold girl like a ship in sail—
What matter to you if their beauty founder,
If belly and breast will never be rounder,
If ready and glad to be mother and wife
They drop, unplucked, from the boughs of life?
"And, having considered all reports,

'Twas agreed that in place of the English courts
They should select a judge by lot
Who would hold enquiry on the spot.
Then Eevul, Queen of the Grey Rock,
That rules all Munster, herd and flock,
Arose and offered to do her share
By putting an end to injustice there,
And the great council swore her in
To judge the women and the men,
To stand by the poor though all ignore them
And humble the pride of the rich before them,
Make might without right conceal its face
And use her might to give right its place.
Her favour money will not buy,
No lawyer will pull the truth awry;
The smartest perjurer will not dare
To make a show of falsehood there.
Her court is sitting today in Feakle,
So off with you now as quick as you're able.
Come on, I say, and give no back chat
Or I'll use my powers and knock you flat."
With the crook of her staff she hooked my cape
And away we went at a terrible rate
Off through the glens in one wild rush
Till we stood at Moinmoy by the ruined church.

Then I saw with an awesome feeling
A building ablaze from floor to ceiling,
Lighted within by guttering torches
Among massive walls and echoing arches,
And the Queen of the Fairies sat alone
At the end of the hall on a gilded throne,
And keeping back the thronged beholders
A great array of guns and soldiers.
I stared at it all, the lighted hall,

Crammed with faces from wall to wall,
And a young woman with downcast eye,
Attractive, good-looking and shy,
With long and sweeping golden locks
Who was standing alone in the witness box;
But the cut of her spoke of some disgrace,
I saw misfortune on her face;
Her tearful eyes were red and hot
And her passions bubbled as in a pot,
And whatever the devil it was provoked her
She was silent, all but the sobs that choked her.
You could see from the way the speaking failed her
That she'd sooner her death than the thing that ailed her.
But unable to express her meaning
She wrung her hands and continued her grieving,
And all we could do was stand and gaze
Till her sobs gave place to a broken phrase,
And little by little she mastered her sorrows,
And dried her eyes and spoke as follows—

"Yourself is the woman we're glad to see
Eevul, Queen of Carriglee,
Our moon at night, our morning light,
Our comfort in the teeth of spite,
Mistress of the host of delight,
Munster and Ireland stand in your sight.
My chief complaint and principal grief?
The thing that gives me no relief,
That sweeps me from harbour in my mind
And blows me like smoke upon every wind,
Is all the women whose charms miscarry
All over the land and who'll never marry;
Bitter old maids without house or home,
Put on one side through no fault of their own.
I know myself from the little I've seen

Enough and to spare of the sort I mean,
And to give an example, here am I
While the tide is flowing left high and dry.
Wouldn't you think I must be a fright
From the way I'm left at the start of life,
Heartsick, bitter, dour and wan,
Unable to sleep for the want of a man,
But how can I lie in a lukewarm bed
With all the thoughts that come into my head?
Indeed, 'tis time that somebody stated
The way that the women are situated,
For if men go on their path to destruction
There will nothing be left to us but abduction.
Their appetite wakes with age and blindness
When you'd let them cover you only from kindness
And offer it up for the wrongs you'd done
In hopes of reward in the life to come;
And if one of them weds in the heat of youth
When the first down is on his mouth
It isn't some woman of his own sort,
Well-shaped, well-mannered or well-taught,
Some mettlesome girl that studied behaviour,
To sit and stand and amuse a neighbour,
But some pious old prude or sour defamer
Who sweated the couple of pounds that shame her.
There you have it. It has me melted,
And makes me feel that the world's demented:
A county's choice for brains and muscle,
Fond of a lark and not scared of a tussle,
Decent and merry and sober and steady,
Good-looking, gamesome and rakish and ready,
A boy in the blush of his youthful vigour
With a gracious flush and a passable figure
Finds a fortune the best attraction
And sires himself off on some bitter extraction,
Some fretful old maid with her heels in the dung

And pious airs and venomous tongue,
Vicious and envious, nagging and whining,
Snoozing and snivelling, plotting, contriving—
Hell to her soul, an unmannerly sow
With a pair of bow legs and hair like tow
Went off this morning to the altar
And here am I still without hope of the halter!
Couldn't some man love me as well?
Amn't I plump and sound as a bell,
Lips for kissing and teeth for smiling,
Blossomy skin and forehead shining?
My eyes are blue and my hair is thick
And coils in streams about my neck—
A man that's looking for a wife,
Here's a face that will keep for life!
Hand and arm and neck and breast,
Each is better than the rest.
Look at my waist! My legs are long,
Limber as willows and light and strong,
There's bottom and belly that claim attention
And the best concealed that I needn't mention.
I'm the sort that a natural man desires,
Not a freak or a death-on-wires,
A sloven that comes to life in flashes,
A creature of moods with her heels in the ashes,
Or a sluggard stewing in her own grease,
But a good-looking girl that's bound to please.
If I were as slow as some I know,
To stand up for my rights and my dress show,
Some brainless, ill-bred country mope,
You could understand if I lost hope;
But ask the first you meet by chance,
Hurling match or race or dance,
Pattern or party, market or fair,
Whatever it was, was I not there?
And didn't I make a good impression,

Turning up in the height of fashion,
My hair was washed and combed and powdered,
My coif like snow and stiffly laundered;
I'd a little white hood with ribbons and ruff
On a spotty dress of the finest stuff
And facings to show off the line
Of a cardinal cloak the colour of wine,
A cambric apron filled with showers
Of fruit and birds and trees and flowers,
Neatly fitting, expensive shoes
And the highest of heels pegged up with screws,
Silken gloves and all in spangles
Of brooches, buckles, rings and bangles.
And you musn't imagine I've been shy,
The sort that slinks with a downcast eye,
Solitary, lonesome, cold and wild,
Like a mountainy girl or an only child.
I tossed my cap for the crowds of the races
And kept my head in the toughest places;
Amn't I always on the watch,
At bonfire, dance or hurling match
Or outside the chapel after Mass
To coax a smile from the fellows that pass?
But I'm wasting my time on a wild-goose chase,
And my spirit is gone—and that's my case!
After all my hopes and sulks and passions,
All my aping of styles and fashions,
All the times that my cards were spread
And my hands were read and my cups were read,
Every old rhyme, pisherogue and rune,
Crescent, full moon and harvest moon,
Whit and All Souls and the First of May,
I've nothing to show for all they say.
Every night as I went to bed
I'd a stocking of apples under my head,

I fasted three canonical hours
To try and come round the heavenly powers,
I washed my shift where the stream ran deep
To hear a lover's voice in sleep;
Often I swept the woodstack bare,
Burned bits of my frock, my nails, my hair,
Up the chimney stuck the flail,
Slept with a spade without avail;
Hid my wool in the limekiln late
And my distaff behind the churchyard gate;
Flax in the road to halt coach and carriage,
And haycocks stuffed with heads of cabbage,
And night and day on the proper occasions
Invoked Old Nick and all his legions,
But 'twas all no good and I'm broken-hearted
For here I am at the place I started,
And this is the cause of all my tears,
I am fast in the rope of the rushing years
With age and want in lessening span
And death at the end and no hopes of a man.
But whatever misfortunes God may send,
Spare me at least that lonesome end!
Do not leave me to cross alone
Without chick nor child when my beauty's gone
As an old maid counting the things I lack
The scowling thresholds that hurl me back.
God, by the lightning and the thunder,
The thought of it makes me ripe for murder.
Every idiot in the country
That marries a man has the right to insult me.
Sal has a slob with a well-stocked farm,
And Molly goes round on her husband's arm;
There's Min and Margery lepping with glee
And never done with their jokes at me.
And the bounce of Susie! and Kitty and Anne

Have children in droves and a proper man,
And all with their kind can mix and mingle
While I go savage and sour and single.

"Now I know in my heart that I've been too quiet
With the remedy there though I scorned to try it
In the matter of draughts and poisonous weeds
And medicine men and darksome deeds
That I know would fetch me a sweetheart plighted
Who'd love me, whether or not he liked it.
Oh, I see 'tis the thing that most prevails
And I'll give it a trial if all fruit fails—
A powerful aid to the making of splices
Is powdered herbs on apples in slices.
A woman I know had the neighbours hopping
When she caught the best match in the county napping,
And 'twas she who told me under a vow,
That from Shrove to All Souls, and she's married now,
She was eating hay as she said by the pail
With bog-roots burned and stuped in ale—
I've waited too long and was too resigned,
And nothing you say can change my mind;
I'll give you a chance to help me first
And I'm off after that to do my worst!"

Then up there jumps from a neighbouring chair
A little old man with a spiteful air,
Staggering legs and sobbing breath
And a look in his eye like poison and death,
And this apparition stumps up the hall
And says to the girl in the hearing of all—
"Damnation take you, you bastard's bitch,
Got by a tinkerman under a ditch,
No wonder the seasons are all upsot
Nor every beating Ireland got,
Decline in decency and manners,

And the cows gone dry and the price of bonhams!
Mavrone, what more can we expect
With Doll and Moll and the way they're decked?
You slut of ill-fame, allow your betters
To tell the court how you learned your letters!
Your seed and breed for all your brag
Were tramps to a man with rag and bag;
I knew your da and what passed for his wife
And he shouldered his traps to the end of his life,
Without knowledge nor niceness, wit nor favour,
An aimless lout without friend nor neighbour.
The breeches he wore were riddled with holes
And his boots without a tack of the soles.
Believe me, friends, if you sold at a fair,
Himself and his wife, his kids and gear,
When the costs were met, by the Holy Martyr,
You'd still go short for a glass of porter.
But the devil's child has the devil's cheek,
You that never owned cow nor sheep
With your buckles and brogues and rings to order—
You that were reared in the reek of solder!
However the rest of the world is cheated,
I knew you when you went half naked,
And I'd venture a guess that in what you lack
A shift would still astonish your back,
And shy as you seem, an inquisitive gent
Might study the same with your full consent.
Bosom and back are tightly laced
Or is it the stays that gives you the waist?
Oh, all can see the way you shine
But your looks are no concern of mine.
Now tell us the truth and don't be shy,
How long are you eating your dinner dry?
A meal of spuds without butter or milk
And the dirt in layers beneath your silk.
Bragging and gab becomes your like

But I know just where you sleep at night,
And blanket or quilt you never saw
But a strip of old mat and a bundle of straw
In a dirty hut without a seat
And the slime that slashes about your feet,
A carpet of weeds from door to wall
And the hens inscribing their tracks on all;
The rafters in with a broken back
And the brown rain lashing through every crack—
'Twas there you learned to look so fine;
But now, may we ask, how you came by the style?
We all admired the way you spoke—
But whisper, treasure, who paid for the cloak?
A sparrow with you would die of hunger—
And how did you come by all the grandeur,
All the tassels and all the lace?
Would you have us believe they were got in grace?
That frock made a hole in somebody's pocket,
And it wasn't yourself that paid for the jacket,
But leaving that and the rest aside,
Tell us, just how did the shoes arrive?

"Your worship, 'tis women's sinful pride
And that alone has the world destroyed!
Every young fellow that's ripe for marriage
Is hooked like this by some tricky baggage,
And no man is secure. For a friend of my own,
As nice a boy as ever I've known
That lives from me only a perch or two,
God help him, married misfortune too.
It breaks my heart to see her go by
With her saucy looks and her head held high,
Cows to pasture and fields of wheat,
And money to spare, and all deceit;
Well-fitted to rear a tinker's clan
She waggles her hips at every man;

With her brazen face and bullock's hide
And such airs and graces, and mad with pride.
And—that God may judge me!—only I hate
A scandalous tongue, I could relate
Things of that woman's previous state
As one with whom every man might mate
In any convenient field or gate
As the chance would come to him, early or late!
But now, of course, we must all forget
Her galloping days and the pace she set,
The race she ran in Ibrackane,
In Manishmore and Teermaclane,
With young and old of the meanest rabble
Of Ennis, Clareabbey and Quin astraddle;
Toughs from Tradree out on a fling
And Cratlee cutthroats sure to swing;
And still I'd say 'twas the neighbours' spite
And the girl did nothing but what was right,
But the devil take her and all she showed
I found her myself on the public road
On the naked earth with a bare backside
And a Garus turfcutter astride!
Is it any wonder my heart is failing
That I feel that the end of the world is nearing
When, ploughed and sown to all men's knowledge,
She can manage the child to arrive with marriage,
And even then, put to the pinch,
Begrudges Charity an inch,
For counting from the final prayer
With the candles quenched and the altar bare
To the day when her offspring takes the air
Is a full nine months with a week to spare?

"But you see the troubles a man takes on;
From the minute he marries his peace is gone,
Forever in fear of a neighbour's sneer,

And my own experience cost me dear.
I lived alone as happy as Larry,
Till I took it into my head to marry;
Tilling my fields with an easy mind
And going wherever I felt inclined,
Welcomed by all as a man of price,
Always ready with good advice;
The neighbours listened, they couldn't refuse
For I'd money and stock to uphold my views;
Everything came at my beck and call
Till a woman appeared and destroyed it all.
A beautiful girl with ripening bosom,
Cheeks as bright as apple blossom,
Hair that glimmered and foamed in the wind
And a face that blazed with the light behind,
A tinkling laugh and a modest carriage
And a twinkling eye that was ripe for marriage.
I goggled and gaped like one born mindless
Till I took her face for a form of kindness,
Though that wasn't quite what the Lord intended
For He marked me down like a man offended
For a vengeance that wouldn't be easy mended
With my folly exposed and my comfort ended.

"Now not to detain ye here all day,
I married the girl without more delay,
And I took my share in the fun that followed;
There was plenty for all and nothing borrowed.
Be fair to me now, there was no man slighted;
The beggarmen took the road delighted,
The clerk and the mummers were elevated
And the priest went home with his purse well weighted.
The lamps were lit; the guests arrived,
The supper was ready; the beer was plied;
The fiddles were flayed and the night advancing
The neighbours joined in the sport and dancing.

"A pity to God I didn't smother
When first I took the milk from my mother
Or any day I ever broke bread
Before I brought that woman to bed!
For though everyone talked of her carouses
As a scratching post of the publichouses
That as sure as ever the glasses would jingle,
Flattened herself to married and single.
Admitting no modesty to mention,
I never believed but 'twas all invention.
They added, in view of the life she led,
I might take to the roads and beg my bread;
But I took it for talk and hardly minded;
Sure a man like me could never be blinded!—
And I smiled and nodded and off I tripped
Till my wedding night when I saw her stripped,
And knew too late that the thing was no libel
Spread in the pub by some jealous rival—
By God, 'twas a fact, and well-supported
I was a father before I started!

"So there I was in the cold daylight
A family man after one short night,
The women around me, scolding, preaching,
The wife in bed and the baby screeching,
Stirring the milk while the kettle boiled,
Making a bottle to give the child.
All the old hags at the hob were cooing
As if they believed it was all my doing,
Flattery worse than ever you heard,
'Glory and praise to Our Blessed Lord,
Though he came in a hurry, the poor little creature,
He's the spit of his da in every feature.
Sal, will you look at the cut of that lip!
There's fingers for you! Feel his grip!
Would you measure the legs and the rolls of fat

Was there ever a seven-months' child like that?'
And they traced away with great preciseness
My matchless face in the baby's likeness;
The same snub nose and frolicsome air
And the way I laugh and the way I stare,
And they swore that never from head to toe
Was a child that resembled his father so.
But they wouldn't let me go near the wonder—
'Sure a draught would blow the poor child asunder!'
All of them out to blind me further—
'The least little breath would be noonday murder!'
Malice and lies, and I took the floor
Mad with rage and I cursed and swore,
And ordered them all to leave my sight,
They shrunk away with their faces white,
And they said as they handed me up the baby,
'Don't crush him now. Can't you handle him easy?
The least thing hurts them. Treat him kindly!
Some fall she got brought it on untimely.
Don't lift his head but leave him lying.
Poor innocent scrap, and to think he's dying!
If he lives at all till the end of day
Till the priest will come 'tis the most we'll pray!'

"I off with the rags and set him free
And studied him well as he lay on my knee,
That too, by God, was nothing but lies
For he staggered myself with his kicks and cries;
A pair of shoulders like my own,
Legs like puddings and hair full grown;
His ears stuck out and his nails were long,
His hands and wrists and elbows strong;
His eyes were bright, his nostrils wide,
And the knee-caps showing beneath his hide—
A champion, begod, a powerful whelp,
Hearty and healthy as myself.

"Young woman, I've made my case entire.
Justice is all that I require.
Once consider the terrible life
We lead from the minute we take a wife,
And you'll find and see that marriage must stop
And the men that's not married must be let off.
And child of grace, don't think of the race,
Plenty will follow to take our place;
There's ways and means to make lovers agree
Without making a show of men like me.
There's no excuse for all the exploiters,
Corner-boys, clerks, and priests and pipers,
Idle fellows that strip you naked
And the jars of malt and the beer that's wasted
When the Mother of God herself conceived,
Without asking the views of clerk or creed;
Healthy and happy, wholesome and sound
The come-by-twilight sort abound;
No one assumes but their lungs are ample
And their hearts as good as the best example.
When did nature display unkindness
To the bastard child in disease or blindness?
Are they not handsomer, better-bred
Than many that comes of a lawful bed?

"I needn't go far to look for proof
For I've always one beneath my roof—
Let him come here for all to view!
Look at him now! You'll see 'tis true.
Agreed, we don't know his father's name,
But his mother admires him just the same,
And if in all things else he shines
Who cares for his baptismal lines?
He isn't a dwarf or an old man's error,
A paralytic or walking terror,
He isn't a hunchback or a cripple,

But a lightsome, laughing, gay young divil.
'Tis easy to see he's no flash in the pan;
No sleepy, good-natured, respectable man
Without sinew or bone or belly or bust
Or venom or vice or love or lust,
Buckled and braced in every limb,
Spouted the seed that flowered in him;
For back and leg and chest and height
Prove him to all in the teeth of spite
A child begotten in fear and wonder
In the blood's millrace and the body's thunder.

"Down with marriage! 'Tis out of date,
It exhausts the stock and cripples the state.
The priest has failed with his whip and blinker
Now give a chance to Tom the Tinker,
And mix and mash in nature's can
The tinker and the gentleman;
Let lovers in every lane extended
Follow their whim as God intended,
And in their pleasure bring to birth
The morning glory of the earth;
The starry litter, girl and boy
That will see the world once more with joy.
Clouds will break and skies will brighten,
Mountains bloom and spirits lighten
And men and women praise your might,
You who restore the old delight."

The girl had listened without dissembling,
Then up she started, hot and trembling,
And she answered him with eyes alight
And a voice that shook with squalls of spite:
"By the Crown of the Rock, I thought in time
Of your age and folly and known decline
And the manners I owe to people and place

Or I'd paint my nails in your ugly face.
I'd scatter your guts and tan your hide
And ferry your soul to the other side
I'd honour you much if I gave the lie
To an impudent speech that needs no reply;
'Tis enough if I tell the sort of life
You led your unfortunate, decent wife.

"This girl was poor, she hadn't a home,
Hadn't a thing to call her own;
Drifting about, ignored, despised,
Doing odd jobs for other men's wives;
As if for drudgery created
Begging a crust from women she hated.
He pretended her troubles were over,
Married to him she'd live in clover;
The cows she milked would be her own,
The feather bed and the decent home;
The stack of turf, the lamp to light,
The sodded wall of a winter's night;
Flax and wool to weave and wind,
The womanly things for which she pined.
Even his friends couldn't have said
That his looks were such that she lost her head.
How else would he come by such a wife
But that ease was the alms she asked of life?
What possible use could she have at night
For dourness, dropsy, bother and blight,
A basket of bones with thighs of lead,
Knees absconded from the dead,
Reddening shanks and temples whitening,
Looking like one that was struck by lightning?
Is there living a girl that could grow fat
Tied to a travelling corpse like that;
That twice a year wouldn't find a wish
To see what was she, flesh or fish,

But dragged the clothes about his head
Like a wintry wind to a woman in bed?

"Now was it too much to expect as right
A little attention once a night?
From all I know she was never accounted
A woman too modest to be mounted;
Gentle, good-humoured and God-fearing,
We need never suppose she denied her rearing.
Whatever the lengths his fancy ran
She wouldn't take fright from a mettlesome man,
And would sooner a boy would be aged a score
Than himself on the job for a week or more;
And dancing at night or Mass at morning,
Fiddle or flute or choir or organ,
She'd sooner the tune that boy would play
As midnight struck or at break of day.
Damn it, you know we're all the same,
A woman nine months in terror and pain,
The minute that Death has lost the game—
Good morrow, my love, and she's off again!
And then imagine what 'twas like
With a fellow like that in the bed at night
That never came close in a friendly way
From All Souls' Night to St. Brigid's Day!
You'd all agree 'twas a horrible fate—
Sixty winters on his pate;
An old dead tree with its timbers drained
And a twenty year old with her heart untamed
It wasn't her fault if things went wrong;
She closed her eyes and held her tongue;
She was no querulous, restless, bawling,
Rearing, leaping, pinching, scrawling,
Hussy from school who smooth and warm
Cushioned him like a sheaf of corn.
Line by line she bade him linger

With gummy lips and groping finger;
Gripping his thighs in a wild embrace,
Rubbing her brush from knee to waist,
Stripping him bare to the cold night air,
Everything that a woman would dare;
But she'd nothing to show for all her pain,
His bleary old eyes looked just the same;
And nothing I said could ever explain
All her misery and shame
Her knees in the air and the clothes beneath her,
Chattering teeth and limbs in fever,
As she sobbed and tossed through a joyless night
And gave it up with the morning light.

"I think you'll agree from the little I've said,
That a man like this must be off his head
To live like a monk to the end of his life,
Muddle his marriage and blame his wife.
The talk about women comes well from him
Without hope in body or help in limb;
If the creature that found him such a sell
Has a lover today, she deserves him well;
A benefit nature never denies
To anything born that swims or flies;
Tell me of one that ever went empty
And died of want in the middle of plenty.
In all the wonders west and east
Did anyone hear of a breed of beast
That turned away from fern and hay
To feed on briars and roots and clay?
You silly old fool, you can't reply
And give us at least one reason why
If your supper is there when you come home late,
You've such hullabaloo about the plate.
Will it lessen your store, will you sigh for more
If twenty millions used it before?

You must fancy women are all like you
If you think they'll go dry for a man or two;
You might as well drink the ocean up
Or empty the Shannon with a cup.
Sure, you must see that you're half insane!
Try cold compresses, avoid all strain,
And stop complaining of the neighbours,
If every man jack enjoyed her favours,
Men by the hundred under her shawl
Would take nothing from you in the heel of all.

"If your jealousy even was based on fact
In some hardy young whelp well used to the act,
Covetous, quarrelsome, keen on scoring,
Or some hairy old villain hardened with whoring;
A vigorous slasher, a rank outsider,
A jockey of note, or a gentleman rider,
But a man disposed in the wrong direction
With a poor mouth shown on a sham erection!

"But oye, my heart will grow grey hairs
Brooding forever on idle cares,
Has the Catholic Church a glimmer of sense
That the priests won't marry like anyone else?
Is it any wonder the way I am,
Out of my mind for the want of a man,
When there's men by the score with looks and leisure,
Walking the roads and scorning pleasure?
The full of a fair of primest beef,
Warranted to afford relief,
Cherry-red cheeks and bull-like voices,
And bellies dripping with fat in slices,
Backs erect and heavy hind quarters,
Hot-blooded men, the best of partners,
Freshness and charm, youth and good looks

And nothing to ease their mind but books!
The best fed men that travel the country,
Beef and mutton, game and poultry,
Whiskey and wine forever in stock,
Sides of bacon, beds of flock.
Mostly they're hardy under the hood,
And we know like ourselves that they're flesh and blood;
I wouldn't ask much of the old campaigners,
The good-for-nothings and born complainers,
But petticoat-tossers aloof and idle
And fillies gone wild for bit and bridle!

"Of course I admit that some more sprightly,
Would like to repent and I'd treat them lightly.
A pardon and a job for life
To every priest that takes a wife!
For many a good man's chance miscarries
If you scuttle the ship for the crooks it carries;
And though some as we know were always savage
Gnashing their teeth at the thought of marriage,
And, modest beyond the needs of merit,
Invoked hell-fire on girls of spirit,
Yet some that took to their pastoral labours
Made very good priests and the best of neighbours.
Many a girl filled byre and stall
And furnished her house through a clerical call.
Everyone's heard the priests extolled
For the lonesome women that they consoled;
People I've heard throughout the county
Have nothing but praise for the curate's bounty;
Or uphold the canon to lasting fame
For the children he reared in another man's name;
But I hate to think of their lonely lives,
The passions they waste on middle-aged wives,
While the women they'd choose if the choice were theirs

Go by the wall and comb grey hairs.
It passes the wit of mortal man
What Ireland has lost by this stupid ban.

"I leave it to you, O Nut of Knowledge,
The girls at home and the boys in college,
I'm blest if I can see the crime,
If they go courting in their prime,
But you that for learning have no rival,
Tell us the teachings of the Bible;
Where are we taught to pervert our senses
And make our natural needs offences?
Fly from lust, advised St. Paul,
He didn't mean men were to fly us all,
But to leave their father and friends behind
And stick to the girl that pleased their mind.
I'm at it again! I must keep my place;
It isn't for me to judge the case,
And you, a spirit born and queen,
Remember the texts and what they mean;
With apt quotations well supplied
From the prophets who took the woman's side,
And the words of Christ that were never belied,
Who chose for His Mother an earthly bride.

"But, oye, what use is pishrogue and spell,
To one like myself in the fires of hell?
What chance can there be for girls like me
With husbands for only one in three?
When there's famine abroad the need advises
To look out for yourself as the chance arises,
And since crops are thin and weeds are plenty
And the young without heart and Ireland empty,
And to fill it again is a hopeless job,
Get me some old fellow to sit by the hob,

Bind him in every way you can—
And leave it to me to make him a man."

Daylight crept in and the lights grew pale
And the girl sat down as she ended her tale;
The princess rose with her face aglow,
And her voice when she spoke was grave and low;
"Oyez," said the clerk, to quell the riot,
And wielded his mace till all sat quiet,
And then from her lips while the hall was hushed
Speech in a rainbow glory gushed.
"My child," she said, "I won't deny
That you've reason enough to scold and cry,
And as a woman, I can't but grieve
To see women like you and Moll and Maeve
With your dues diminished, your favours gone,
While none can enjoy a likely man
But misers sucking a lonely bone
Or hairy old harpies living alone.
I do enact according then
That all the young unmarried men
Shall be arrested by the guard,
Detained within the chapel yard,
Stripped and tied beside the gate,
While you decide upon their fate.
Those that you find whom the years have thwarted
With masculine parts that were never exerted,
To the palpable loss of some woman's employment,
The thrill of the milk and their own enjoyment,
Who having the chance of wife and home,
Took to the hills and lived alone,
Are only a burden on the earth,
So give it to them for all you're worth;
Roast or pickle them; some reflection
Will frame a suitable correction;

That you can fix at your own tribunal
And whatever you do will have my approval.
Fully grown men too old to function
You may punish without the least compunction,
Nothing you do can have consequences
To middle-aged men with failing senses,
And whatever is lost or whatever survives
We need never suppose will affect their wives,
Young men, of course, are another affair.
You may find them of use, so strike with care!

"There are poor men working in rain and sleet
Half out of their minds with the troubles they meet,
But men in name and in deed according,
They comfort their women by night and morning,
As their fathers did to console their mothers,
And these are the men I'd have for lovers.
In the matter of priests a change is due,
And I think I may say that it's coming too,
For any day now it may come to their knowledge
That the case has been judged by the cardinals' college,
And we'll hear no more of the ban on marriage
Before the priests go entirely savage;
And the cry of the blood in the body's fire
You can quicken or quell to your heart's desire,
But anyone else of woman born,
Flay him alive if he won't reform;
Abolish wherever my judgment reaches
The nancy boy and the flapper in breeches,
And when their rule is utterly ended
Give us the world that God intended.

"The rest of the work must only wait,
I'm due elsewhere and already late,
I have business there that I must attend
Though you and I are far from the end,

But I'll sit next month and God help the men
If they haven't improved their ways by then;
And mostly those who sin from pride
With women whose names they do not hide,
Who keep their tally of ruined lives
In whispers, nudges, winks and gibes.
Was ever vanity more misplaced
Than in married women and girls disgraced?
It isn't desire that gives the thrust,
The smoking blood and the ache of lust,
Weakness of love and the body's blindness,
But to punish the fools who show them kindness.
Thousands are born without a name
That braggarts may boast of their mothers' shame,
Men lost to nature through conceit,
And their manhood killed by their own deceit,
For 'tis sure, however, their wives may weep,
It's never because they go short of sleep."

I had listened to every word she uttered,
And then as she stopped my midriff fluttered,
I was took with a sort of sudden reeling
Till my feet seemed resting on the ceiling;
People and place went round and round,
And her words came back as a jumble of sound,
As the bailiff strode along the aisle,
And reached for me with an ugly smile;
She nipped my ear as if in sport
And dragged me out and up the court.
Then the girl who complained of the way she was slighted
Spotted my face and sprang up, delighted.
"Is it you?" says she. "Of all the old crocks,
I'm waiting for years to comb your locks;
You had your chance and missed your shot,
And devil's cure to you now you're caught!
Is there anyone here will speak in your favour,

Or would anyone think you worth the labour?
What little affair would you care to mention
Or whom have you honoured with your attention?
Though we'll all agree that the man's no beauty,
You must admit that he's fit for duty.
I know he's ill-made and as ugly as sin,
But isn't he sound in wind and limb?
I'd sooner him pale and not so plump,
But I've no objection to his hump.
It isn't a feature that intrudes,
Or one that especially goes with prudes;
You find bandy legs with a frolicsome figure
And arms like pegs on a man of vigour;
To be sure the wretch has some secret reason
That kept him single out of season.
As welcome at the country houses,
As at the villagers' carouses;
Called in wherever the fun was going,
And the fiddles being tuned and the whiskey flowing—
I'll never believe that there's truth in a name;
A wonder the Merrymans stand the shame!
The doggedest divil that tramps the hill
With the grey in his hair and a virgin still.
O leave me alone till I settle the savage,
You can spare your breath to cool your porridge
The truth of it's plain upon your forehead,
You're thirty at least and still unmarried!
Listen to me, O Fount of Luck,
This fellow's the worst that ever I struck,
The venom of years that I've locked inside
Won't let me rest till I tan his hide.
Can't you all help me? Catch him! Mind him!
Winnie, girl, run and get ropes to bind him!
Where are you, Annie, or are you blind?
Sally, tie up his hands behind!
Molly and Maeve, you fools, what ails you?

Isn't it soon the courage fails you?
Take the rope and give him a crack,
Earth it up in the small of his back.
That, young man, is the place to hurt you,
We'll teach you to respect your virtue,
Steady now, till we give you a sample—
Women alive, he's a grand example!
Hurry now and we'll nourish him well!
One good clout till we hear him yell!
And the more he yells the harder we'll strike
Till we teach his friends to be more polite.
No blesseder act restored the nation,
We must write the date as a famous occasion,
The First of January, Seventeen Eighty—"

And there I stood, half stripped, half crazy;
For nothing, I felt, could save my skin,
And she opened her book and immersed her pen,
And she wrote it down with careful art,
While the women sighed for the fun to start,
I shivered and gave myself a shake,
Opened my eyes and was wide awake.

Translator Frank O'Connor.

I Am Raftery

BY Anthony Raftery (c. 1784-1835)

I am Raftery the poet,
Full of hope and love,
My eyes without sight,
My mind without torment.

Going west on my journey
By the light of my heart,
Tired and weary
To the end of the road.

Behold me now
With my back to a wall,
Playing music
To empty pockets.

Translator James Stephens

The County Mayo

BY Anthony Raftery

Now with the coming in of the spring the days will stretch a bit,
And after the Feast of Brigid I shall hoist my flag and go,
For since the thought got into my head I can neither stand
nor sit
Until I find myself in the middle of the County of Mayo.

In Claremorris I would stop a night and sleep with decent men,
And then go on to Balla just beyond and drink galore,
And next to Kiltimagh for a visit of about a month, and then
I would only be a couple of miles away from Ballymore.

I say and swear my heart lifts up like the lifting of a tide,
Rising up like the rising wind till fog or mist must go,
When I remember Carra and Gallen close beside,
And the Gap of the Two Bushes, and the wide plains of Mayo.

To Killaden then, to the place where everything grows that is
best,
There are raspberries there and strawberries there and all that
is good for men;
And if I were only there in the middle of my folk my heart
could rest,
For age itself would leave me there and I'd be young again.

Translator James Stephens.

The Brow of Nephin

Did I stand on the bald top of Nefin
And my hundred-times loved one with me,
We should nestle together as safe in
Its shade as the birds on a tree.

From your lips such a music is shaken,
When you speak it awakens my pain,
And my eyelids by sleep are forsaken,
And I seek for my slumber in vain.

But were I on the fields of the ocean,
I should sport on its infinite room,
I should plough through the billow's commotion
Though my friends should look dark at my doom.

For the flower of all maidens of magic
Is beside me where'er I may be,
Not a woman takes pity on me.
And my heart like a coal is extinguished,

How well for the birds in all weather,
They rise up on high in the air
And then sleep upon one bough together
Without sorrow or trouble or care;

But so it is not in this world
For myself and my thousand times fair,
For away, far apart from each other,
Each day rises barren and bare.

19TH CENTURY.
Translator Douglas Hyde.

My Grief on the Sea

My grief on the sea,
  How the waves of it roll!
For they heave between me
  And the love of my soul!

Abandoned, forsaken,
  To grief and to care,
Will the sea ever waken
  Relief from despair?

My grief and my trouble!
  Would he and I were
In the province of Leinster
  Or the county of Clare.

Were I and my darling—
  Oh, heart-bitter wound!—
On board of the ship
  For America bound.

On a green bed of rushes
  All last night I lay,
And I flung it abroad
  With the heat of the day.

And my love came behind me—
  He came from the South;
His breast to my bosom.
  His mouth to my mouth.

19TH CENTURY.
Translator Douglas Hyde.

Ringleted Youth of My Love

RINGLETED youth of my love,
With thy locks bound loosely behind thee,
You passed by the road above,
But you never came in to find me;
Where were the harm for you
If you came for a little to see me;
Your kiss is a wakening dew
Were I ever so ill or so dreamy.

If I had golden store
I would make a nice little boreen
To lead straight up to his door,
The door of the house of my storeen;
Hoping to God not to miss
The sound of his footfall in it,
I have waited so long for his kiss
That for days I have slept not a minute.

I thought, O my love! you were so—
As the moon is, or sun on a fountain,
And I thought after that you were snow,
The cold snow on top of the mountain;
And I thought after that you were more
Like God's lamp shining to find me,
Or the bright star of knowledge before,
And the star of knowledge behind me.

You promised me high-heeled shoes,
And satin and silk, my storeen,
And to follow me, never to lose,
Though the ocean were round us roaring;
Like a bush in a gap in a wall
I am now left lonely without thee,
And this house, I grow dead of, is all
That I see around or about me.

19TH CENTURY.
Translator Douglas Hyde.

I Shall Not Die For Thee

For thee I shall not die,
Woman high of fame and name;
Foolish men thou mayest slay,
I and they are not the same.

Why should I expire
For the fire of any eye,
Slender waist or swan-like limb,
Is't for them that I should die?

The round breasts, the fresh skin,
Cheeks crimson, hair so long and rich;
Indeed, indeed, I shall not die,
Please God, not I, for any such.

The golden hair, the forehead then,
The chaste mien, the gracious ease,
The rounded heel, the languid tone,
Fools alone find death from these.

Thy sharp wit, thy perfect calm,
    Thy thin palm like foam of sea;
Thy white neck, thy blue eye,
    I shall not die for thee.

Woman, graceful as the swan,
    A wise man did nurture me,
Little palm, white neck, bright eye,
    I shall not die for thee.

19TH CENTURY.
Translator Douglas Hyde.

PART V

Irish Literature in English

The Irish Dancer

I am of Ireland,
And of the holy land
   Of Ireland.
Good Sir, pray I thee,
For of *saint charité*
Come and dance with me
   In Ireland.

14TH CENTURY.

A Rhyme-beginning Fragment[1]

Love hath me brought in evil thought,
  Thought I have to blinne;[2]
Blinne to think it is for nought,
  Nought is love of sin.

Sin me hath in care ibrought,
  Brought in much unwinne;[3]
Winne to weld[4] I had ithought,
  Thought is that I am in.

In me is care, how I shall fare,
  Fare I will and funde;[5]
Funde I with outen are,[6]
  Ere I be brought to ground.

14TH CENTURY.

Cokaygne[7]

Far in sea, west of Spain,
Is a land that's named Cokaygne,
There is no land under heavenriche[8]

---

1 See Bibliographical Notes, p. 589. The poem may be paraphrased thus. *Love has led me to sinful thoughts. I have intended to stop. But merely to intend is to do nothing, and nothing is the love of sin. Sin, in turn, has brought me only worry and much unhappiness. I thought I could achieve happiness but have got no farther than the thought. And now I am worried about how I shall go on. But go on I must and fare. I shall go on without honor until I perish.* 2 Stop. 3 Unhappiness. 4 Happiness. 5 Go. 6 Honor.

7 See Bibliographical Notes, p. 589. 8 The kingdom of heaven.

Of wealth, of goodness, it iliche,[1]
Though Paradise be merry and bright
Cokaygne is of fairer sight.
What is there in Paradise
But grass, and flowers, and green ris?[2]
Though there be joy and great dute[3]
There is no food only fruit;
There is no hall, bower, nor bench,
But water man his thirst to quench.
There be no men, but two,
Hely and Enok[4] also;
Elinglich[5] may they go
Where there dwelleth man no mo.[6]

In Cokaygne is meat and drink
Without care, thought, and swink;[7]
The meat is choice, the drink is clear,
At noon, russin,[8] and supper.
I say for sooth, boute were,[9]
There is no land on earth its peer,
Under heaven's no land, iwis,[10]
Of so great joy and bliss.
There is many a sweete sight,
All is day, there is no night.
There is neither quarrel nor strife,
There is no death, but ever life,
There is no lack of meat nor cloth,
There is no man nor woman wroth,
There is no serpent, wolf, nor fox,
Horse nor capil,[11] cow nor ox,
There is no sheep, nor swine, nor goat,
Nothing unclean, lo! God it wot.[12]
Neither harace nor stode,[13]

---

1 Equal to it. 2 Twigs, branches. 3 Pleasure. 4 Enoch and Elijah. 5 Mournfully. 6 No other men. 7 Toil. 8 Mid-day meal. 9 Without a doubt. 10 In truth. 11 Nag. 12 God knows it. 13 Stud of horses or stable.

The land is full of every good.
There is no fly, flea, nor louse,
In cloth, in farm, in bed, nor house;
There is no thunder, sleet, nor hail,
Neither a vile worm nor snail,
Nor no storm, rain, or wind,
There is no man nor woman blind.
But all is sport, joy and glee,
Lucky's he who there may be.
There are rivers great and fine
Of oil, milk, honey, and wine,
Water serveth there to no thing
But to boil and to washing,
There is all manner of fruit,
All is solace and dedute.[1]

There is a right fair abbey
Both of white monks and of grey.
There be bowers and halls,
All of pastys be the walls,
Of flesh, of fish, and of rich meat,
The pleasantest that men may eat.
Flouren cakes be the shingles all
Of church, and cloister, bower, and hall.
The pins be fat puddings,
Rich meat for princes and kings.
Men may thereof eat enow

---

1 Delight.

All with right, and not with wogh.[1]
All is common to young and old,
To stout and stern, weak and bold.
There is a cloister fair and light,
Broad and long, of seemly sight.
The pillars of that cloister all
Be iturned of crystal,
With their base and capital
Of green jasper and red coral.

In the lawn there is a tree
Very pleasant for to see.
The root is ginger and galingale[2]
The scions be all sedwale,[3]
Choice maces[4] be the flower,
The rind canel[5] of sweet odour,
The fruit gillyflower of good smack,[6]
Of cubebs there is no lack;
There be roses of red ble,[7]
And lilies pleasant for to see,
That never fade day nor night,
This should be a sweet sight.
There be four wells in the abbey,

---

1 Altogether with right and not with wrongdoing.
2 A plant from the aromatic root of which a spice is prepared.
3 Zedoary, a root resembling ginger. 4 Spice made of dried outer covering of nutmeg. 5 Cinnamon. 6 Scent, taste. 7 Color.

Of triacle and of halwei,[1]
Of balm and also piement,[2]
Ever flowing to right rent.[3]
Of the streams all the mould[4]
Stones precious, and gold.
There is sapphire and uniune[5]
Carbuncle and astiune,[6]
Emerald, lugre,[7] and prassiune,[8]
Beryl, onyx, and topasiune,[9]
Amethyst and chrysolite,
Chalcedony and epetite.[10]

There be birds many and fale,[11]
Throstle, thrush, and nightingale,
Chalandre and woodwale,[12]
And other birds without tale,[13]
That cease never by their might
Merry to sing day and night.
Yet I do you more to wit:[14]
The geese iroasted on the spit
Fly to that abbey, God it wot,
And cry out "Geese, all hot, all hot!"
They bring of garlic great plenty,
The best prepared that man may see.
The leverokes that be cuth[15]
Alight down to man his mouth,
Prepared in stew-pan very well,
Stuffed with gillyflowers and canel.
There is no talk of no drink,
But take enough without swink.

---

1 Healing medicine, and balsam. 2 Mixed drink of wine, honey and spices. 3 To good profit. 4 All the beds of the streams are composed of, etc. 5 Pearl. 6 Unidentified precious stone. 7 Jacynth. 8 Chrysoprase. 9 Topaz. 10 Bloodstone. 11 Numerous. 12 Goldfinch, or perhaps some sort of lark: woodlark. 13 Beyond count. 14 I let you know in addition. 15 The larks that are trained.

When the monks go to mass
All the windows that be of glass
Turn into crystal bright
To give the monks more light.
When the masses be isaid,
And the books up ilaid,
The crystal turneth into glass
In the state it rather[1] was.

The young monks each day
After meat go to play.
There is no hawk nor fowl so swift
Better flying in the lift[2]
Than the monks high of mood
With their sleeves and their hood.
When the abbot seeth them flee
That he holds for much glee,
But nathless all there among
He biddeth them light to evensong.
But the monks alight not down
But fly in a randown.[3]
When the abbot him iseeth
That his monks from him fleeth,
He taketh maiden of the route,
And turneth up her white toute
And beateth the tabor with his hand,
To make his monks 'light to land.
When his monks that iseeth,
To the maid down they fleeth,
And goeth the wench all about,
And thwacketh all her white toute,
And then after their swink,
Turn meekly home to drink,
And go to their collation,
A right fair procession.

---

1 Formerly. 2 Air. 3 In a furious course.

Another abbey is thereby,
Forsooth a great fair nunnery,
Upon a river of sweet milk
Where is plenty great of silk.
When the summer day is hot
The young nuns take a boat
And do them forth in that river
Both with oars and with stere.[1]
When they be far from the abbey
They make them naked for to play,
And leap down into the brim,
And do them slyly for to swim.

The young monks that them seeth,
They hie them up, and forth they fleeth,
And come to the nuns anon.
And each monk him taketh one,
And snellich[2] beareth forth their prey
To the mochil[3] grey abbey.
And teacheth the nuns an orison
With *jambleuc*[4] up and down.
The monk that will be staluu[5] good,
And can set aright his hood,
He shall have, without danger,[6]
Twelve wives each year:
All through right, and nought through grace,

1 Rudder.
2 Swiftly. 3 Great. 4 Gambols. 5 Stout. (?) 6 Punishment.

For to do himself solace.
And this monk that clepith[1] best,
Of him is hope, God it wot,
To be soon father abbot.

Whoso will that land come to
Full great penance he must do:
Seven years in swine's dirt
He must wade, well ye wit,
All anon up to the chin,
So he shall that land win.

Lordlinges good and hend[2]
May ye never of world wend
For ye stand to your chance[3]
And fulfil that penance,
That ye might that land isee
And nevermore turn age.[4]
Pray we God, so mote it be.
Amen, *pour saint charité*.

13TH CENTURY.

1 Declared, or perhaps *clippeth*, i.e. embraces. 2 Courteous. 3 May you never leave the world till you try your fortune about getting to that land. 4 Again.

An Anglo-Irishman's Complaint[1]

By granting charters of peace
To false English, without lease
  This land shall be much undo.
But gossipred[2] and alterage,[3]
And losing of our language
  Have mickly holp[4] thereto.

16TH CENTURY.

---

1 See Bibliographical Notes, p. 589. The poet complains that the English settlers in Ireland are fraternizing with the Irish to the extent of adopting native customs and speaking Irish. He resents the fact that a weak government, instead of reducing to obedience these disloyal Anglo-Norman families who are "false English," appeases them with "charters of peace" and other legal concessions. The poet's sentiments find reinforcement in the preamble to the Statutes of Kilkenny (1366) which deplored the fact that "now many English of the said land, forsaking the English language, manners, mode of riding, laws and usages, live and govern themselves according to the manners, fashion and language of the Irish enemies and also have made divers marriages between themselves and the Irish enemies . . ."

2 Standing sponsor at baptism.

3 Fostering—an Irish custom whereby a man, to guarantee friendship or seal an agreement, would send one of his children to be brought up in the house of another man. The custom continued into the 17th century.

4 Greatly helped.

A Modest Proposal for Preventing the Children of Ireland From Being a Burden to Their Parents or Country

BY Jonathan Swift (1667-1745)

IT IS A melancholy object to those who walk through this great town or travel in the country, when they see the streets, the roads, and cabin doors, crowded with beggars of the female sex, followed by three, four, or six children, all in rags and importuning every passenger for an alms. These mothers, instead of being able to work for their honest livelihood, are forced to employ all their time in strolling to beg sustenance for their helpless infants: who as they grow up either turn thieves for want of work, or leave their dear native country to fight for the pretender in Spain, or sell themselves to the Barbadoes.

I think it is agreed by all parties that this prodigious number of children in the arms, or on the backs, or at the heels of their mothers, and frequently of their fathers, is in the present deplorable state of the kingdom a very great additional grievance; and, therefore, whoever could find out a fair, cheap, and easy method of making these children sound, useful members of the commonwealth, would deserve so well of the public as to have his statue set up for a preserver of the nation.

But my intention is very far from being confined to provide only for the children of professed beggars; it is of a much greater extent, and shall take in the whole number of infants at a certain age who are born of parents in effect as little able to support them as those who demand our charity in the streets.

As to my own part, having turned my thoughts for many years upon this important subject, and maturely weighed the several schemes of our projectors, I have always found them grossly mistaken in their computation. It is true, a child just dropped from its dam may be supported by her milk for a solar year, with little other nourishment; at most not above the value of 2s., which the mother may certainly get, or the value in scraps, by her lawful occupation of begging; and it is exactly at one year old that I propose to provide for them in such a manner as instead of being a charge upon their parents or the parish, or wanting food and raiment for the rest of their lives, they shall on the contrary contribute to the feeding, and partly to the clothing, of many thousands.

There is likewise another great advantage in my scheme, that it will prevent those voluntary abortions, and that horrid practice of women murdering their bastard children, alas! too frequent among us! sacrificing the poor innocent babes I doubt more to avoid the expense than the shame, which would move tears and pity in the most savage and inhuman breast.

The number of souls in this kingdom being usually reckoned one million and a half, of these I calculate there may be about 200,000 couple whose wives are breeders; from which number I subtract 30,000 couple who are able to maintain their own children (although I apprehend there cannot be so many, under the present distresses of the kingdom); but this being granted, there will remain 170,000 breeders. I again subtract 50,000 for those women who miscarry, or whose children die by accident or disease within the year. There only remains 120,000 children of poor parents annually born. The question therefore is, how this number shall be reared and provided for? which, as I have already said, under the present situation of affairs, is utterly impossible by all the methods hitherto proposed. For we can neither employ them in handicraft or agriculture; we neither build houses (I mean in the country) nor cultivate land; they can very seldom pick up a livelihood by stealing, till they arrive at six years old, except where they are of towardly parts; although I confess they learn the rudiments much earlier; during which time, they can however be properly looked upon only as probationers; as I have been informed by a principal gentleman in the county of Cavan, who protested to me that he never knew above one or two instances under the age of six, even in a part of the kingdom so renowned for the quickest proficiency in that art.

I am assured by our merchants, that a boy or a girl before twelve years old is no saleable commodity; and even when they come to this age they will not yield above £3 or £3 and half a crown at most on the exchange; which cannot turn to account either to the parents or kingdom, the charge of nutriment and rags having been at least four times that value.

I shall now therefore humbly propose my own thoughts, which I hope will not be liable to the least objection.

I have been assured by a very knowing American of my acquaintance in London, that a young healthy child well nursed is at a year old a most delicious, nourishing, and wholesome food, whether stewed, roasted, baked, or boiled; and I make no doubt that it will equally serve in a fricassee or a ragout.

I do therefore humbly offer it to public consideration that of the 120,000 children already computed, 20,000 may be reserved for breed, whereof only one-fourth part to be males; which is more than we allow to sheep, black cattle, or swine; and my reason is, that these children are seldom the fruits of marriage, a circumstance not much regarded by our savages, therefore one male will be sufficient to serve four females. That the remaining 100,000 may, at a year old, be offered in sale to the persons of quality and fortune through the kingdom; always advising the mother to let them suck plentifully in the last month, so as to render them plump and fat for a good table. A child will make two dishes at an entertainment for friends; and when the family dines alone, the fore or hind quarter will make a reasonable dish, and seasoned with a little pepper or salt will be very good boiled on the fourth day, especially in winter.

I have reckoned upon a medium that a child just born will weigh 12 pounds, and in a solar year, if tolerably nursed, will increase to 28 pounds.

I grant this food will be somewhat dear, and therefore very proper for landlords, who, as they have already devoured most of the parents, seem to have the best title to the children.

Infant's flesh will be in season throughout the year, but more plentifully in March, and a little before and after: for we are told by a grave author, an eminent French physician, that fish being a prolific diet, there are more children born in Roman Catholic countries about nine months after Lent than at any other season; therefore, reckoning a year after Lent, the markets will be more glutted than usual, because the number of popish infants is at least three to one in this kingdom: and therefore it will have one other collateral advantage, by lessening the number of papists among us.

I have already computed the charge of nursing a beggar's child (in which list I reckon all cottagers, laborers, and four-fifths of the farmers) to be about 2s. per annum, rags included; and I believe no gentleman would repine to give 10s. for the carcass of a good fat child, which, as I have said, will make four dishes of excellent nutritive meat, when he has only some particular friend or his own family to dine with him. Thus the squire will learn to be a good landlord, and grow popular among the tenants; the mother will have 8s. net profit, and be fit for work till she produces another child.

Those who are more thrifty (as I must confess the times require) may flay the carcass; the skin of which artificially dressed will make admirable gloves for ladies, and summer boots for fine gentlemen.

As to our city of Dublin, shambles may be appointed for this purpose in the most convenient parts of it, and butchers we may be assured will not be wanting; although I rather recommend buying the children alive, and dressing them hot from the knife as we do roasting pigs.

A very worthy person, a true lover of his country, and whose virtues I highly esteem, was lately pleased in discoursing on this matter to offer a refinement upon my scheme. He said that many gentlemen of this kingdom, having of late destroyed their deer, he conceived that the want of venison might be well supplied by the bodies of young lads and maidens, not exceeding fourteen years of age nor under twelve; so great a number of both sexes in every country being now ready to starve for want of work and service; and these to be disposed of by their parents, if alive, or otherwise by their nearest relations. But with due deference to so excellent a friend and so deserving a patriot, I cannot be altogether in his sentiments; for as to the males, my American acquaintance assured me, from frequent experience that their flesh was generally tough and lean, like that of our school-boys by continual exercise, and their taste disagreeable; and to fatten them would not answer the charge. Then as to the females, it would, I think, with humble submission be a loss to the public, because they soon would become breeders themselves: and besides, it is not improbable that some scrupulous people might be apt to censure such a practice (although indeed very unjustly), as a little bordering upon cruelty; which, I confess, has always been with me the strongest objection against any project, how well soever intended.

But in order to justify my friend, he confessed that this expedient was put into his head by the famous Psalmanazar, a native of the island Formosa, who came from thence to London about twenty years ago: and in conversation told my friend, that in his country when any young person happened to be put to death, the executioner sold the carcass to persons of quality as a prime dainty; and that in his time the body of a plump girl of fifteen, who was crucified for an attempt to poison the emperor, was sold to his imperial majesty's prime minister of state, and other great mandarins of the court, in joints from the gibbet, at 400 crowns. Neither indeed can I deny, that if the same use were made of several plump young girls in this town, who without one single groat to their fortunes cannot stir abroad without a chair, and appear at playhouse and assemblies in foreign fineries which they never will pay for, the kingdom would not be the worse.

Some persons of a desponding spirit are in great concern about that vast number of poor people, who are aged, diseased, or maimed, and I have been desired to employ my thoughts what course may be taken to ease the nation of so grievous an encumbrance. But I am not in the least pain upon that matter, because it is very well known that they are every day dying and rotting by cold and famine, and filth and vermin, as fast as can be reasonably expected. And as to the young laborers, they are now in as hopeful a condition; they cannot get work, and consequently pine away for want of nourishment, to a degree that if at any time they are accidentally hired to common labor, they have not strength to perform it; and thus the country and themselves are happily delivered from the evils to come.

I have too long digressed, and therefore shall return to my subject. I think the advantages by the proposal which I have made are obvious and many, as well as of the highest importance.

For first, as I have already observed, it would greatly lessen the number of papists, with whom we are yearly overrun, being the principal breeders of the nation as well as our most dangerous enemies; and who stay at home on purpose to deliver the kingdom to the Pretender, hoping to take their advantage by the absence of so many good protestants, who have chosen rather to leave their country than stay at home and pay tithes against their conscience to an episcopal curate.

Secondly, The poorer tenants will have something valuable of their own, which by law may be made liable to distress and help to pay their landlord's rent, their corn and cattle being already seized, and money a thing unknown.

Thirdly, Whereas the maintenance of 100,000 children, from two years old and upward, cannot be computed at less than 10s. a-piece per annum, the nation's stock will be thereby increased £50,000 per annum, beside the profit of a new dish introduced to the tables of all gentlemen of fortune in the kingdom who have any refinement in taste. And the money will circulate among ourselves, the goods being entirely of our own growth and manufacture.

Fourthly, The constant breeders, beside the gain of 8s. sterling per annum by the sale of their children, will be rid of the charge of maintaining them after the first year.

Fifthly, This food would likewise bring great custom to taverns; where the vintners will certainly be so prudent as to procure the best receipts for dressing it to perfection, and consequently have their houses frequented by all the fine gentlemen, who justly value themselves upon their knowledge in good eating: and a skilful cook who understands how to oblige his guests, will contrive to make it as expensive as they please.

Sixthly, This would be a great inducement to marriage, which all wise nations have either encouraged by rewards or enforced by laws and penalties. It would increase the care and tenderness of mothers toward their children, when they were sure of a settlement for life to the poor babes, provided in some sort by the public, to their annual profit instead of expense. We should see an honest emulation among the married women, which of them could bring the fattest child to the market. Men would become as fond of their wives during the time of their pregnancy as they are now of their mares in foal, their cows in calf, their sows when they are ready to farrow; nor offer to beat or kick them (as is too frequent a practice) for fear of a miscarriage.

Many other advantages might be enumerated. For instance, the addition of some thousand carcasses in our exportation of barreled beef, the propagation of swine's flesh, and improvement in the art of making good bacon, so much wanted among us by the great destruction of pigs, too frequent at our table; which are no way comparable in taste or magnificence to a well-grown, fat, yearling child, which roasted whole will make a considerable figure at a lord mayor's feast or any other public entertainment. But this and many others I omit, being studious of brevity.

Supposing that 1000 families in this city would be constant

customers for infants' flesh, beside others who might have it at merry-meetings, particularly at weddings and christenings, I compute that Dublin would take off annually about 20,000 carcasses; and the rest of the kingdom (where probably they will be sold somewhat cheaper) the remaining 80,000.

I can think of no one objection that will possibly be raised against this proposal, unless it should be urged that the number of people will be thereby much lessened in the kingdom. This I freely own, and it was indeed one principal design in offering it to the world. I desire the reader will observe, that I calculate my remedy for this one individual kingdom of Ireland and for no other that ever was, is, or I think ever can be upon earth. Therefore let no man talk to me of other expedients: of taxing our absentees at 5s. a pound: of using neither clothes nor household furniture except what is of our own growth and manufacture: of utterly rejecting the materials and instruments that promote foreign luxury: of curing the expensiveness of pride, vanity, idleness, and gaming in our women: of introducing a vein of parsimony, prudence, and temperance: of learning to love our country, in the want of which we differ even from LAPLANDERS and the inhabitants of TOPINAMBOO: of quitting our animosities and factions, nor acting any longer like the Jews, who were murdering one another at the very moment their city was taken: of being a little cautious not to sell our country and conscience for nothing: of teaching landlords to have at least one degree of mercy toward their tenants: lastly, of putting a spirit of honesty, industry, and skill into our shopkeepers; who, if a resolution could now be taken to buy only our native goods, would immediately unite to cheat and exact upon us in the price, the measure, and the goodness, nor could ever yet be brought to make one fair proposal of just dealing, though often and earnestly invited to it.

Therefore I repeat, let no man talk to me of these and the like expedients, till he has at least some glimpse of hope that there will be ever some hearty and sincere attempt to put them in practice.

But as to myself, having been wearied out for many years with offering vain, idle, visionary thoughts, and at length utterly despairing of success, I fortunately fell upon this proposal; which, as it is wholly new, so it has something solid and real, of no expense and little trouble, full in our own power, and whereby we can incur no danger in disobliging ENGLAND. For this kind of commodity will not bear exportation, the flesh being of too tender a consistence to admit a long continuance in salt, although perhaps I could name a country which would be glad to eat up our whole nation without it.

After all, I am not so violently bent upon my own opinion as to reject any offer proposed by wise men, which shall be found equally innocent, cheap, easy, and effectual. But before something of that kind shall be advanced in contradiction to my scheme, and offering a better, I desire the author or authors will be pleased maturely to consider two points. First, as things now stand, how they will be able to find food and raiment for 100,000 useless mouths and backs. And secondly, there being a round million of creatures in human figure throughout this kingdom, whose whole subsistence put into a common stock would leave them in debt £2,000,000 sterling, adding those who are beggars by profession to the bulk of farmers, cottagers, and laborers, with the wives and children who are beggars in effect; I desire those politicians who dislike my overture, and may perhaps be so bold as to attempt an answer, that they will first ask the parents of these mortals, whether they would not at this day think it a great happiness to have been sold for food at a year old in the manner I prescribe, and thereby have avoided such a perpetual scene of misfortunes as they have since gone through by the oppression of landlords, the impossibility of paying rent without money or trade, the want of common sustenance, with neither house nor clothes to cover them from the inclemencies of the weather, and the most inevitable prospect of entailing the like or greater miseries upon their breed for ever.

I profess, in the sincerity of my heart, that I have not the least personal interest in endeavoring to promote this necessary work, having no other motive than the public good of my country, by advancing our trade, providing for infants, relieving the poor, and giving some pleasure to the rich. I have no children by which I can propose to get a single penny; the youngest being nine years old, and my wife past child-bearing.

Adventure in Cork[1]

BY Oliver Goldsmith (1728-1774)

MY DEAR MOTHER,

If you will sit down and calmly listen to what I say, you shall be fully resolved in every one of those many questions you have asked me. I went to Cork and converted my horse, which you prize so much higher than Fiddleback, into cash, took my passage in a ship bound for America, and at the same time paid the captain for my freight and all the other expenses of my voyage. But it so happened that the wind did not answer for three weeks; and you know, mother, that I could not command the elements. My misfortune was that when the wind served I happened to be with a party in the country, and my friend the captain never inquired after me, but set sail with as much indifference as if I had been on board. The remainder of my time I employed in the city and its environs, viewing everything curious; and you know no one can starve while he has money in his pocket.

Reduced, however, to my last two guineas, I began to think of my dear mother and friends whom I had left behind me, and so bought that generous beast Fiddleback and bade adieu to Cork with only five shillings in my pocket. This to be sure was a scanty allowance for man and horse towards a journey of above an hundred miles; but I did not despair, for I knew I must find friends on the road.

1 See Bibliographical Notes, p. 589.

I recollected particularly an old and faithful acquaintance I made at college, who had often and earnestly pressed me to spend a summer with him; and he lived but eight miles from Cork. This circumstance of vicinity he would expatiate on to me with particular emphasis.—"We shall," says he, "enjoy the delights of both city and country, and you shall command my stable and my purse."

However, upon the way I met a poor woman all in tears, who told me her husband had been arrested for a debt he was not able to pay, and that his eight children must now starve, bereaved as they were of his industry, which had been their only support. I thought myself at home, being not far from my good friend's house, and therefore parted with a moiety of all my store; and pray, mother, ought I not to have given her the other half-crown, for what she got would be of little use to her?—However, I soon arrived at the mansion of my affectionate friend, guarded by the vigilance of a huge mastiff, who flew at me and would have torn me to pieces, but for the assistance of a woman whose countenance was not less grim than that of the dog; yet she with great humanity relieved me from the jaws of this Cerberus, and was prevailed on to carry up my name to her master.

Without suffering me to wait long, my old friend, who was then recovering from a severe fit of sickness, came down in his night-cap, night-gown, and slippers, and embraced me with the most cordial welcome, showed me in, and after giving me a history of his indisposition, assured me that he considered himself as peculiarly fortunate in having under his roof the man he most loved on earth, and whose stay with him must, above all things, contribute to perfect his recovery. I now repented sorely I had not given the poor woman the other half-crown, as I thought all my bills of humanity would be punctually answered by this worthy man. I revealed to him my whole soul; and freely owned that I had but one half-crown in my pocket; but that now, like a ship after weathering out the storm, I considered myself secure in a safe and hospitable harbour. He made no answer, but walked about the room, rubbing his hands as one in a deep study. This I imputed to the sympathetic feelings of a tender heart, which increased my esteem for him, and as that increased I gave the most favourable interpretation to his silence. I construed it into delicacy of sentiment, as if he dreaded to wound my pride by expressing his commiseration in words, leaving his generous conduct to speak for itself.

It now approached six o'clock in the evening, and as I had eaten no breakfast, and as my spirits were raised, my appetite for dinner grew uncommonly keen. At length the old woman came into the room, with two plates, one spoon, and a dirty cloth, which she laid upon the table. This appearance, without increasing my spirits, did not diminish my appetite. My protectress soon returned with a small bowl of sago, a small porringer of sour milk, a loaf of stale brown bread, and the heel of an old cheese all over crawling with mites. My friend apologized that his illness obliged him to live on slops, and that better fare was not in the house; observing at the same time that a milk diet was certainly the most healthful; and at eight o'clock he again recommended a regular life, declaring that for his part he would *lie down with the lamb and rise with the lark*. My hunger was at this time so exceedingly sharp that I wished for another slice of the loaf, but was obliged to go to bed without even that refreshment.

The Lenten entertainment I had received made me resolve to depart as soon as possible; accordingly next morning, when I spoke of going, he did not oppose my resolution; he rather commended my design, adding some very sage counsel upon the occasion. "To be sure," said he, "the longer you stay away from your mother, the more you will grieve her and your other friends; and possibly they are already afflicted at hearing of this foolish expedition you have made." Notwithstanding all this, and without any hope of softening such a sordid heart, I again renewed the tale of my distress, and asking "how he thought I could travel above an hundred miles upon one half-crown?" I begged to borrow a single guinea, which I assured him should be repaid with thanks. "And you know, Sir," said I, "it is no more than I have often done for you." To which he firmly answered, "Why, look you, Mr. Goldsmith, that is neither here nor there. I have paid you all you ever lent me, and this sickness of mine has left me bare of cash. But I have bethought myself of a conveyance for you; sell your horse and I will furnish you a much better one to ride on." I readily grasped at his proposal, and begged to see the nag; on which he led me to his bed-chamber, and from under the bed he pulled out a stout oak stick. "Here he is," said he; "take this in your hand, and it will carry you to your mother's with more safety than such a horse as you ride." I was in doubt when I got it into my hand whether I should not, in the first place, apply it to his pate; but a rap at the street-door made the wretch fly to it, and when I returned to the parlour, he introduced me, as if nothing of the kind had happened, to the gentleman who entered, as Mr. Goldsmith, his most ingenious and worthy friend, of whom he had so often heard him speak with rapture. I could scarcely compose myself; and must have betrayed indignation in my mien to the stranger, who was a counsellor at law in the neighbourhood, a man of engaging aspect and polite address.

After spending an hour, he asked my friend and me to dine with him at his house. This I declined at first, as I wished to have no further communication with my old hospitable friend; but at the solicitation of both I at last consented, determined as I was by two motives; one, that I was prejudiced in favour of the looks and manner of the counsellor; and the other that I stood in need of a comfortable dinner. And there indeed I found every thing that I could wish, abundance without profusion, and elegance without affectation. In the evening when my old friend, who had eaten very plentifully at his neighbour's table, but talked again of lying down with the lamb, made a motion to me for retiring, our generous host requested I should take a bed with him, upon which I plainly told my old friend that he might go home and take care of the horse he had given me, but that I should never re-enter his doors. He went away with a laugh, leaving me to add this to the other little things the counsellor already knew of his plausible neighbour.

And now, my dear mother, I found sufficient to reconcile me to all my follies; for here I spent three whole days. The counsellor had two sweet girls to his daughters, who played enchantingly on the harpsichord; and yet it was but a melancholy pleasure I felt the first time I heard them; for that being the first time also that either of them had touched the instrument since their mother's death, I saw the tears in silence trickle down their father's cheeks. I every day endeavoured to go away, but every day was pressed and obliged to stay. On my going the counsellor offered me his purse, with a horse and servant to convey me home; but the latter I declined, and only took a guinea to bear my necessary expenses on the road.

OLIVER GOLDSMITH.

To Mrs. Anne Goldsmith, Ballymahon.

The Shan Van Vocht[1]

Oh! the French are on the sea,
  Says the Shan Van Vocht;
The French are on the sea,
  Says the Shan Van Vocht:
Oh! the French are in the Bay,
They'll be here without delay,
And the Orange will decay,
  Says the Shan Van Vocht.
    Oh! the French are in the Bay,
    They'll be here by break of day,
    And the Orange will decay,
      Says the Shan Van Vocht.

[1] This ballad and the two that follow deal with the abortive invasion of Ireland by the French in 1796 and again in 1798 when the landing was supplemented by the uprising of the United Irishmen. *Shan Van Vocht* means *poor old woman* and is a name for Ireland.

And where will they have their camp?
Says the Shan Van Vocht;
Where will they have their camp?
Says the Shan Van Vocht;
On the Curragh of Kildare,
The boys they will be there,
With their pikes in good repair,
Says the Shan Van Vocht.
To the Curragh of Kildare
The boys they will repair,
And Lord Edward[2] will be there,
Says the Shan Van Vocht.

Then what will the yeomen do?
Says the Shan Van Vocht;
What will the yeomen do?
Says the Shan Van Vocht;
What should the yeomen do
But throw off the Red and Blue,
And swear that they'll be true
To the Shan Van Vocht?
What should the yeomen do
But throw off the red and blue,
And swear that they'll be true
To the Shan Van Vocht?

---

[2] Lord Edward Fitzgerald, younger brother of the Duke of Leinster a rebel leader in the uprising of 1798.

And what colour will they wear?
  Says the Shan Van Vocht;
What colour will they wear?
  Says the Shan Van Vocht;
What colour should be seen
Where our fathers' homes have been,
But our own immortal Green?
  Says the Shan Van Vocht.
What colour should be seen
    Where our father's homes have been.
    But our own immortal Green?
      Says the Shan Van Vocht.

And will Ireland then be free?
  Says the Shan Van Vocht;
Will Ireland then be free?
  Says the Shan Van Vocht;
Yes! Ireland shall be free,
From the centre to the sea;
Then hurrah for Liberty!
  Says the Shan Van Vocht.
    Yes! Ireland shall be free,
    From the centre to the sea:
    Then hurrah for Liberty!
      Says the Shan Van Vocht.

18TH CENTURY.

The Wearin' o' the Green

O Paddy dear, an' did ye hear the news that's goin' round?
The shamrock is by law forbid to grow on Irish ground!
No more Saint Patrick's Day we'll keep, his colour can't be seen,
For there's a cruel law agin the wearin' o' the Green!
I met wid Napper Tandy,[1] and he took me by the hand,
And he said, "How's poor ould Ireland, and how does she stand?"
She's the most disthressful country that iver yet was seen,
For they're hangin' men an' women there for the wearin' o' the Green.

And if the colour we must wear is England's cruel Red,
Let it remind us of the blood that Ireland has shed;
Then pull the shamrock from your hat, and throw it on the sod,
And never fear, 'twill take root there, tho' under foot 'tis trod!
When law can stop the blades of grass from growin' as they grow,
And when the leaves in summer-time their colour dare not show,
Then I will change the colour, too, I wear in my caubeen,[2]
But till that day, plase God, I'll stick to wearin' o' the Green.

---

[1] James Napper Tandy was a Protestant merchant who defended the rights of Catholics, helped found the Society of United Irishmen, and escaped, first to America, then to the continent before he could be arrested for treason.

[2] Hat.

The Croppy Boy[1]

It was very early in the spring,
The birds did whistle and sweetly sing,
Changing their notes from tree to tree,
And the song they sang was Old Ireland free.

It was early in the night
The yeoman cavalry gave me a fright;
The yeoman cavalry was my downfall
And taken was I by Lord Cornwall.[2]

'Twas in the guard-house where I was laid
And in a parlor where I was tried;
My sentence passed and my courage low
When to Dungannon I was forced to go.

As I was passing by my father's door,
My brother William stood at the door;
My aged father stood at the door;
And my tender mother her hair she tore.

As I was walking up Wexford Street
My own first cousin I chanced to meet:
My own first cousin did me betray,
And for one bare guinea swore my life away.

My sister Mary heard the express,
She ran upstairs in her mourning-dress—
Five hundred guineas I will lay down,
To see my brother through Wexford town.

---

[1] A name given to the Wexford rebels of 1798 who were peasants and wore closely-cropped hair.

[2] Lord Cornwallis, viceroy and commander-in-chief in Ireland in 1798.

As I was walking up Wexford Hill,
Who could blame me to cry my fill?
I looked behind and I looked before,
But my tender mother I shall ne'er see more.

As I was mounted on the platform high,
My aged father was standing by;
My aged father did me deny,
And the name he gave me was the Croppy Boy.

It was in Dungannon this young man died,
And in Dungannon his body lies;
And you good Christians that do pass by
Just drop a tear for the Croppy Boy.

18TH CENTURY.

Thomas Moore (1779-1852)

Oh, Breathe Not His Name[1]

Oh, breathe not his name! let it sleep in the shade,
Where cold and unhonored his relics are laid;
Sad, silent, and dark be the tears that we shed,
As the night-dew that falls on the grass o'er his head.

But the night-dew that falls, though in silence it weeps,
Shall brighten with verdure the grave where he sleeps;
And the tear that we shed, though in secret it rolls,
Shall long keep his memory green in our souls.

---

[1] This lyric has generally been supposed to refer to Robert Emmet, the rebel leader of 1803.

The Harp That Once Through Tara's Halls

The harp that once through Tara's halls
  The soul of music shed,
Now hangs as mute on Tara's walls
  As if that soul were fled.
So sleeps the pride of former days,
  So glory's thrill is o'er,
And hearts that once beat high for praise
  Now feel that pulse no more!

No more to chiefs and ladies bright
  The harp of Tara swells;
The chord alone that breaks at night
  Its tale of ruin tells.
Thus Freedom now so seldom wakes,
  The only throb she gives
Is when some heart indignant breaks,
  To show that still she lives.

The Meeting of the Waters

There is not in the wide world a valley so sweet
As that vale in whose bosom the bright waters meet;
O, the last rays of feeling and life must depart,
Ere the bloom of that valley shall fade from my heart.

Yet it was not that nature had shed o'er the scene
Her purest of crystal and brightest of green;
'Twas *not* her soft magic of streamlet or hill,
O, no, it was something more exquisite still.

'Twas that friends, the belov'd of my bosom, were near,
Who made every dear scene of enchantment more dear,
And who felt how the best charms of nature improve,
When we see them reflected from looks that we love.

Sweet vale of Avoca! how calm could I rest
In thy bosom of shade, with the friends I love best,
Where the storms that we feel in this cold world should cease,
And our hearts, like thy waters, be mingled in peace.

The Song of Fionnuala[1]

Silent, O Moyle, be the roar of thy water,
  Break not, ye breezes, your chain of repose,
While, murmuring mournfully, Lir's lonely daughter
  Tells to the night star her tale of woes.
When shall the swan, her death note singing,
  Sleep, with wings in darkness furl'd?
When will heaven, its sweet bell ringing,
  Call my spirit from this stormy world?

[1] Fionnuala, the daughter of Lir, was changed into a swan along with her three brothers by a cruel step-mother. They had the power of speech and the gift of singing and for three hundred years they sang to the men of Ireland. When finally they were captured by the king of Connaught they were changed back into three old men and an old woman and died. "The Tragedy of the Children of Lir," with two other stories, is preserved in a manuscript of the 15th or 16th century entitled *The Three Sorrowful Stories*.

Sadly, O Moyle, to thy winter wave weeping,
  Fate bids me languish long ages away;
Yet still in her darkness doth Erin lie sleeping,
  Still doth the pure light its dawning delay.
When will that daystar, mildly springing,
  Warm our isle with peace and love?
When will heaven, its sweet bell ringing,
  Call my spirit to the fields above?

She Is Far from the Land[1]

She is far from the land where her young hero sleeps,
  And lovers are round her, sighing:
But coldly she turns from their gaze, and weeps,
  For her heart in his grave is lying.

She sings the wild song of her dear native plains,
  Every note which he loved awaking;—
Ah! little they think who delight in her strains,
  How the heart of the Minstrel is breaking.

He had lived for his love, for his country he died,
  They were all that to life had entwined him;
Nor soon shall the tears of his country be dried,
  Nor long will his love stay behind him.

Oh! make her a grave where the sun-beams rest,
  When they promise a glorious morrow;
They'll shine o'er her sleep, like a smile from the West,
  From her own loved island of sorrow.

---

[1] This lyric commemorates the love of Sarah Curran for Robert Emmet.

The Minstrel Boy

The Minstrel Boy to the war is gone,
In the ranks of death you'll find him;
His father's sword he has girded on,
And his wild harp slung behind him.—
"Land of song!" said the warrior-bard,
"Though all the world betray thee,
One sword, at least, thy rights shall guard,
One faithful harp shall praise thee!"

The Minstrel fell!—but the foeman's chain
Could not bring his proud soul under;
The harp he loved ne'er spoke again,
For he tore its cords asunder;
And said, "No chains shall sully thee,
Thou soul of love and bravery!
Thy songs were made for the brave and free,
They shall never sound in slavery!"

Dear Harp of my Country

Dear Harp of my Country! in darkness I found thee,
The cold chain of silence had hung o'er thee long,
When proudly, my own Island Harp, I unbound thee,
And gave all thy chords to light, freedom, and song!
The warm lay of love and the light note of gladness
Have waken'd thy fondest, thy liveliest thrill;
But, so oft hast thou echoed the deep sigh of sadness,
That ev'n in thy mirth it will steal from thee still.

Dear Harp of my Country! farewell to thy numbers,
This sweet wreath of song is the last we shall twine!
Go, sleep with sunshine of Fame on thy slumbers,
Till touch'd by some hand less unworthy than mine;
If the pulse of the patriot, soldier, or lover,
Have throbb'd at our lay, 'tis thy glory alone;
I was *but* as the wind, passing heedlessly over,
And all the wild sweetness I wak'd was thy own.

The Hedge School

BY William Carleton (1794-1869)

THE VILLAGE of Findramore was situated at the foot of a long green hill, the outline of which formed a low arch, as it rose to the eye against the horizon. This hill was studded with clumps of beeches, and sometimes enclosed as a meadow. In the month of July, when the grass on it was long, many an hour have I spent in solitary enjoyment, watching the wavy motion produced upon its pliant surface by the sunny winds, or the flight of the cloud-shadows, like gigantic phantoms, as they swept rapidly over it, whilst the murmur of the rocking trees, and the glancing of their bright leaves in the sun, produced a heartfelt pleasure, the very memory of which rises in my imagination like some fading recollection of a brighter world.

At the foot of this hill ran a clear, deep-banked river, bounded on one side by a slip of rich, level meadow, and on the other by a kind of common for the village geese, whose white feathers, during the summer season lay scattered over its green surface. It was also the play-ground for the boys of the village school; for there ran that part of the river which, with very correct judgment, the urchins had selected as their bathing-place. A little slope, or watering-ground in the bank, brought them to the edge of the stream, where the bottom fell away into the fearful depths of the whirlpool, under the hanging oak on the other bank. Well do I remember the first time I ventured to swim across it, and even yet do I see, in imagination, the two bunches of water flaggons on which the inexperienced swimmers trusted themselves in the water.

About two hundred yards above this, the *boreen*,[1] which led from the village to the main road, crossed the river, by one of those old narrow bridges whose arches rise like round ditches across the road—an almost impassable barrier to horse and car. On passing the bridge, in a northern direction, you found a range of low thatched houses on each side of the road: and if one o'clock, the hour of dinner, drew near, you might observe columns of blue smoke curling up from a row of chimneys, some made of wicker creels plastered over with a rich coat of mud; some, of old, narrow, bottomless tubs; and others, with a greater appearance of taste, ornamented with thick, circular ropes of straw, sewed together like bees' skeps,[2] with the peel of a brier; and many having nothing but the open vent above. But the smoke by no means escaped by its legitimate aperture, for you might observe little clouds of it bursting out of the doors and windows; the panes of the latter being mostly stopped at other times with old hats and rags, were now left entirely open for the purpose of giving it a free escape.

Before the doors, on right and left, was a series of dunghills, each with its concomitant sink of green, rotten water; and if it happened that a stout-looking woman, with watery eyes, and a yellow cap hung loosely upon her matted locks, came, with a chubby urchin on one arm, and a pot of dirty water in her hand, its unceremonious ejection in the aforesaid sink would be apt to send you up the village with your finger and thumb (for what purpose you would yourself perfectly understand) closely, but not knowingly, applied to your nostrils. But, independently of this, you would be apt to have other

[1] A little road.
[2] Hives.

reasons for giving your horse, whose heels are by this time surrounded by a dozen of barking curs, and the same number of shouting urchins, a pretty sharp touch of the spurs, as well as for complaining bitterly of the odour of the atmosphere. It is no landscape without figures; and you might notice, if you are, as I suppose you to be, a man of observation, in every sink as you pass along, a "slip-of-a-pig," stretched in the middle of the mud, the very *beau ideal* of luxury, giving occasionally a long, luxuriant grunt, highly expressive of his enjoyment; or, perhaps, an old farrower, lying in indolent repose, with half a dozen young ones jostling each other for their draught, and punching her belly with their little snouts, reckless of the fumes they are creating; whilst the loud crow of the cock, as he confidently flaps his wings on his own dunghill, gives the warning note for the hour of dinner.

As you advance, you will also perceive several faces thrust out of the doors, and rather than miss a sight of you, a grotesque visage peeping by a short cut through the paneless windows—or a tattered female flying to snatch up her urchin that has been tumbling itself, heels up, in the dust of the road, lest "the gintleman's horse might ride over it"; and if you happen to look behind, you may observe a shaggy-headed youth in tattered frize,[1] with one hand thrust indolently in his breast, standing at the door in conversation with the inmates, a broad grin of sarcastic ridicule on his face, in the act of breaking a joke or two upon yourself, or your horse; or, perhaps, your jaw may be saluted with a lump of clay, just hard enough not to fall asunder as it flies, cast by some ragged gorsoon[2] from behind a hedge, who squats himself in a ridge of corn to avoid detection.

Seated upon a hob at the door, you may observe a toil-worn man, without coat or waistcoat; his red, muscular, sunburnt shoulder peering through the remnant of a shirt, mending his

[1] I.e. frieze—a kind of coarse woollen cloth, with a nap, usually on one side only. NED

[2] A boy; from the French *garçon*.

shoes with a piece of twisted flax, called a *lingel*, or, perhaps, sewing two footless stockings (or *martyeens*) to his coat, as a substitute for sleeves.

In the gardens, which are usually fringed with nettles, you will see a solitary labourer, working with that carelessness and apathy that characterise an Irishman when he labours *for himself*—leaning upon his spade to look after you, and glad of any excuse to be idle.

The houses, however, are not all such as I have described—far from it. You see here and there, between the more humble cabins, a stout, comfortable-looking farm-house, with ornamental thatching and well-glazed windows; adjoining to which is a hay-yard, with five or six large stacks of corn, well-trimmed and roped, and a fine, yellow, weather-beaten old hay-rick, half cut—not taking into account twelve or thirteen circular strata of stones, that mark out the foundations on which others has been raised. Neither is the rich smell of oaten or wheaten bread, which the good wife is baking on the griddle, unpleasant to your nostrils; nor would the bubbling of a large pot, in which you might see, should you chance to enter, a prodigious square of fat, yellow, and almost transparent bacon tumbling about, to be an unpleasant object; truly, as it hangs over a large fire, with well-swept hearthstone, it is in good keeping with the white settle and chairs, and the dresser with noggins, wooden trenchers, and pewter dishes, perfectly clean, and as well polished as a French courtier.

As you leave the village, you have, to the left, a view of the hill which I have already described, and to the right a level expanse of fertile country, bounded by a good view of respectable mountains, peering decently into the sky; and in a line that forms an acute angle from the point of the road where you ride, is a delightful valley, in the bottom of which shines a pretty lake; and a little beyond, on the slope of a green hill, rises a splendid house, surrounded by a park, well-wooded and stocked with deer. You have now topped the little hill above the village, and a straight line of level road, a mile long, goes forward to a country town, which lies immediately behind that white church with its spire cutting into the sky, before you. You descend on the other side, and, having advanced a few perches, look to the left, where you see a long, thatched chapel, only distinguished from a dwelling-house by its want of chimneys, and a small stone cross that stands on the top of the eastern gable; behind it is a graveyard; and beside it a snug public-house, well white-washed; then, to the right, you observe a door apparently in the side of a clay bank, which rises considerably above the pavement of the road. What! you ask yourself, can this be a human habitation?—but ere you have time to answer the question, a confused buzz of voices from within reaches your ear, and the appearance of a little "gorsoon," with a red, close-cropped head and Milesian[1] face, having in his hand a short, white stick, or the thigh-bone of a horse, which you at once recognise as "the pass" of a village school, gives you the full information. He has an ink-horn, covered with leather, dangling at the button-hole (for he has long since played away the buttons) of his frize jacket—his mouth is circumscribed with a streak of ink—his pen is stuck knowingly behind his ear—his shins are dotted over with fire-blisters, black, red, and blue—on each heel a kibe—his "leather crackers," *videlicet*—breeches, shrunk up upon him, and only reaching as far down as the caps of his knees. Having spied you, he places his hand over his brows, to throw back the dazzling light of the sun, and peers at you from under it, till he breaks out into a laugh, exclaiming, half to himself, half to you,

"You a gintleman!—no, nor one of your breed never was, you procthorin' thief, you!"

You are now immediately opposite the door of the seminary, when half a dozen of those seated next it notice you.

"Oh, sir, here's a gintleman on a horse!—masther, sir, here's a gintleman on a horse, wid boots and spurs on him, that's looking in at us."

---

[1] The Irish were fond of describing themselves as Milesians, i.e., the descendants of the sons of Mil, legendary conquerors of Ireland.

"Silence!" exclaims the master; "back from the door; boys rehearse; every one of you rehearse, I say, you Bœotians, till the gintleman goes past!"

"I want to go out, if you plase, sir."

"No, you don't, Phelim."

"I do, indeed, sir."

"What!—is it afther conthradictin' me you'd be? Don't you see the porter's' out, and you can't go."

"Well, 'tis Mat Meehan has it, sir: and he's out this half-hour, sir; I can't stay in, sir—iphfff—iphfff!"

"You want to be idling your time looking at the gintleman, Phelim."

"No, indeed, sir—iphfff!"

"Phelim, I know you of ould—go to your sate. I tell you, Phelim, you were born for the encouragement of the hemp manufacture, and you'll die promoting it."

In the meantime, the master puts his head out of the door, his body stooped to a "half bend"—a phrase, and the exact curve which it forms, I leave for the present to your own sagacity—and surveys you until you pass. That is an Irish hedge-school, and the personage who follows you with his eye, a hedge-schoolmaster.

James Clarence Mangan (1803-1849)

A Vision of Connaught in the Thirteenth Century

I walked entranced
Through a land of Morn;
The sun, with wondrous excess of light,
Shone down and glanced
Over seas of corn

And lustrous gardens aleft and right
Even in the clime
Of resplendent Spain,
Beams no such sun upon such a land;
But it was the time,
'Twas in the reign,
Of Cáhal Mór of the Wine-red Hand.[1]

Anon stood nigh
By my side a man
Of princely aspect and port sublime.
Him queried I—
"O, my Lord and Khan,
What clime is this, and what golden time?"
When he—"The clime
Is a clime to praise,
The clime is Erin's, the green and bland;
And it is the time,
These be the days,
Of Cáhal Mór of the Wine-red Hand!"

Then saw I thrones,
And circling fires,
And a Dome rose near me, as by a spell,
Whence flowed the tones
Of silver lyres,

[1] Cathal of the Red Hand was the illegitimate son of Turlogh Mor O'Conor, King of Connaught. When Turlogh's wife by magic turned one of Cathal's hands red, he fled and took service as a farm hand. When Turlogh died Cathal made his identity known by exhibiting his red hand and established a claim to the throne. There were other claimants however and Cathal did not become king until 1202. In 1224 he abdicated in favor of his son and with his bard, Morrogh O'Daly, entered the abbey of Grey Friars of Knockmoy which he had founded in 1189. He instituted tithes, built magnificent abbeys and was apparently a favorite with the poets and chroniclers.

And many voices in wreathèd swell;
And their thrilling chime
Fell on mine ears
As the heavenly hymn of an angel-band—
"It is now the time,
These be the years,
Of Cáhal Mór of the Wine-red Hand!"

I sought the hall,
And, behold!—a change
From light to darkness, from joy to woe!
King, nobles, all,
Looked aghast and strange;
The minstrel-group sat in dumbest show!
Had some great crime
Wrought this dread amaze,
This terror? None seemed to understand
'Twas then the time
We were in the days,
Of Cáhal Mór of the Wine-red Hand.

I again walked forth;
But lo! the sky
Showed fleckt with blood, and an alien sun
Glared from the north,
And there stood on high,
Amid his shorn beams, a skeleton!
It was by the stream
Of the castled Maine,
One Autumn eve, in the Teuton's land,
That I dreamed this dream
Of the time and reign
Of Cáhal Mór of the Wine-red Hand!

To My Native Land

AWAKE! arise! shake off thy dreams!
  Thou art not what thou wert of yore:
Of all those rich, those dazzling beams,
  That once illum'd thine aspect o'er
Show me a solitary one
Whose glory is not quenched and gone.

The harp remaineth where it fell,
  With mouldering frame and broken chord;
Around the song there hangs no spell—
  No laurel wreath entwines the sword;
And startlingly the footstep falls
Along thy dim and dreary halls.

When other men in future years,
  In wonder ask, how this could be?
Then answer only by thy tears,
  That ruin fell on thine and thee;
Because thyself wouldst have it so—
Because thou welcomedst the blow!

To stamp dishonour on thy brow
  Was not within the power of earth;
And art thou agonised, when now
  The hour that lost thee all thy worth
And turned thee to the thing thou art,
Rushes upon thy bleeding heart?

Weep, weep, degraded one—the deed,
  The desperate deed was all thine own:
Thou madest more than maniac speed
  To hurl thine honours from their throne.
Thine honours fell, and when they fell
The nations rang thy funeral knell.

Well may thy sons be seared in soul,
  Their groans be deep by night and day;
Till day and night forget to roll,
  Their noblest hopes shall morn decay—
Their freshest flowers shall die by blight—
Their brightest sun shall set at night.

The stranger, as he treads thy sod,
  And views thy universal wreck,
May execrate the foot that trod
  Triumphant on a prostrate neck;
But what is that to thee? Thy woes
May hope in vain for pause or close.

Awake! arise! shake off thy dreams!
  'Tis idle all to talk of power,
And fame and glory—these are themes
  Befitting ill so dark an hour;
'Till miracles be wrought for thee,
Nor fame nor glory shalt thou see.

Thou art forsaken by the earth,
  Which makes a byword of thy name;
Nations, and thrones, and powers whose birth
  As yet is not, shall rise to fame,
Shall flourish and may fail—but thou
Shalt linger as thou lingerest now.

And till all earthly power shall wane,
  And Time's grey pillar, groaning, fall;
Thus shall it be, and still in vain
  Thou shalt essay to burst the thrall
Which binds, in fetters forged by fate,
The wreck and ruin of what once was great.

The Hunt

BY Charles Lever (1806-1872)

. . . Mr. Blake and his family, though estranged from my uncle for several years past, had been always most kind and good-natured to me; and although I could not, with propriety, have cultivated any close intimacy with them, I had every reason to suppose that they entertained towards me nothing but sentiments of good-will. The head of the family was a Galway squire of the oldest and most genuine stock, a great sportsman, a negligent farmer, and most careless father; he looked upon a fox as an infinitely more precious part of the creation than a French governess, and thought that riding well with hounds was a far better gift than all the learning of a Porson.[1] His daughters were after his own heart,—the best-tempered, least-educated, most high-spirited, gay, dashing, ugly girls in the county, ready to ride over a four-foot paling without a saddle, and to dance the "Wind that shakes the barley" for four consecutive hours, against all the officers that their hard fate, and the Horse Guards, ever condemned to Galway.

The mamma was only remarkable for her liking for whist, and her invariable good fortune thereat,—a circumstance the world were agreed in ascribing less to the blind goddess than her own natural endowments.

1 Richard Porson (1759-1808), an English scholar.

Lastly, the heir of the house was a stripling of about my own age, whose accomplishments were limited to selling spavined and broken-winded horses to the infantry officers, playing a safe game at billiards, and acting as jackal-general to his sisters at balls, providing them with a sufficiency of partners, and making a strong fight for a place at the supper-table for his mother. These fraternal and filial traits, more honored at home than abroad, had made Mr. Matthew Blake a rather well-known individual in the neighborhood where he lived.

Though Mr. Blake's property was ample, and strange to say for his county, unencumbered, the whole air and appearance of his house and grounds betrayed anything rather than a sufficiency of means. The gate lodge was a miserable mud-hovel with a thatched and falling roof; the gate itself, a wooden contrivance, one half of which was boarded and the other railed; the avenue was covered with weeds, and deep with ruts; and the clumps of young plantation, which had been planted and fenced with care, were now open to the cattle, and either totally uprooted or denuded of their bark and dying. The lawn, a handsome one of some forty acres, had been devoted to an exercise-ground for training horses, and was cut up by their feet beyond all semblance of its original destination; and the house itself, a large and venerable structure of above a century old, displayed every variety of contrivance, as well as the usual one of glass, to exclude the weather. The hall-door hung by a single hinge, and required three persons each morning and evening to open and shut it; the remainder of the day it lay pensively open; the steps which led to it were broken and falling; and the whole aspect of things without was ruinous in the extreme. Within, matters were somewhat better, for though the furniture was old, and none of it clean, yet an appearance of comfort was evident; and the large grate, blazing with its pile of red-hot turf, the deep-cushioned chairs, the old black mahogany dinner-table, and the soft carpet, albeit deep with dust, were not to be despised on a winter's evening, after a hard day's run with the "Blazers." Here it was, however, that Mr. Philip Blake had dispensed his hospitalities for above fifty years, and his father before him; and here, with a retinue of servants as *gauches* and ill-ordered as all about them, was he accustomed to invite all that the county possessed of rank and wealth, among which the officers quartered in his neighborhood were never neglected, the Miss Blakes having as decided a taste for the army as any young ladies of the west of Ireland; and while the Galway squire, with his cords and tops, was detailing the latest news from Ballinasloe in one corner, the dandy from St. James's Street might be seen displaying more arts of seductive flattery in another than his most accurate *insouciance* would permit him to practise in the elegant salons of London or Paris, and the same man who would have "cut his brother," for a solecism of dress or equipage, in Bond Street, was now to be seen quietly domesticated, eating family dinners, rolling silk for the young ladies, going down the middle in a country dance, and even descending to the indignity of long whist at "tenpenny" points, with only the miserable consolation that the company were not honest.

It was upon a clear frosty morning, when a bright blue sky and a sharp but bracing air seem to exercise upon the feelings a sense no less pleasurable than the balmiest breeze and warmest sun of summer, that I whipped my leader short round, and entered the precincts of "Gurt-na-Morra." As I proceeded along the avenue, I was struck by the slight traces of repairs here and there evident,—a gate or two that formerly had been parallel to the horizon had been raised to the perpendicular; some ineffectual efforts at paint were also perceptible upon the palings; and, in short, everything seemed to have undergone a kind of attempt at improvement.

When I reached the door, instead of being surrounded, as of old, by a tribe of menials frieze-coated, bare-headed, and bare-legged, my presence was announced by a tremendous ringing of bells from the hands of an old functionary in a very formidable livery, who peeped at me through the hall-window, and whom, with the greatest difficulty, I recognized as my quondam acquaintance, the butler. His wig alone would have graced a king's counsel; and the high collar of his coat, and the stiff pillory of his cravat denoted an eternal adieu to so humble a vocation as drawing a cork. Before I had time for any conjecture as to the altered circumstances about, the activity of my friend at the bell had surrounded me with "four others worse than himself," at least they were exactly similarly attired; and probably from the novelty of their costume, and the restraints of so unusual a thing as dress, were as perfectly unable to assist themselves or others as the Court of Aldermen would be were they to rig out in plate armor of the fourteenth century. How much longer I might have gone on conjecturing the reasons for the masquerade around, I cannot say; but my servant, an Irish disciple of my uncle's, whispered in my ear, "It's a red-breeches day, Master Charles,—they'll have the hoith of company in the house." From the phrase, it needed little explanation to inform me that it was one of those occasions on which Mr. Blake attired all the hangers-on of his house in livery, and that great preparations were in progress for a more than usually splendid reception.

In the next moment I was ushered into the breakfast-room, where a party of above a dozen persons were most gayly enjoying all the good cheer for which the house had a well-deserved repute. After the usual shaking of hands and hearty greetings were over, I was introduced in all form to Sir George Dashwood, a tall and singularly handsome man of about fifty, with an undress military frock and ribbon. His reception of me was somewhat strange; for as they mentioned my relationship to Godfrey O'Malley, he smiled slightly, and whispered something to Mr. Blake, who replied, "Oh, no, no; not the least. A mere boy; and besides—" What he added I lost, for at that moment Nora Blake was presenting me to Miss Dashwood.

If the sweetest blue eyes that every beamed beneath a forehead of snowy whiteness, over which dark brown and waving hair fell less in curls than masses of locky richness, could only have known what wild work they were making of my poor heart, Miss Dashwood, I trust, would have looked at her teacup or her muffin rather than at me, as she actually did on that fatal morning. If I were to judge from her costume, she had only just arrived, and the morning air had left upon her cheek a bloom that contributed greatly to the effect of her lovely countenance. Although very young, her form had all the roundness of womanhood; while her gay and sprightly manner indicated all the *sans gêne* which only very young girls possess, and which, when tempered with perfect good taste, and accompanied by beauty and no small share of talent, forms an irresistible power of attraction.

Beside her sat a tall, handsome man of about five-and-thirty or perhaps forty years of age, with a most soldierly air, who as I was presented to him scarcely turned his head, and gave me a half-nod of very unequivocal coldness. There are moments in life in which the heart is, as it were, laid bare to any chance or casual impression with a wondrous sensibility of pleasure or its opposite. This to me was one of those; and as I turned from the lovely girl, who had received me with a marked courtesy, to the cold air and repelling *hauteur* of the dark-browed captain, the blood rushed throbbing to my forehead; and as I walked to my place at the table, I eagerly sought his eye, to return him a look of defiance and disdain, proud and contemptuous as his own. Captain Hammersley, however, never took further notice of me, but continued to recount, for the amusement of those about him, several excellent stories of his military career, which, I confess, were heard with every test of delight by all save me. One thing galled me particularly,—and how easy is it, when you have begun by disliking a person, to supply food for your antipathy,—all his allusions to his military life were coupled with half-hinted and ill-concealed sneers at civilians of every kind, as though every man not a soldier were absolutely unfit for common intercourse with the world, still more for any favorable reception in ladies' society.

The young ladies of the family were a well-chosen auditory, for their admiration of the army extended from the Life Guards to the Veteran Battalion, the Sappers and Miners included; and as Miss Dashwood was the daughter of a soldier, she of course coincided in many of, if not all, his opinions. I turned towards my neighbor, a Clare gentleman, and tried to engage him in conversation, but he was breathlessly attending to the captain. On my left sat Matthew Blake, whose eyes were firmly riveted upon the same person, and who heard his marvels with an interest scarcely inferior to that of his sisters. Annoyed and in ill-temper, I ate my breakfast in silence, and resolved that the first moment I could obtain a hearing from Mr. Blake I would open my negotiation, and take my leave at once of Gurt-na-Morra.

We all assembled in a large room, called by courtesy the library, when breakfast was over; and then it was that Mr. Blake, taking me aside, whispered, "Charley, it's right I should inform you that Sir George Dashwood there is the Commander of the Forces, and is come down here at this moment to—" What for, or how it should concern me, I was not to learn; for at that critical instant my informant's attention was called off by Captain Hammersley asking if the hounds were to hunt that day.

"My friend Charley here is the best authority upon that matter," said Mr. Blake, turning towards me.

"They are to try the Priest's meadows," said I, with an air of some importance; "but if your guests desire a day's sport, I'll send word over to Brackely to bring the dogs over here, and we are sure to find a fox in your cover."

"Oh, then, by all means," said the captain, turning towards Mr. Blake, and addressing himself to him,—"by all means; and Miss Dashwood, I'm sure, would like to see the hounds throw off."

Whatever chagrin the first part of his speech caused me, the latter set my heart a-throbbing; and I hastened from the room to despatch a messenger to the huntsman to come over to Gurt-na-Morra, and also another to O'Malley Castle to bring my best horse and my riding equipments as quickly as possible.

"Matthew, who is this captain?" said I, as young Blake met me in the hall.

"Oh, he is the aide-de-camp of General Dashwood. A nice fellow, is n't he?"

"I don't know what you may think," said I, "but I take

him for the most impertinent, impudent, supercilious—"

The rest of my civil speech was cut short by the appearance of the very individual in question, who, with his hands in his pockets and a cigar in his mouth, sauntered forth down the steps, taking no more notice of Matthew Blake and myself than the two fox-terriers that followed at his heels.

However anxious I might be to open negotiations on the subject of my mission, for the present the thing was impossible; for I found that Sir George Dashwood was closeted closely with Mr. Blake, and resolved to wait till evening, when chance might afford me the opportunity I desired.

As the ladies had retired to dress for the hunt, and as I felt no peculiar desire to ally myself with the unsocial captain, I accompanied Matthew to the stable to look after the cattle, and make preparations for the coming sport.

"There's Captain Hammersley's mare," said Matthew, as he pointed out a highly bred but powerful English hunter. "She came last night; for as he expected some sport, he sent his horses from Dublin on purpose. The others will be here today."

"What is his regiment?" said I, with an appearance of carelessness, but in reality feeling curious to know if the captain was a cavalry or infantry officer.

"The —th Light Dragoons."

"You never saw him ride?" said I.

"Never; but his groom there says he leads the way in his own country."

"And where may that be?"

"In Leicestershire, no less," said Matthew.

"Does he know Galway?"

"Never was in it before. It's only this minute he asked Moses Daly if the ox-fences were high here."

"Ox-fences! Then he does not know what a wall is?"

"Devil a bit; but we'll teach him."

"That we will," said I, with as bitter a resolution to impart the instruction as ever schoolmaster did to whip Latin grammar into one of the great unbreeched.

"But I had better send the horses down to the Mill," said Matthew; "we'll draw that cover first."

So saying, he turned towards the stable, while I sauntered alone towards the road by which I expected the huntsman. I had not walked half a mile before I heard the yelping of the dogs, and a little farther on I saw old Brackely coming along at a brisk trot, cutting the hounds on each side, and calling after the stragglers.

"Did you see my horse on the road, Brackely?" said I.

"I did, Misther Charles; and troth, I'm sorry to see him. Sure yerself knows better than to take out the Badger, the best steeple-chaser in Ireland, in such a country as this,—nothing but awkward stone-fences, and not a foot of sure ground in the whole of it."

"I know it well, Brackely; but I have my reasons for it."

"Well, may be you have; what cover will your honor try first?"

"They talk of the Mill," said I; "but I'd much rather try Morran-a-Gowl."

"Morran-a-Gowl! Do you want to break your neck entirely?"

"No, Brackely, not mine."

"Whose, then, alannah?"

"An English captain's, the devil fly away with him! He's come down here to-day, and from all I can see is a most impudent fellow; so, Brackely—"

"I understand. Well, leave it to me; and though I don't like the only deer-park wall on the hill, we'll try it this morning with the blessing. I'll take him down by Woodford, over the Devil's Mouth,—it's eighteen foot wide this minute with the late rains,—into the four callows; then over the stone walls, down to Dangan; then take a short cast up the hill, blow him a bit, and give him the park wall at the top. You must come in then fresh, and give him the whole run home over Sleibhmich. The Badger knows it all, and takes the road always in a fly,—a mighty distressing thing for the horse that follows, more particularly if he does not understand a stony country. Well, if he lives through this, give him the sunk fence and the stone wall at Mr. Blake's clover-field, for the hounds will run into the fox about there; and though we never ride that leap since Mr. Malone broke his neck at it, last October, yet upon an occasion like this, and for the honor of Galway—"

"To be sure, Brackely; and here's a guinea for you, and now trot on towards the house. They must not see us together, or they might suspect something. But, Brackely," said I, calling out after him, "if he rides at all fair, what's to be done?"

"Troth, then, myself does n't know. There is nothing so bad west of Athlone. Have ye a great spite again him?"

"I have," said I, fiercely.

"Could ye coax a fight out of him?"

"That's true," said I; "and now ride on as fast as you can."

Brackely's last words imparted a lightness to my heart and my step, and I strode along a very different man from what I had left the house half an hour previously.

Although we had not the advantages of a southerly wind and cloudy sky, the day towards noon became strongly overcast, and promised to afford us good scenting weather; and as we assembled at the meet, mutual congratulations were exchanged upon the improved appearance of the day. Young Blake had provided Miss Dashwood with a quiet and well-trained horse, and his sisters were all mounted as usual upon their own animals, giving to our turnout quite a gay and lively aspect. I myself came to cover upon a hackney, having sent Badger with a groom, and longed ardently for the moment when, casting the skin of my great-coat and overalls, I should appear before the world in my well-appointed "cords and tops." Captain Hammersley had not as yet made his appearance, and many conjectures were afloat as to whether "he might have missed the road, or changed his mind," or "forgot all about it," as Miss Dashwood hinted.

"Who, pray, pitched upon this cover?" said Caroline Blake, as she looked with a practised eye over the country on either side.

"There is no chance of a fox late in the day at the Mill," said the huntsman, inventing a lie for the occasion.

"Then of course you never intend us to see much of the sport; for after you break cover, you are entirely lost to us."

"I thought you always followed the hounds," said Miss Dashwood, timidly.

"Oh, to be sure we do, in any common country, but here it is out of the question; the fences are too large for any one, and if I am not mistaken, these gentlemen will not ride far over this. There, look yonder, where the river is rushing down the hill: that stream, widening as it advances, crosses the cover nearly midway,—well, they must clear that; and then you may see these walls of large loose stones nearly five feet in height. This is the usual course the fox takes, unless he heads towards the hills and goes towards Dangan, and then there's an end of it; for the deer-park wall is usually a pull up to every one except perhaps, to our friend Charley yonder, who has tried his fortune against drowning more than once there."

"Look, here he comes," said Matthew Blake, "and looking splendidly too,—a little too much in flesh perhaps, if anything."

"Captain Hammersley!" said the four Miss Blakes, in a breath. "Where is he?"

"No; it's the Badger I'm speaking of," said Matthew, laughing, and pointing with his finger towards a corner of the field where my servant was leisurely throwing down a wall about two feet high to let him pass.

"Oh, how handsome! What a charger for a dragoon!" said Miss Dashwood.

Any other mode of praising my steed would have been much more acceptable. The word "dragoon" was a thorn in my tenderest part that rankled and lacerated at every stir. In a moment I was in the saddle, and scarcely seated when at once all the *mauvais honte* of boyhood left me, and I felt every inch a man. I often look back to that moment of my life, and comparing it with similar ones, cannot help acknowledging how purely is the self-possession which so often wins success the result of some slight and trivial association. My confidence in my horsemanship suggested moral courage of a very different kind; and I felt that Charles O'Malley curveting upon a thorough-bred, and the same man ambling upon a shelty, were two and very dissimilar individuals.

"No chance of the captain," said Matthew, who had returned from a *reconnaissance* upon the road; "and after all it's a pity, for the day is getting quite favorable."

While the young ladies formed pickets to look out for the gallant *militaire*, I seized the opportunity of prosecuting my acquaintance with Miss Dashwood, and even in the few and passing observations that fell from her, learned how very different an order of being she was from all I had hitherto seen of country belles. A mixture of courtesy with *naïveté*; a wish to please, with a certain feminine gentleness, that always flatters a man, and still more a boy that fain would be one,—gained momentarily more and more upon me, and put me also on my mettle to prove to my fair companion that I was not altogether a mere uncultivated and unthinking creature, like the remainder of those about me.

"Here he is at last," said Helen Blake, as she cantered across a field waving her handkerchief as a signal to the captain, who was now seen approaching at a brisk trot.

As he came along, a small fence intervened; he pressed his horse a little, and as he kissed hands to the fair Helen, cleared it in a bound, and was in an instant in the midst of us.

"He sits his horse like a man, Misther Charles," said the old huntsman; "troth, we must give him the worst bit of it."

Captain Hammersley was, despite all the critical acumen with which I canvassed him, the very beau-ideal of a gentleman rider; indeed, although a very heavy man, his powerful English thorough-bred, showing not less bone than blood, took away all semblance of overweight; his saddle was well fitting and well placed, as also was his large and broad-reined snaffle; his own costume of black coat, leathers, and tops was in perfect keeping, and even to his heavy-handled hunting-whip I could find nothing to cavil at. As he rode up he paid his respects to the ladies in his usual free and easy manner, expressed some surprise, but no regret, at hearing that he was late, and never deigning any notice of Matthew or myself, took his place beside

Miss Dashwood, with whom he conversed in a low undertone.

"There they go!" said Matthew, as five or six dogs, with their heads up, ran yelping along a furrow, then stopped, howled again, and once more set off together. In an instant all was commotion in the little valley below us. The huntsman, with his hand to his mouth, was calling off the stragglers, and the whipper-in followed up the leading dogs with the rest of the pack. "They've found! They're away!" said Matthew; and as he spoke a yell burst from the valley, and in an instant the whole pack were off at full speed. Rather more intent that moment upon showing off my horsemanship than anything else, I dashed spurs into Badger's sides, and turned him towards a rasping ditch before me; over we went, hurling down behind us a rotten bank of clay and small stones, showing how little safety there had been in topping instead of clearing it at a bound. Before I was well-seated again the captain was beside me. "Now for it, then," said I; and away we went. What might be the nature of his feelings I cannot pretend to state, but my own were a strange *mélange* of wild, boyish enthusiasm, revenge, and recklessness. For my own neck I cared little,—nothing; and as I led the way by half a length, I muttered to myself, "Let him follow me fairly this day, and I ask no more."

The dogs had got somewhat the start of us; and as they were in full cry, and going fast, we were a little behind. A thought therefore struck me that, by appearing to take a short cut upon the hounds, I should come down upon the river where its breadth was greatest, and thus, at one *coup*, might try my friend's mettle and his horse's performance at the same time. On we went, our speed increasing, till the roar of the river we were now approaching was plainly audible. I looked half around, and now perceived the captain was standing in his stirrups, as if to obtain a view of what was before him; otherwise his countenance was calm and unmoved, and not a muscle betrayed that he was not cantering on a parade. I fixed myself firmly in my seat, shook my horse a little together, and with a shout whose import every Galway hunter well knows rushed him at the river. I saw the water dashing among the large stones; I heard it splash; I felt a bound like the *ricochet* of a shot, and we were over, but so narrowly that the bank had yielded beneath his hind legs, and it needed a bold effort of the noble animal to regain his footing. Scarcely was he once more firm, when Hammersley flew by me, taking the lead, and sitting quietly in his saddle, as if racing. I know of little in my after-life like the agony of that moment; for although I was far, very far, from wishing real ill to him, yet I would gladly have broken my leg or my arm if he could not have been able to follow me. And now, there he was, actually a length and a half in advance! and worse than all, Miss Dashwood must have witnessed the whole, and doubtless his leap over the river was better and bolder than mine. One consolation yet remained, and while I whispered it to myself I felt comforted again. "His is an English mare. They understand these leaps; but what can he make of a Galway wall?" The question was soon to be solved. Before us, about three fields, were the hounds still in full cry; a large stone-wall lay between, and to it we both directed our course together. "Ha!" thought I, "he is floored at last," as I perceived that the captain held his course rather more in hand, and suffered me to lead. "Now, then, for it!" So saying, I rode at the largest part I could find, well knowing that Badger's powers were here in their element. One spring, one plunge, and away we were galloping along at the other side. Not so the captain; his horse had refused the fence, and he was now taking a circuit of the field for another trial of it.

"Pounded, by Jove!" said I, as I turned round in my saddle to observe him. Once more she came at it, and once more balked, rearing up, at the same time, almost so as to fall backward.

My triumph was complete; and I again was about to follow the hounds, when, throwing a look back, I saw Hammersley clearing the wall in a most splendid manner, and taking a stretch of at least thirteen feet beyond it. Once more he was on my flanks, and the contest renewed. Whatever might be the sentiments of the riders (mine I confess to), between the horses it now became a tremendous struggle. The English mare, though evidently superior in stride and strength, was slightly overweighted, and had not, besides, that cat-like activity an Irish horse possesses; so that the advantages and disadvantages on either side were about equalized. For about half an hour now the pace was awful. We rode side by side, taking our leaps at exactly the same instant, and not four feet apart. The hounds were still considerably in advance, and were heading towards the Shannon, when suddenly the fox doubled, took the hillside, and made for Dangan. "Now, then, comes the trial of strength," I said, half aloud, as I threw my eye up a steep and rugged mountain, covered with wild furze and tall heath, around the crest of which ran, in a zigzag direction, a broken and dilapidated wall, once the enclosure of a deer park. This wall, which varied from four to six feet in height, was of solid masonry, and would, in the most favorable ground, have been a bold leap. Here, at the summit of a mountain, with not a yard of footing, it was absolutely desperation.

By the time that we reached the foot of the hill, the fox, followed closely by the hounds, had passed through a breach in the wall; while Matthew Blake, with the huntsmen and whipper-in, was riding along in search of a gap to lead the horses through. Before I put spurs to Badger to face the hill, I turned one look towards Hammersley. There was a slight curl, half-smile, half-sneer, upon his lip that actually maddened me, and had a precipice yawned beneath my feet, I should have dashed at it after that. The ascent was so steep that I was obliged to take the hill in a slanting direction; and even thus, the loose footing rendered it dangerous in the extreme.

At length I reached the crest, where the wall, more than five feet in height, stood frowning above and seeming to defy me. I turned my horse full round, so that his very chest almost touched the stones, and with a bold cut of the whip and a loud halloo, the gallant animal rose, as if rearing, pawed for an instant to regain his balance, and then, with a frightful struggle, fell backwards, and rolled from top to bottom of the hill, carrying me along with him; the last object that crossed my sight, as I lay bruised and motionless, being the captain as he took the wall in a flying leap, and disappeared at the other side. After a few scrambling efforts to rise, Badger regained his legs and stood beside me; but such was the shock and concussion of my fall that all the objects around seemed wavering and floating before me, while showers of bright sparks fell in myriads before my eyes. I tried to rise, but fell back helpless. Cold perspiration broke over my forehead, and I fainted. From that moment I can remember nothing, till I felt myself galloping along at full speed upon a level table-land, with the hounds about three fields in advance, Hammersley riding foremost, and taking all his leaps coolly as ever. As I swayed to either side upon my saddle, from weakness, I was lost to all thought or recollection, save a flickering memory of some plan of vengeance, which still urged me forward. The chase had now lasted above an hour, and both hounds and horses began to feel the pace at which they were going. As for me, I rode mechanically; I neither knew nor cared for the dangers before me. My eye rested on but one object; my whole being was concentrated upon one vague and undefined sense of revenge. At this instant the huntsman came alongside of me.

"Are you hurted, Misther Charles? Did you fall? Your cheek is all blood, and your coat is torn in two; and, Mother o' God! his boot is ground to powder; he does not hear me! Oh, pull up! pull up, for the love of the Virgin! There's the clover-field and the sunk fence before you, and you'll be killed on the spot!"

"Where?" cried I, with the cry of a madman. "Where's the clover-field; where's the sunk fence? Ha! I see it; I see it now."

So saying, I dashed the rowels into my horse's flanks, and in an instant was beyond the reach of the poor fellow's remonstrances. Another moment I was beside the captain. He turned round as I came up; the same smile was upon his mouth; I could have struck him. About three hundred yards before us lay the sunk fence; its breadth was about twenty feet, and a wall of close brickwork formed its face. Over this the hounds were now clambering; some succeeded in crossing, but by far the greater number fell back, howling, into the ditch.

I turned towards Hammersley. He was standing high in his stirrups, and as he looked towards the yawning fence, down which the dogs were tumbling in masses, I thought (perhaps it was but a thought) that his cheek was paler. I looked again; he was pulling at his horse. Ha! it was true then; he would not face it. I turned round in my saddle, looked him full in the face, and as I pointed with my whip to the leap, called out in a voice hoarse with passion, "Come on!" I saw no more. All objects were lost to me from that moment. When next my senses cleared, I was standing amidst the dogs, where they had just killed. Badger stood blown and trembling beside me, his head drooping and his flanks gored with spur-marks. I looked about, but all consciousness of the past had fled; the concussion of my fall had shaken my intellect, and I was like one but half-awake. One glimpse, short and fleeting, of what was taking place shot through my brain, as old Brackely whispered to me, "By my soul, ye did for the captain there." I turned a vague look upon him, and my eyes fell upon the figure of a man that lay stretched and bleeding upon a door before me. His pale face was crossed with a purple stream of blood that trickled from a wound beside his eyebrow; his arms lay motionless and heavily at either side. I knew him not. A loud report of a pistol aroused me from my stupor; I looked back. I saw a crowd that broke suddenly asunder and fled right and left. I heard a heavy crash upon the ground; I pointed with my finger, for I could not utter a word.

"It is the English mare, yer honor; she was a beauty this morning, but she's broke her shoulder-bone and both her legs, and it was best to put her out of pain."

Samuel Ferguson (1810-1886)

The Abdication of Fergus Mac Roy

Once, ere God was crucified,
I was King o'er Uladh[1] wide:
King, by law of choice and birth,
O'er the fairest realm of Earth.

I was head of Rury's race;
Emain was my dwelling-place;
Right and Might were mine; nor less
Stature, strength, and comeliness.

Neither lacked I love's delight,
Nor the glorious meeds of fight.
All on earth was mine could bring
Life's enjoyment to a king.

Much I loved the jocund chase,
Much the horse and chariot race:
Much I loved the deep carouse,
Quaffing in the Red Branch House.

But, in Council call'd to meet,
Loved I not the judgment seat;
And the suitors' questions hard
Won but scantly my regard.

Rather would I, all alone,
Care and state behind me thrown,
Walk the dew through showery gleams
O'er the meads, or by the streams,

[1] Ulster.

Chanting, as the thoughts might rise,
Unimagined melodies;
While with sweetly-pungent smart
Secret happy tears would start.

Such was I, when in the dance,
Nessa did bestow a glance,
And my soul that moment took
Captive in a single look.

I am but an empty shade,
Far from life and passion laid;
Yet does sweet remembrance thrill
All my shadowy being still.

Nessa had been Fathna's spouse,
Fathna of the Royal house,
And a beauteous boy had borne him:
Fourteen summers did adorn him:

Yea; thou deem'st it marvellous,
That a widow's glance should thus
Turn from lure of maidens' eyes
All a young king's fantasies.

Yet if thou hadst known but half
Of the joyance of her laugh,
Of the measures of her walk,
Of the music of her talk,

Of the witch'ry of her wit,
Even when smarting under it,—
Half the sense, the charm, the grace,
Thou hadst worshipp'd in my place.

And, besides, the thoughts I wove
Into songs of war and love,
She alone of all the rest
Felt them with a perfect zest.

"Lady, in thy smiles to live
Tell me but the boon to give,
Yea, I lay in gift complete
Crown and sceptre at thy feet."

"Not so great the boon I crave:
Hear the wish my soul would have";
And she glanc'd a loving eye
On the stripling standing by:—

"Conor is of age to learn;
Wisdom is a king's concern;
Conor is of royal race,
Yet may sit in Fathna's place.

"Therefore, king, if thou wouldst prove
That I have indeed thy love,
On the judgment seat permit
Conor by thy side to sit,

"That by use the youth may draw
Needful knowledge of the Law."
I with answer was not slow,
"Be thou mine, and be it so."

I am but a shape of air,
Far removed from love's repair;
Yet, were mine a living frame
Once again I'd say the same.

Thus, a prosperous wooing sped,
Took I Nessa to my bed,
While in council and debate
Conor daily by me sate.

Modest was his mien in sooth,
Beautiful the studious youth,
Questioning with earnest gaze
All the reasons and the ways

In the which, and why because,
Kings administer the Laws.
Silent so with looks intent
Sat he till the year was spent.

But the strifes the suitors raised
Bred me daily more distaste,
Every faculty and passion
Sunk in sweet intoxication.

Till upon a day in court
Rose a plea of weightier sort:
Tangled as a briary thicket
Were the rights and wrongs intricate

Which the litigants disputed,
Challenged, mooted, and confuted;
Till, when all the plea was ended,
Naught at all I comprehended.

Scorning an affected show
Of the thing I did not know,
Yet my own defect to hide,
I said "Boy-judge, thou decide."

Conor, with unalter'd mien,
In a clear sweet voice serene,
Took in hand the tangled skein
And began to make it plain.

As a sheep-dog sorts his cattle,
As a king arrays his battle,
So, the facts on either side
He did marshal and divide.

Every branching side-dispute
Traced he downward to the root
Of the strife's main stem, and there
Laid the ground of difference bare.

Then to scope of either cause
Set the compass of the laws,
This adopting, that rejecting,—
Reasons to a head collecting,—

As a charging cohort goes
Through and over scatter'd foes,
So, from point to point, he brought
Onward still the weight of thought

Through all error and confusion,
Till he set the clear conclusion
Standing like a king alone,
All things adverse overthrown,

And gave judgment clear and sound:—
Praises fill'd the hall around;
Yea, the man that lost the cause
Hardly could withhold applause.

By the wondering crowd surrounded
I sat shamefaced and confounded.
Envious ire awhile oppress'd me
Till the nobler thought possess'd me;

And I rose, and on my feet
Standing by the judgment-seat,
Took the circlet from my head,
Laid it on the bench, and said,

"Men of Uladh, I resign
That which is not rightly mine,
That a worthier than I
May your judge's place supply.

"Lo, it is no easy thing
For a man to be a king
Judging well, as should behove
One who claims a people's love.

"Uladh's judgment-seat to fill
I have neither wit nor will.
One is here may justly claim
Both the function and the name.

"Conor is of royal blood;
Fair he is; I trust him good;
Wise he is we all may say
Who have heard his words to-day.

"Take him therefore in my room,
Letting me the place assume—
Office but with life to end—
Of his councillor and friend."

So young Conor gain'd the crown;
So I laid the kingship down;
Laying with it as it went
All I knew of discontent.

The Burial of King Cormac[1]

"Crom Cruach[2] and his sub-gods twelve,"
Said Cormac, "are but carven treene;
The axe that made them, haft or helve,
Had worthier of our worship been.

"But He who made the tree to grow,
And hid in earth the iron-stone,
And made the man with mind to know
The axe's use, is God alone."

Anon to priests of Crom was brought—
Where, girded in their service dread,
They minister'd on red Moy Slaught—
Word of the words King Cormac said.

They loosed their curse against the king;
They cursed him in his flesh and bones;
And daily in their mystic ring
They turn'd the maledictive stones,

Till, where at meat the monarch sate,
Amid the revel and the wine,
He choked upon the food he ate,
At Sletty, southward of the Boyne.

---

[1] Cormac Mac Art, who reigned in the third century A.D. is one of the most famous of Irish kings.

[2] God of Winter and patron of agriculture, who stood on Mag Slecht (Moy Slaught) in County Cavan and was worshiped at Samhain, the Celtic New Year.

High vaunted then the priestly throng,
  And far and wide they noised abroad
With trump and loud liturgic song
  The praise of their avenging God.

But ere the voice was wholly spent
  That priest and prince should still obey,
To awed attendants o'er him bent
  Great Cormac gather'd breath to say,—

"Spread not the beds of Brugh for me
  When restless death-bed's use is done:
But bury me at Rossnaree
  And face me to the rising sun.

"For all the kings who lie in Brugh
  Put trust in gods of wood and stone;
And 'twas at Ross that first I knew
  One, Unseen, who is God alone.

"His glory lightens from the east;
  His message soon shall reach our shore;
And idol-god, and cursing priest
  Shall plague us from Moy Slaught no more."

Dead Cormac on his bier they laid:—
  "He reign'd a king for forty years,
And shame it were," his captains said,
  "He lay not with his royal peers.

"His grandsire, Hundred-Battle,[1] sleeps
  Serene in Brugh: and, all around,
Dead kings in stone sepulchral keeps
  Protect the sacred burial ground.

[1] Cormac was the grandson of Conn of the Hundred Battles, also called Conn the Hundred Fighter.

"What though a dying man should rave
Of changes o'er the eastern sea?
In Brugh of Boyne shall be his grave,
And not in noteless Rossnaree."

Then northward forth they bore the bier,
And down from Sletty side they drew,
With horsemen and with charioteer,
To cross the fords of Boyne to Brugh.

There came a breath of finer air
That touch'd the Boyne with ruffling wings,
It stirr'd him in his sedgy lair
And in his mossy moorland springs.

And as the burial train came down
With dirge and savage dolorous shows,
Across their pathway, broad and brown
The deep, full-hearted river rose;

From bank to bank through all his fords,
'Neath blackening squalls he swell'd and boil'd;
And thrice the wondering gentile lords
Essay'd to cross, and thrice recoil'd.

Then forth stepp'd grey-hair'd warriors four:
They said, "Through angrier floods than these,
On link'd shields once our king we bore
From Dread-Spear and the hosts of Deece.

"And long as loyal will holds good,
And limbs respond with helpful thews,
Nor flood, nor fiend within the flood,
Shall bar him of his burial dues."

With slanted necks they stoop'd to lift;
They heaved him up to neck and chin;
And, pair and pair, with footsteps swift,
Lock'd arm and shoulder, bore him in.

'Twas brave to see them leave the shore;
To mark the deep'ning surges rise,
And fall subdued in foam before
The tension of their striding thighs.

'Twas brave, when now a spear-cast out,
Breast-high the battling surges ran;
For weight was great, and limbs were stout,
And loyal man put trust in man.

But ere they reach'd the middle deep,
Nor steadying weight of clay they bore,
Nor strain of sinewy limbs could keep
Their feet beneath the swerving four.

And now they slide, and now they swim,
And now, amid the blackening squall,
Grey locks afloat, with clutching grim,
They plunge around the floating pall.

While, as a youth with practised spear
Through justling crowds bears off the ring,
Boyne from their shoulders caught the bier
And proudly bore away the king.

At morning, on the grassy marge
Of Rossnaree, the corpse was found,
And shepherds at their early charge
Entomb'd it in the peaceful ground.

A tranquil spot: a hopeful sound
Comes from the ever youthful stream,
And still on daisied mead and mound
The dawn delays with tenderer beam.

Round Cormac Spring renews her buds:
In march perpetual by his side,
Down come the earth-fresh April floods,
And up the sea-fresh salmon glide:

And life and time rejoicing run
From age to age their wonted way;
But still he waits the risen Sun,
For still 'tis only dawning Day.

The Wedding of the Clans

BY Aubrey De Vere (1814-1902)

I go to knit two clans together;
Our clan and this clan unseen of yore:—
Our clan fears nought! but I go, whither?
This day I go from my mother's door.

Thou redbreast sing'st the old song over,
Though many a time thou hast sung it before;
They never sent thee to some strange new lover:—
I sing a new song by my mother's door.

I stepp'd from my little room down by the ladder,
The ladder that never so shook before;
I was sad last night; to-day I am sadder,
Because I go from my mother's door.

The last snow melts upon bush and bramble;
The gold bars shine on the forest's floor;
Shake not, thou leaf! it is I must tremble
Because I go from my mother's door.

From a Spanish sailor a dagger I bought me;
I trail'd a rose-three our grey bawn[1] o'er;
The creed and my letters our bard taught me;
My days were sweet by my mother's door.

My little white goat that with raised feet huggest
The oak stock, thy horns in the ivies frore,[2]
Could I wrestle like thee—how the wreaths thou tuggest!—
I never would move from my mother's door.

Oh weep no longer, my nurse and mother!
My foster-sister, weep not so sore!
You cannot come with me, Ir, my brother—
Along I go from my mother's door.

Farewell, my wolf-hound, that slew Mac Owing
As he caught me and far through the thickets bore:
My heifer, Alb, in the green vale lowing,
My cygnet's nest upon Lorna's shore!

He has kill'd ten chiefs, this chief that plights me;
His hand is like that of the giant Balor:[3]
But I fear his kiss; and his beard affrights me,
And the great stone dragon above his door.

---

[1] Meadow.
[2] Frozen, frosty. NED
[3] A Celtic god famous because of his poisonous eye.

Had I daughters nine with me they should tarry;
They should sing old songs; they should dance at my door;
They should grind at the quern;—no need to marry;
Oh when will this marriage-day be o'er?

Had I buried, like Moirin, three mates already
I might say, "Three husbands! then why not four?"
But my hand is cold and my foot unsteady
Because I never was married before!

The Fairies

BY William Allingham (1824-1889)

Up the airy mountain,
Down the rushy glen,
We daren't go a-hunting
For fear of little men;
Wee folk, good folk,
Trooping all together;
Green jacket, red cap,
And white owl's feather!

Down along the rocky shore
Some make their home—
They live on crispy pancakes
Of yellow tide-foam;
Some in the reeds
Of the black mountain lake,
With frogs for their watch-dogs,
All night awake.

High on the hill-top
The old King sits;
He is now so old and gray
He's nigh lost his wits.
With a bridge of white mist,
Columbkill he crosses,
On his stately journeys
From Slieveleague to Rosses;
Or going up with music
On cold starry nights,
To sup with the Queen
Of the gay Northern Lights.

They stole little Bridget
For seven years long;
When she came down again
Her friends were all gone.
They took her lightly back,
Between the night and morrow,
They thought that she was fast asleep,
But she was dead with sorrow.
They have kept her ever since
Deep within the lakes,
On a bed of flag-leaves,
Watching till she wakes.

By the craggy hill-side,
Through the mosses bare,
They have planted thorn-trees
For pleasure here and there.
Is any man so daring
As dig one up in spite,
He shall find their sharpest thorns
In his bed at night.

Up the airy mountain,
Down the rushy glen,
We daren't go a-hunting
For fear of little men;
Wee folk, good folk,
Trooping all together;
Green jacket, red cap,
And white owl's feather!

Aghadoe

BY John Todhunter (1839-1916)

There's a glade in Aghadoe, Aghadoe, Aghadoe,
There's a green and silent glade in Aghadoe,
Where we met, my Love and I, Love's fair planet in the sky,
O'er that sweet and silent glade in Aghadoe.

There's a glen in Aghadoe, Aghadoe, Aghadoe,
There's a deep and secret glen in Aghadoe,
Where I hid him from the eyes of the red-coats and their spies
That year the trouble came to Aghadoe!

Oh! my curse on one black heart in Aghadoe, Aghadoe,
On Shaun Dhuv, my mother's son in Aghadoe,
When your throat fries in hell's drouth salt the flame be in your mouth,
For the treachery you did in Aghadoe!

For they tracked me to that glen in Aghadoe, Aghadoe,
When the price was on his head in Aghadoe;
O'er the mountain through the wood, as I stole to him with food,
When in hiding lone he lay in Aghadoe.

But they never took him living in Aghadoe, Aghadoe;
With the bullets in his heart in Aghadoe,
There he lay, the head—my breast keeps the warmth where once 'twould rest—
Gone, to win the traitor's gold from Aghadoe!

I walked to Mallow Town from Aghadoe, Aghadoe,
Brought his head from the gaol's gate to Aghadoe,
Then I covered him with fern, and I piled on him the cairn,
Like an Irish king he sleeps in Aghadoe.

Oh, to creep into that cairn in Aghadoe, Aghadoe!
There to rest upon his breast in Aghadoe!
Sure your dog for you could die with no truer heart than I—
Your own love cold on your cairn in Aghadoe.

The Peeler[1] and the Goat

A Bansha Peeler wint won night
On duty and pathrollin' O,
An' met a goat upon the road,
And tuck her for a sthroller O.
Wud bay'net fixed he sallied forth,
An' caught her by the wizzen O,
An' then he swore a mighty oath,
"I'll send you off to prison O."

[1] Policeman, so called after Sir Robert Peel, Chief Secretary for Ireland, later Prime Minister of England, who was largely responsible for establishing an Irish police force.

"Oh, mercy, sir!" the goat replied,
"Pray let me tell my story O!
I am no rogue, no Ribbonman,[1]
No Croppy, Whig, or Tory O;
I'm guilty not of any crime
Of petty or high thraison O,
I'm sadly wanted at this time,
For this is the milkin' saison O."

"It is in vain for to complain
Or give your tongue such bridle O,
You're absent from your dwellin' place,
Disorderly and idle O.
Your hoary locks will not prevail,
Nor your sublime oration O,
You'll be thransported by Peel's Act,
Upon my information O."

"No penal law did I transgress
By deeds or combination O.
I have no certain place to rest,
No home or habitation O.
But Bansha is my dwelling-place,
Where I was bred and born O.
Descended from an honest race,
That's all the trade I've learned O."

"I will chastise your insolince
And violent behaviour O;
Well bound to Cashel you'll be sint,
Where you will gain no favor O.
The magistrates will all consint
To sign your condemnation O;
From there to Cork you will be sint
For speedy thransportation O."

[1] Member of a secret revolutionary society opposing the English government and Orangeism.

"This parish an' this neighborhood
Are paiceable and thranquil O;
There's no disturbance here, thank God!
An' long may it continue so,
I don't regard your oath a pin,
Or sign for my committal O,
My jury will be gintlemin
And grant me my acquittal O."

"The consequince be what it will,
A peeler's power I'll let you know,
I'll handcuff you, at all events,
And march you off to Bridewell O.
An' sure, you rogue, you can't deny
Before the judge or jury O,
Intimidation with your horns,
An' threatening me with fury O."

"I make no doubt but you are dhrunk,
Wud whiskey, rum, or brandy O,
Or you wouldn't have such gallant spunk
To be so bould or manly O.
You readily would let me pass
If I had money handy O,
To thrate you to a potheen[1] glass—
Oh! it's then I'd be the dandy O."

---

[1] Illegally distilled whiskey.

The Nameless Dun[1]

BY William Larminie (1850-1900)

WHO were the builders? Question not the silence
That settles on the lake for evermore,
Save when the sea-bird screams and to the islands
The echo answers from the steep-cliffed shore.

O half-remaining ruin, in the lore
Of human life a gap shall all deplore
Beholding thee; since thou art like the dead
Found slain, no token to reveal the why,
The name, the story. Some one murder'd
We know, we guess; and gazing upon thee,
And, filled by thy long silence of reply,
We guess some garnered sheaf of tragedy;—
Of tribe or nation slain so utterly
That even their ghosts are dead, and on their grave
Springeth no bloom of legend in its wildness;
And age by age weak washing round the islands
No faintest sign of story lisps the wave.

---

[1] A *dun* was a fortified dwelling.

The Murrigan

BY George Moore (1852-1933)

One day in my walks in the high wood I spied a man standing on a boulder in the midst of the river, seemingly undecided whether he should jump to the next one; and knowing the pool to be deep between the boulders I tried to dissuade him. There's no chance of drowning, he cried to me, but if I miss my step I'll be up to my belt. I called out that to cross the river he would be trespassing on private rights, but he did not heed my warning. He jumped again; and, laying hold of a protruding root, began to climb the bank, telling me as he made his way up that the master (the gentleman in whose house I was staying) would have nothing to say against the gathering of a few ferns along the river's bank. A fern-gatherer, I said, and followed him asking questions, not so much for the answers he gave as for the pleasure it was to listen to his low, musical voice, a tenor voice, in keeping, it seemed to me, with his pale, almost affectionate eyes, shining like jewels in a pointed oval face; a young man who had just passed out of his first youth, an Irish peasant, but far from the typical, I said, when I left him to his search and continued my walk through the beech wood, not able to forget his spare chestnut beard, his moustache and his comely, well-knit figure. These, so it seemed to me, I had seen before and many times, but where I had seen them I could not remember, and it was not till after long soul searching it occurred to me that I had seen him in pictures. Yes, I murmured to myself, he is the Jesus that has come down to us from the fifteenth century, imagined first perhaps by Fra Angelico, and repeated ever since by many thousands of painters, inclining more and more to the feminine and epicene type, becoming a woman in Holman Hunt's picture, *The Light of the World*, Miss Christina Rossetti, with a blonde beard and moustache. But, I continued, my fern-gatherer does not reproduce the fond emptiness of Jesus's face; he is with it all a man; and there can be no doubt that I am doing him an injustice by associating him with Holman Hunt's version of Christina Rossetti in a blonde beard. My fern-gatherer is a man and altogether himself in the life he has chosen for himself. A romantic figure, I added, one which does honour to the town of Westport.

He had already captured my imagination by dinnertime, and at the first pause in the conversation, when the girls' narratives of the day's doings had ceased, I related our meeting, and learnt that legends had already begun to collect about him. His name? I asked anxiously, feeling I should be disappointed if his name were among those that one wearies of in Ireland —Higgins, Walsh, O'Connor, Murphy. That it might not be Murphy I prayed inly. Alec Trusselby! It would be strange, indeed, I exclaimed, if legends had not begun to collect about a name like that, and begged that all that was known about him should be told to me at once. Everybody was willing to tell, and the biographical scraps uttered from different ends and sides of the dinner-table were in keeping with his name.

I learnt from one member of the family that Alec had been to America and had suffered from sunstroke, from another that he lived in the woods all the summer-time, bringing back beech and oak ferns to Westport and getting for them a fair share of money; and from another that his voice and manner were so winning that it was difficult not to be his customer, and as every customer became a patron, Alec had no cause for complaint. Even if he had he is not the kind of man that would complain, a girl suddenly interjected, and turning to her I asked: How is that? She replied that he was a very shy man who would remain silent for long intervals to break into speech suddenly like a bird. This seemed to me a good description, but I had not seen enough of Alec at that time to be able to vouch for its accuracy. A girl told me the report was that Alec had built himself a summer dwelling in a great tree, and I answered that what she said did not surprise me. Lying in his bed under the boughs, I said, he caught his style from the moody blackbird who fills the wood at dawn with his exalted lay; more likely still from the meditative thrush. But how does Alec live through the winter? I asked, and it was delightful to hear that in the winter he related stories about the firesides in the cottages, and that no one refused Alec bed and board if he could help it; Alec's company was sought for by everybody; and a suspicion was abroad that to treat him ill was to bring ill luck upon oneself. Gathering ferns in the summer and telling stories in the winter, I repeated, becoming possessed in a moment of an absorbing interest in Alec Trusselby. Is he an Irish speaker? I asked, and heard that he was one of the best in the county of Mayo. But, a girl cried across the table, mind, if he suspects you of laughing at him he will run away at once, and don't tell him you're a Protestant, he might refuse to go into the woods with you. With a heretic? I added.

A custard pudding interrupted the conversation about Alec, but as soon as everybody had been helped it returned to him, and I learnt that the gentle winning personality that had awakened fellow-feeling in me was only one side of Alec Trusselby; there was another, and one well known to the Westport police —staunch friends of his, always ready to take his part when Alec's less reputable associates mocked him in the street after drinking his money away in the public-house, their joke being to try to grab the Murrigan, not an easy thing to do, for it never left his hand, and where the Murrigan was concerned Alec was resolute and strong. The Murrigan? I interjected. He calls his blackthorn the Murrigan, one of the girls answered, but we don't know what the word means, whether it's an Irish word or a word invented by himself. I wonder if the police could tell me? I said. Now why should the police be bothering their heads with what Alec means when he calls his stick the Murrigan? my friend, the girl's father, blurted out; and he laughed the short, quick, intelligent laugh whereby I remember him. Haven't they enough to do to keep him out of jail? And he told a story how, returning home late one night, he had come upon Trusselby and the police—the sergeant and the constable engaged in trying to persuade Alec to return to his lodging You see, Alec, you're free to follow them if you like:

the constable has let go your arm, the sergeant was saying. But if you take my advice you'll be taking yourself and the Murrigan home like the quiet, good man that you are, the divil a better. If they insult you again we'll let yourself and the Murrigan at them, but this time we'll be asking you to let them pass on, for to break their skulls with the Murrigan would be conferring too much honour upon them. You see, said mine host, we have all a kindly feeling for Trusselby, myself as well as the police; to keep him out of jail takes us all our time, and we haven't that much over to be ferreting out the meaning of all the talk that goes on between himself and his stick as he walks the roads. But he's not half-witted? I asked, looking round the dinner-table, preferring a general to an individual opinion, and the company was agreed that Alec could not be held to be a loon. And his stories? I asked; but none at the table had felt sufficient curiosity to ask him to tell one. I'd give a great deal, I said, to hear Trusselby tell a story, and was warned not to offer him a big sum of money, but to wait an occasion to win his confidence. If you offer him a sovereign to tell you a story you'll frighten him; he'll begin to suspect some evil and you'll get nothing out of him. But I may not meet Trusselby again, and if I did, to the end of my visit is not a long time to win his confidence—I shall be leaving in a few days. You can stay as long as you like, my host and hostess interjected, we would like to see you friends with Trusselby before you leave.

The next day one of the girls rushed into the room in which I was writing: Trusselby is coming down the hill, she said, and I bolted out after him. You sell ferns, don't you? I asked; he answered that he did, and I asked him to get me some. He said he would and passed on, and I returned to the house disappointed. But luck was with me, and two evenings later, returning home after dining with a friend, I met Trusselby at the riverside, whirling the Murrigan and apparently in a convivial mood. Well, Alec, I said, have you come upon the royal or the hart's tongue in your walks? You're the gentleman I met the other day up at the old mill, aren't you? he asked. I answered that I was, and we walked on together, myself making conversation, afraid every moment that Trusselby would say: I must be wishing you goodnight, sir, or I'll be locked out. But it was unlikely that Trusselby had a latchkey, it was more probable that he contemplated spending the night out, which would be no great hardship, for the night was warm and still, and were it not that a bench is a hard bed, the most home-loving and respectable man in Westport might have liked to have lain out of doors, sooner or later to be hushed to sleep by the almost inaudible sound of water rippling past and the soft cawing of sleepy rooks. A night it was that would keep anybody out of his bed till midnight at least, except, perhaps, a dry old curmudgeon. A breathless night, full of stars, and perchance stories, I said to myself, and then aloud to Alec: Yes, we met up at the old mill, but you didn't find the ferns you were looking for? Is it the royal you're after? Alec asked, and I answered that that was what I had in mind, and having listened to Trusselby for some time on the rarity of the fern, I broke in with the remark that I'd never seen a finer blackthorn than the one he was carrying.

He had come upon it in a brake, he said, in a thicket that often served him as a bedroom in a summer's night when his quest for ferns had led him far from Westport. And it was one morning at sunrise that I spied her; she was no thicker that morning than one of my fingers, and I said to myself: In about three years' time that stem will be the finest in Ireland if the top be cut at once so that it may be throwing out little knots and spikes. The knots begin almost at the top, sir, and at every knot there is three spikes. You would be lost if you started counting them, just as you might be if you were to start on the stars in the skies. It was the blessing of God that I saw the Murrigan that morning, for a year later it would have been too late to cut the top. I was only in time, and there it stayed for its three years sprouting, with three spikes coming out on every knot. You can see them, sir, all the way up. Faith, there isn't half-an-inch of the stick without its three spikes. But if somebody had gone into the brake and seen the stick before you? I asked. I had to risk that, sir, for it takes three full years for the stick to furnish, and often I didn't like going to the brake for fear a person might spy me and be wondering what I was after and perhaps be coming in behind me and find out the stick; but sure I had the luck all the time and nobody came. In three years to the day, your honour, I was down in the dingle cutting my stick, my heart filled with joy so furnished was it. Mind you, sir, the seasoning of a blackthorn isn't understood by every man, for when you've cut your stick you must season it, and the place I was living in then had a fine old chimney with a flue inside of it on which you could rest a stick, and there the Murrigan rested seasoning. After six good months I took it down and gave it a rub with an oil rag, and I'll tell you, mister, it was good for sore eyes to see the way it was coming up. Take a look at it yourself now and tell me, is there a bit of Spanish mahogany in the country is its equal for colour. To this I agreed, and asked: Is that the reason you call it the Murrigan? Well, it isn't, your honour. Do you see, Murrigan means "great queen" in the Irish, and my stick here is the queen of the fair this many a day. The stick knows it too, for if I'm not at the fair off goes the Murrigan without me; I look round in the morning, but not a stick can I see, so I say: The Murrigan's gone, and she'll be breaking the head of some poor chap out of sheer light-heartedness and divilment. That's the way it does be, sir, for after she's gone there's somebody has a cracked head somewhere. No one knows who breaks it, barring the Murrigan, and she tells nobody, but just flies back unbeknownst to anybody, and finds her old place in the corner just as any creature would. And there I find her, waiting for me. Have a look at the Murrigan, sir, for you'll never see another like her. She's as beautifully ornamented as the Brooch of Tara itself. So the Murrigan goes to the fair by herself? She does so, your honour, and she flies round the heads of the people, urging them on the way the old Murrigan used to do when Brian Boru was in it, waking up the spirit of fight in them. The Murrigan whirls like an eagle over the heads of the people, prodding them here and poking them there, and putting them at each other. When I'm there, and the Murrigan with me, I feel my hand rise up and my head is that elated I don't know whether it's me or the Murrigan is doing the deeds, and I don't know if the stars that are in my head aren't thicker and twice as thick than they are in the sky. All I can see is the Murrigan about me and she whirling like a bird, but never leaving me five fingers; a faithful thing the Murrigan, bless her soul, and she saved my life many a time, good luck to her!

Trusselby kissed his blackthorn and we leaned our backs against the parapet of the bridge, looking up into the sky, the town asleep, nothing to be heard about us but the ripple of the river. Trusselby seemed to have forgotten me, and I wondered of what he could be thinking, of some battle long ago, I thought, in which doubtless the Murrigan played a great part, and seeing a smile playing over his bland, almost holy face, I said: There used to be great fighting long ago? It was about fighting I was thinking, your honour, a great fair at Castlebar, when there were more two-year-olds than three-year-olds about. To check the story that was on his lips with a question would have been fatal, so I held my peace, hoping to learn whether the fair was lacking in three-year-old bullocks or three-year-old colts and fillies. He began again after a pause. You see, sir, in the old times when your ancestors were in it, God rest their souls, in the days of your grandfather, there was an O'Brien sold a heifer to a Fitzgerald for a two-year-old, but the heifer itself was a three-year-old; and the next fair day there was a fight between Fitzgerald and O'Brien; and at the next fair the Fitzgerald brothers and the O'Brien brothers were fighting; and the fair day after that the cousins were in the fight, and after the cousins the friends came in on one side and the other, until it was a dangerous thing to hold any fair in the country at all, so great was the fighting; after whacking with all the blackthorns in the country over all the skulls in the country for more than fifty years the war finished, and it was only at the heel of the hunt that I strolled in one fair day to Castlebar. There was a man there, and somebody made a cake of his skull with a tap of a stick. Nobody knew who did it. He said it was the policeman, and he took out a summons against the policeman. Well, I was a witness in the case, your honour, and I couldn't see an innocent man condemned even if he was a peeler itself. When I came before the magistrate he asked if I was standing by at the time. I was, your Worship, says I; and he says: Was it the policeman broke the man's head? and I said: It was not, your Worship; the policeman didn't hit the man that tap. A tap, you call it, said the man, Michael Joyce was his name, and he lifted up the bloody bandage that was upon his brow. 'Tis more than a tap, your Worship, says I, it's a clout; but tap or clout, it wasn't the policeman gave it to him. You're on your oath, Alec Trusselby, he said. And I said: Before God! and I gave a swear that it wasn't the policeman. Now what do you think but the magistrate was looking into Joyce's face, and he saw three little weeney holes around his eye, and he took notice of them three little holes, and when I picked up the Murrigan and was going out of the box he said: Let me have a look at your stick, Trusselby, so I gave it to him, and he said: Wasn't it you gave the man the tap? And I said: It was so, your Worship. Tell me, says he, why did you strike that blow? So I ups and I told him the story of the two-year-olds and the three-year-olds. Which was he, said the magistrate, was he a two-year-old or a three-year-old? Your Worship, says I, he was like myself, he was a two-year-old. And why did you assault and batter the man? Well, you see, your Worship, says I, there was only a few of us in that fair. We was outnumbered altogether by the three-year-olds, and Joyce yonder was saying he'd like well to see the man who'd tread on the tail of his coat, and seeing that there would be a fight in which we might be worsted I just gave him a tap to make him quiet like, and to keep him out of harm's way.

So that's the story of the Murrigan? It is, your honour, I've told you the whole of it. A wonderful stick she is; look at her; every knob with three little spikes like the blessed shamrock that St. Patrick picked so that he would be able to explain the Holy Trinity to the pagans. A beautiful stick, I said, and a very interesting story. You know many stories, Alec, and can tell them better than any man now living. It's puffing me up with pride and goster you'd be, your honour, and after reminding him that he had promised to bring me some beech and oak ferns we parted, myself regretting that my shyness had prevented me from asking Alec to tell me a story.

The Rising of the Moon

BY Lady Gregory (1852-1932)

PERSONS: *Sergeant.*
Policeman X.
Policeman B.
A Ragged Man.

Scene: Side of a quay in a seaport town. Some posts and chains. A large barrel. Enter three policemen. Moonlight.

(Sergeant, who is older than the others, crosses the stage to right and looks down steps. The others put down a paste-pot and unroll a bundle of placards.)

POLICEMAN B: I think this would be a good place to put up a notice. *(He points to barrel.)*

POLICEMAN X: Better ask him. *(Calls to Sergt.)* Will this be a good place for a placard?

(No answer.)

POLICEMAN B: Will we put up a notice here on the barrel?

(No answer.)

SERGEANT: There's a flight of steps here that leads to the water. This is a place that should be minded well. If he got down here, his friends might have a boat to meet him; they might send it in here from outside.

POLICEMAN B: Would the barrel be a good place to put a notice up?

SERGEANT: It might; you can put it there.

(They paste the notice up.)

SERGEANT: *(Reading it.)* Dark hair—dark eyes, smooth face, height five feet five—there's not much to take hold of in that—It's a pity I had no chance of seeing him before he broke out of gaol. They say he's a wonder, that it's he makes all the plans for the whole organization. There isn't another man in Ireland would have broken gaol the way he did. He must have some friends among the gaolers.

POLICEMAN B: A hundred pounds is little enough for the Government to offer for him. You may be sure any man in the force that takes him will get promotion.

SERGEANT: I'll mind this place myself. I wouldn't wonder at all if he came this way. He might come slipping along there *(points to side of quay)*, and his friends might be waiting for him there *(points down steps)*, and once he got away it's little chance we'd have of finding him; it's maybe under a load of kelp he'd be in a fishing boat, and not one to help a married man that wants it to the reward.

POLICEMAN X: And if we get him itself, nothing but abuse on our heads for it from the people, and maybe from our own relations.

SERGEANT: Well, we have to do our duty in the force. Haven't we the whole country depending on us to keep law and order? It's those that are down would be up and those that are up would be down, if it wasn't for us. Well, hurry on, you have plenty of other places to placard yet, and come back here then to me. You can take the lantern. Don't be too long now. It's very lonesome here with nothing but the moon.

POLICEMAN B: It's a pity we can't stop with you. The Government should have brought more police into the town, with *him* in gaol, and at assize time too. Well, good luck to your watch.

(They go out.)

SERGEANT: *(Walks up and down once or twice and looks at placard.)* A hundred pounds and promotion sure. There must be a great deal of spending in a hundred pounds. It's a pity some honest man not to be the better of that.

(A ragged man appears at left and tries to slip past. Sergeant suddenly turns.)

SERGEANT: Where are you going?

MAN: I'm a poor ballad-singer, your honour. I thought to sell some of these *(holds out bundle of ballads)* to the sailors. *(He goes on.)*

SERGEANT: Stop! Didn't I tell you to stop? You can't go on there.

MAN: Oh, very well. It's a hard thing to be poor. All the world's against the poor!

SERGEANT: Who are you?

MAN: You'd be as wise as myself if I told you, but I don't mind. I'm one Jimmy Walsh, a ballad-singer.

SERGEANT: Jimmy Walsh? I don't know that name.

MAN: Ah, sure, they know it well enough in Ennis. Were you ever in Ennis, sergeant?

SERGEANT: What brought you here?

MAN: Sure, it's to the assizes I came, thinking I might make a few shillings here or there. It's in the one train with the judges I came.

SERGEANT: Well, if you came so far, you may as well go farther, for you'll walk out of this.

MAN: I will, I will; I'll just go on where I was going. *(Goes towards steps.)*

SERGEANT: Come back from those steps; no one has leave to pass down them to-night.

MAN: I'll just sit on the top of the steps till I see will some sailor buy a ballad off me that would give me my supper. They do be late going back to the ship. It's often I saw them in Cork carried down the quay in a hand-cart.

SERGEANT: Move on, I tell you. I won't have any one lingering about the quay to-night.

MAN: Well, I'll go. It's the poor have the hard life! Maybe yourself might like one, sergeant. Here's a good sheet now. *(Turns one over.)* "Content and a pipe"—that's not much. "The Peeler and the goat"—you wouldn't like that. "Johnny Hart"—that's a lovely song.

SERGEANT: Move on.

MAN: Ah, wait till you hear it. *(Sings:)*

There was a rich farmer's daughter lived near the town of Ross;
She courted a Highland soldier, his name was Johnny Hart;
Says the mother to her daughter, "I'll go distracted mad
If you marry that Highland soldier dressed up in Highland plaid."

SERGEANT: Stop that noise.

(Man wraps up his ballads and shuffles towards the steps.)

SERGEANT: Where are you going?

MAN: Sure you told me to be going, and I am going.

SERGEANT: Don't be a fool. I didn't tell you to go that way; I told you to go back to the town.

MAN: Back to the town, is it?

SERGEANT: *(Taking him by the shoulder and shoving him before him.)* Here, I'll show you the way. Be off with you. What are you stopping for?

MAN: *(Who has been keeping his eye on the notice, points to it.)* I think I know what you're waiting for, sergeant.

SERGEANT: What's that to you?

MAN: And I know well the man you're waiting for—I know him well—I'll be going.

(He shuffles on.)

SERGEANT: You know him? Come back here. What sort is he?

MAN: Come back is it, sergeant? Do you want to have me killed?

SERGEANT: Why do you say that?

MAN: Never mind. I'm going. I wouldn't be in your shoes if the reward was ten times as much. *(Goes on off stage to left.)* Not if it was ten times as much.

SERGEANT: *(Rushing after him.)* Come back here, come back. *(Drags him back.)* What sort is he? Where did you see him?

MAN: I saw him in my own place, in the County Clare. I tell you you wouldn't like to be looking at him. You'd be afraid to be in the one place with him. There isn't a weapon he doesn't know the use of, and as to strength, his muscles are as hard as that board *(slaps barrel)*.

SERGEANT: Is he as bad as that?

MAN: He is then.

SERGEANT: Do you tell me so?

MAN: There was a poor man in our place, a sergeant from Ballyvaughan.—It was with a lump of stone he did it.

SERGEANT: I never heard of that.

MAN: And you wouldn't, sergeant. It's not everything that happens gets into the papers. And there was a policeman in plain clothes, too . . . It is in Limerick he was. . . . It was after the time of the attack on the police barrack at Kilmallock. . . . Moonlight . . . just like this . . . waterside. . . . Nothing was known for certain.

SERGEANT: Do you say so? It's a terrible county to belong to.

MAN: That's so, indeed! You might be standing there, looking out that way, thinking you saw him coming up this side of the quay *(points)*, and he might be coming up this other side *(points)*, and he'd be on you before you knew where you were.

SERGEANT: It's a whole troop of police they ought to put here to stop a man like that.

MAN: But if you'd like me to stop with you, I could be looking down this side. I could be sitting up here on this barrel.

SERGEANT: And you know him well, too?

MAN: I'd know him a mile off, sergeant.

SERGEANT: But you wouldn't want to share the reward?

MAN: Is it a poor man like me, that has to be going the roads and singing in fairs, to have the name on him that he took a reward? But you don't want me. I'll be safer in the town.

SERGEANT: Well, you can stop.

MAN: *(Getting up on barrel.)* All right, sergeant. I wonder, now, you're not tired out, sergeant, walking up and down the way you are.

SERGEANT: If I'm tired I'm used to it.

MAN: You might have hard work before you to-night yet. Take it easy while you can. There's plenty of room up here on the barrel, and you see farther when you're higher up.

SERGEANT: Maybe so. *(Gets up beside him on barrel, facing right. They sit back to back, looking different ways.)* You made me feel a bit queer with the way you talked.

MAN: Give me a match, sergeant *(he gives it and man lights pipe)*; take a draw yourself? It'll quiet you. Wait now till I give you a light, but you needn't turn round. Don't take your eye off the quay for the life of you.

SERGEANT: Never fear, I won't. *(Lights pipe. They both smoke.)* Indeed it's a hard thing to be in the force, out at night and no thanks for it, for all the danger we're in. And it's little we get but abuse from the people, and no choice but to obey our orders, and never asked when a man is sent into danger, if you are a married man with a family.

MAN: *(Sings)*—

As through the hills I walked to view the hills and shamrock plain,
I stood awhile where nature smiles to view the rocks and streams,
On a matron fair I fixed my eyes beneath a fertile vale,
As she sang her song it was on the wrong of poor old Granuaile.

SERGEANT: Stop that; that's no song to be singing in these times.

MAN: Ah, sergeant, I was only singing to keep my heart up. It sinks when I think of him. To think of us two sitting here, and he creeping up the quay, maybe, to get to us.

SERGEANT: Are you keeping a good lookout?

MAN: I am; and for no reward too. Amn't I the foolish man? But when I saw a man in trouble, I never could help trying to get him out of it. What's that? Did something hit me? *(Rubs his heart.)*

SERGEANT: *(Patting him on the shoulder.)* You will get your reward in heaven.

MAN: I know that, I know that, sergeant, but life is precious.

SERGEANT: Well, you can sing if it gives you more courage.

MAN: *(Sings)*—

Her head was bare, her hands and feet with iron bands were bound,
Her pensive strain and plaintive wail mingles with the evening gale,
And the song she sang with mournful air, I am old Granuaile.

Her lips so sweet that monarchs kissed . . .

SERGEANT: That's not it. . . . "Her gown she wore was stained with gore." . . . That's it—you missed that.

MAN: You're right, sergeant, so it is; I missed it. *(Repeats line.)* But to think of a man like you knowing a song like that.

SERGEANT: There's many a thing a man might know and might not have any wish for.

MAN: Now, I daresay, sergeant, in your youth, you used to be sitting up on a wall, the way you are sitting up on this barrel now, and the other lads beside you, and you singing "Granuaile"? . . .

SERGEANT: I did then.

MAN: And the "Shan Bhean Bhocht"? . . .

SERGEANT: I did then.

MAN: And the "Green on the Cape?"

SERGEANT: That was one of them.

MAN: And maybe the man you are watching for to-night used to be sitting on the wall, when he was young, and singing those same songs. . . . It's a queer world. . . .

SERGEANT: Whisht! . . . I think I see something coming. . . . It's only a dog.

MAN: And isn't it a queer world? . . . Maybe it's one of the boys you used to be singing with that time you will be arresting to-day or to-morrow, and sending into the dock. . . .

SERGEANT: That's true indeed.

MAN: And maybe one night, after you had been singing, if

the other boys had told you some plan they had, some plan to free the country, you might have joined with them . . . and maybe it is you might be in trouble now.

SERGEANT: Well, who knows but I might? I had a great spirit in those days.

MAN: It's a queer world, sergeant, and it's little any mother knows when she sees her child creeping on the floor what might happen to it before it has gone through its life, or who will be who in the end.

SERGEANT: That's a queer thought now, and a true thought. Wait now till I think it out. . . . If it wasn't for the sense I have, and for my wife and family, and for me joining the force the time I did, it might be myself now would be after breaking gaol and hiding in the dark, and it might be him that's hiding in the dark and that got out of gaol would be sitting up where I am on this barrel. . . . And it might be myself would be creeping up trying to make my escape from himself, and it might be himself would be keeping the law, and myself would be breaking it, and myself would be trying maybe to put a bullet in his head, or to take up a lump of a stone the way you said he did . . . no, that myself did. . . . Oh! *(Gasps. After a pause.)* What's that? *(Grasps man's arm.)*

MAN: *(Jumps off barrel and listens, looking out over water.)* It's nothing, sergeant.

SERGEANT: I thought it might be a boat. I had a notion there might be friends of his coming about the quays with a boat.

MAN: Sergeant, I am thinking it was with the people you were, and not with the law you were, when you were a young man.

SERGEANT: Well, if I was foolish then, that time's gone.

MAN: Maybe, sergeant, it comes into your head sometimes, in spite of your belt and your tunic, that it might have been as well for you to have followed Granuaile.

SERGEANT: It's no business of yours what I think.

MAN: Maybe, sergeant, you'll be on the side of the country yet.

SERGEANT: *(Gets off barrel.)* Don't talk to me like that. I have my duties and I know them. *(Looks round.)* That was a boat; I hear the oars.

(Goes to the steps and looks down.)

MAN: *(Sings)*—

O, then, tell me, Shawn O'Farrell,
Where the gathering is to be.
In the old spot by the river
Right well known to you and me!

SERGEANT: Stop that! Stop that, I tell you!

MAN: *(Sings louder)*—

One word more, for signal token,
Whistle up the marching tune,
With your pike upon your shoulder,
At the Rising of the Moon.

SERGEANT: If you don't stop that, I'll arrest you.

(A whistle from below answers, repeating the air.)

SERGEANT: That's a signal. *(Stands between him and steps.)* You must not pass this way. . . . Step farther back. . . . Who are you? You are no ballad-singer.

MAN: You needn't ask who I am; that placard will tell you. *(Points to placard.)*

SERGEANT: You are the man I am looking for.

MAN: *(Takes off hat and wig. Sergeant seizes them.)* I am. There's a hundred pounds on my head. There is a friend of mine below in a boat. He knows a safe place to bring me to.

SERGEANT: *(Looking still at hat and wig.)* It's a pity! It's a pity. You deceived me. You deceived me well.

MAN: I am a friend of Granuaile. There is a hundred pounds on my head.

SERGEANT: It's a pity, it's a pity!

MAN: Will you let me pass, or must I make you let me?

SERGEANT: I am in the force. I will not let you pass.

MAN: I thought to do it with my tongue. *(Puts hand in breast.)* What is that?

(Voice of Policeman X outside:) Here, this is where we left him.

SERGEANT: It's my comrades coming.

MAN: You won't betray me . . . the friend of Granuaile. *(Slips behind barrel.)*

(Voice of Policeman B:) That was the last of the placards.

POLICEMAN X: *(As they come in.)* If he makes his escape it won't be unknown he'll make it.

(Sergeant puts hat and wig behind his back.)

POLICEMAN B: Did any one come this way?

SERGEANT: *(After a pause.)* No one.

POLICEMAN B: No one at all?

SERGEANT: No one at all.

POLICEMAN B: We had no orders to go back to the station; we can stop along with you.

SERGEANT: I don't want you. There is nothing for you to do here.

POLICEMAN B: You bade us to come back here and keep watch with you.

SERGEANT: I'd sooner be alone. Would any man come this way and you making all that talk? It is better the place to be quiet.

POLICEMAN B: Well, we'll leave you the lantern anyhow. *(Hands it to him.)*

SERGEANT: I don't want it. Bring it with you.

POLICEMAN B: You might want it. There are clouds coming up and you have the darkness of the night before you yet. I'll leave it over here on the barrel. *(Goes to barrel.)*

SERGEANT: Bring it with you I tell you. No more talk.

POLICEMAN B: Well, I thought it might be a comfort to you. I often think when I have it in my hand and can be flashing it about into every dark corner *(doing so)* that it's the same as being beside the fire at home, and the bits of bogwood blazing up now and again.

(Flashes it about, now on the barrel, now on Sergeant.)

SERGEANT: *(Furious.)* Be off the two of you, yourselves and your lantern!

(They go out. Man comes from behind barrel. He and Sergeant stand looking at one another.)

SERGEANT: What are you waiting for?

MAN: For my hat, of course, and my wig. You wouldn't wish me to get my death of cold?

(Sergeant gives them.)

MAN: *(Going towards steps.)* Well, good-night, comrade, and thank you. You did me a good turn to-night, and I'm obliged to you. Maybe I'll be able to do as much for you when the small rise up and the big fall down . . . when we all change places at the Rising *(waves his hand and disappears)* of the Moon.

SERGEANT: *(Turning his back to audience and reading placard.)* A hundred pounds reward! A hundred pounds! *(Turns towards audience.)* I wonder, now, am I as great a fool as I think I am?

Curtain.

The Grave of Rury[1]

BY T. W. Rolleston (1857-1920)

Clear as air, the western waters.
Evermore their sweet, unchanging song
Murmur in their stony channels
Round O'Conor's sepulchre in Cong.

Crownless, hopeless, here he lingered;
Year on year went by him like a dream,
While the far-off roar of conquest
Murmured faintly like the singing stream.

---

1 Rory O'Conor was the last High King of Ireland because in submitting to Henry II in 1171 he acknowledged the fact that Ireland was no longer independent. He spent the closing years of his life in the monastery of St. Fechin at Cong, County Mayo. He had no successor.

Here he died, and here they tombed him,
Men of Fechin, chanting round his grave.
Did they know, ah! did they know it,
What they buried by the babbling wave?

Now above the sleep of Rury
Holy things and great have passed away;
Stone by stone the stately Abbey
Falls and fades in passionless decay.

Darkly grows the quiet ivy,
Pale the broken arches glimmer through;
Dark upon the cloister-garden
Dreams the shadow of the ancient yew.

Through the roofless aisles the verdure
Flows, the meadow-sweet and fox-glove bloom.
Earth, the mother and consoler,
Winds soft arms about the lonely tomb.

Peace and holy gloom possess him,
Last of Gaelic monarchs of the Gael,
Slumbering by the young, eternal
River-voices of the western vale.

Poisson D'Avril

BY E. Œ. Somerville (1859-1949)
AND Martin Ross (1862-1915)

THE atmosphere of the waiting-room set at naught at a single glance the theory that there can be no smoke without fire. The station-master, when remonstrated with, stated, as an incontrovertible fact, that any chimney in the world would smoke in a south-easterly wind, and further, said there wasn't a poker, and that if you poked the fire the grate would fall out. He was, however, sympathetic, and went on his knees before the smouldering mound of slack, endeavouring to charm it to a smile by subtle proddings with the handle of the ticket punch. Finally, he took me to his own kitchen fire and talked politics and salmon fishing, the former with judicious attention to my presumed point of view, and careful suppression of his own, the latter with no less tactful regard for my admission that for three days I had not caught a fish, while the steam rose from my wet boots, in witness of the ten miles of rain through which an outside car had carried me.

Before the train was signalled I realized for the hundredth time the magnificent superiority of the Irish mind to the trammels of officialdom, and the inveterate supremacy in Ireland of the personal element.

"You might get a foot-warmer at Carrig Junction," said a species of lay porter in a knitted jersey, ramming my suit-case upside down under the seat. "Sometimes they're in it, and more times they're not."

The train dragged itself rheumatically from the station, and a cold spring rain—the time was the middle of a most inclement April—smote it in flank as it came into the open. I pulled up both windows and began to smoke; there is, at least, a semblance of warmth in a thoroughly vitiated atmosphere.

It is my wife's habit to assert that I do not read her letters, and being now on my way to join her and my family in Gloucestershire, it seemed a sound thing to study again her latest letter of instructions.

"I am starting to-day, as Alice wrote to say we must be there two days before the wedding, so as to have a rehearsal for the pages. Their dresses have come, and they look too delicious in them—"

(I here omit profuse particulars not pertinent to this tale)—

"It is sickening for you to have had such bad sport. If the worst comes to the worst couldn't you buy one?—"

I smote my hand upon my knee. I had forgotten the infernal salmon! What a score for Philippa! If these *contretemps* would only teach her that I was not to be relied upon, they would have their uses, but experience is wasted upon her; I have no objection to being called an idiot, but, that being so, I ought to be allowed the privileges and exemptions proper to idiots. Philippa had, no doubt, written to Alice Hervey, and assured her that Sinclair would be only too delighted to bring her a salmon, and Alice Hervey, who was rich enough to find much enjoyment in saving money, would reckon upon it, to its final fin in mayonnaise.

Plunged in morose meditations, I progressed through a country parcelled out by shaky and crooked walls into a patchwood of hazel scrub and rocky fields, veiled in rain. About every six miles there was a station, wet and windswept; at one the sole occurrence was the presentation of a newspaper to the guard by the station-master; at the next the guard read aloud some choice excerpts from the same to the porter. The Personal Element was potent on this branch of the Munster and Connaught Railway. Routine, abhorrent to all artistic minds, was sheathed in conversation; even the engine-driver, a functionary ordinarily as aloof as the Mikado, alleviated his enforced isolation by sociable shrieks to every level crossing, while the long row of public-houses that formed, as far as I could judge, the town of Carrig, received a special and, as it seemed, humorous salutation.

The time-table decreed that we were to spend ten minutes at Carrig Junction; it was fifteen before the crowd of market people on the platform had been assimilated; finally, the window of a neighbouring carriage was flung open, and a wrathful English voice asked how much longer the train was going to wait. The station-master, who was at the moment engrossed in conversation with the guard and a man who was carrying a long parcel wrapped in newspaper, looked round, and said gravely:

"Well now, that's a mystery!"

The man with the parcel turned away, and convulsively studied a poster. The guard put his hand over his mouth.

The voice, still more wrathfully, demanded the earliest hour at which its owner could get to Belfast.

"Ye'll be asking me next when I take me breakfast," replied the station-master, without haste or palpable annoyance.

The window went up again with a bang, the man with the parcel dug the guard in the ribs with his elbow, and the parcel slipped from under his arm and fell on the platform.

"Oh my! oh my! Me fish!" exclaimed the man, solicitously picking up a remarkably good-looking salmon that had slipped from its wrapping of newspaper.

Inspiration came to me, and I, in my turn, opened my window and summoned the station-master.

Would his friend sell me the salmon? The station-master entered upon the mission with ardour, but without success.

No; the gentleman was only just after running down to the town for it in the delay, but why wouldn't I run down and get one for myself? There was half a dozen more of them below at Coffey's, selling cheap; there would be time enough, the mail wasn't signalled yet.

I jumped from the carriage and doubled out of the station at top speed, followed by an assurance from the guard that he would not forget me.

Congratulating myself on the ascendancy of the personal element, I sped through the soapy limestone mud towards the public-houses. En route I met a heated man carrying yet another salmon, who, without preamble, informed me that there were three or four more good fish in it, and that he was after running down from the train himself.

"Ye have whips o' time!" he called after me. "It's the first house that's not a public-house. Ye'll see boots in the window—she'll give them for tenpence a pound if ye're stiff with her!"

I ran past the public-houses.

"Tenpence a pound!" I exclaimed inwardly, "at this time of year! That's good enough."

Here I perceived the house with boots in the window, and dived into its dark doorway.

A cobbler was at work behind a low counter. He mumbled something about herself, through lengths of waxed thread that hung across his mouth, a fat woman appeared at an inner door, and at that moment I heard, appallingly near, the whistle of the incoming mail. The fat woman grasped the situation in an instant, and with what appeared but one movement, snatched a large fish from the floor of the room behind her and flung a newspaper round it.

"Eight pound weight!" she said swiftly. "Ten shillings!"

A convulsive effort of mental arithmetic assured me that this was more than tenpence a pound, but it was not the moment for stiffness. I shoved a half-sovereign into her fishy hand, clasped my salmon in my arms, and ran.

Needless to say it was uphill, and at the steepest gradient another whistle stabbed me like a spur; above the station roof successive and advancing puffs of steam warned me that the worst had probably happened, but still I ran. When I gained the platform my train was already clear of it, but the personal element held good. Every soul in the station, or so it seemed to me, lifted up his voice and yelled. The station-master put his fingers in his mouth and sent after the departing train an unearthly whistle, with a high trajectory and a serrated edge. It took effect; the train slackened, I plunged from the platform and followed it up the rails, and every window in both trains blossomed with the heads of deeply interested spectators. The guard met me on the line, very apologetic and primed with an explanation that the gentleman going for the boat train wouldn't let him wait any longer, while from our rear came an exultant cry from the station-master.

"Ye *told* him ye wouldn't forget him!"

"There's a few countrywomen in your carriage, sir," said the guard, ignoring the taunt, as he shoved me and my salmon up the side of the train, "but they'll be getting out in a couple of stations. There wasn't another seat in the train for them!"

My sensational return to my carriage was viewed with the utmost sympathy by no less than seven shawled and cloaked countrywomen. In order to make room for me one of them seated herself on the floor with her basket in her lap, another, on the seat opposite to me, squeezed herself under the central elbow flap that had been turned up to make room. The aromas of wet cloaks, turf smoke, and salt fish formed a potent blend. I was excessively hot, and the eyes of the seven women were fastened upon me with intense and unwearying interest.

"Move west a small piece, Mary Jack, if you please," said a voluminous matron in the corner, "I declare we're as throng as three in a bed this minute!"

"Why then, Julia Casey, there's little throubling yourself," grumbled the woman under the flap. "Look at the way meself is! I wonder is it to be putting humps on themselves the gentry has them things down on top o' them! I'd sooner be carrying a basket of turnips on me back than to be scrooged this way!"

The woman on the floor at my feet rolled up at me a glance of compassionate amusement at this rustic ignorance, and tactfully changed the conversation by supposing that it was at Coffey's I got the salmon.

I said it was.

There was a silence, during which it was obvious that one question burnt in every heart.

"I'll go bail she axed him tinpence!" said the woman under the flap, as one who touches the limits of absurdity.

"It's a beautiful fish!" I said defiantly. "Eight pounds weight. I gave her ten shillings for it."

What is described in newspapers as "sensation in court" greeted this confession.

"Look!" said the woman under the flap, darting her head out of the hood of her cloak, like a tortoise, " 'tis what it is, ye haven't as much roguery in your heart as 'd make ye a match for her!"

"Divil blow the ha'penny Eliza Coffey paid for that fish!" burst out the fat woman in the corner. "Thim lads o' her's had a creel full o' thim snatched this morning before it was making day!"

"How would the gentleman be a match for her!" shouted the woman on the floor through a long-drawn whistle that told of a coming station. "Sure a Turk itself wouldn't be a match for her! That one has a tongue that'd clip a hedge!"

At the station they clambered out laboriously, and with groaning. I handed down to them their monster baskets, laden, apparently, with ingots of lead; they told me in return that I was a fine *grauver* man, and it was a pity there weren't more like me; they wished, finally, that my journey might well thrive with me, and passed from my ken, bequeathing to me, after the agreeable manner of their kind, a certain comfortable mental sleekness that reason cannot immediately dispel. They also left me in possession of the fact that I was about to present the irreproachable Alice Hervey with a contraband salmon.

The afternoon passed cheerlessly into evening, and my journey did not conspicuously thrive with me. Somewhere in the dripping twilight I changed trains, and again later on, and at each change the salmon moulted some more of its damp raiment of newspaper, and I debated seriously the idea of interring it, regardless of consequences, in my portmanteau. A lamp was banged into the roof of my carriage, half an inch of orange flame, poised in a large glass globe, like a gold fish, and of about as much use as an illuminant. Here also was handed in the dinner basket that I had wired for, and its contents, arid though they were, enabled me to achieve at least some measure of mechanical distension, followed by a dreary lethargy that was not far from drowsiness.

At the next station we paused long; nothing whatever occurred, and the rain drummed patiently upon the roof. Two nuns and some schoolgirls were in the carriage next door, and their voices came plaintively and in snatches through the partition; after a long period of apparent collapse, during which I closed my eyes to evade the cold gaze of the salmon through the netting, a voice in the next carriage said resourcefully:

"Oh, girls, I'll tell you what we'll do! We'll say the Rosary!"

"Oh, that will be lovely!" said another voice; "well, who'll give it out? Theresa Condon, you'll give it out."

Theresa Condon gave it out, in a not unmelodious monotone, interspersed with the responses, always in a lower cadence; the words were indistinguishable, but the rise and fall of the western voices was lulling as the hum of bees. I fell asleep.

I awoke in total darkness; the train was motionless, and complete and profound silence reigned. We were at a station, that much I discerned by the light of the dim lamp at the far end of a platform glistening with wet. I struck a match and ascertained that it was eleven o'clock, precisely the hour at which I was to board the mail train. I jumped out and ran down the platform; there was no one in the train; there was no one even on the engine, which was forlornly hissing to itself in the silence. There was not a human being anywhere. Every door was closed, and all was dark. The name-board of the station was faintly visible; with a lighted match I went along it letter by letter. It seemed as if the whole alphabet were in it, and by the time I had got to the end I had forgotten the beginning. One fact I had, however, mastered, that it was not the junction at which I was to catch the mail.

I was undoubtedly awake, but for a moment I was inclined to entertain the idea that there had been an accident, and that I had entered upon existence in another world. Once more I assailed the station house and the appurtenances thereof, the ticket office, the waiting-room, finally, and at some distance, the goods store, outside which the single lamp of the station commented feebly on the drizzle and the darkness. As I approached it a crack of light under the door became perceptible, and a voice was suddenly uplifted within.

"Your best now agin that! Throw down your jack!"

I opened the door with pardonable violence, and found the guard, the station-master, the driver, and the stoker, seated on barrels round a packing-case, on which they were playing a game of cards.

To have too egregiously the best of a situation is not, to a generous mind, a source of strength. In the perfection of their overthrow I permitted the driver and stoker to wither from their places, and to fade away into the outer darkness without any suitable send-off; with the guard and the station-master I dealt more faithfully, but the pleasure of throwing water on drowned rats is not a lasting one. I accepted the statements that they thought there wasn't a Christian in the train, that a few minutes here or there wouldn't signify, that they would have me at the junction in twenty minutes, and it was often the mail was late.

Fired by this hope I hurried back to my carriage, preceded at an emulous gallop by the officials. The guard thrust in with me the lantern from the card table, and fled to his van.

"Mind the Goods, Tim!" shouted the station-master, as he slammed my door, "she might be coming any time now!"

The answer travelled magnificently back from the engine.

"Let her come! She'll meet her match!" A war-whoop upon the steam whistle fittingly closed the speech, and the train sprang into action.

We had about fifteen miles to go, and we banged and bucketed over it in what was, I should imagine, record time. The carriage felt as if it were galloping on four wooden legs, my teeth chattered in my head, and the salmon slowly churned its way forth from its newspaper, and moved along the netting with dreadful stealth.

All was of no avail.

"Well," said the guard, as I stepped forth on to the deserted platform of Loughranny, "that owld Limited Mail's th' un-punctualest thrain in Ireland! If you're a minute late she's gone from you, and maybe if you were early you might be half an hour waiting for her!"

On the whole the guard was a gentleman. He said he would show me the best hotel in the town, though he feared I would be hard set to get a bed anywhere because of the "*Feis*" (a Feis, I should explain, is a festival, devoted to competitions in Irish songs and dances). He shouldered my portmanteau, he even grappled successfully with the salmon, and, as we traversed the empty streets, he explained to me how easily I could catch the morning boat from Rosslare, and how it was, as a matter of fact, quite the act of providence that my original scheme had been frustrated.

All was dark at the uninviting portals of the hotel favoured by the guard. For a full five minutes we waited at them, ringing hard: I suggested that we should try elsewhere.

"He'll come," said the guard, with the confidence of the Pied Piper of Hamelin, retaining an implacable thumb upon the button of the electric bell. "He'll come. Sure it rings in his room!"

The victim came, half awake, half dressed, and with an inch of dripping candle in his fingers. There was not a bed there, he said, nor in the town neither.

I said I would sit in the dining-room till the time for the early train.

"Sure there's five beds in the dining-room," replied the boots, "and there's mostly two in every bed."

His voice was firm, but there was a wavering look in his eye.

"What about the billiard-room, Mike?" said the guard, in wooing tones.

"Ah, God bless you! we have a mattress on the table this minute!" answered the boots, wearily, "and the fellow that got the First Prize for Reels asleep on top of it!"

"Well, and can't ye put the palliasse on the floor under it, ye omadhawn?" said the guard, dumping my luggage and the salmon in the hall, "sure there's no snugger place in the house! I must run away home now, before Herself thinks I'm dead altogether!"

His retreating footsteps went lightly away down the empty street.

"Annything don't throuble *him!*" said the boots bitterly.

As for me, nothing save the Personal Element stood between me and destitution.

It was in the dark of the early morning that I woke again to life and its troubles. A voice, dropping, as it were, over the edge of some smothering over-world, had awakened me. It was the voice of the First Prize for Reels, descending through a pocket of the billiard-table.

"I beg your pardon, sir, are ye going on the 5 to Cork?"

I grunted a negative.

"Well, if ye were, ye'd be late," said the voice.

I received this useful information in indignant silence, and endeavoured to wrap myself again in the vanishing skirts of a dream.

"I'm going on the 6:30 meself," proceeded the voice, "and it's unknown to me how I'll put on me boots. Me feet is swelled the size o' three-pound loaves with the dint of the little dancing-shoes I had on me in the competition last night. Me feet's delicate that way, and I'm a great epicure about me boots."

I snored aggressively, but the dream was gone. So, for all practical purposes was the night.

The First Prize for Reels arose, presenting an astonishing spectacle of grass-green breeches, a white shirt, and pearl-grey stockings, and accomplished a toilet that consisted of removing these and putting on ordinary garments, completed by the apparently excruciating act of getting into his boots. At any other hour of the day I might have been sorry for him. He then removed himself and his belongings to the hall, and there entered upon a resounding conversation with the boots, while I crawled forth from my lair to renew the strife with circumstances and to endeavour to compose a telegram to Alice Hervey of explanation and apology that should cost less than seven and six-pence. There was also the salmon to be dealt with.

Here the boots intervened, opportunely, with a cup of tea, and the intelligence that he had already done up the salmon in straw bottle-covers and brown paper, and that I could travel Europe with it if I liked. He further informed me that he would run up to the station with the luggage now, and that maybe I wouldn't mind carrying the fish myself; it was on the table in the hall.

My train went at 6:15. The boots had secured for me one of many empty carriages, and lingered conversationally till the train started; he regretted politely my bad night at the hotel, and assured me that only for Jimmy Durkan having a little drink taken—Jimmy Durkan was the First Prize for Reels—he would have turned him off the billiard-table for my benefit. He finally confided to me that Mr. Durkan was engaged to his sister, and was a rising baker in the town of Limerick; "indeed," he said, "any girl might be glad to get him. He dances like whalebone, and he makes grand bread!"

Here the train started.

It was late that night when, stiff, dirty, with tired eyes blinking in the dazzle of electric lights, I was conducted by the Herveys' beautiful footman into the Herveys' baronial hall, and was told by the Herveys' imperial butler that dinner was over, and the gentlemen had just gone into the drawing-room. I was in the act of hastily declining to join them there, when a voice cried:

"Here he is!"

And Philippa, rustling and radiant, came forth into the hall, followed in shimmers of satin, and flutterings of lace, by Alice Hervey, by the bride elect, and by the usual festive rout of exhilarated relatives, male and female, whose mission it is to keep things lively before a wedding.

"Is this a wedding present for me, Uncle Sinclair?" cried the bride elect, through a deluge of questions and commiserations, and snatched from under my arm the brown paper parcel that had remained there from force of direful habit.

"I advise you not to open it!" I exclaimed; "it's a salmon!"

The bride elect, with a shriek of disgust, and without an instant of hesitation, hurled it at her nearest neighbour, the head bridesmaid. The head bridesmaid, with an answering shriek, sprang to one side, and the parcel that I had cherished with a mother's care across two countries and a stormy Channel fell, with a crash, on the flagged floor.

Why did it crash?

"A salmon!" screamed Philippa, gazing at the parcel, round which a pool was already forming, "why, that's whisky! Can't you smell it?"

The footman here respectfully interposed, and kneeling down, cautiously extracted from folds of brown paper a straw bottle-cover full of broken glass and dripping with whisky.

"I'm afraid the other things are rather spoiled, sir," he said seriously, and drew forth, successively, a very large pair of high-low shoes, two long grey worsted stockings, and a pair of grass-green breeches.

They brought the house down, in a manner doubtless familiar to them when they shared the triumphs of Mr. Jimmy Durkan, but they left Alice Hervey distinctly cold.

"You know, darling," she said to Philippa afterwards, "I don't think it was very clever of dear Sinclair to take the wrong parcel. I *had* counted on that salmon."

From the Preface to John Bull's Other Island

BY George Bernard Shaw (1856-1950)

WHAT IS AN IRISHMAN?

When I say that I am an Irishman I mean that I was born in Ireland, and that my native language is the English of Swift and not the unspeakable jargon of the mid-XIX century London newspapers. My extraction is the extraction of most Englishmen: that is, I have no trace in me of the commercially imported North Spanish strain which passes for aboriginal Irish: I am a genuine typical Irishman of the Danish, Norman, Cromwellian, and (of course) Scotch invasions. I am violently and arrogantly Protestant by family tradition; but let no English Government therefore count on my allegiance: I am English enough to be an inveterate Republican and Home Ruler. It is true that one of my grandfathers was an Orangeman; but then his sister was an abbess; and his uncle, I am proud to say, was hanged as a rebel. When I look round me on the hybrid cosmopolitans, slum poisoned or square pampered, who call themselves Englishmen today, and see them bullied by the Irish Protestant garrison as no Bengalee now lets himself be bullied by an Englishman; when I see the Irishman everywhere standing clearheaded, sane, hardily callous to the boyish sentimentalities, susceptibilities, and credulities that make the Englishman the dupe of every charlatan and the idolater of every numskull, I perceive that Ireland is the only spot on earth which still produces the ideal Englishman of history. Blackguard, bully, drunkard, liar, foulmouth, flatterer, beggar, backbiter, venal functionary, corrupt judge, envious friend, vindictive opponent, unparalleled political traitor: all these your Irishman may easily be, just as he may be a gentleman (a species extinct in England, and nobody a penny the worse); but he is never quite the hysterical, nonsense-crammed, fact-proof, truth-terrified, unballasted sport of all the bogey panics and all the silly enthusiasms that now calls itself "God's Englishman." England cannot do without its Irish and its Scots today, because it cannot do without at least a little sanity.

THE PROTESTANT GARRISON

The more Protestant an Irishman is—the more English he is, if it flatters you to have it put that way, the more intolerable he finds it to be ruled by English instead of Irish folly. A "loyal" Irishman is an abhorrent phenomenon, because it is an unnatural one. No doubt English rule is vigorously exploited in the interests of the property, power, and promotion of the Irish classes as against the Irish masses. Our delicacy is part of a keen sense of reality which makes us a very practical, and even, on occasion, a very coarse people. The Irish soldier takes the King's shilling and drinks the King's health; and the Irish squire takes the title deeds of the English settlement and rises uncovered to the strains of the English national anthem. But do not mistake this cupboard loyalty for anything deeper. It gains a broad base from the normal attachment of every reasonable man to the established government as long as it is bearable; for we all, after a certain age, prefer peace to revolution and order to chaos, other things being equal. Such considerations produce loyal Irishmen as they produce loyal Poles and Fins, loyal Hindoos, loyal Filipinos, and faithful slaves. But there is nothing more in it than that. If there is an entire lack of gall in the feeling of the Irish gentry towards the English, it is because the Englishman is always gaping admiringly at the Irishman as at some clever child prodigy. He overrates him with a generosity born of a traditional conviction of his own superiority in the deeper aspects of human character. As the Irish gentleman, tracing his pedigree to the conquest or one of the invasions, is equally convinced that if this superiority really exists, he is the genuine true blue heir to it, and as he is easily able to hold his own in all the superficial social accomplishments, he finds English society agreeable, and English houses very comfortable, Irish establishments being generally straitened by an attempt to keep a park and a stable on an income which would not justify an Englishman in venturing upon a wholly detached villa.

OUR TEMPERAMENTS CONTRASTED

But however pleasant the relations between the Protestant garrison and the English gentry may be, they are always essentially of the nature of an *entente cordiale* between foreigners. Personally I like Englishmen much better than Irishmen (no doubt because they make more of me) just as many Englishmen like Frenchmen better than Englishmen, and never go on board a Peninsular and Oriental steamer when one of the ships of the Messageries Maritimes is available. But I never think of an Englishman as my countryman. I should as soon think of applying that term to a German. And the Englishman has the same feeling. When a Frenchman fails to make the distinction, we both feel a certain disparagement involved in the misapprehension. Macaulay, seeing that the Irish had in Swift an author worth stealing, tried to annex him by contending that he must be classed as an Englishman because he was not an aboriginal Celt. He might as well have refused the name of Briton to Addison because he did not stain himself blue and attach scythes to the poles of his sedan chair. In spite of all such trifling with facts, the actual distinction between the idolatrous Englishman and the fact-facing Irishman, of the same extraction though they be, remains to explode those two hollowest of fictions, the Irish and English "races." There is no Irish race any more than there is an English race or a Yankee race. There is an Irish climate, which will stamp an immigrant more deeply and durably in two years, apparently, than the English climate will in two hundred. It is reinforced by an artificial economic climate which does some of the work attributed to the natural geographic one; but the geographic climate is eternal and irresistible, making a mankind and a womankind that Kent, Middlesex, and East Anglia cannot produce and do not want to imitate.

How can I sketch the broad lines of the contrast as they strike me? Roughly I should say that the Englishman is wholly at the mercy of his imagination, having no sense of reality to check it. The Irishman, with a far subtler and more fastidious imagination, has one eye always on things as they are. If you compare Moore's visionary Minstrel Boy with Mr Rudyard Kipling's quasi-realistic Soldiers Three, you may yawn over Moore or gush over him, but you will not suspect him of having had any illusions about the contemporary British private; whilst as to Mr Kipling, you will see that he has not, and unless he settles in Ireland for a few years will always remain constitutionally and congenitally incapable of having, the faintest inkling of the reality which he idolizes as Tommy Atkins. Perhaps you have never thought of illustrating the contrast between English and Irish by Moore and Mr Kipling, or even by Parnell and Gladstone. Sir Boyle Roche and Shakespear may seem more to your point. Let me find you a more dramatic instance. Think of the famous meeting between the

Duke of Wellington, that intensely Irish Irishman, and Nelson, that intensely English Englishman. Wellington's contemptuous disgust at Nelson's theatricality as a professed hero, patriot, and rhapsode, a theatricality which in an Irishman would have been an insufferably vulgar affectation, was quite natural and inevitable. Wellington's formula for that kind of thing was a well-known Irish one: "Sir: dont be a damned fool." It is the formula of all Irishmen for all Englishmen to this day. It is the formula of Larry Doyle for Tom Broadbent in my play, in spite of Doyle's affection for Tom. Nelson's genius, instead of producing intellectual keenness and scrupulousness, produced mere delirium. He was drunk with glory, exalted by his fervent faith in the sound British patriotism of the Almighty, nerved by the vulgarest anti-foreign prejudice, and apparently unchastened by any reflections on the fact that he had never had to fight a technically capable and properly equipped enemy except on land, where he had never been successful. Compare Wellington, who had to fight Napoleon's armies, Napoleon's marshals, and finally Napoleon himself, without one moment of illusion as to the human material he had to command, without one gush of the "Kiss me, Hardy" emotion which enabled Nelson to idolize his crews and his staff, without forgetting even in his dreams that the normal British officer of that time was an incapable amateur (as he still is) and the normal British soldier a never-do-well (he is now a depressed and respectable young man). No wonder Wellington became an accomplished comedian in the art of anti-climax, scandalizing the unfortunate Croker, responding to the demand for glorious sentiments by the most disenchanting touches of realism, and, generally, pricking the English windbag at its most explosive crises of distention. Nelson, intensely nervous and theatrical, made an enormous fuss about victories so cheap that he would have deserved shooting if he had lost them, and, not content with lavishing splendid fighting on helpless adversaries like the heroic De Brueys or Villeneuve (who had not even the illusion of heroism when he went like a lamb to the slaughter), got himself killed by his passion for exposing himself to death in that sublime defiance of it which was perhaps the supreme tribute of the exquisite coward to the King of Terrors (for, believe me, you cannot be a hero without being a coward: supersense cuts both ways), the result being a tremendous effect on the gallery. Wellington, most capable of captains, was neither a hero nor a patriot: perhaps not even a coward; and had it not been for the Nelsonic anecdotes invented for him—"Up guards, and at em" and so forth—and the fact that the antagonist with whom he finally closed was such a master of theatrical effect that Wellington could not fight him without getting into his limelight, nor overthrow him (most unfortunately for us all) without drawing the eyes of the whole world to the catastrophe, the Iron Duke would have been almost forgotten by this time. Now that contrast is English against Irish all over, and is the more delicious because the real Irishman in it is the Englishman of tradition, whilst the real Englishman is the traditional theatrical foreigner.

The value of the illustration lies in the fact that Nelson and Wellington were both in the highest degree efficient, and both in the highest degree incompatible with one another on any other footing than one of independence. The government of Nelson by Wellington or of Wellington by Nelson is felt at once to be a dishonorable outrage to the governed and a finally impossible task for the governor.

I daresay some Englishman will now try to steal Wellington as Macaulay tried to steal Swift. And he may plead with some truth that though it seems impossible that any other country than England could produce a hero so utterly devoid of common sense, intellectual delicacy, and international chivalry as Nelson, it may be contended that Wellington was rather an eighteenth century aristocratic type, than a specifically Irish type. George IV and Byron, contrasted with Gladstone, seem Irish in respect of a certain humorous blackguardism, and a power of appreciating art and sentiment without being duped by them into mistaking romantic figments for realities. But faithlessness and the need for carrying off the worthlessness and impotence that accompany it, produce in all nations a gay, sceptical, amusing, blaspheming, witty fashion which suits the flexibility of the Irish mind very well; and the contrast between this fashion and the energetic infatuations that have enabled intellectually ridiculous men, without wit or humor, to go on crusades and make successful revolutions, must not be confused with the contrast between the English and Irish idiosyncrasies. The Irishman makes a distinction which the Englishman is too lazy intellectually (the intellectual laziness and slovenliness of the English is almost beyond belief) to make. The Englishman, impressed with the dissoluteness of the faithless wits of the Restoration and the Regency, and with the victories of the wilful zealots of the patriotic, religious, and revolutionary wars, jumps to the conclusion that wilfulness is the main thing. In this he is right. But he overdoes his jump so far as to conclude also that stupidity and wrong-headedness are better guarantees of efficiency and trustworthiness than intellectual vivacity, which he mistrusts as a common symptom of worthlessness, vice, and instability. Now in this he is most dangerously wrong. Whether the Irishman grasps the truth as firmly as the Englishman may be open to question; but he is certainly comparatively free from the error. That affectionate and admiring love of sentimental stupidity for its own sake, both in men and women, which shines so steadily through the novels of Thackeray, would hardly be possible in the works of an Irish novelist. Even Dickens, though too vital a genius and too severely educated in the school of shabby-genteel poverty to have any doubt of the national danger of fatheadedness in high places, evidently assumes rather too hastily the superiority of Mr Meagles to Sir John Chester and Harold Skimpole. On the other hand, it takes an Irishman years of residence in England to learn to respect and like a blockhead. An Englishman will not respect nor like anyone else. Every English statesman has to maintain his popularity by pretending to be ruder, more ignorant, more sentimental, more superstitious, more stupid than any man who has lived behind the scenes of public life for ten minutes can possibly be. Nobody dares to publish really intimate memoirs of him or really private letters of his until his whole generation has passed away, and his party can no longer be compromised by the discovery that the platitudinizing twaddler and hypocritical opportunist was really a man of some perception as well as of strong constitution, peg-away industry, personal ambition, and party keenness.

ENGLISH STUPIDITY EXCUSED

I do not claim it as a natural superiority in the Irish nation that it dislikes and mistrusts fools, and expects its political leaders to be clever and humbug-proof. It may be that if our resources included the armed force and virtually unlimited money which push the political and military figureheads of England through bungled enterprises to a muddled success, and create an illusion of some miraculous and divine innate English quality that enables a general to become a conqueror with abilities that would not suffice to save a cabman from having his license marked, and a member of parliament to become Prime Minister with the outlook on life of a sporting country solicitor educated by a private governess, we should lapse into gross intellectual sottishness, and prefer leaders who encouraged our vulgarities by sharing them, and flattered us by associating them with purchased successes, to our betters. But as it is, we cannot afford that sort of encouragement and flattery in Ireland. The odds against which our leaders have to fight would be too heavy for the fourth-rate Englishman whose leadership consists for the most part in marking time ostentatiously until they are violently shoved, and then stumbling blindly forward (or backward) wherever the shove sends them. We cannot crush England as a Pickford's van might crush a perambulator. We are the perambulator and England the Pickford. We must study her and our real weaknesses and real strength; we must practise upon her slow conscience and her quick terrors; we must deal in ideas and political principles since we cannot deal in bayonets; we must outwit, outwork, outstay her; we must embarrass, bully, even conspire and assassinate when nothing else will move her, if we are not all to be driven deeper and deeper into the shame and misery of our servitude. Our leaders must be not only determined enough, but clever enough to do this. We have no illusions as to the existence of any mysterious Irish pluck, Irish honesty, Irish bias on the part of Providence, or sterling Irish solidity of character, that will enable an Irish blockhead to hold his own against England. Blockheads are of no use to us: we were compelled to follow a supercilious, unpopular, tongue-tied, aristocratic Protestant Parnell, although there was no lack among us of fluent imbeciles, with majestic presences and oceans of dignity and sentiment, to promote into his place could they have done his work for us. It is obviously convenient that Mr Redmond should be a better speaker and rhetorician than Parnell; but if he began to use his powers to make himself agreeable instead of making himself reckoned with by the enemy; if he set to work to manufacture and support English shams and hypocrisies instead of exposing and denouncing them; if he constituted himself the permanent apologist of doing nothing, and, when the people insisted on his doing something, only roused himself to discover how to pretend to do it without really changing anything, he would lose his leadership as certainly as an English politician would, by the same course, attain a permanent place on the front bench. In short, our circumstances place a premium on political ability whilst the circumstances of England discount it; and the quality of the supply naturally follows the demand. If you miss in my writings that hero-worship of dotards and duffers which is planting England with statues of disastrous statesmen and absurd generals, the explanation is simply that I am an Irishman and you an Englishman.

IRISH PROTESTANTISM REALLY PROTESTANT

When I repeat that I am an Irish Protestant, I come to a part of the relation between England and Ireland that you will never understand unless I insist on explaining it to you with that Irish insistence on intellectual clarity to which my English critics are so intensely recalcitrant.

First, let me tell you that in Ireland Protestantism is really Protestant. It is true that there is an Irish Protestant Church (disestablished some 35 years ago) in spite of the fact that a Protestant Church is, fundamentally, a contradiction in terms. But this means only that the Protestants use the word Church to denote their secular organization, without troubling themselves about the metaphysical sense of Christ's famous pun, "Upon this rock I will build my church." The Church of England, which is a reformed Anglican Catholic Anti-Protestant Church, is quite another affair. An Anglican is acutely conscious that he is not a Wesleyan; and many Anglican clergymen do not hesitate to teach that all Methodists incur damnation. In Ireland all that the member of the Irish Protestant Church knows is that he is not a Roman Catholic. The decorations of even the "lowest" English Church seem to him to be extravagantly Ritualistic and Popish. I myself entered the Irish Church by baptism, a ceremony performed by my uncle in "his own church." But I was sent, with many boys of my own denomination, to a Wesleyan school where the Wesleyan catechism was taught without the least protest on the part of the parents, although there was so little presumption in favor of any boy there being a Wesleyan that if all the Church boys had been withdrawn at any moment, the school would have become bankrupt. And this was by no means analogous to the case of those working class members of the Church of England in London, who send their daughters to Roman Catholic schools rather than to the public elementary schools. They do so for the definite reason that the nuns teach girls good manners and sweetness of speech, which have no place in the County Council curriculum. But in Ireland the Church parent sends his son to a Wesleyan school (if it is convenient and socially eligible) because he is indifferent to the form of Protestantism, provided it is Protestantism. There is also in Ireland a characteristically Protestant refusal to take ceremonies and even sacraments very seriously except by way of strenuous objection to them when they are conducted with candles or incense. For example, I was never confirmed, although the ceremony was specially needed in my case as the failure of my appointed godfather to appear at my baptism had led to his responsibilities being assumed on the spot, at my uncle's order, by the sexton. And my case was a very common one, even among people quite untouched by modern scepticisms. Apart from the weekly churchgoing, which holds its own as a respectable habit, the initiations are perfunctory, the omissions regarded as negligible. The distinction between churchman and dissenter, which in England is a class distinction, a political distinction, and even occasionally a religious distinction, does not exist. Nobody is surprised in Ireland to find that the squire who is the local pillar of the formerly established Church is also a Plymouth Brother, and, except on certain special or fashionable occasions, attends the Methodist meeting-house. The parson has no priestly character and no priestly influence: the High Church curate of course exists and has his vogue among religious epicures of the other sex; but the general attitude of his congregation towards him is that of Dr Clifford. The clause in the Apostles' creed professing belief in a Catholic Church is a standing puzzle to Protestant children; and when they grow up they dismiss it from their minds more often than they solve it, because they really are not Catholics but Protestants to the extremest practicable degree of individualism. It is true that they talk of church and chapel with all the Anglican contempt for chapel; but in Ireland the chapel means the Roman Catholic church, for which the Irish Protestant reserves all the class rancor, the political hostility, the religious bigotry, and the bad blood generally that in England separates the Establishment from the nonconforming Protestant organizations. When a vulgar Irish Protestant speaks of a "Papist" he feels exactly as a vulgar Anglican vicar does when he speaks of a Dissenter. And when the vicar is Anglican enough to call himself a Catholic priest, wear a cassock, and bless his flock with two fingers, he becomes horrifically incomprehensible to the Irish Protestant Churchman, who, on his part, puzzles the Anglican by regarding a Methodist as tolerantly as an Irishman who likes grog regards an Irishman who prefers punch.

A FUNDAMENTAL ANOMALY

Now nothing can be more anomalous, and at bottom impossible, than a Conservative Protestant party standing for the established order against a revolutionary Catholic party. The Protestant is theoretically an anarchist as far as anarchism is practicable in human society: that is, he is an individualist, a freethinker, a self-helper, a Whig, a Liberal, a mistruster and vilifier of the State, a rebel. The Catholic is theoretically a Collectivist, a self-abnegator, a Tory, a Conservative, a supporter of Church and State one and undivisible, an obeyer. This would be a statement of fact as well as of theory if men were Protestants and Catholics by temperament and adult choice instead of by family tradition. The peasant who supposed that Wordsworth's son would carry on the business now the old gentleman was gone was not a whit more foolish than we who laugh at his ignorance of the nature of poetry whilst we take it as a matter of course that a son should "carry on" his father's religion. Hence, owing to our family system, the Catholic Churches are recruited daily at the font by temperamental Protestants, and the Protestant organizations by temperamental Catholics, with consequences most disconcerting to those who expect history to be deducible from the religious professions of the men who make it.

Still, though the Roman Catholic Church may occasionally catch such Tartars as Luther and Voltaire, or the Protestant organizations as Newman and Manning, the general run of mankind takes its impress from the atmosphere in which it is brought up. In Ireland the Roman Catholic peasant cannot escape the religious atmosphere of his Church. Except when he breaks out like a naughty child he is docile; he is reverent; he is content to regard knowledge as something not his business; he is a child before his Church, and accepts it as the highest authority in science and philosophy. He speaks of himself as a son of the Church, calling his priest father instead of brother or Mister. To rebel politically, he must break away from parish tutelage and follow a Protestant leader on national questions. His Church naturally fosters his submissiveness. The British Government and the Vatican may differ very vehemently as to whose subject the Irishman is to be; but they are quite agreed as to the propriety of his being a subject. Of the two, the British Government allows him more liberty, giving him as complete a democratic control of local government as his means will enable him to use, and a voice in the election of a formidable minority in the House of Commons, besides allowing him to read and learn what he likes—except when it makes a tufthunting onslaught on a seditious newspaper. But if he dared to claim a voice in the selection of his parish priest, or a representative at the Vatican, he would be denounced from the altar as an almost inconceivable blasphemer; and his educational opportunities are so restricted by his Church that he is heavily handicapped in every walk of life that requires any literacy. It is the aim of his priest to make him and keep him a submissive Conservative; and nothing but gross economic oppression and religious persecution could have produced the strange phenomenon of a revolutionary movement not only tolerated by the Clericals, but, up to a certain point, even encouraged by them. If there is such a thing as political science, with natural laws like any other science, it is certain that only the most violent external force could effect and maintain this unnatural combination of political revolution with Papal reaction, and of hardy individualism and independence with despotism and subjugation.

That violent external force is the clumsy thumb of English rule. If you would be good enough, ladies and gentlemen of England, to take your thumb away and leave us free to do something else than bite it, the unnaturally combined elements in Irish politics would fly asunder and recombine according to their proper nature with results entirely satisfactory to real Protestantism.

THE NATURE OF POLITICAL HATRED

Just reconsider the Home Rule question in the light of that very English characteristic of the Irish people, their political hatred of priests. Do not be distracted by the shriek of indignant denial from the Catholic papers and from those who have witnessed the charming relations between the Irish peasantry and their spiritual fathers. I am perfectly aware that the Irish love their priests as devotedly as the French loved them before the Revolution or as the Italians loved them before they imprisoned the Pope in the Vatican. They love their landlords too: many an Irish gentleman has found in his nurse a foster-mother more interested in him than his actual mother. They love the English, as every Englishman who travels in Ireland can testify. Please do not suppose that I speak satirically: the world is full of authentic examples of the concurrence of human kindliness with political rancor. Slaves and schoolboys often love their masters; Napoleon and his soldiers made desperate efforts to save from drowning the Russian soldiers under whom they had broken the ice with their cannon; even the relations between nonconformist peasants and country parsons in England are not invariably unkindly; in the southern States of America planters are often traditionally fond of negroes and kind to them, with substantial returns in humble affection; soldiers and sailors often admire and cheer their officers sincerely and heartily; nowhere is actual personal intercourse found compatible for long with the intolerable friction of hatred and malice. But people who persist in pleading these amiabilities as political factors must be summarily bundled out of the room when questions of State are to be discussed. Just as an Irishman may have English friends whom he may prefer to any Irishman of his acquaintance, and be kind, hospitable, and serviceable in his intercourse with Englishmen, whilst being perfectly prepared to make the Shannon run red with English blood if Irish freedom could be obtained at that price; so an Irish Catholic may like his priest as a man and revere him as a confessor and spiritual pastor whilst being implacably determined to seize the first opportunity of throwing off his yoke. This is political hatred: the only hatred that civilization allows to be mortal hatred.

THE REVOLT AGAINST THE PRIEST

Realize, then, that the popular party in Ireland is seething with rebellion against the tyranny of the Church. Imagine the feelings of an English farmer if the parson refused to marry him for less than £20, and if he had virtually no other way of getting married! Imagine the Church Rates revived in the form of an unofficial Income Tax scientifically adjusted to your taxable capacity by an intimate knowledge of your affairs verified in the confessional! Imagine being one of a peasantry reputed the poorest in the world, under the thumb of a priesthood reputed the richest in the world! Imagine a Catholic middle class continually defeated in the struggle of professional, official, and fashionable life by the superior education of its Protestant competitors, and yet forbidden by its priests to resort to the only efficient universities in the country! Imagine trying to get a modern education in a seminary of priests, where every modern book worth reading is on the index, and the earth is still regarded, not perhaps as absolutely flat, yet as being far from so spherical as Protestants allege! Imagine being forbidden to read this preface because it proclaims your own grievance! And imagine being bound to submit to all this because the popular side must hold together at all costs in the face of the Protestant enemy! That is, roughly, the predicament of Roman Catholic Ireland.

PROTESTANT LOYALTY: A FORECAST

Now let us have a look at Protestant Ireland. I have already said that a "loyal" Irishman is an abhorrent phenomenon, because he is an unnatural one. In Ireland it is not "loyalty" to drink the English king's health and stand uncovered to the English national anthem: it is simply exploitation of English rule in the interests of the property, power, and promotion of the Irish classes as against the Irish masses. From any other point of view it is cowardice and dishonor. I have known a Protestant go to Dublin Castle to be sworn in as a special constable, quite resolved to take the baton and break the heads of a patriotic faction just then upsetting the peace of the town, yet back out at the last moment because he could not bring himself to swallow the oath of allegiance tendered with the baton. There is no such thing as genuine loyalty in Ireland. There is a separation of the Irish people into two hostile camps: one Protestant, gentlemanly, and oligarchical; the other Roman Catholic, popular, and democratic. The oligarchy governs Ireland as a bureaucracy deriving authority from the king of England. It cannot cast him off without casting off its own ascendancy. Therefore it naturally exploits him sedulously, drinking his health, waving his flag, playing his anthem, and using the foolish word "traitor" freely in its cups. But let the English Government make a step towards the democratic party, and the Protestant garrison revolts at once, not with tears and prayers and anguish of soul and years of trembling reluctance, as the parliamentarians of the XVII century revolted against Charles I, but with acrid promptitude and strident threatenings. When England finally abandons the garrison by yielding to the demand for Home Rule, the Protestants will not go under, nor will they waste much time in sulking over their betrayal, and comparing their fate with that of Gordon left by Gladstone to perish on the spears of heathen fanatics. They cannot afford to retire into an Irish Faubourg St Germain. They will take an energetic part in the national government, which will be sorely in need of parliamentary and official forces independent of Rome. They will get not only the Protestant votes, but the votes of Catholics in that spirit of toleration which is everywhere extended to heresies that happen to be politically serviceable to the orthodox. They will not relax their determination to hold every inch of the government of Ireland that they can grasp; but as that government will then be a national Irish government instead of as now an English government, their determination will make them the vanguard of Irish Nationalism and Democracy as against Romanism and Sacerdotalism, leaving English Unionists grieved and shocked at their discovery of the true value of an Irish Protestant's loyalty.

But there will be no open break in the tradition of the party. The Protestants will still be the party of Union, which will then mean, not the Repeal of Home Rule, but the maintenance of the Federal Union of English-speaking commonwealths, now theatrically called the Empire. They will pull down the Union Jack without the smallest scruple; but they know the value of the Channel Fleet, and will cling closer than brothers to that and any other Imperial asset that can be exploited for the protection of Ireland against foreign aggression or the sharing of expenses with the British taxpayer. They know that the Irish coast is for the English invasion-scare-monger the heel of Achilles, and that they can use this to make him pay for the boot.

PROTESTANT PUGNACITY

If any Englishman feels incredulous as to this view of Protestantism as an essentially Nationalist force in Ireland, let him ask himself which leader he, if he were an Irishman, would rather have back from the grave to fight England: the Catholic Daniel O'Connell or the Protestant Parnell. O'Connell organized the Nationalist movement only to draw its teeth, to break its determination, and to declare that Repeal of the Union was not worth the shedding of a drop of blood. He died in the bosom of his Church, not in the bosom of his country. The Protestant leaders, from Lord Edward Fitzgerald to Parnell, have never divided their devotion. If any Englishman thinks that they would have been more sparing of blood than the English themselves are, if only so cheap a fluid could have purchased the honor of Ireland, he greatly mistakes the Irish Protestant temper. The notion that Ireland is the only country in the world not worth shedding a drop of blood for is not a

Protestant one, and certainly not countenanced by English practice. It was hardly reasonable to ask Parnell to shed blood *quant. suff.* in Egypt to put an end to the misgovernment of the Khedive and replace him by Lord Cromer for the sake of the English bondholders, and then to expect him to become a Tolstoyan or an O'Connellite in regard to his own country. With a wholly Protestant Ireland at his back he might have bullied England into conceding Home Rule; for the insensibility of the English governing classes to philosophical, moral, social considerations—in short, to any considerations which require a little intellectual exertion and sympathetic alertness—is tempered, as we Irish well know, by an absurd susceptibility to intimidation.

For let me halt a moment here to impress on you, O English reader, that no fact has been more deeply stamped into us than that we can do nothing with an English Government unless we frighten it, any more than you can yourself. When power and riches are thrown haphazard into children's cradles as they are in England, you get a governing class without industry, character, courage, or real experience; and under such circumstances reforms are produced only by catastrophes followed by panics in which "something must be done." Thus it costs a cholera epidemic to achieve a Public Health Act, a Crimean War to reform the Civil Service, and a gunpowder plot to disestablish the Irish Church. It was by the light, not of reason, but of the moon, that the need for paying serious attention to the Irish land question was seen in England. It cost the American War of Independence and the Irish Volunteer movement to obtain the Irish parliament of 1782, the constitution of which far overshot the nationalist mark of today in the matter of independence.

It is vain to plead that this is human nature and not class weakness. The Japanese have proved that it is possible to conduct social and political changes intelligently and providentially instead of drifting along helplessly until public disasters compel a terrified and inconsiderate rearrangement. Innumerable experiments in local government have shewn that when men are neither too poor to be honest nor too rich to understand and share the needs of the people—as in New Zealand, for example—they can govern much more providently than our little circle of aristocrats and plutocrats.

THE JUST ENGLISHMAN

English Unionists, when asked what they have to say in defence of their rule of subject peoples, often reply that the Englishman is just, leaving us divided between our derision of so monstrously inhuman a pretension, and our impatience with so gross a confusion of the mutually exclusive functions of judge and legislator. For there is only one condition on which a man can do justice between two litigants, and that is that he shall have no interest in common with either of them, whereas it is only by having every interest in common with both of them that he can govern them tolerably. The indispensable preliminary to Democracy is the representation of every interest: the indispensable preliminary to justice is the elimination of every interest. When we want an arbitrator or an umpire, we turn to a stranger: when we want a government, a stranger is the one person we will not endure. The Englishman in India, for example, stands, a very statue of justice, between two natives. He says, in effect, "I am impartial in your religious disputes because I believe in neither of your religions. I am impartial in your conflicts of custom and sentiment because your customs and sentiments are different from, and abysmally inferior to, my own. Finally, I am impartial as to your interests because they are both equally opposed to mine, which is to keep you both equally powerless against me in order that I may extract money from you to pay salaries and pensions to myself and my fellow Englishmen as judges and rulers over you. In return for which you get the inestimable benefit of a government that does absolute justice as between Indian and Indian, being wholly preoccupied with the maintenance of absolute injustice as between India and England."

It will be observed that no Englishman, without making himself ridiculous, could pretend to be perfectly just or disinterested in English affairs, or would tolerate a proposal to establish the Indian or Irish system in Great Britain. Yet if the justice of the Englishman is sufficient to ensure the welfare of India or Ireland, it ought to suffice equally for England. But the English are wise enough to refuse to trust to English justice themselves, preferring democracy. They can hardly blame the Irish for taking the same view.

In short, dear English reader, the Irish Protestant stands outside that English Mutual Admiration Society which you call the Union or the Empire. You may buy a common and not ineffective variety of Irish Protestant by delegating your powers to him, and in effect making him the oppressor and you his sorely bullied and bothered catspaw and military maintainer; but if you offer him nothing for his loyalty except the natural superiority of the English character, you will—well, try the experiment, and see what will happen! You would have a ten-times better chance with the Roman Catholic; for he has been saturated from his youth up with the Imperial idea of foreign rule by a spiritually superior international power, and is trained to submission and abnegation of his private judgment. A Roman Catholic garrison would take its orders from England and let her rule Ireland if England were Roman Catholic. The Protestant garrison simply seizes on the English power; uses it for its own purposes; and occasionally orders the English Government to remove an Irish secretary who has dared to apply English ideas to the affairs of the garrison. Whereupon the English Government abjectly removes him, and implores him, as a gentleman and a loyal Englishman, not to reproach it in the face of the Nationalist enemy.

Such incidents naturally do not shake the sturdy conviction of the Irish Protestant that he is more than a match for any English Government in determination and intelligence. Here, no doubt, he flatters himself; for his advantage is not really an advantage of character, but of comparative directness of interest, concentration of force on one narrow issue, simplicity of aim, with freedom from the scruples and responsibilities of world-politics. The business is Irish business, not English; and he is Irish. And his object, which is simply to secure the dominance of his own caste and creed behind the power of England, is simpler and clearer than the confused aims of English Cabinets struggling ineptly with the burdens of empire, and biassed by the pressure of capital anywhere rather than in Ireland. He has no responsibility, no interest, no status outside his own country and his own movement, which means that he has no conscience in dealing with England; whereas England, having a very uneasy conscience, and many hindering and hampering responsibilities and interests in dealing with him, gets bullied and driven by him, and finally learns sympathy with Nationalist aims by her experience of the tyranny of the Orange party.

IRISH CATHOLICISM FORECAST

Let us suppose that the establishment of a national government were to annihilate the oligarchic party by absorbing the Protestant garrison and making it a Protestant National Guard. The Roman Catholic laity, now a cipher, would organize itself; and a revolt against Rome and against the priesthood would ensue. The Roman Catholic Church would become the official Irish Church. The Irish parliament would insist on a voice in the promotion of churchmen; fees and contributions would be regulated; blackmail would be resisted; sweating in conventual factories and workshops would be stopped; and the ban would be taken off the universities. In a word, the Roman Catholic Church, against which Dublin Castle is powerless, would meet the one force on earth that can cope with it victoriously. That force is Democracy, a thing far more Catholic than itself. Until that force is let loose against it, the Protestant garrison can do nothing to the priesthood except consolidate it and drive the people to rally round it in defence of their altars against the foreigner and the heretic. Where it *is* let loose, the Catholic laity will make as short work of sacerdotal tyranny in Ireland as it has done in France and Italy. And in doing so it will be forced to face the old problem of the relations of Church and State. A Roman Catholic party must submit to Rome: an anti-clerical Catholic party must of necessity become an Irish Catholic party. The Holy Roman Empire, like the other Empires, has no future except as a Federation of national Catholic Churches; for Christianity can no more escape Democracy than Democracy can escape Socialism. It is noteworthy in this connection that the Anglican Catholics have played and are playing a notable part in the Socialist movement in England in opposition to the individualist Secularists of the urban proletariat; but they are quit of the preliminary dead lift that awaits the Irish Catholic. Their Church has thrown off the yoke of Rome, and is safely and permanently Anglicized. But the Catholic Church in Ireland is still Roman. Home Rule will herald the day when the Vatican will go the way of Dublin Castle, and the island of the saints assume the headship of her own Church. It may seem incredible that long after the last Orangeman shall lay down his chalk for ever, the familiar scrawl on every blank wall in the north of Ireland "To hell with the Pope!" may reappear in the south, traced by the hands of Catholics who shall have forgotten the traditional counter legend, "To hell with King William!" (of glorious, pious, and immortal memory); but it may happen so. "The island of the saints" is no idle phrase. Religious genius is one of our national products; and Ireland is no bad rock to build a Church on. Holy and beautiful is the soul of Catholic Ireland: her prayers are lovelier than the teeth and claws of Protestantism, but not so effective in dealing with the English.

ENGLISH VOLTAIREANISM

Let me familiarize the situation by shewing how closely it reproduces the English situation in its essentials. In England, as in France, the struggle between the priesthood and the laity has produced a vast body of Voltaireans. But the essential identity of the French and English movements has been obscured by the ignorance of the ordinary Englishman, who, instead of knowing the distinctive tenets of his church or sect, vaguely believes them to be the eternal truth as opposed to the damnable error of all the other denominations. He thinks of Voltaire as a French "infidel," instead of as the champion of the laity against the official theocracy of the State Church. The Nonconformist leaders of our Free Churches are all Voltaireans. The warcry of the Passive Resisters is Voltaire's warcry, "Ecrasez l'infâme." No account need be taken of the technical difference between Voltaire's "infâme" and Dr Clifford's. One was the unreformed Roman Church of France: the other is the reformed Anglican Church; but in both cases the attack has been on a priestly tyranny and a professional monopoly. Voltaire convinced the Genevan ministers that he was the philosophic champion of their Protestant, Individualistic, Democratic Deism against the State Church of Roman Catholic France; and his heroic energy and beneficence as a philanthropist, which now only makes the list of achievements on his monument at Ferney the most impressive epitaph in Europe, then made the most earnest of the Lutheran ministers glad to claim a common inspiration with him. Unfortunately Voltaire had an irrepressible sense of humor. He joked about Habakkuk; and jokes about Habakkuk smelt too strongly of brimstone to be tolerated by Protestants to whom the Bible was not a literature but a fetish and a talisman. And so Voltaire, in spite of the church he "erected to God," became in England the bogey-atheist of three generations of English ignoramuses, instead of the legitimate successor of Martin Luther and John Knox.

Nowadays, however, Voltaire's jokes are either forgotten or else fall flat on a world which no longer venerates Habakkuk; and his true position is becoming apparent. The fact that Voltaire was a Roman Catholic layman, educated at a Jesuit college, is the conclusive reply to the shallow people who imagine that Ireland delivered up to the Irish democracy—

that is, to the Catholic laity—would be delivered up to the tyranny of the priesthood.

SUPPOSE!

Suppose, now, that the conquest of France by Henry V of England had endured, and that France in the XVIII century had been governed by an English viceroy through a Huguenot bureaucracy and a judicial bench appointed on the understanding that loyalty for them meant loyalty to England, and patriotism a willingness to die in defence of the English conquest and of the English Church, would not Voltaire in that case have been the meanest of traitors and self-seekers if he had played the game of England by joining in its campaign against his own and his country's Church? The energy he threw into the defence of Calas and Sirven would have been thrown into the defence of the Frenchmen whom the English would have called "rebels"; and he would have been forced to identify the cause of freedom and democracy with the cause of "l'infâme." The French revolution would have been a revolution against England and English rule instead of against aristocracy and ecclesiasticism; and all the intellectual and spiritual forces in France, from Turgot to De Tocqueville, would have been burnt up in mere anti-Anglicism and nationalist dithyrambs instead of contributing to political science and broadening the thought of the world.

What would have happened in France is what has happened in Ireland; and that is why it is only the small-minded Irish, incapable of conceiving what religious freedom means to a country, who do not loathe English rule. For in Ireland England is nothing but the Pope's policeman. She imagines she is holding the Vatican cardinals at bay when she is really strangling the Voltaires, the Foxes and Penns, the Cliffords, Hortons, Campbells, Walters, and Silvester Hornes, who are to be found among the Roman Catholic laity as plentifully as among the Anglican Catholic laity in England. She gets nothing out of Ireland but infinite trouble, infinite confusion and hindrance in her own legislation, a hatred that circulates through the whole world and poisons it against her, a reproach that makes her professions of sympathy with Finland and Macedonia ridiculous and hypocritical, whilst the priest takes all the spoils, in money, in power, in pride, and in popularity.

IRELAND'S REAL GRIEVANCE

But it is not the spoils that matter. It is the waste, the sterilization, the perversion of fruitful brain power into flatulent protest against unnecessary evil, the use of our very entrails to tie our own hands and seal our own lips in the name of our honor and patriotism. As far as money or comfort is concerned, the average Irishman has a more tolerable life—especially now that the population is so scanty—than the average Englishman. It is true that in Ireland the poor man is robbed and starved and oppressed under judicial forms which confer the imposing title of justice on a crude system of bludgeoning and perjury. But so is the Englishman. The Englishman, more docile, less dangerous, too lazy intellectually to use such political and legal power as lies within his reach, suffers more and makes less fuss about it than the Irishman. But at least he has nobody to blame but himself and his fellow countrymen. He does not doubt that if an effective majority of the English people made up their minds to alter the Constitution, as the majority of the Irish people have made up their minds to obtain Home Rule, they could alter it without having to fight an overwhelmingly powerful and rich neighboring nation, and fight, too, with ropes round their necks. He can attack any institution in his country without betraying it to foreign vengeance and foreign oppression. True, his landlord may turn him out of his cottage if he goes to a Methodist chapel instead of to the parish church. His customers may stop their orders if he votes Liberal instead of Conservative. English ladies and gentlemen who would perish sooner than shoot a fox do these things without the smallest sense of indecency and dishonor. But they cannot muzzle his intellectual leaders. The English philosopher, the English author, the English orator can attack every abuse and expose every superstition without strengthening the hands of any common enemy. In Ireland every such attack, every such exposure, is a service to England and a stab to Ireland. If you expose the tyranny and rapacity of the Church, it is an argument in favor of Protestant ascendency. If you denounce the nepotism and jobbery of the new local authorities, you are demonstrating the unfitness of the Irish to govern themselves, and the superiority of the old oligarchical grand juries.

And there is the same pressure on the other side. The Protestant must stand by the garrison at all costs: the Unionist must wink at every bureaucratic abuse, connive at every tyranny, magnify every official blockhead, because their exposure would be a victory for the Nationalist enemy. Every Irishman is in Lancelot's position: his honor rooted in dishonor stands; and faith unfaithful keeps him falsely true.

THE CURSE OF NATIONALISM

It is hardly possible for an Englishman to understand all that this implies. A conquered nation is like a man with cancer: he can think of nothing else, and is forced to place himself, to the exclusion of all better company, in the hands of quacks who profess to treat or cure cancer. The windbags of the two rival platforms are the most insufferable of all windbags. It requires neither knowledge, character, conscience, diligence in public affairs, nor any virtue, private or communal, to thump the Nationalist or Orange tub: nay, it puts a premium on the rancor or callousness that has given rise to the proverb that if you put an Irishman on a spit you can always get another Irishman to baste him. Jingo oratory in England is sickening enough to serious people: indeed one evening's mafficking in London produced a determined call for the police. Well, in Ireland all political oratory is Jingo oratory; and all political demonstrations are maffickings. English rule is such an intolerable abomination that no other subject can reach the people. Nationalism stands between Ireland and the light of the world. Nobody in Ireland of any intelligence likes Nationalism any more than a man with a broken arm likes having it set. A healthy nation is as unconscious of its nationality as a healthy man of his bones. But if you break a nation's nationality it will think of nothing else but getting it set again. It will listen to no reformer, to no philosopher, to no preacher, until the demand of the Nationalist is granted. It will attend to no business, however vital, except the business of unification and liberation.

That is why everything is in abeyance in Ireland pending the achievement of Home Rule. The great movements of the human spirit which sweep in waves over Europe are stopped on the Irish coast by the English guns of the Pigeon House Fort. Only a quaint little offshoot of English pre-Raphaelitism called the Gaelic movement has got a footing by using Nationalism as a stalking-horse, and popularizing itself as an attack on the native language of the Irish people, which is most fortunately also the native language of half the world, including England. Every election is fought on nationalist grounds; every appointment is made on nationalist grounds; every judge is a partisan in the nationalist conflict; every speech is a dreary recapitulation of nationalist twaddle; every lecture is a corruption of history to flatter nationalism or defame it; every school is a recruiting station; every church is a barrack; and every Irishman is unspeakably tired of the whole miserable business, which nevertheless is and perforce must remain his first business until Home Rule makes an end of it, and sweeps the nationalist and the garrison back together into the dustbin.

There is indeed no greater curse to a nation than a nationalist movement, which is only the agonizing symptom of a suppressed natural function. Conquered nations lose their place in the world's march because they can do nothing but strive to get rid of their nationalist movements by recovering their national liberty. All demonstrations of the virtues of a foreign government, though often conclusive, are as useless as demonstrations of the superiority of artificial teeth, glass eyes, silver windpipes, and patent wooden legs to the natural products. Like Democracy, national self-government is not for the good of the people: it is for the satisfaction of the people. One Antonine emperor, one St Louis, one Richelieu, may be worth ten democracies in point of what is called good government; but there is no satisfaction for the people in them. To deprive a dyspeptic of his dinner and hand it over to a man who can digest it better is a highly logical proceeding; but it is not a sensible one. To take the government of Ireland away from the Irish and hand it over to the English on the ground that they can govern better would be a precisely parallel case if the English had managed their own affairs so well as to place their superior faculty for governing beyond question. But as the English are avowed muddlers—rather proud of it, in fact—even the logic of that case against Home Rule is not complete. Read Mr Charles Booth's account of London, Mr Rowntree's account of York, and the latest official report on Dundee; and then pretend, if you can, that Englishmen and Scotchmen have not more cause to hand over their affairs to an Irish parliament than to clamor for another nation's cities to devastate and another people's business to mismanage.

A NATURAL RIGHT

The question is not one of logic at all, but of natural right. English universities have for some time past encouraged an extremely foolish academic exercise which consists in disproving the existence of natural rights on the ground that they cannot be deduced from the principles of any known political system. If they could, they would not be natural rights but acquired ones. Acquired rights are deduced from political constitutions; but political constitutions are deduced from natural rights. When a man insists on certain liberties without the slightest regard to demonstrations that they are not for his own good, nor for the public good, nor moral, nor reasonable, nor decent, nor compatible with the existing constitution of society, then he is said to claim a natural right to that liberty. When, for instance, he insists on living, in spite of the irrefutable demonstrations of many able pessimists, from the author of the book of Ecclesiastes to Schopenhauer, that life is an evil, he is asserting a natural right to live. When he insists on a vote in order that his country may be governed according to his ignorance instead of the wisdom of the Privy Council, he is asserting a natural right to self-government. When he insists on guiding himself at 21 by his own inexperience and folly and immaturity instead of by the experience and sagacity of his father, or the well-stored mind of his grandmother, he is asserting a natural right to independence. Even if Home Rule were as unhealthy as an Englishman's eating, as intemperate as his drinking, as filthy as his smoking, as licentious as his domesticity, as corrupt as his elections, as murderously greedy as his commerce, as cruel as his prisons, and as merciless as his streets, Ireland's claim to self-government would still be as good as England's. King James the First proved so cleverly and conclusively that the satisfaction of natural rights was incompatible with good government that his courtiers called him Solomon. We, more enlightened, call him Fool, solely because we have learnt that nations insist on being governed by their own consent—or, as they put it, by themselves and for themselves—and that they will finally upset a good government which denies them this even if the alternative be a bad government which at least creates and maintains an illusion of democracy. America, as far as one can ascertain, is much worse governed, and has a much more disgraceful political history than England under Charles I; but the American Republic is the stabler government because it starts from a formal concession of natural rights, and keeps up an illusion of safeguarding them by an elaborate machinery of democratic election. And the final reason why Ireland must have Home Rule is that she has a natural right to it.

A WARNING

Finally, some words of warning to both nations. Ireland has been deliberately ruined again and again by England. Unable to compete with us industrially, she has destroyed our industries by the brute force of prohibitive taxation. She was perfectly right. That brute force was a more honorable weapon than the poverty which we used to undersell her. We lived with and as our pigs, and let loose our wares in the Englishman's market at prices which he could compete with only by living like a pig himself. Having the alternative of stopping our industry altogether, he very naturally and properly availed himself of it. We should have done the same in his place. To bear malice against him on that score is to poison our blood and weaken our constitutions with unintelligent rancor. In wrecking all the industries that were based on the poverty of our people England did us an enormous service. In omitting to do the same on her own soil, she did herself a wrong that has rotted her almost to the marrow. I hope that when Home Rule is at last achieved, one of our first legislative acts will be to fortify the subsistence of our people behind the bulwark of a standard wage, and to impose crushing import duties on every English trade that flourishes in the slum and fattens on the starvation of our unfortunate English neighbors.

W. B. Yeats (1865-1939)

Cuchulain's Fight With the Sea[1]

A Man came slowly, from the setting sun,
To Emer, raddling[2] raiment in her dun,
And said, "I am that swineherd whom you bid
Go watch the road between the wood and tide,
But now I have no need to watch it more."

Then Emer cast the web upon the floor,
And raising arms all raddled with the dye,
Parted her lips with a loud sudden cry.
That swineherd stared upon her face and said,
"No man alive, no man among the dead,
Has won the gold his cars of battle bring."

"But if your master comes home triumphing
Why must you blench and shake from foot to crown?"

Thereon he shook the more and cast him down
Upon the web-heaped floor, and cried his word:
"With him is one sweet-throated like a bird."

---

[1] How Cuchulain unknowingly killed his own son is told in a ninth century story entitled "The Tragic Death of Connla" (see p. 61). Yeats' poem, however, is not based directly on the Old Irish tale but on later ballad versions in which the roles of Emer and Aife have been reversed and in which Cuchulain is deluded by a druid's spell into fighting the waves. Yeats dealt with the same story in his play *On Baile's Strand* (1904).

[2] Coloring coarsely with red or rouge. NED

"You dare me to my face," and thereupon
She smote with raddled fist, and where her son
Herded the cattle came with stumbling feet,
And cried with angry voice, "It is not meet
To idle life away, a common herd."

"I have long waited, mother, for that word:
But wherefore now?"
"There is a man to die;
You have the heaviest arm under the sky."

"Whether under its daylight or its stars
My father stands amid his battle-cars."

"But you have grown to be the taller man."

"Yet somewhere under starlight or the sun
My father stands."
"Aged, worn out with wars
On foot, on horseback or in battle-cars."

"I only ask what way my journey lies,
For He who made you bitter made you wise."

"The Red Branch camp in a great company
Between wood's rim and the horses of the sea.
Go there, and light a camp-fire at wood's rim;
But tell your name and lineage to him
Whose blade compels, and wait till they have found
Some feasting man that the same oath has bound."

Among those feasting men Cuchulain dwelt
And his young sweetheart close beside him knelt,
Stared on the mournful wonder of his eyes,
Even as Spring upon the ancient skies,
And pondered on the glory of his days;
And all around the harp-string told his praise,
And Conchubar, the Red Branch king of kings,
With his own fingers touched the brazen strings.

At last Cuchulain spake, "Some man has made
His evening fire amid the leafy shade.
I have often heard him singing to and fro,
I have often heard the sweet sound of his bow.
Seek out what man he is."

One went and came.
"He bade me let all know he gives his name
At the sword-point, and waits till we have found
Some feasting man that the same oath has bound."

Cuchulain cried, "I am the only man
Of all this host so bound from childhood on."

After short fighting in the leafy shade,
He spake to the young man, "Is there no maid
Who loves you, no white arms to wrap you round,
Or do you long for the dim sleepy ground,
That you have come and dared me to my face?"

"The dooms of men are in God's hidden place."

"Your head a while seemed like a woman's head
That I loved once."
Again the fighting sped,
But now the war-rage in Cuchulain woke,
And through that new blade's guard the old blade broke,
And pierced him.
"Speak before your breath is done."

"Cuchulain I, mighty Cuchulain's son."

"I put you from your pain. I can no more."

While day its burden on to evening bore,
With head bowed on his knees Cuchulain stayed;
Then Conchubar sent that sweet-throated maid,
And she, to win him, his grey hair caressed;
In vain her arms, in vain her soft white breast.
Then Conchubar, the subtlest of all men,
Ranking his Druids round him ten by ten,
Spake thus: "Cuchulain will dwell there and brood
For three days more in dreadful quietude,
And then arise, and raving slay us all.
Chaunt in his ear delusions magical,
That he may fight the horses of the sea."

The Druids took them to their mystery,
And chaunted for three days.
Cuchulain stirred,
Stared on the horses of the sea, and heard
The cars of battle and his own name cried;
And fought with the invulnerable tide.

The Folly of Being Comforted

One that is ever kind said yesterday:
"Your well-belovèd's hair has threads of grey,
And little shadows come about her eyes;
Time can but make it easier to be wise
Though now it seems impossible, and so
All that you need is patience."
Heart cries, "No,
I have not a crumb of comfort, not a grain.
Time can but make her beauty over again:
Because of that great nobleness of hers
The fire that stirs about her, when she stirs,
Burns but more clearly. O she had not these ways
When all the wild summer was in her gaze."

O heart! O heart! if she'd but turn her head,
You'd know the folly of being comforted.

To A Shade

If you have revisited the town, thin Shade,
Whether to look upon your monument
(I wonder if the builder has been paid)
Or happier-thoughted when the day is spent
To drink of that salt breath out of the sea
When grey gulls flit about instead of men,
And the gaunt houses put on majesty:
Let these content you and be gone again;
For they are at their old tricks yet.

A man
Of your own passionate serving kind who had brought
In his full hands what, had they only known,
Had given their children's children loftier thought,
Sweeter emotion, working in their veins
Like gentle blood, has been driven from the place,
And insult heaped upon him for his pains,
And for his open-handedness, disgrace;
Your enemy, an old foul mouth, had set
The pack upon him.
Go, unquiet wanderer,
And gather the Glasnevin coverlet
About your head till the dust stops your ear,
The time for you to taste of that salt breath
And listen at the corners has not come;
You had enough of sorrow before death—
Away, away! You are safer in the tomb.
September 29, 1913

In Memory of Major Robert Gregory

I

Now that we're almost settled in our house
I'll name the friends that cannot sup with us
Beside a fire of turf in th' ancient tower,
And having talked to some late hour
Climb up the narrow winding stairs to bed:
Discoverers of forgotten truth
Or mere companions of my youth,
All, all are in my thoughts to-night being dead.

II

Always we'd have the new friend meet the old
And we are hurt if either friend seem cold,
And there is salt to lengthen out the smart
In the affections of our heart,
And quarrels are blown up upon that head;
But not a friend that I would bring
This night would set us quarrelling,
For all that come into my mind are dead.

III

Lionel Johnson comes the first to mind,
That loved his learning better than mankind,
Though courteous to the worst; much falling he
Brooded upon sanctity
Till all his Greek and Latin learning seemed
A long blast upon the horn that brought
A little nearer to his thought
A measureless consummation that he dreamed.

IV

And that enquiring man John Synge comes next,
That dying chose the living world for text
And never could have rested in the tomb
But that, long travelling, he had come
Towards nightfall upon certain set apart
In a most desolate stony place,
Towards nightfall upon a race
Passionate and simple like his heart.

V

And then I think of old George Pollexfen,
In muscular youth well known to Mayo men
For horsemanship at meets or at racecourses,
That could have shown how pure-bred horses
And solid men, for all their passion, live
But as the outrageous stars incline
By opposition, square and trine;
Having grown sluggish and contemplative.

VI

They were my close companions many a year,
A portion of my mind and life, as it were,
And now their breathless faces seem to look
Out of some old picture-book;
I am accustomed to their lack of breath,
But not that my dear friend's dear son,
Our Sidney and our perfect man,
Could share in that discourtesy of death.

VII

For all things the delighted eye now sees
Were loved by him: the old storm-broken trees
That cast their shadows upon road and bridge;
The tower set on the stream's edge;
The ford where drinking cattle make a stir
Nightly, and startled by that sound
The water-hen must change her ground;
He might have been your heartiest welcomer.

VIII

When with the Galway foxhounds he would ride
From Castle Taylor to the Roxborough side
Or Esserkelly plain, few kept his pace;
At Mooneen he had leaped a place
So perilous that half the astonished meet
Had shut their eyes; and where was it
He rode a race without a bit?
And yet his mind outran the horses' feet.

IX

We dreamed that a great painter had been born
To cold Clare rock and Galway rock and thorn,
To that stern colour and that delicate line
That are our secret discipline
Wherein the gazing heart doubles her might.
Soldier, scholar, horseman, he,
And yet he had the intensity
To have published all to be a world's delight.

X

What other could so well have counselled us
In all lovely intricacies of a house
As he that practised or that understood
All work in metal or in wood,
In moulded plaster or in carven stone?
Soldier, scholar, horseman, he,
And all he did done perfectly
As though he had but that one trade alone.

XI

Some burn damp faggots, others may consume
The entire combustible world in one small room
As though dried straw, and if we turn about
The bare chimney is gone black out
Because the work had finished in that flare.
Soldier, scholar, horseman, he,
As 'twere all life's epitome.
What made us dream that he could comb grey hair?

XII

I had thought, seeing how bitter is that wind
That shakes the shutter, to have brought to mind
All those that manhood tried, or childhood loved
Or boyish intellect approved,
With some appropriate commentary on each;
Until imagination brought
A fitter welcome; but a thought
Of that late death took all my heart for speech.

Sailing to Byzantium

I

That is no country for old men. The young
In one another's arms, birds in the trees
—Those dying generations—at their song,
The salmon-falls, the mackerel-crowded seas,
Fish, flesh, or fowl, commend all summer long
Whatever is begotten, born, and dies.
Caught in that sensual music all neglect
Monuments of unageing intellect.

II

An aged man is but a paltry thing,
A tattered coat upon a stick, unless
Soul clap its hands and sing, and louder sing
For every tatter in its mortal dress,
Nor is there singing school but studying
Monuments of its own magnificence;
And therefore I have sailed the seas and come
To the holy city of Byzantium.

III

O sages standing in God's holy fire
As in the gold mosaic of a wall,
Come from the holy fire, perne in a gyre,
And be the singing-masters of my soul.
Consume my heart away; sick with desire
And fastened to a dying animal
It knows not what it is; and gather me
Into the artifice of eternity.

IV

Once out of nature I shall never take
My bodily form from any natural thing,
But such a form as Grecian goldsmiths make
Of hammered gold and gold enamelling
To keep a drowsy Emperor awake;
Or set upon a golden bough to sing
To lords and ladies of Byzantium
Of what is past, or passing, or to come.

1927

Leda and the Swan

A sudden blow: the great wings beating still
Above the staggering girl, her thighs caressed
By the dark webs, her nape caught in his bill,
He holds her helpless breast upon his breast.

How can those terrified vague fingers push
The feathered glory from her loosening thighs?
And how can body, laid in that white rush,
But feel the strange heart beating where it lies?

A shudder in the loins engenders there
The broken wall, the burning roof and tower
And Agamemnon dead.
Being so caught up,
So mastered by the brute blood of the air,
Did she put on his knowledge with his power
Before the indifferent beak could let her drop?
1923

Among School Children

I

I walk through the long school room questioning;
A kind old nun in a white hood replies;
The children learn to cipher and to sing,
To study reading-books and histories,
To cut and sew, be neat in everything
In the best modern way—the children's eyes
In momentary wonder stare upon
A sixty-year-old smiling public man.

II

I dream of a Ledaean body, bent
Above a sinking fire, a tale that she
Told of a harsh reproof, or trivial event
That changed some childish day to tragedy—
Told, and it seemed that our two natures blent
Into a sphere from youthful sympathy,
Or else, to alter Plato's parable,
Into the yolk and white of the one shell.

III

And thinking of that fit of grief or rage
I look upon one child or t'other there
And wonder if she stood so at that age—
For even daughters of the swan can share
Something of that paddler's heritage—
And had that colour upon cheek or hair,
And thereupon my heart is driven wild:
She stands before me as a living child.

IV

Her present image floats into the mind—
Did Quattrocento finger fashion it
Hollow of cheek as though it drank the wind
And took a mess of shadows for its meat?
And I though never of Ledaean kind
Had pretty plumage once—enough of that,
Better to smile on all that smile, and show
There is a comfortable kind of old scarecrow.

V

What youthful mother, a shape upon her lap
Honey of generation had betrayed,
And that must sleep, shriek, struggle to escape
As recollection or the drug decide,
Would think her son, did she but see that shape
With sixty or more winters on its head,
A compensation for the pang of his birth,
Or the uncertainty of his setting forth?

VI

Plato thought nature but a spume that plays
Upon a ghostly paradigm of things;
Soldier Aristotle played the taws
Upon the bottom of a king of kings;
World-famous golden-thighed Pythagoras
Fingered upon a fiddle-stick or strings
What a star sang and careless Muses heard:
Old clothes upon old sticks to scare a bird.

VII

Both nuns and mothers worship images,
But those the candles light are not as those
That animate a mother's reveries,
But keep a marble or a bronze repose.
And yet they too break hearts—O Presences
That passion, piety or affection knows,
And that all heavenly glory symbolise—
O self-born mockers of man's enterprise;

VIII

Labour is blossoming or dancing where
The body is not bruised to pleasure soul,
Nor beauty born out of its own despair,
Nor blear-eyed wisdom out of midnight oil.
O chestnut-tree, great-rooted blossomer,
Are you the leaf, the blossom or the bole?
O body swayed to music, O brightening glance,
How can we know the dancer from the dance?

The Wild Old Wicked Man

"Because I am mad about women
I am mad about the hills,"
Said that wild old wicked man
Who travels where God wills.
"Not to die on the straw at home,
Those hands to close these eyes,
That is all I ask, my dear,
From the old man in the skies.
Daybreak and a candle-end.

"Kind are all your words, my dear,
Do not the rest withhold.
Who can know the year, my dear,
When an old man's blood grows cold?
I have what no young man can have
Because he loves too much.
Words I have that can pierce the heart,
But what can he do but touch?"
Daybreak and a candle-end.

Then said she to that wild old man,
His stout stick under his hand,
"Love to give or to withhold
Is not at my command.
I gave it all to an older man:
That old man in the skies.
Hands that are busy with His beads
Can never close those eyes."
Daybreak and a candle-end.

"Go your ways, O go your ways,
I choose another mark,
Girls down on the seashore
Who understand the dark;
Bawdy talk for the fishermen;
A dance for the fisher-lads;
When dark hangs upon the water
They turn down their beds.
Daybreak and a candle-end.

"A young man in the dark am I,
But a wild old man in the light,
That can make a cat laugh, or
Can touch by mother wit
Things hid in their marrow-bones
From time long passed away,
Hid from all those warty lads
That by their bodies lay.
Daybreak and a candle-end.

"All men live in suffering,
I know as few can know,
Whether they take the upper road
Or stay content on the low,
Rower bent in his row-boat
Or weaver bent at his loom,
Horseman erect upon horseback
Or child hid in the womb.
Daybreak and a candle-end.

"That some stream of lightning
From the old man in the skies
Can burn out that suffering
No right-taught man denies.
But a coarse old man am I,
I choose the second-best,
I forget it all awhile
Upon a woman's breast."
Daybreak and a candle-end.

The Statues

Pythagoras planned it. Why did the people stare?
His numbers, though they moved or seemed to move
In marble or in bronze, lacked character.
But boys and girls, pale from the imagined love
Of solitary beds, knew what they were,
That passion could bring character enough,
And pressed at midnight in some public place
Live lips upon a plummet-measured face.

No! Greater than Pythagoras, for the men
That with a mallet or a chisel modelled these
Calculations that look but casual flesh, put down
All Asiatic vague immensities,
And not the banks of oars that swam upon
The many-headed foam at Salamis.
Europe put off that foam when Phidias
Gave women dreams and dreams their looking-glass.

One image crossed the many-headed, sat
Under the tropic shade, grew round and slow,
No Hamlet thin from eating flies, a fat
Dreamer of the Middle Ages. Empty eyeballs knew
That knowledge increases unreality, that
Mirror on mirror mirrored is all the show.
When gong and conch declare the hour to bless
Grimalkin crawls to Buddha's emptiness.

When Pearse[1] summoned Cuchulain to his side,
What stalked through the Post Office? What intellect,
What calculation, number, measurement, replied?
We Irish, born into that ancient sect
But thrown upon this filthy modern tide
And by its formless spawning fury wrecked,
Climb to our proper dark, that we may trace
The lineaments of a plummet-measured face.
April 9, 1938

---

[1] Padraic Pearse (1879-1916) was one of the leaders in the Rising of 1916, when the General Post Office in Dublin was occupied by the insurrectionists and besieged by English forces.

AE (George Russell) (1867-1935)

Truth

THE hero first thought it
To him 'twas a deed:
To those who retaught it,
A chain on their speed.

The fire that we kindled,
A beacon by night,
When darkness has dwindled
Grows pale in the light.

For life has no glory
Stays long in one dwelling,
And time has no story
That's true twice in telling.

And only the teaching
That never was spoken
Is worthy thy reaching,
The fountain unbroken.

The Twilight of Earth

THE wonder of the world is o'er:
The magic from the sea is gone:
There is no unimagined shore,
No islet yet to venture on.
The Sacred Hazels' blooms are shed,
The Nuts of Knowledge harvested.

Oh, what is worth this lore of age
  If time shall never bring us back
Our battle with the gods to wage
  Reeling along the starry track.
The battle rapture here goes by
In warring upon things that die.

Let be the tale of him whose love
  Was sighed between white Deirdre's breasts,
It will not lift the heart above
  The sodden clay on which it rests.
Love once had power the gods to bring
All rapt on its wild wandering.

We shiver in the falling dew,
  And seek a shelter from the storm:
When man these elder brothers knew
  He found the mother nature warm,
A hearth fire blazing through it all,
A home without a circling wall.

We dwindle down beneath the skies,
  And from ourselves we pass away:
The paradise of memories
  Grows ever fainter day by day.
The shepherd stars have shrunk within,
The world's great night will soon begin.

Will no one, ere it is too late,
  Ere fades the last memorial gleam,
Recall for us our earlier state?
  For nothing but so vast a dream
That it would scale the steeps of air
Could rouse us from so vast despair.

The power is ours to make or mar
  Our fate as on the earliest morn,
The Darkness and the Radiance are
  Creatures within the spirit born.
Yet, bathed in gloom too long, we might
Forget how we imagined light.

Not yet are fixed the prison bars;
  The hidden light the spirit owns
If blown to flame would dim the stars
  And they who rule them from their thrones:
And the proud sceptred spirits thence
Would bow to pay us reverence.

Oh, while the glory sinks within
  Let us not wait on earth behind,
But follow where it flies, and win
  The glow again, and we may find
Beyond the Gateways of the Day
Dominion and ancestral sway.

On Behalf of Some Irishmen Not Followers of Tradition

THEY call us aliens, we are told,
Because our wayward visions stray
From that dim banner they unfold,
The dreams of worn-out yesterday.
The sum of all the past is theirs,
The creeds, the deeds, the fame, the name,
Whose death-created glory flares
And dims the spark of living flame.
They weave the necromancer's spell,
And burst the graves where martyrs slept,
Their ancient story to retell,

Renewing tears the dead have wept.
And they would have us join their dirge,
This worship of an extinct fire
In which they drift beyond the verge
Where races all outworn expire.
The worship of the dead is not
A worship that our hearts allow,
Though every famous shade were wrought
With woven thorns above the brow.
We fling our answer back in scorn:
"We are less children of this clime
Than of some nation yet unborn
Or empire in the womb of time.
We hold the Ireland in the heart
More than the land our eyes have seen,
And love the goal for which we start
More than the tale of what has been."
The generations as they rise
May live the life men lived before,
Still hold the thought once held as wise,
Go in and out by the same door.
We leave the easy peace it brings:
The few we are shall still unite
In fealty to unseen kings
Or unimaginable light.
We would no Irish sign efface,
But yet our lips would gladlier hail
The firstborn of the Coming Race
Than the last splendour of the Gael.
No blazoned banner we unfold—
One charge alone we give to youth,
Against the sceptred myth to hold
The golden heresy of truth.

A Prisoner

Brixton, September 1920

SEE, though the oil be low, more purely still and higher
The flame burns in the body's lamp. The watchers still
Gaze with unseeing eyes while the Promethean will,
The Uncreated Light, the Everlasting Fire,
Sustain themselves against the torturer's desire,
Even as the fabled Titan chained upon the hill.
Burn on, shine here, thou immortality, until
We too can light our lamps at the funereal pyre;
Till we too can be noble, unshakeable, undismayed
Till we too can burn with the holy flame, and know
There is that within us can conquer the dragon pain,
And go to death alone, slowly and unafraid.
The candles of God already are burning row on row:
Farewell, light-bringer; fly to thy fountain again.

The King of Ireland's Son

BY Nora Hopper (1871-1906)

All the way to Tir na n'Og are many roads that run,
But the darkest road is trodden by the King of Ireland's Son.
The world wears on to sundown, and love is lost and won,
But he recks not of loss or gain, the King of Ireland's Son.
He follows on for ever, when all your chase is done,
He follows after shadows—the King of Ireland's Son.

From Deirdre of the Sorrows[1]

BY J. M. Synge (1871-1909)

ACT III

SCENE. *Tent below Emain, with shabby skins and benches. There is an opening at each side and at back, the latter closed. Old Woman comes in with food and fruits and arranges them on table. Conchubor comes in on right.*

CONCHUBOR (*sharply*). Has no one come with news for me?

OLD WOMAN. I've seen no one at all, Conchubor.

CONCHUBOR (*watches her working for a moment, then makes sure opening at back is closed*). Go up then to Emain, you're not wanting here. (*A noise heard left.*) Who is that?

OLD WOMAN (*going left*). It's Lavarcham coming again. She's a great wonder for jogging back and forward through the world, and I made certain she'd be off to meet them; but she's coming alone, Conchubor, my dear child Deirdre isn't with her at all.

CONCHUBOR. Go up so and leave us.

OLD WOMAN (*pleadingly*). I'd be well pleased to set my eyes on Deirdre if she's coming this night, as we're told.

---

[1] See p. 76 for the story from Old Irish literature upon which Synge's play is based. The third act begins at the point where Deirdre, her nurse Lavarcham and the sons of Usna have just returned to Emain Macha after their exile in Scotland. King Conchubor, from whom the lovers fled seven years before, has promised no harm to them if they will return and has sent Fergus to accompany them as surety. From the beginning Deirdre has looked with suspicion on the king's offer of a safe return. The first inkling Naisi has that they are to be betrayed comes when Fergus is separated from the lovers as soon as they arrive in Ireland by an offer of a feast, which he is under taboo not to refuse.

CONCHUBOR (*impatiently*). It's not long till you'll see her. But I've matters with Lavarcham, and let you go now, I'm saying.

[*He shows her out right, as Lavarcham comes in on the left.*]

LAVARCHAM (*looking round her with suspicion*). This is a queer place to find you, and it's a queer place to be lodging Naisi and his brothers, and Deirdre with them, and the lot of us tired out with the long way we have been walking.

CONCHUBOR. You've come along with them the whole journey?

LAVARCHAM. I have, then, though I've no call now to be wandering that length to a wedding or a burial, or the two together. (*She sits down wearily.*) It's a poor thing the way me and you is getting old, Conchubor, and I'm thinking you yourself have no call to be loitering this place getting your death, maybe, in the cold of night.

CONCHUBOR. I'm waiting only to know is Fergus stopped in the north.

LAVARCHAM (*more sharply*). He's stopped, surely, and that's a trick has me thinking you have it in mind to bring trouble this night on Emain and Ireland and the big world's east beyond them. (*She goes to him.*) And yet you'd do well to be going to your dun, and not putting shame on her meeting the High King, and she seamed and sweaty and in great disorder from the dust of many roads. (*Laughing derisively*). Ah, Conchubor, my lad, beauty goes quickly in the woods, and you'd let a great gasp, I tell you, if you set your eyes this night on Deirdre.

CONCHUBOR (*fiercely*). It's little I care if she's white and worn, for it's I did rear her from a child. I should have a good right to meet and see her always.

LAVARCHAM. A good right, is it? Haven't the blind a good right to be seeing, and the lame to be dancing, and the dummies[1] singing tunes? It's that right you have to be looking for gaiety on Deirdre's lips. (*Coaxingly.*) Come on to your dun, I'm saying, and leave her quiet for one night itself.

[1] The dumb.

CONCHUBOR (*with sudden anger*). I'll not go, when it's long enough I am above in my dun stretching east and west without a comrade, and I more needy, maybe, than the thieves of Meath. . . . You think I'm old and wise, but I tell you the wise know the old must die, and they'll leave no chance for a thing slipping from them they've set their blood to win.

LAVARCHAM (*nodding her head*). If you're old and wise, it's I'm the same, Conchubor, and I'm telling you you'll not have her though you're ready to destroy mankind and skin the gods to win her. There's things a king can't have, Conchubor, and if you go rampaging this night you'll be apt to win nothing but death for many, and a sloppy face of trouble on your own self before the day will come.

CONCHUBOR. It's too much talk you have. (*Goes right.*) Where is Owen? Did you see him no place and you coming the road?

LAVARCHAM. I seen him surely. He went spying on Naisi, and now the worms is spying on his own inside.

CONCHUBOR (*exultingly*). Naisi killed him?

LAVARCHAM. He did not, then. It was Owen destroyed himself running mad because of Deirdre. Fools and kings and scholars are all one in a story with her like, and Owen thought he'd be a great man, being the first corpse in the game you'll play this night in Emain.

CONCHUBOR. It's yourself should be the first corpse, but my other messengers are coming, men from the clans that hated Usna.

LAVARCHAM (*drawing back hopelessly*). Then the gods have pity on us all!

[*Men with weapons come in.*]

CONCHUBOR (*to Soldiers*). Are Ainnle and Ardan separate from Naisi?

MEN. They are, Conchubor. We've got them off, saying they were needed to make ready Deirdre's house.

CONCHUBOR. And Naisi and Deirdre are coming?

SOLDIER. Naisi's coming, surely, and a woman with him is putting out the glory of the moon is rising and the sun is going down.

CONCHUBOR (*looking at Lavarcham*). That's your story that she's seamed and ugly?

SOLDIER. I have more news. (*Pointing to Lavarcham.*) When that woman heard you were bringing Naisi this place, she sent a horse-boy to call Fergus from the north.

CONCHUBOR (*to Lavarcham*). It's for that you've been playing your tricks, but what you've won is a nearer death for Naisi. (*To Soldiers.*) Go up and call my fighters, and take that woman up to Emain.

LAVARCHAM. I'd liefer stay this place. I've done my best, but if a bad end is coming, surely it would be a good thing maybe I was here to tend her.

CONCHUBOR (*fiercely*). Take her to Emain; it's too many tricks she's tried this day already. (*A Soldier goes to her.*)

LAVARCHAM. Don't touch me. (*She puts her cloak round her and catches Conchubor's arm.*) I thought to stay your hand with my stories till Fergus would come to be beside them, the way I'd save yourself, Conchubor, and Naisi and Emain Macha; but I'll walk up now into your halls, and I'll say (*with a gesture*) it's here nettles will be growing, and beyond thistles and docks. I'll go into your high chambers, where you've been figuring yourself stretching out your neck for the kisses of a queen of women; and I'll say it's here there'll be deer stirring and goats scratching, and sheep waking and coughing when there is a great wind from the north. (*Shaking herself loose. Conchubor makes a sign to Soldiers.*) I'm going, surely. In a short space I'll be sitting up with many listening to the flames crackling, and the beams breaking, and I looking on the great blaze will be the end of Emain.

[*She goes out.*]

CONCHUBOR (*looking out*). I see two people in the trees; it should be Naisi and Deirdre. (*To Soldier.*) Let you tell them they'll lodge here to-night.

[*Conchubor goes out right. Naisi and Deirdre come in on left, very weary.*]

NAISI (*to Soldiers*). Is it this place he's made ready for myself and Deirdre?

SOLDIER. The Red Branch House is being aired and swept and you'll be called there when a space is by; till then you'd find fruits and drink on this table, and so the gods be with you.

[Goes *out right.*]

NAISI (*looking round*). It's a strange place he's put us camping and we come back as his friends.

DEIRDRE. He's likely making up a welcome for us, having curtains shaken out and rich rooms put in order; and it's right he'd have great state to meet us, and you his sister's son.

NAISI (*gloomily*). It's little we want with state or rich rooms or curtains, when we're used to the ferns only and cold streams and they making a stir.

DEIRDRE (*roaming round room*). We want what is our right in Emain (*looking at hangings*), and though he's riches in store for us it's a shabby, ragged place he's put us waiting, with frayed rugs and skins are eaten by the moths.

NAISI (*a little impatiently*). There are few would worry over skins and moths on this first night that we've come back to Emain.

DEIRDRE (*brightly*). You should be well pleased it's for that I'd worry all times, when it's I have kept your tent these seven years as tidy as a bee-hive or a linnet's nest. If Conchubor'd a queen like me in Emain he'd not have stretched these rags to meet us. (*She pulls hanging, and it opens.*) There's new earth on the ground and a trench dug. . . . It's a grave, Naisi, that is wide and deep.

NAISI (*goes over and pulls back curtain showing grave*). And that'll be our home in Emain. . . . He's dug it wisely at the butt of a hill, with fallen trees to hide it. He'll want to have us killed and buried before Fergus comes.

DEIRDRE. Take me away. . . . Take me to hide in the rocks, for the night is coming quickly.

NAISI (*pulling himself together*). I will not leave my brothers.

DEIRDRE (*vehemently*). It's of us two he's jealous. Come away to the places where we're used to have our company. . . .

Wouldn't it be a good thing to lie hid in the high ferns together? (*She pulls him left.*) I hear strange words in the trees.

NAISI. It should be the strange fighters of Conchubor. I saw them passing as we came.

DEIRDRE (*pulling him towards the right*). Come to this side. Listen, Naisi!

NAISI. There are more of them. . . . We are shut in, and I have not Ainnle and Ardan to stand near me. Isn't it a hard thing that we three who have conquered many may not die together?

DEIRDRE (*sinking down*). And isn't it a hard thing that you and I are in this place by our opened grave; though none have lived had happiness like ours those days in Alban that went by so quick?

NAISI. It's a hard thing, surely, we've lost those days for ever; and yet it's a good thing, maybe, that all goes quick, for when I'm in that grave it's soon a day'll come you'll be too wearied to be crying out, and that day'll bring you ease.

DEIRDRE. I'll not be here to know if that is true.

NAISI. It's our three selves he'll kill to-night, and then in two months or three you'll see him walking down for courtship with yourself.

DEIRDRE. I'll not be here.

NAISI (*hard*). You'd best keep him off, maybe, and then, when the time comes, make your way to some place west in Donegal, and it's there you'll get used to stretching out lonesome at the fall of night, and waking lonesome for the day.

DEIRDRE. Let you not be saying things are worse than death.

NAISI (*a little recklessly*). I've one word left. If a day comes in the west that the larks are cocking their crests on the edge of the clouds, and the cuckoos making a stir, and there's a man you'd fancy, let you not be thinking that day I'd be well pleased you'd go on keening always.

DEIRDRE (*turning to look at him*). And if it was I that died, Naisi, would you take another woman to fill up my place?

NAISI (*very mournfully*). It's little I know, saving only that it's a hard and bitter thing leaving the earth, and a worse and harder thing leaving yourself alone and desolate to be making lamentation on its face always.

DEIRDRE. I'll die when you do, Naisi. I'd not have come here from Alban but I knew I'd be along with you in Emain, and you living or dead. . . . Yet this night it's strange and distant talk you're making only.

NAISI. There's nothing, surely, the like of a new grave of open earth for putting a great space between two friends that love.

DEIRDRE. If there isn't, it's that grave when it's closed will make us one for ever, and we two lovers have had great space without weariness or growing old or any sadness of the mind.

CONCHUBOR (*coming in on right*). I'd bid you welcome, Naisi.

NAISI (*standing up*). You're welcome, Conchubor. I'm well pleased you've come.

CONCHUBOR (*blandly*). Let you not think bad of this place where I've put you till other rooms are readied.

NAISI (*breaking out*). We know the room you've readied. We know what stirred you to send your seals and Fergus into Alban and stop him in the north, (*opening curtain and pointing to the grave*) and dig that grave before us. Now I ask what brought you here?

CONCHUBOR. I've come to look on Deirdre.

NAISI. Look on her. You're a knacky fancier, and it's well you chose the one you'd lure from Alban. Look on her, I tell you, and when you've looked I've got ten fingers will squeeze your mottled goose neck, though you're king itself.

DEIRDRE (*coming between them*). Hush, Naisi! Maybe Conchubor'll make peace. . . . Do not mind him, Conchubor; he has cause to rage.

CONCHUBOR. It's little I heed his raging, when a call would bring my fighters from the trees. . . . But what do you say, Deirdre?

DEIRDRE. I'll say so near that grave we seem three lonesome

people, and by a new made grave there's no man will keep brooding on a woman's lips, or on the man he hates. It's not long till your own grave will be dug in Emain, and you'd go down to it more easy if you'd let call Ainnle and Ardan, the way we'd have a supper all together, and fill that grave, and you'll be well pleased from this out, having four new friends the like of us in Emain.

CONCHUBOR (*looking at her for a moment*). That's the first friendly word I've heard you speaking, Deirdre. A game the like of yours should be the proper thing for softening the heart and putting sweetness in the tongue; and yet this night when I hear you I've small blame left for Naisi that he stole you off from Ulster.

DEIRDRE (*to Naisi*). Now, Naisi, answer gently, and we'll be friends to-night.

NAISI (*doggedly*). I have no call but to be friendly. I'll answer what you will.

DEIRDRE (*taking Naisi's hand*). Then you'll call Conchubor your friend and king, the man who reared me up upon Slieve Fuadh.

[*As Conchubor is going to clasp Naisi's hand cries are heard behind.*]

CONCHUBOR. What noise is that?

AINNLE (*behind*). Naisi. . . . Naisi! Come to us; we are betrayed and broken.

NAISI. It's Ainnle crying out in a battle.

CONCHUBOR. I was near won this night, but death's between us now.

[*He goes out.*]

DEIRDRE (*clinging to Naisi*). There is no battle. . . . Do not leave me, Naisi.

NAISI. I must go to them.

DEIRDRE (*beseechingly*). Do not leave me, Naisi. Let us creep up in the darkness behind the grave. If there's a battle, maybe the strange fighters will be destroyed, when Ainnle and Ardan are against them.

[*Cries heard.*]

NAISI (*wildly*). I hear Ardan crying out. Do not hold me from my brothers.

DEIRDRE. Do not leave me, Naisi. Do not leave me broken and alone.

NAISI. I cannot leave my brothers when it is I who have defied the king.

DEIRDRE. I will go with you.

NAISI. You cannot come. Do not hold me from the fight. [*He throws her aside almost roughly*.]

DEIRDRE (*with restraint*). Go to your brothers. For seven years you have been kindly, but the hardness of death has come between us.

NAISI (*looking at her aghast*). And you'll have me meet death with a hard word from your lips in my ear?

DEIRDRE. We've had a dream, but this night has waked us surely. In a little while we've lived too long, Naisi, and isn't it a poor thing we should miss the safety of the grave, and we trampling its edge?

AINNLE (*behind*). Naisi, Naisi, we are attacked and ruined!

DEIRDRE. Let you go where they are calling. (*She looks at him for an instant coldly*.) Have you no shame loitering and talking, and a cruel death facing Ainnle and Ardan in the woods?

NAISI (*frantic*). They'll not get a death that's cruel, and they with men alone. It's women that have loved are cruel only; and if I went on living from this day I'd be putting a curse on the lot of them I'd meet walking in the east or west, putting a curse on the sun that gave them beauty, and on the madder and the stonecrop[1] put red upon their cloaks.

DEIRDRE (*bitterly*). I'm well pleased there's no one in this place to make a story that Naisi was a laughing-stock the night he died.

NAISI. There'd not be many'd make a story, for that mockery is in your eyes this night will spot the face of Emain with a plague of pitted graves.
[*He goes out*.]

---

[1] Plants from which reddish die is extracted.

CONCHUBOR (*outside*). This is Naisi. Strike him! (*Tumult. Deirdre crouches down on Naisi's cloak. Conchubor comes in hurriedly.*) They've met their death—the three that stole you, Deirdre, and from this out you'll be my queen in Emain.

[*A keen of men's voices is heard behind.*]

DEIRDRE (*bewildered and terrified*). It is not I will be a queen.

CONCHUBOR. Make your lamentation a short while if you will, but it isn't long till a day'll come when you begin pitying a man is old and desolate, and High King also. . . . Let you not fear me, for it's I'm well pleased you have a store of pity for the three that were your friends in Alban.

DEIRDRE. I have pity, surely. . . . It's the way pity has me this night, when I think of Naisi, that I could set my teeth into the heart of a king.

CONCHUBOR. I know well pity's cruel, when it was my pity for my own self destroyed Naisi.

DEIRDRE (*more wildly*). It was my words without pity gave Naisi a death will have no match until the ends of life and time. (*Breaking out into a keen.*) But who'll pity Deirdre has lost the lips of Naisi from her neck and from her cheek for ever? Who'll pity Deirdre has lost the twilight in the woods with Naisi, when beech-trees were silver and copper, and ash-trees were fine gold?

CONCHUBOR (*bewildered*). It's I'll know the way to pity and care you, and I with a share of troubles has me thinking this night it would be a good bargain if it was I was in the grave, and Deirdre crying over me, and it was Naisi who was old and desolate.

[*Keen heard.*]

DEIRDRE (*wild with sorrow*). It is I who am desolate; I, Deirdre, that will not live till I am old.

CONCHUBOR. It's not long you'll be desolate, and I seven years saying, "It's a bright day for Deirdre in the woods of Alban"; or saying again, "What way will Deirdre be sleeping this night, and wet leaves and branches driving from the north?" Let you not break the thing I've set my life on, and you giving yourself up to your sorrow when it's joy and sorrow do burn out like straw blazing in an east wind.

DEIRDRE (*turning on him*). Was it that way with your sorrow, when I and Naisi went northward from Slieve Fuadh and let raise our sails for Alban?

CONCHUBOR. There's one sorrow has no end surely—that's being old and lonesome. (*With extraordinary pleading.*) But you and I will have a little peace in Emain, with harps playing, and old men telling stories at the fall of night. I've let build rooms for our two selves, Deirdre, with red gold upon the walls and ceilings that are set with bronze. There was never a queen in the east had a house the like of your house, that's waiting for yourself in Emain.

SOLDIER (*running in*). Emain is in flames. Fergus has come back and is setting fire to the world. Come up, Conchubor, or your state will be destroyed!

CONCHUBOR (*angry and regal again*). Are the Sons of Usna buried?

SOLDIER. They are in their grave, but no earth is thrown.

CONCHUBOR. Let me see them. Open the tent! (*Soldier opens back of tent and shows grave.*) Where are my fighters?

SOLDIER. They are gone to Emain.

CONCHUBOR (*to Deirdre*). There are none to harm you. Stay here until I come again.

[*Goes out with Soldier. Deirdre looks round for a moment, then goes up slowly and looks into grave. She crouches down and begins swaying herself backwards and forwards, keening softly. At first her words are not heard, then they become clear.*]

DEIRDRE. It's you three will not see age or death coming—you that were my company when the fires on the hill-tops were put out and the stars were our friends only. I'll turn my thoughts back from this night, that's pitiful for want of pity, to the time it was your rods and cloaks made a little tent for me where there'd be a birch tree making shelter and a dry stone; though from this day my own fingers will be making a tent for me, spreading out my hairs and they knotted with the rain.

[*Lavarcham and Old Woman come in stealthily on right.*]

DEIRDRE (*not seeing them*). It is I, Deirdre, will be crouching in a dark place; I, Deirdre, that was young with Naisi, and brought sorrow to his grave in Emain.

OLD WOMAN. Is that Deirdre broken down that was so light and airy?

LAVARCHAM. It is, surely, crying out over their grave. [*She goes to Deirdre.*]

DEIRDRE. It will be my share from this out to be making lamentation on this stone always, and I crying for a love will be the like of a star shining on a little harbour by the sea.

LAVARCHAM (*coming forward*). Let you rise up, Deirdre, and come off while there are none to heed us, the way I'll find you shelter and some friend to guard you.

DEIRDRE. To what place would I go away from Naisi? What are the woods without Naisi or the sea shore?

LAVARCHAM (*very coaxingly*). If it is that way you'd be, come till I find you a sunny place where you'll be a great wonder they'll call the queen of sorrows; and you'll begin taking a pride to be sitting up pausing and dreaming when the summer comes.

DEIRDRE. It was the voice of Naisi that was strong in summer —the voice of Naisi that was sweeter than pipes playing, but from this day will be dumb always.

LAVARCHAM (*to Old Woman*). She doesn't heed us at all. We'll be hard set to rouse her.

OLD WOMAN. If we don't the High King will rouse her, coming down beside her with the rage of battle in his blood, for how could Fergus stand against him?

LAVARCHAM (*touching Deirdre with her hand*). There's a score of woman's years in store for you, and you'd best choose will you start living them beside the man you hate, or being your own mistress in the west or south?

DEIRDRE. It is not I will go on living after Ainnle and after Ardan. After Naisi I will not have a lifetime in the world.

OLD WOMAN *(with excitement)*. Look, Lavarcham! There's a light leaving the Red Branch. Conchubor and his lot will be coming quickly with a torch of bog-deal for her marriage, throwing a light on her three comrades.

DEIRDRE *(startled)*. Let us throw down clay on my three comrades. Let us cover up Naisi along with Ainnle and Ardan, they that were the pride of Emain. *(Throwing in clay.)* There is Naisi was the best of three, the choicest of the choice of many. It was a clean death was your share, Naisi; and it is not I will quit your head, when it's many a dark night among the snipe and plover that you and I were whispering together. It is not I will quit your head, Naisi, when it's many a night we saw the stars among the clear trees of Glen da Ruadh, or the moon pausing to rest her on the edges of the hills.

OLD WOMAN. Conchubor is coming, surely. I see the glare of flames throwing a light upon his cloak.

LAVARCHAM *(eagerly)*. Rise up, Deirdre, and come to Fergus, or be the High King's slave for ever!

DEIRDRE *(imperiously)*. I will not leave Naisi, who has left the whole world scorched and desolate. I will not go away when there is no light in the heavens, and no flower in the earth under them, but is saying to me that it is Naisi who is gone for ever.

CONCHUBOR *(behind)*. She is here. Stay a little back. *(Lavarcham and Old Woman go into the shadow on left as Conchubor comes in. With excitement, to Deirdre.)* Come forward and leave Naisi the way I've left charred timber and a smell of burning in Emain Macha, and a heap of rubbish in the storehouse of many crowns.

DEIRDRE *(more awake to what is round her)*. What are crowns and Emain Macha, when the head that gave them glory is this place, Conchubor, and it stretched upon the gravel will be my bed to-night?

CONCHUBOR. Make an end of talk of Naisi, for I've come to bring you to Dundealgan since Emain is destroyed.

[*Conchubor makes a movement towards her.*]

DEIRDRE (*with a tone that stops him*). Draw a little back from Naisi, who is young for ever. Draw a little back from the white bodies I am putting under a mound of clay and grasses that are withered—a mound will have a nook for my own self when the end is come.

CONCHUBOR (*roughly.*) Let you rise up and come along with me in place of growing crazy with your wailings here.

DEIRDRE. It's yourself has made a crazy story, and let you go back to your arms, Conchubor, and to councils where your name is great, for in this place you are an old man and a fool only.

CONCHUBOR. If I've folly, I've sense left not to lose the thing I've bought with sorrow and the deaths of many.

[*He moves towards her.*]

DEIRDRE. Do not raise a hand to touch me.

CONCHUBOR. There are other hands to touch you. My fighters are set round in among the trees.

DEIRDRE. Who'll fight the grave, Conchubor, and it opened on a dark night?

LAVARCHAM (*eagerly*). There are steps in the wood. I hear the call of Fergus and his men.

CONCHUBOR (*furiously*). Fergus cannot stop me. I am more powerful than he is, though I am defeated and old.

FERGUS (*comes in to Deirdre; a red glow is seen behind the grove*). I have destroyed Emain, and now I'll guard you all times, Deirdre, though it was I, without knowledge, brought Naisi to his grave.

CONCHUBOR. It's not you will guard her, for my whole armies are gathering. Rise up, Deirdre, for you are mine surely.

FERGUS (*coming between them*). I am come between you.

CONCHUBOR (*wildly*). When I've killed Naisi and his brothers, is there any man that I will spare? And is it you will stand against me, Fergus, when it's seven years you've seen me getting my death with rage in Emain?

FERGUS. It's I, surely, will stand against a thief and a traitor.

DEIRDRE *(stands up and sees the light from Emain).* Draw a little back with the squabbling of fools when I am broken up with misery. *(She turns round.)* I see the flames of Emain starting upward in the dark night; and because of me there will be weasels and wild cats crying on a lonely wall where there were queens and armies and red gold, the way there will be a story told of a ruined city and a raving king and a woman will be young for ever. *(She looks round.)* I see the trees naked and bare, and the moon shining. Little moon, little moon of Alban, it's lonesome you'll be this night, and to-morrow night, and long nights after, and you pacing the woods beyond Glen Laoi, looking every place for Deirdre and Naisi, the two lovers who slept so sweetly with each other.

FERGUS *(going to Conchubor's right and whispering).* Keep back, or you will have the shame of pushing a bolt on a queen who is out of her wits.

CONCHUBOR. It is I who am out of my wits, with Emain in flames, and Deirdre raving, and my own heart gone within me.

DEIRDRE *(in a high and quiet tone).* I have put away sorrow like a shoe that is worn out and muddy, for it is I have had a life that will be envied by great companies. It was not by a low birth I made kings uneasy, and they sitting in the halls of Emain. It was not a low thing to be chosen by Conchubor, who was wise, and Naisi had no match for bravery. It is not a small thing to be rid of grey hairs, and the loosening of the teeth. *(With a sort of triumph.)* It was the choice of lives we had in the clear woods, and in the grave, we're safe, surely. . . .

CONCHUBOR. She will do herself harm.

DEIRDRE *(showing Naisi's knife).* I have a little key to unlock the prison of Naisi you'd shut upon his youth for ever. Keep back, Conchubor; for the High King who is your master has put his hands between us. *(She half turns to the grave.)* It was sorrows were foretold, but great joys were my share always;

yet it is a cold place I must go to be with you, Naisi; and it's cold your arms will be this night that were warm about my neck so often. . . . It's a pitiful thing to be talking out when your ears are shut to me. It's a pitiful thing, Conchubor, you have done this night in Emain; yet a thing will be a joy and triumph to the ends of life and time.

[*She presses knife into her heart and sinks into the grave. Conchubor and Fergus go forward. The red glow fades, leaving stage very dark.*]

FERGUS. Four white bodies are laid down together; four clear lights are quenched in Ireland. (*He throws his sword into the grave.*) There is my sword that could not shield you—my four friends that were the dearest always. The names of Emain have gone out: Deirdre is dead and there is none to keen her. That is the fate of Deirdre and the children of Usna, and for this night, Conchubor, our war is ended.

[*He goes out.*]

LAVARCHAM. I have a little hut where you can rest, Conchubor; there is a great dew falling.

CONCHUBOR (*with the voice of an old man*). Take me with you. I'm hard set to see the way before me.

OLD WOMAN. This way, Conchubor.

[*They go out.*]

LAVARCHAM (*beside the grave*). Deirdre is dead, and Naisi is dead; and if the oaks and stars could die for sorrow, it's a dark sky and a hard and naked earth we'd have this night in Emain.

CURTAIN

Oliver St. John Gogarty (1878-)

The Crab Tree

Here is the crab tree,
Firm and erect,
In spite of the thin soil,
In spite of neglect.
The twisted root grapples
For sap with the rock,
And draws the hard juice
To the succulent top:
Here are wild apples,
Here's a tart crop!

No outlandish grafting
That ever grew soft
In a sweet air of Persia,
Or safe Roman croft;
Unsheltered by steading,
Rock-rooted and grown,
A great tree of Erin,
It stands up alone,
A forest tree spreading
Where forests are gone.

Of all who pass by it
How few in it see
A westering remnant
Of days when Lough Neagh
Flowed up the long dingles
Its blossom had lit,
Old days of glory
Time cannot repeat;
And therefore it mingles
The bitter and sweet.

It takes from the West Wind
The thrust of the main;
It makes from the tension
Of sky and of plain,
Of what clay enacted,
Of living alarm,
A vitalised symbol
Of earth and of storm,
Of Chaos contracted
To intricate form.

Unbreakable wrestler!
What sapling or herb
Has core of such sweetness
And fruit so acerb?
So grim a transmitter
Of life through mishap,
That one wonders whether
If that in the sap,
Is sweet or is bitter
Which makes it stand up.

Ringsend

(After Reading Tolstoi)

I will live in Ringsend
With a red-headed whore,
And the fan-light gone in
Where it lights the hall-door;
And listen each night
For her querulous shout,
As at last she streels in
And the pubs empty out.

To soothe that wild breast
With my old-fangled songs,
Till she feels it redressed
From inordinate wrongs,
Imagined, outrageous,
Preposterous wrongs,
Till peace at last comes,
Shall be all I will do,
Where the little lamp blooms
Like a rose in the stew;
And up the back-garden
The sound comes to me
Of the lapsing, unsoilable,
Whispering sea.

Exorcism

To banish your shape from my mind
I thought of the dangerous wood
Where a man might wander and find,
By a stream in the solitude,
The Queen it is death if one sees,
Death by a merciless dart;
But how could that bring me release,
Shot as I am to the heart?

Beauty will cure me, I cried;
By Beauty is Beauty dislodged.
And I worked on a dream till I eyed
The Queens whom the young man judged.
But the vision faded and slipt;
And the cure was a cure of no worth;
For I said, when the Queens were stript,
I have given the prize to a fourth.

Ugliness, Chaos and War
I know, but I would not invoke;
They would feed you as darkness a star,
And strengthen the beam of my yoke.
If Love be reborn in a song
I with my fate will not quarrel,
But you, if you do him a wrong,
May be changed to a reed or a laurel.

To the Liffey With the Swans[1]

Keep you these calm and lovely things,
  And float them on your clearest water;
For one would not disgrace a King's
  Transformed beloved and buoyant daughter.

And with her goes this sprightly swan,
  A bird of more than royal feather,
With alban beauty clothed upon:
  O keep them fair and well together!

As fair as was that doubled Bird,
  By love of Leda so besotten,
That she was all with wonder stirred,
  And the Twin Sportsmen were begotten!

---

[1] The poet, imprisoned in a deserted house on the edge of the Liffey, escaped from his enemies by plunging into the water. As he swam the stream he promised it, in return for safe passage, two swans. Later, in the presence of W. B. Yeats, he fulfilled his vow.

Per Iter Tenebricosum

Enough! Why should a man bemoan
A Fate that leads the natural way?
Or think himself a worthier one
Than those who braved it in their day?
If only gladiators died,
Or Heroes, Death would be his pride;
But have not little maidens gone,
And Lesbia's sparrow—all alone?

Verse

What should we know,
For better or worse,
Of the Long Ago,
Were it not for Verse:
What ships went down;
What walls were razed;
Who won the crown;
What lads were praised?
A fallen stone,
Or a waste of sands;
And all is known
Of Art-less lands.
But you need not delve
By the sea-side hills
Where the Muse herself
All Time fulfils,
Who cuts with his scythe
All things but hers;
All but the blithe
Hexameters.

To the Maids Not to Walk In the Wind

When the wind blows, walk not abroad,
For, Maids, you may not know
The mad, quaint thoughts which incommode
Me when the winds do blow.

What though the tresses of the treen
In doubled beauty move,
With silver added to their green,
They were not made for Love.

But when your clothes reveal your thighs
And surge around your knees,
Until from foam you seem to rise,
As Venus from the seas . . .

Though ye are fair, it is not fair!
Unless you will be kind,
Till I am dead, and changed to AIR,
O walk not in the wind!

To W. B. Yeats Who Says That His Castle of Ballylee Is His Monument

To stones trust not your monument
To make a living fame endure.
Who built Dun Angus battlement?
O'Flaherty is forgotten in Auchnanure.

And he who told how Troy was sacked
And what men clipt the lovely Burd,[1]
Had seven Mayors to swear, in fact,
Their towns first heard his babbling word.

Leda and the Swan

Though her Mother told her
  Not to go a-bathing,
Leda loved the river
  And she could not keep away:
Wading in its freshets
  When the noon was heavy;
Walking by the water
  At the close of day.

Where between its waterfalls,
  Underneath the beeches,
Gently flows a broader
  Hardly moving stream,
And the balanced trout lie
  In the quiet reaches;
Taking all her clothes off,
  Leda went to swim.

There was not a flag-lead
  By the river's margin
That might be a shelter
  From a passer-by;
And a sudden whiteness
  In the quiet darkness,
Let alone the splashing,
  Was enough to catch an eye.

---

1 Lady, i.e., Helen.

But the place was lonely,
  And her clothes were hidden;
Even cattle walking
  In the ford had gone away;
Every single farm-hand
  Sleeping after dinner,—
What's the use of talking?
  There was no one in the way.

In, without a stitch on,
  Peaty water yielded,
Till her head was lifted
  With its ropes of hair;
It was more surprising
  Than a lily gilded
Just to see how golden
  Was her body there:

Lolling in the water,
  Lazily uplifting
Limbs that on the surface
  Whitened into snow;
Leaning on the water,
  Indolently drifting,
Hardly any faster
  Than the foamy bubbles go.

You would say to see her
  Swimming in the lonely
Pool, or after, dryer,
  Putting on her clothes:
"O but she is lovely,
  Not a soul to see her,
And how lovely only
  Leda's Mother knows!"

Under moving branches
  Leisurely she dresses,
And the leafy sunlight
  Made you wonder were
All its woven shadows
  But her golden tresses,
Or a smock of sunlight
  For her body bare.

When on earth great beauty
  Goes exempt from danger,
It will be endangered
  From a source on high;
When unearthly stillness
  Falls on leaves, the ranger,
In his wood-lore anxious,
  Gazes at the sky.

While her hair was drying,
  Came a gentle languor,
Whether from the bathing
  Or the breeze she didn't know.
Anyway she lay there,
  And her Mother's anger
(Worse if she had wet hair)
  Could not make her dress and go.

Whitest of all earthly
  Things, the white that's rarest,
Is the snow on mountains
  Standing in the sun;
Next the clouds above them,
  Then the down is fairest
On the breast and pinions
  Of a proudly sailing swan.

And she saw him sailing
  On the pool where lately
She had stretched unnoticed,
  As she thought, and swum;
And she never wondered
  Why, erect and stately,
Where no river weed was
  Such a bird had come.

What was it she called him:
  Goosey-goosey gander?
For she knew no better
  Way to call a swan;
And the bird responding
  Seemed to understand her,
For he left his sailing
  For the bank to waddle on.

Apple blossoms under
  Hills of Lacedæmon,
With the snow beyond them
  In the still blue air,
To the swan who hid them
  With his wings asunder,
Than the breasts of Leda,
  Were not lovelier!

Of the tales that daughters
  Tell their poor old mothers,
Which by all accounts are
  Often very odd;
Leda's was a story
  Stranger than all others.
What was there to say but:
  Glory be to God?

And she half-believed her,
  For she knew her daughter;
And she saw the swan-down
  Tangled in her hair.
Though she knew how deeply
  Runs the stillest water;
How could she protect her
  From the winged air?

Why is it effects are
  Greater than their causes?
Why should causes often
  Differ from effects?
Why should what is lovely
  Fill the world with harness?
And the most deceived be
  She who least suspects?

When the hyacinthine
  Eggs were in the basket,—
Blue as at the whiteness
  Where a cloud begins;
Who would dream there lay there
  All that Trojan brightness;
Agamemnon murdered;
  And the mighty Twins?

Joseph Campbell (1879-1944)

The Old Age Pensioner

He sits over the glimmering coal
With ancient face and folded hands:
His eye glasses his quiet soul,
He blinks and nods and understands.
In dew wetted, in tempest blown,
A Lear at last come to his own.

For fifty years he trenched his field
That he might eat a freeman's bread:
The seasons balked him of their yield,
His children's children wished him dead.
But ransom came to him at length
At the ebb-tide of life and strength.

And so he sits with folded hands
Over the flag of amber fire:
He blinks and nods and understands,
He has his very soul's desire.
In dew wetted, in tempest blown,
A Lear at last come to his own.

The Unfrocked Priest

He leant at the door
In his priest's clothes—
Greasy black they were:
And he bled at the nose.

He leant at the door,
And the blood trickled down:
A man of the country,
More than the town.

He was of God's anointed,
A priest, no less:
But he had been unfrocked
For drunkenness.

For that, or worse,
And flesh is only human,
For some wrong-doing
With a woman.

And in his father's house
He lived at ease,
Reading his books,
As quiet as the trees.

No one troubled him
As he went in and out,
And he smoked his clay,
And he grew stout.

And he tramped the parish
In the summer days,
Thinking high thoughts
And giving God praise.

None but blessed him
As he walked the hills,
For he gave to the poor
And he cured their ills.

There was no herb
That grew in the grass,
But he saw its virtue
As in a glass.

No rath, no Mass-bush
No ogham stone,
But he knew its story
As his own.

He had a scholar's knowledge
Of Greek,
And dabbled in Hebrew
And Arabic.

And in his time
    (He died in 'eighty-seven)
He wrote two epics
    And a "Dream of Heaven."

I saw him once only
    In his priest's clothes
At his father's door:
    And he bled at the nose.

I Am the Mountainy Singer

I am the mountainy singer—
The voice of the peasant's dream,
The cry of the wind on the wooded hill,
The leap of the fish in the stream.

Quiet and love I sing—
The carn[1] on the mountain crest,
The cailin[2] in her lover's arms,
The child at its mother's breast.

Beauty and peace I sing—
The fire on the open hearth,
The cailleach[3] spinning at her wheel,
The plough in the broken earth.

Travail and pain I sing—
The bride on the childing bed,
The dark man laboring at his rhymes,
The ewe in the lambing shed.

---

[1] Cairn—a pyramid of rough stones raised as a memorial or a sepulchral monument. NED

[2] Colleen, girl.

[3] Old woman.

Sorrow and death I sing—
The canker come on the corn,
The fisher lost in the mountain loch,
The cry at the mouth of morn.

No other life I sing,
For I am sprung of the stock
That broke the hilly land for bread,
And built the nest in the rock!

I Am the Gilly of Christ

I AM the gilly[1] of Christ,
The mate of Mary's Son;
I run the roads at seeding time,
And when the harvest's done.

I sleep among the hills,
The heather is my bed;
I dip the termon[2]-well for drink,
And pull the sloe for bread.

No eye has ever seen me,
But shepherds hear me pass,
Singing at fall of even
Along the shadowed grass.

The beetle is my bellman,
The meadow-fire my guide,
The bee and bat my ambling nags
When I have need to ride.

---

[1] Servant.
[2] Land belonging to a religious house. NED

All know me only the Stranger,
Who sits on the Saxons' height:
He burned the bacach's[1] little house
On last St. Brigid's Night.

He sups off silver dishes,
And drinks in a golden horn,
But he will wake a wiser man
Upon the Judgment Morn!

I am the gilly of Christ,
The mate of Mary's Son;
I run the roads at seeding time,
And when the harvest's done.

The seed I sow is lucky,
The corn I reap is red,
And whoso sings the Gilly's Rann[2]
Will never cry for bread.

As I Came Over the Grey, Grey Hills

As I came over the grey, grey hills
And over the grey, grey water,
I saw the gilly leading on,
And the white Christ following after.

Where and where does the gilly lead?
And where is the white Christ faring?
They've travelled the four grey sounds of Orc,
And the four grey seas of Eirinn.

---

[1] Lame man's.
[2] A verse, quatrain or stanza.

The moon it set and the wind's away,
And the song in the grass is dying,
And a silver cloud on the silent sea
Like a shrouding sheet is lying.

But Christ and the gilly will follow on
Till the ring in the east is showing,
And the awny[1] corn is red on the hills,
And the golden light is glowing!

I Will Go With My Father A-Ploughing

I will go with my father a-ploughing
To the green field by the sea,
And the rooks and the crows and the seagulls
Will come flocking after me.
I will sing to the patient horses
With the lark in the white of the air,
And my father will sing the plough-song
That blesses the cleaving share.

I will go with my father a-sowing
To the red field by the sea,
And the rooks and the gulls and the starlings
Will come flocking after me.
I will sing to the striding sowers
With the finch on the flowering sloe,
And my father will sing the seed-song
That only the wise men know.

[1] Bearded, bristly.

I will go with my father a-reaping
To the brown field by the sea,
And the geese and the crows and the children
Will come flocking after me.
I will sing to the weary reapers
With the wren in the heat of the sun,
And my father will sing the scythe-song
That joys for the harvest done.

The Herb-Leech

I HAVE gathered *luss*[1]
At the wane of the moon,
And supped its sap
With a yewen[2] spoon.
I have set a spell
By the carn of Medb,
And smelt the mould
Of the red queen's grave.
I have dreamed a dearth
In the darkened sun,
And felt the hand
Of the Evil One.
I have fathomed war
In the comet's tail,
And heard the crying
Of Gall[3] and Gael.
I have seen the spume
On the dead priest's lips,
And the "holy fire"
On the spars of ships;
And the shooting stars

[1] Foxglove.
[2] Made of yew.
[3] Englishman.

On Barthelmy's Night,
Blanching the dark
With ghostly light;
And the corpse-candle
Of the seer's dream,
Bigger in girth
Than a weaver's beam;
And the shy hearth-fairies
About the grate,
Blowing the turves
To a whiter heat.
All things on earth
To me are known,
For I have the gift
Of the Murrain Stone!

The Raid[1]

BY Sean O'Casey (1880-)

THE cold beauty of frost glittered everywhere outside, unseen, unfelt, for the slum was asleep. An uneasy silence echoed over the house, for awake or asleep, everyone knew that death with his comrade, the inflictor of wounds, roamed the darkened streets. Stretched out in a truckle bed in a tenement room, its murky window facing on to the street, Sean thought of the tapestry of the day. He could see the street stretching along outside, its roughly cobbled roadway beset with empty match-boxes, tattered straws, tattered papers, scattered mounds of horse-dung, and sprinkled deep with slumbering dust waiting for an idle wind to come and raise it to irritating life again. Lean-looking gas-lamps stood at regular intervals on the foot-

[1] The action takes place during the Anglo-Irish war (1918-1921). The Black and Tans, so called because they wore makeshift uniforms of half English khaki and half Royal Irish Constabulary black, were temporary policemen. The Auxiliaries were recruited from ex-officers of the Royal Navy, Army and Air Force and were a military force.

paths, many of them deformed from the play of swinging children, bending over like old men standing to gasp, and wait for a pain in the back to go. The melancholy pathway meandered along by the side of the tall houses, leading everywhere to tarnishing labour, to consumption's cough, to the writhings of fever, to bitter mutterings against life, and frantic calls on St. Anthony, The Little Flower, and Bernadette of Missabielle to be absent helps in time of trouble. Upon these stones, I will build my church.

There were the houses, too—a long, lurching row of discontented incurables, smirched with the age-long marks of ague, fevers, cancer, and consumption, the soured tears of little children, and the sighs of disappointed newly-married girls. The doors were scarred with time's spit and anger's hasty knocking; the pillars by their sides were shaky, their stuccoed bloom long since peeled away, and they looked like crutches keeping the trembling doors standing on their palsied feet. The gummy-eyed windows blinked dimly out, lacquered by a year's tired dust from the troubled street below. Dirt and disease were the big sacraments here—outward and visible signs of an inward and spiritual disgrace. The people bought the cheapest things in food they could find in order to live, to work, to worship: the cheapest spuds, the cheapest tea, the cheapest meat, the cheapest fat; and waited for unsold bread to grow stale that they might buy that cheaper, too. Here they gathered up the fragments so that nothing would be lost. The streets were long haggard corridors of rottenness and ruin. What wonderful mind of memory could link this shrinking wretchedness with the flaunting gorgeousness of silk and satin; with bloom of rose and scent of lavender? A thousand years must have passed since the last lavender lady was carried out feet first from the last surviving one of them. Even the sun shudders now when she touches a roof, for she feels some evil has chilled the glow of her garment. The flower that here once bloomed is dead forever. No wallflower here has crept into a favoured cranny; sight and sign of the primrose were far away; no room here for a dance of daffodils; no swallow twittering under a shady eave; and it was sad to see an odd sparrow seeking a yellow grain from the mocking dust; not even a spiky-headed thistle, purple mitred, could find a corner here for a sturdy life. No Wordsworth here wandered about as lonely as a cloud.

> The decent dead provoke no blood-congealing fear,
> Like the dread death that lives to fester here.
> Here children, lost to every sense but life,
> Indulge in play that mimics social strife;
> And learn from strenuous practice that they may
> Act well their part at home some future day:
> The girl trains her lungs to scream and shout,
> The boy his arms to knock a wife about.

And yet his riddled horridness had given root to the passion flower. What had been lost was found; what had been dead came to life again. The spirit beneath the coat brocaded, with slender sword quivering, had come into being again, not in brocade, but in rags; not with sword or dainty phrases, elegant in comedy and satire; but with bitter curses, blows as hard as an arm can give, and a rank, savage spit into a master's face. Fought these frantic fools did, led by Larkin and by Connolly; fought till the day-star arose in their shivering hearts, the new and glorious light, the red evangel, the light of the knowledge of the glory of God, manifested in the active mind and vital bodies of men and women and little children. And now something stronger than bare hands were in the battle. Many a spearpoint flame from a gun frightened a dark corner or a shadowy street, making armed men in khaki or black crouch low in their rushing lorries, firing rapidly back at the street grown shadowy again, or the corner now darker than ever before.

Now the old house was still. Comely Bessie Ballynoy, on her way up, had knocked; but finding Sean in bed, had bid good-night, and gone. Lazy sleep had crawled in by the dark hallway to soothe restlessness and to hush the clamour from the attic above to the basement below. A lousy sleep, dreary-eyed, in loosely slippered feet, torn and muddy, calling in a shoddy whisper for quietness; creeping in yawning, leaving no-one on watch, though every night now was a perilous night for Dublin. In all the rooms, all the cheap crockery stood quiet on the shelves; the chairs leaned against the shaky walls; rosy-faced fires had all gone pale; the patter of children's feet had long since ceased; only dreams crept slyly in to fill the ugly rooms with sparkling peace for a few dark moments, clothing the sleepers with a cautious splendour; setting them, maybe, to sip rare wines from bulging bottles, or led them to yellow sands bordering a playful sea. A younger lass, perhaps, dreamed of scanty night attire between snowy sheets, with a colour-robed prince by the bedroom door in haste to come in, and bid her a choice goodnight; while the younger men saw themselves, sword in hand, driving the khaki cut-throats out of Eire's five beautiful fields.

Every guardian angel relaxed now, and nodded sleepily by tattered counterpane and ragged sheet, for sin usually curled up like a dog to sleep at their feet, waiting for the tenement life to go on again in the morning. So after Curfew the silent tenement slept, unconscious even that every whining wail of every passing motor sang a song of death to someone; for in sleep the slimy roof above them had slid aside, and left the stars but a hand's breadth out of reach.

When will the day break in Eirinn; when will her day-star arise? How often had he heard these words sung in a languishing voice after an eight-hand reel or a high-cauled cap at *ceilidh* or *sgoruidheacht!* Well, no day would ever break here, nor would the shadows ever flee away. Sean's eyes were closing, and dimming thoughts swooned faintly from his mind into the humming whine of motor-engines coming quick along the road outside. Up on his elbow he shot as he heard the sound of braking, telling him that the lorries were outside of his house, or of those on either side. Then he shot down again to hide as a blinding beam from a searchlight poured through the window, skimming the cream of the darkness out of the room. It silvered the old walls for a few moments, then withdrew like a receding tide to send its beam on another part of the house. Then there was a volley of battering blows on the obstinate wooden door, mingled with the crash of falling glass that told Sean the panels on each side of it had been shattered by hammer or rifle-butt.

A raid! All the winsome dreams of the house had vanished; sleep had gone; and children dug arms and legs into the tensing bodies of their mothers.

Which were they—the Tommies or the Tans? Tans, thought Sean, for the Tommies would not shout so soullessly, nor smash the glass panels so suddenly; they would hammer on the door with a rifle-butt, and wait for it to be opened. No; these were the Tans.

He heard the quick pit-put, pit-put of stockinged feet, faint as it was, coming down the stairs, turning left at the bottom of them, and hurrying along the hall towards the back-yard. His ears were so cocked that he heard the soft, silkly pad of the hurrying feet plainly through the storm of blows falling on the street door; then he thought he heard the back door open softly and gently close again.

—Who could that be? he thought. Might be anyone of the men. Those who didn't take part in ambushes often carried ammunition to those who did; and the dockers and seamen gave a ready hand to the smuggling in of arms. If it wasn't for his own poor sight, he'd probably be doing it himself. All were friendly, save the thin and delicate husband of Mrs. Ballynoy, who cared for no manner of politics. Someone, anyway, slipping into the back to dodge over the wall into the dark lanes, with fear but without fuss. The Dublin slums at war with the British Empire; all the power of an army, flanked by gangs of ruthless ruffians; all the ordered honour of a regal cabinet and the mighty-moneyed banks fighting the ragged tits of the tenements. An unequal fight, by God, but the slums would win! There goes the door!

A great crash shook the old house and shook the heart of Sean, for well he knew the ordeal that might be in front of him once the light from a Tan's torch smote the darkness of the room. A mad rush of heavy feet went past his door, to spread over the stilly house; for no-one had come from a room to risk sudden death in the dark and draughty hallway. He remembered the two boys brought bound from Dublin Castle to a dump-field on the edge of the city by two Auxie-Tan officers, who set them sitting against an old stone wall, extinguishing each young head under an old bucket picked from a rubbish heap. Then going away forty paces or so, they fired away at the buckets till they were full of holes, leaving what they had done behind them to put the fear of the Tans into the hearts of the surviving I.R.A. men. He thought, too, of Clancy, Clune, and McKee, caught and brought to the Castle, where the Tans interviewed them with the stimulant of bayonets, prodding them gamely till none of the three could sigh any longer, for each at last was dead. Now he could hear neither sound nor murmur—all had gone quiet after the crashing fall of the door. No sound even of a child's protest, though that wasn't surprising, for all of them would be too frightened to squeal till a gun exploded somewhere: all was quiet—the sad silence of a sleeping slum. Yet Sean knew that the house must be alive with crawling men, slinking up and down the stairs, hovering outside this door or that one, each with a gun tensed to the last hair, with a ready finger touching the trigger. He guessed that a part of them were the Auxies, the classic members of sibilant and sinister raiders. The Tans alone would make more noise, slamming themselves into a room, shouting to shake off the fear that slashed many of their faces. The Auxies were too proud to show a sign of it. The Tommies would be warm, always hesitant at knocking a woman's room about; they would even be jocular in their funny English way, encouraging the women and even the children to grumble at being taken away from their proper sleep.

All Sean could do was to try to lie dead still, digging down deeper without a sound into the hard mattress of his truckle bed; stifling any desire to steal to the door to listen; to try to modify his breathing till it became unnoticed by himself; for a profound silence might make the Tans disinclined to probe a way in to find out the cause of it; though the Auxies cared nothing for silence, but would lift a corpse from a coffin to search for a gun. He always left his door unlocked now, for past experience had shown him that the slightest obstacle to a swift entrance to a room always irritated them.

From the corner of an eye he could see through the window the searchlight gliding, now up, now down the street, and once for a few moments it blinded him by flooding the room. Then he heard sullen, but loud, thuds of heavy iron falling on heavy wood, coming from the back, and he guessed they were breaking in the entrance to the large shed that was said to be used as a carpenter's shop, and in which Mrs. Ballynoy's husband sometimes worked. Now he heard soft, sly steps going down the hallway to the back. After whomsoever had crept away while the door was being broken down. He had climbed the wall, thought Sean, and somewhere—maybe just behind it—crouched silently in the darkest corner of the narrow lane, a revolver tight in his hand, his shoes slung round his neck, so that, if he had to run, no sound of running feet would give an enemy a cue of a direction through which to send a hail of bullets: a bitter night for a pair of bare feet.

Sean could sense the women, and, maybe, the men, praying while the hammering lasted, to cease at once when silence came again, for it wouldn't serve them to let the Auxies hear them trying to talk to God. These silences were the worst: during the hammering one knew where they were; throughout the silences one didn't. Then they might be anywhere; might be opening his very own door snakily, softly, now; some of them might be even in the room, for their black uniforms fitted the darkness they loved, and black juices, smeared over their cheeks and brows, mixed them cosily with the darker shadows of the night. Any moment a brilliant torch might blind his slatted eyes, and a string of shouted questions blast his ear; a pressed-in, cold pistol barrel make a tiny livid rim on his naked chest. He tried to forget thought, making his mind one with the darkness, losing his fear in the vastness of space; but it was no use, for thought never got farther than that the Tans were there, and his mind came back to think of how it would feel to have a bullet burning a swift channel through the middle of his belly.

Azrael, Azrael, gentle, dignified being of spirit, graceful spirit of death, come, and minister unto us, and save us merry gentlemen!

> Come lovely and soothing death,
> Undulate round the world, serenely arriving,
> Arriving
> In the day, in the night, to all, to each,
> Sooner or later, delicate death.

Ah! Whitman, Walt Whitman, you never knew the Tans! Death doesn't arrive serenely here, his hands are desperate, and neither is delicately formed. Here the angel of death is a biting bitch!

The silence was startled by the sound of a motor-engine warming up, getting ready to go. He heard steps now in the hall, and the sound of *bravura* jests from a few voices. They were going. They mightn't be, though: they pretended that at times, driving the lorries away a bit, but leaving the men behind, to come with a rush into the house again among foolish people hurrying in their nightclothes out of their rooms to ask questions of each other. Stay still; don't move; not a stir: some of them still might be just beyond the door.

He lay there for what seemed a long time, the sweat of fear damping his body, and making him shiver. Stay still; don't move—someone was beside the door. He heard the handle giving a faint, brassy murmur. Soon, a black-clothed arm would thrust itself within, and a shot might go off that he would never hear. He silently squirmed deeper into the bed, and left the rest to God.

—Eh! he heard the voice of Mrs. Ballynoy whisper from the darkness, Are you there, or did they take you? Are you gone, or are you asleep, or wha'?

—That woman again! he thought resentfully—what a fright she gave me! Awake, Mrs. Ballynoy, he whispered back.

—Well, she said softly, you can take your ayse now, an' sleep tranquil, or get up, an' talk about th' queer things done in a Christian age.

—Wait till I light a candle, he said, making a great creak as he heaved himself out of the bed's hollow.

—You'll light no candle while I'm here, young man, said her voice, dressed in a titter, for a slip of overall's th' only shelter between me and a piercin' look from a young man's eyes; an' it wouldn't be good to go from one exthreme to another on an identical night.

—Did they discover anything? asked Sean.

—Not a thing, though they took two o' th' men away with them. A sudden end to them all, an' a short fall to th' hottest hob that hell can heat! Don't light that candle yet, she added, for minds that have safely passed a danger near them are often reckless in their dealin' with an innocent female; though you're not that kind of a man, I know.

He heard the door softly closing and her hand fumbling with the lock. He hoped she wasn't going to stay. Ah! here's the key, for it's safer to put a locked door between eyes that pry into other people's affairs day an' night, tintin' everything with the colour of their own minds.

—Hadn't you better go back to your room, Mrs. Ballynoy, he warned. You need all the sleep you can get these days. We all do; and someone might be prowlin' round an' see an' think th' worst.

—Ay, she said; bad minds, th' lot o' them—that's why I've locked th' door. An' call me Nellie, for you know me well enough be now. Light th' candle now you can, but leave it on th' far side of where I'll be, for it's only a flimsy apron-overall I have between me an' all harm; and she tittered gaily as Sean very slowly lighted a candle on a box beside his bed.

She was a fine-looking heifer, right enough: long reddish hair coiled up into a bunch that rested neatly on the nape of a white neck; a well-chiselled, pale face, with large grey innocent eyes that seemed to be shrouded in a mist from the valley of the Missabielle; a fine figure set these charms off, and when she slyly waved this sweet figure in front of a man, he no longer saw, or wanted to see, the mist of Missabielle. A rose of Tralee, without the flower's serenity, maybe; but certainly a lovely rose of the tenements. But Sean was in no mood now to enjoy the charm of her fine figure and face. Once let a soul see she had been in his room and the whole house would be declaring that he was carrying on with Mrs. Ballynoy. He should have had the courage to get up and push her out. He almost wished now that the Auxies had stayed a little longer.

In the sober light of the candle he saw that she had just decorated her delightful body in a pair of brown slippers and a flowered overall reaching only half-way down her thighs, and showing a wide part of her white swelling bosom; a show that was very charming, but damned uncomfortable to one who was determined to take no notice of it.

—Oh! There y'are, she said, when the candle-light got steady, nice an' snug an' all alone. She came over and sat down on the edge of the bed beside him. I'm askin' meself why a land, overflowin' with prayer an' devotion, should be so often plunged into dhread in the dead o' night for nothin'? An' they tellin' me it's for Ireland's sake. Them politics'll be the death of us some day. I feel terrible shy in this get-up, she said suddenly. Afther washin' the one good nightgown I have, I was sleepin' in me skin, an' this overall was th' first thing I laid hands on when the Tans came thundherin' at the door.

Pansies on it, she said, giggling, pulling it a little from her thigh, pansies for thought! and she poked Sean in the breast, playfully, with a hand reddened by the soda she used in the washing of clothes.

—Isn't Mr. Ballynoy at home, said Sean, trying to get her mind away from the overall, while he thought of a way to get rid of her.

—Didn't I tell you this mornin', on the stairs, that he was on a counthry job! He would be when the Tans come; though it's little good he'd be in any emergency, bein' born timid, with a daisy in his mouth. So I'm a poor lone lassie now, and she gave him another poke—this time in the thigh.

Don't you think you ought to get back, he warned; the Tans might come again.

—Ay, indeed, they might; a body can never know what them fellas'll do. An' it only a little way from Christmas, too. Ah! she said suddenly, looking away into a dream distance; it's good to be near one of your own: th' only two protestants in th' house, not countin' me husband. Of the crowd, not countin' him, only two who have th' proper way o' worshippin' an' are able to foresee th' genuine meanin' of th' holy text.

—There's me for you, said Sean, thinking neither you nor your husband bothered about religion, one way or another.

—Then you're sadly mistaken. I can't remember a year we missed feelin' the curious chantin' glow in th' air of a Christmas mornin', an' us on our way to church. In a proper mood, an' that was often, I could see what you'd think's th' star, ashine on the tip of the spire's top; an' me ears can hear th' dull plod of the three camels' feet in th' deep sand, bearin' th' three kings with th' three rich gifts from Persia, or some other place in th' wilds of a faraway world; an' all th' time an anxious man seekin' shelter for his good woman, with the valleys levelled an' th' hills hidden be th' fallin' snow, dyein' her rich hair grey with its fallin' flakes, a sly soft carpet for her sandalled feet, an' sore they were from th' sting in its frosty tendherness; while th' tired Joseph thrudged demented behind, wondherin' if they'd find their lodgins only on the cowld, cowld ground. But God was good, an' found the shelther of a stable for the bewildhered, half-perished man, with his thin gown sodden, his toil-marked hands a hot ache, an' his poor feet blue with the bitther penetration of th' clingin' snow; an' afther Joseph had shooed th' puzzled animals to a safe an' ordherly distance, th' little fella was soon snug in a manger on top o' warm heaps of sainfoin, thyme, rosemary, an' lavender.

—You're wrong there, said Sean; for how in such a bitther season could anyone come on spring and summer plants like those?

—I dunno, she murmured, unless God turned th' hay an' th' sthraw into th' sweet-savourin' herbs. But it's far betther not to thry to go into them things. Are you afraid to look at me, or what? she ejaculated, turning away from her dream; for Sean had turned his head away to escape the charm of the white bosom and soft thighs. As long as you don't make too free, I don't mind, though I feel a little shy in this scarce get-up.

A shoulder-band of the overall had slipped down, and she had saucily drawn an arm out of it altogether so that near half of her body to the waist was bare, and he saw a breast, rather lovely in the light of the candle, looking like a golden cup with a misty ruby in its centre. If he only had her in a shady corner of the Phoenix Park, or in a room of his own in a house where she wasn't known, the world would be well lost for a period of ecstasy. But not here.

—Your husband's a good fellow, he said trying to keep his mind off her, and would rejoice to see you as you are now. He thinks a lot of you.

—He oughtn't, she said sarcastically; where'd he get another like me? He means well, poor man, but honest, it's pathetic when we're alone, an' he thries to get goin'. Askin' me to tell him when he's hurtin' me! She went into a soft, gay, gurgling laugh, putting a hand over her mouth to quench the merry sound of it. It's funny to talk of it here, but maddenin' when

I'm with him. I'm often near worn out thryin', thryin' to coax a little flash of endeavour outa him. He does his best, but the little sting he once had's gone with the wind—joy go with it! She now laughed venomously and loud, making Sean fearful of someone hearing her. Wait till I tell you, she went on—you'll die laughin'! You should see Charlie when he's at the he-man business—are you sure you won't get faint, Nellie? Don't forget to say if I'm hurtin' you, dearie! One night, when he was—you know—I jerked him clean outa th' bed on to th' floor—th' bump shook th' house! D'ye know, honest t'God, he just lay stunned there. Put th' heart across me. Ever afther, d'ye know, I've had to handle him like a delicate piece of china! No; poor Charlie's style's too shy for me. Not like Jim Achree's. J'ever hear o' his?

She slid down till she was half lying over him, and sang sedulously beside his ear:

> Jim Achree's style has a wondherful way with it,
> All th' girls' minds are in sad disarray with it;
> Whenever they venture to have a short play with it,
> Good girls want to stay with it, ever an' aye.
> Oh! Jimmy Achree, shure your style is your own,
> Amazin' th' way it has flourished an' grown,
> With lovely threats shakin,' tense with mischief makin',
> Knockin' poor women flat like a gorgeous cyclone!

—Looka, she said breathlessly, th' least bit o' fondlin' now, an' I'd swoon away, helpless an' benighted.

—In the midst of death we are in life, thought Sean. He tried to turn his head away so that he wouldn't be prompted by the white breast that was like a golden cup with a misty ruby in its centre; but his head refused to stir. Instead, he found his hand sliding over her fair bosom. He felt her arm pushing a way under his head till it was firmly round his neck, while the other pushed the clothes from covering him. He was lost, unless he yelled for help, and that he couldn't do.

—You're a good young man, he heard her whispering, an' would never take advantage of a woman alone in your room in th' dead o' night, with but a loose slip between you an' a swift lie-down on a bed o' meadow-sweet. Don't sthruggle, man, or you'll upset things! Why'r you thryin' to keep me from gettin' the clothes down? You've far too many on you; a little cool air'll do you good. Take th' good things while they're goin'. She whipped the clothes down with a fierce jerk, and lying beside him, pressed her mouth to his. Her big innocent eyes looked frantic now.

—G'won, she muttered, panting, be as rough as you like with me—it's what I'm longin' for for weeks! And half mad himself now, he gripped her like a vice, and sank his fingers into her flesh.

Then they suddenly went still as death, listening; listening to the whine of a motor-engine cruising down the road outside. Then another whine followed that, and another, the last, till they mingled into one shrill, threatening whine that went echoing round the walls of the old house.

—Out in strength tonight, thought Sean; more'n three of them; each of them crooning a song of death to someone. Ireland's modern, senseless Tanshee!

Suddenly the shrill whine lifted into a shrill, quavering scream, the scream fading into the throb, throb of active engines as the lorries stopped outside, or very near, the house.

—They've stopped at this house, or th' next one! said Nellie, loosening her arm from around his neck, and sliding swift from the bed to the door. Who' ha' thought th' bastards would bother to come twice th' same night? Christ! It's this house they're makin' for! And swiftly came a great hammering on the door again. Nellie frantically twisted and turned at the key, but she couldn't get the door of the room open.

—In they'll come, she squealed softly, an' I'll be exposed to th' world as a fast woman. She tugged and writhed till the slip fell from her shoulders, leaving her naked, fuming, at the door. You it was, she half shouted, turning a red and bitter face towards Sean, that lured me into this predicument, never able to let any decent woman pass without thryin' to meddle her!

Sean as eager as she was herself that she should go unseen, leaped out of bed, hurried over, and with a hard twist, turned the key. Snatching up her flowered overall, she whipped the door open, rushed out, and up the stairs, without another word. Shutting the door again, he fled back to bed, digging himself down deep into it once again, listening to hear if it was Tan or Tommy who had entered the house.

The door spun open, and a torchlight shot terror into his eyes. Silently he waited for a blow or a shot, but neither came. He opened his eyes, and saw a young khaki-clad officer just inside the door, a torch in one hand, a revolver in the other. Behind him were two soldiers with rifles at ready. The officer stared at Sean, then slowly returned the gun to a holster, and the soldiers, at this sign, stood at ease, and rested the butts of the rifles on the dirty floor.

—Get up; dress; go out to the street, said the officer tersely; this house has to be searched room by room. Don't try to go farther than the wire cordon ringing the district: orders are to fire on any who do. He watched Sean dressing, and when he saw him clap a cap on his head, asked, Haven't you an overcoat?

—A sort of a one, said Sean.

—Better than nothing; you'd better put it on—it's damned cold outside.

—Decent man, thought Sean, putting on his old coat; has an occasional thought for others. Thank God, the Tans are absent!

He went out into the dark hall, and near bumped into a Tan standing there, fingering a heavy revolver. A cold shiver trickled down his spine.

—Where are you going? he asked.

—Outside to street—officer's orders, said Sean.

—What officer? asked the Tan.

—Military officer, sir.

—Oh! Military officer, eh? Well, we give the orders here—understand?

—Yessir, said Sean promptly.

—Are you a Sinn Feiner? he questioned, twisting the gun in his hand.

—A Sinn Feiner? Me? No fear.

—You were one, then.

—No; never, said Sean emphatically. Thank God, thought Sean, he didn't ask if I had ever been a Republican. The ignorant English bastard doesn't know the difference.

—Well, you're an Irishman, anyway—you can't deny that!

—No, sir, I can't deny that: I'm an Irishman, right enough.

—Well, shout To Hell with Ireland, and you can go—no mutter, but a shout the house can hear. Now!

But Sean fell silent. God damn him if he'd do that! He knew his face was white; he felt his legs tremble; but he fell silent, with a stubborn look on his face.

—Go on, you Sinn Fein rat, shout it!

A streak of light fell on them, and Sean saw the young officer coming to them. He stopped, looked at Sean, then looked at the Tan.

—What's wrong here? he asked. Let that man go into the street.

—You mind your own damned business, snarled the Tan.

—I am minding it, said the young officer. I happen to be an Irishman, too. Have you any objection to it?

—I don't take orders from you! said the Tan roughly.

—I'm not sorry for that, the officer said; but this man does—didn't I give you an order to go into the street? he asked, turning to Sean.

—Yessir.

—Carry it out, then, he said sharply; and Sean, turning swiftly, made a quick march through the hall, out by the door, into the street.

It was very cold, and from the timid gleams from a waning moon, Sean saw that path and road were white with a covering of rich rime frost. Groups of people were standing, huddled up against the railings of the houses, while more were oozing sleepily out of the remaining ones, shepherded into bunches by armed soldiers. The women were trying to coax warmth into their tearful and shivering children by wrapping flimsy rags round their shoulders, and tucking the little ones under them into their arms.

Several searchlights wandered through the street, flashing over the groups of people, or tinselling along the walls of the houses. At one end stood an armoured car, the lids raised, showing the heads of several Tommies who were quietly chanting an advice to the shivering people to pack up their troubles in their old kit-bags. Along the road, over the calm, quiet chastity of the white frost, slid a diamond-shaped tank, looking like a dirty, dangerous crawling slug, machine-guns sticking out from slits, like ugly protruding eyes staring at the cowering people.

He saw a commotion round the door of the house he lived in. He mooched over till he was beside the steps to look over the shoulders of a rank of soldiers. A prisoner! Who could it be? He whisperingly asked the soldier in front of him what had happened.

—An awrsenal! whispered the soldier hoarsely. Rear of th' ouse, an awrsenal discovered! 'Nough gelignite to blow up 'ole neighbourhood. A blighter there drew a gun, but was shot through hand afore 'ee could pull trigger. 'Ere's the bawstard coming!

Amid a group of soldiers with rifles at the ready marched a thin forlorn figure, but the lips in the pale face were tight together, and the small head was held high. Peering closer, Sean saw that handcuffs kept the two small hands locked together, and that from one of them red blobs were dripping on to the white frost on the path, leaving little spots behind like crimson berries that had fallen on to snow. In the hall he heard the voice of Nellie shouting.

—That's me husband! he heard her shout; a good man an' a brave one! Yous'll never shoot the life outa Ireland, yous gang o' armed ruffians! Here, take me, too, if yous aren't afraid. Keep your pecker up, Charlie—Ireland's with you!

Sean peered closer. Good God—the prisoner was the timid, insignificant Charlie Ballynoy who took no interest in politics! A lorry, full of soldiers, swirled into the kerb. The handcuffed prisoner was pushed and lifted into it. Standing there in the middle of the soldiers, with the searchlight covering him with glory, he held up his iron-locked hands from which clouts of blood still dripped.

—Up th' Republic! he shouted with the full force of his voice.

The lorry drove off, and the red specks in the rime turned brown and lonely. Heads that had lifted bent again, and all was quiet once more. A bleak dawn at last began to peel the deeper darkness from the sky, and the scene crept into a ghostly glamour, brightened by the pale faces of the waiting people; the pale moon sinking deeper into a surly sky, and the rimy frost on pathway, road, and roof grew whiter. Dirty-yellow-clad figures moved into the whiteness from one dark doorway, to move out of it again into another blacker still; while the brown, slug-like tank crept up and down the road, charring the dainty rime with its grinding treads—the new leviathan that God could ne'er control.

Padraic Colum (1881-)

A Drover

To Meath of the pastures,
From wet hills by the sea,
Through Leitrim and Longford,
Go my cattle and me.

I hear in the darkness
Their slipping and breathing—
I name them the by-ways
They're to pass without heeding;

Then the wet, winding roads,
Brown bogs with black water,
And my thoughts on white ships
And the King o' Spain's daughter.

O farmer, strong farmer!
You can spend at the fair,
But your face you must turn
To your crops and your care;

And soldiers, red soldiers!
You've seen many lands,
But you walk two by two,
And by captain's commands!

O the smell of the beasts,
The wet wind in the morn,
And the proud and hard earth
Never broken for corn!

And the crowds at the fair,
The herds loosened and blind,
Loud words and dark faces,
And the wild blood behind!

(O strong men with your best
I would strive breast to breast,
I could quiet your herds
With my words, with my words!)

I will bring you, my kine,
Where there's grass to the knee,
But you'll think of scant croppings
Harsh with salt of the sea.

A Poor Scholar of the 'Forties

My eyelids red and heavy are
With bending o'er the smold'ring peat.
I know the Æneid now by heart,
My Virgil read in cold and heat,
In loneliness and hunger smart.
  And I know Homer, too, I ween,
  As Munster poets know Ossian.

And I must walk this road that winds
'Twixt bog and bog, while east there lies
A city with its men and books;
With treasures open to the wise,
Heart-words from equals, comrade-looks;
  Down here they have but tale and song,
  They talk Repeal[1] the whole night long.

---

[1] Repeal of the Act of Union (1800) which disestablished the Irish Parliament and provided Ireland instead with representation at Westminster.

"You teach Greek verbs and Latin nouns,"
The dreamer of Young Ireland said,
"You do not hear the muffled call,
The sword being forged, the far-off tread
Of hosts to meet as Gael and Gall—
  What good to us your wisdom-store,
  Your Latin verse, your Grecian lore?"

And what to me is Gael or Gall?
Less than the Latin or the Greek—
I teach these by the dim rush-light
In smoky cabins night and week.
But what avail my teaching slight?
  Years hence, in rustic speech, a phrase,
  As in wild earth a Grecian vase!

James Stephens (1882-1950)

The Wind

The wind stood up, and gave a shout;
He whistled on his fingers, and

Kicked the withered leaves about,
And thumped the branches with his hand,

And said he'll kill, and kill, and kill;
And so he will! And so he will!

The College of Surgeons

As I stood at the door
Sheltered out of the wind,
Something flew in
Which I hardly could find.

In the dim gloomy doorway
I searched till I found
A dry withered leaf
Lying down on the ground.

With thin pointed claws
And a dry dusty skin,
—Sure, a hall is no place
For a leaf to be in!

Oh where is your tree,
And your summer and all,
Poor dusty leaf,
Whistled into a hall!

Check

The Night was creeping on the ground!
She crept and did not make a sound,

Until she reached the tree: And then
She covered it, and stole again

Along the grass beside the wall!
—I heard the rustling of her shawl

(4)

It has been writ in wisdom old—
This is the last word to be told:

—There is no dissolution! No
Creation! There are none in woe!

There is no teacher, teaching, taught!
Are none who long for, lack for aught!

Are none who pine for freedom! None
Are liberated under sun!

—And this is absolutely true
In Him who dreams in me and you.

Ivy Day in the Committee Room

BY James Joyce (1882-1941)

OLD JACK raked the cinders together with a piece of cardboard and spread them judiciously over the whitening dome of coals. When the dome was thinly covered his face lapsed into darkness but, as he set himself to fan the fire again, his crouching shadow ascended the opposite wall and his face slowly re-emerged into light. It was an old man's face, very bony and hairy. The moist blue eyes blinked at the fire and the moist mouth fell open at times, munching once or twice mechanically when it closed. When the cinders had caught he laid the piece of cardboard against the wall, sighed and said:

"That's better now, Mr. O'Connor."

Mr. O'Connor, a grey-haired young man, whose face was disfigured by many blotches and pimples, had just brought the tobacco for a cigarette into a shapely cylinder but when spoken to he undid his handiwork meditatively. Then he began to roll the tobacco again meditatively and after a moment's thought decided to lick the paper.

"Did Mr. Tierney say when he'd be back?" he asked in a husky falsetto.

"He didn't say."

Mr. O'Connor put his cigarette into his mouth and began to search his pockets. He took out a pack of thin pasteboard cards.

"I'll get you a match," said the old man.

"Never mind, this'll do," said Mr. O'Connor.

He selected one of the cards and read what was printed on it:

MUNICIPAL ELECTIONS

ROYAL EXCHANGE WARD

Mr. Richard J. Tierney, P.L.G., respectfully solicits the favour of your vote and influence at the coming election in the Royal Exchange Ward.

Mr. O'Connor had been engaged by Tierney's agent to canvass one part of the ward but, as the weather was inclement and his boots let in the wet, he spent a great part of the day sitting by the fire in the Committee Room in Wicklow Street with Jack, the old caretaker. They had been sitting thus since the short day had grown dark. It was the sixth of October, dismal and cold out of doors.

Mr. O'Connor tore a strip off the card and, lighting it, lit his cigarette. As he did so the flame lit up a leaf of dark glossy ivy in the lapel of his coat. The old man watched him attentively and then, taking up the piece of cardboard again, began to fan the fire slowly while his companion smoked.

"Ah, yes," he said, continuing, "it's hard to know what way to bring up children. Now who'd think he'd turn out like that! I sent him to the Christian Brothers and I done what I could for him, and there he goes boosing about. I tried to make him someway decent."

He replaced the cardboard wearily.

"Only I'm an old man now I'd change his tune for him. I'd take the stick to his back and beat him while I could stand over him—as I done many a time before. The mother, you know, she cocks him up with this and that. . . ."

"That's what ruins children," said Mr. O'Connor.

"To be sure it is," said the old man. "And little thanks you get for it, only impudence. He takes th'upper hand of me whenever he sees I've a sup taken. What's the world coming to when sons speaks that way to their fathers?"

"What age is he?" said Mr. O'Connor.

"Nineteen," said the old man.

"Why don't you put him to something?"

"Sure, amn't I never done at the drunken bowsy ever since he left school? 'I won't keep you,' I says. 'You must get a job for yourself.' But, sure, it's worse whenever he gets a job; he drinks it all."

Mr. O'Connor shook his head in sympathy, and the old man fell silent, gazing into the fire. Someone opened the door of the room and called out:

"Hello! Is this a Freemason's meeting?"

"Who's that?" said the old man.

"What are you doing in the dark?" asked a voice.

"Is that you, Hynes?" asked Mr. O'Connor.

"Yes. What are you doing in the dark?" said Mr. Hynes, advancing into the light of the fire.

He was a tall, slender young man with a light brown moustache. Imminent little drops of rain hung at the brim of his hat and the collar of his jacket-coat was turned up.

"Well, Mat," he said to Mr. O'Connor, "how goes it?"

Mr. O'Connor shook his head. The old man left the hearth, and after stumbling about the room returned with two candlesticks which he thrust one after the other into the fire and carried to the table. A denuded room came into view and the fire lost all its cheerful colour. The walls of the room were bare except for a copy of an election address. In the middle of the room was a small table on which papers were heaped.

Mr. Hynes leaned against the mantelpiece and asked:

"Has he paid you yet?"

"Not yet," said Mr. O'Connor. "I hope to God he'll not leave us in the lurch to-night."

Mr. Hynes laughed.

"O, he'll pay you. Never fear," he said.

"I hope he'll look smart about it if he means business," said Mr. O'Connor.

"What do you think, Jack?" said Mr. Hynes satirically to the old man.

The old man returned to his seat by the fire, saying:

"It isn't but he has it, anyway. Not like the other tinker."

"What other tinker?" said Mr Hynes.

"Colgan," said the old man scornfully.

"It is because Colgan's a working-man you say that? What's the difference between a good honest bricklayer and a publican—eh? Hasn't the working-man as good as right to be in the Corporation as anyone else—ay, and a better right than those shoneens that are always hat in hand before any fellow with a handle to his name? Isn't that so, Mat?" said Mr. Hynes, addressing Mr. O'Connor.

"I think you're right," said Mr. O'Connor.

"One man is a plain honest man with no hunker-sliding about him. He goes in to represent the labour classes. This fellow you're working for only wants to get some job or other."

"Of course, the working-classes should be represented," said the old man.

"The working-man," said Mr. Hynes, "gets all kicks and no halfpence. But it's labour produces everything. The working-man is not looking for fat jobs for his sons and nephews and cousins. The working-man is not going to drag the honour of Dublin in the mud to please a German monarch."

"How's that?" said the old man.

"Don't you know they want to present an address of welcome to Edward Rex if he comes here next year? What do we want kowtowing to a foreign king?"

"Our man won't vote for the address," said Mr. O'Connor. "He goes in on the Nationalist ticket."

"Won't he?" said Mr. Hynes. "Wait till you see whether he will or not. I know him. Is it Tricky Dicky Tierney?"

"By God! perhaps you're right, Joe," said Mr. O'Connor. "Anyway, I wish he'd turn up with the spondulics."

The three men fell silent. The old man began to rake more cinders together. Mr. Hynes took off his hat, shook it and then turned down the collar of his coat, displaying, as he did so, an ivy leaf in the lapel.

"If this man was alive," he said, pointing to the leaf, "we'd have no talk of an address of welcome."

"That's true," said Mr. O'Connor.

"Musha, God be with them times!" said the old man. "There was some life in it then."

The room was silent again. Then a bustling little man with a snuffling nose and very cold ears pushed in the door. He walked over quickly to the fire, rubbing his hands as if he intended to produce a spark from them.

"No money, boys," he said.

"Sit down here, Mr. Henchy," said the old man, offering him his chair.

"O, don't stir, Jack, don't stir," said Mr. Henchy.

He nodded curtly to Mr. Hynes and sat down on the chair which the old man vacated.

"Did you serve Aungier Street?" he asked Mr. O'Connor.

"Yes," said Mr. O'Connor, beginning to search his pockets for memoranda.

"Did you call on Grimes?"

"I did."

"Well? How does he stand?"

"He wouldn't promise. He said: 'I won't tell anyone what way I'm going to vote.' But I think he'll be all right."

"Why so?"

"He asked me who the nominators were; and I told him. I mentioned Father Burke's name. I think it'll be all right."

Mr. Henchy began to snuffle and to rub his hands over the fire at a terrific speed. Then he said:

"For the love of God, Jack, bring us a bit of coal. There must be some left."

The old man went out of the room.

"It's no go," said Mr. Henchy, shaking his head. "I asked the little shoeboy, but he said: 'O, now, Mr. Henchy, when I see the work going on properly I won't forget you, you may be sure.' Mean little tinker! 'Usha, how could he be anything else?"

"What did I tell you, Mat?" said Mr. Hynes. "Tricky Dicky Tierney."

"O, he's as tricky as they make 'em," said Mr. Henchy. "He hasn't got those little pigs' eyes for nothing. Blast his soul! Couldn't he pay up like a man instead of: 'O, now, Mr. Henchy, I must speak to Mr. Fanning. . . . I've spent a lot of money'? Mean little schoolboy of hell! I suppose he forgets the time his little old father kept the hand-me-down shop in Mary's Lane."

"But is that a fact?" asked Mr. O'Connor.

"God, yes," said Mr. Henchy. "Did you never hear that? And the men used to go in on Sunday morning before the houses were open to buy a waistcoat or a trousers—moya! But Tricky Dicky's little old father always had a tricky little black bottle up in a corner. Do you mind now? That's that. That's where he first saw the light."

The old man returned with a few lumps of coal which he placed here and there on the fire.

"That's a nice how-do-you-do," said Mr. O'Connor. "How does he expect us to work for him if he won't stump up?"

"I can't help it," said Mr. Henchy. "I expect to find the bailiffs in the hall when I go home."

Mr. Hynes laughed and, shoving himself away from the mantelpiece with the aid of his shoulders, made ready to leave.

"It'll be all right when King Eddie comes," he said. "Well, boys, I'm off for the present. See you later. 'Bye, 'bye."

He went out of the room slowly. Neither Mr. Henchy nor the old man said anything, but, just as the door was closing, Mr. O'Connor, who had been staring moodily into the fire, called out suddenly:

" 'Bye, Joe."

Mr. Henchy waited a few moments and then nodded in the direction of the door.

"Tell me," he said across the fire, "what brings our friend in here? What does he want?"

" 'Usha, poor Joe!" said Mr. O'Connor, throwing the end of his cigarette into the fire, "he's hard up, like the rest of us."

Mr. Henchy snuffled vigorously and spat so copiously that he nearly put out the fire, which uttered a hissing protest.

"To tell you my private and candid opinion," he said, "I think he's a man from the other camp. He's a spy of Colgan's, if you ask me. Just go round and try and find out how they're getting on. They won't suspect you. Do you twig?"

"Ah, poor Joe is a decent skin," said Mr. O'Connor.

"His father was a decent, respectable man," Mr. Henchy admitted. "Poor old Larry Hynes! Many a good turn he did in his day! But I'm greatly afraid our friend is not nineteen carat. Damn it, I can understand a fellow being hard up, but what I can't understand is a fellow sponging. Couldn't he have some spark of manhood about him?"

"He doesn't get a warm welcome from me when he comes," said the old man. "Let him work for his own side and not come spying around here."

"I don't know," said Mr. O'Connor dubiously, as he took out cigarette-papers and tobacco. "I think Joe Hynes is a straight man. He's a clever chap, too, with the pen. Do you remember that thing he wrote . . . ?"

"Some of these hillsiders and fenians are a bit too clever if you ask me," said Mr. Henchy. "Do you know what my private and candid opinion is about some of those little jokers? I believe half of them are in the pay of the Castle."

"There's no knowing," said the old man.

"O, but I know it for a fact," said Mr. Henchy. "They're Castle hacks. . . . I don't say Hynes. . . . No, damn it, I think he's a stroke above that. . . . But there's a certain little nobleman with a cock-eye—you know the patriot I'm alluding to?"

Mr. O'Connor nodded.

"There's a lineal descendant of Major Sirr[1] for you if you like! O, the heart's blood of a patriot! That's a fellow now that'd sell his country for fourpence—ay—and go down on his bended knees and thank the Almighty Christ he had a country to sell."

There was a knock at the door.

"Come in!" said Mr. Henchy.

A person resembling a poor clergyman or a poor actor appeared in the doorway. His black clothes were tightly buttoned on his short body and it was impossible to say whether he wore a clergyman's collar or a layman's, because the collar of his shabby frock-coat, the uncovered buttons of which reflected the candlelight, was turned up about his neck. He wore a round hat of hard black felt. His face, shining with raindrops, had the appearance of damp yellow cheese save where two rosy spots indicated the cheekbones. He opened his very long mouth suddenly to express disappointment and at the same time opened wide his very bright blue eyes to express pleasure and surprise.

"O Father Keon!" said Mr. Henchy, jumping up from his chair. "Is that you? Come in!"

"O, no, no, no!" said Father Keon quickly, pursing his lips as if he were addressing a child.

"Won't you come in and sit down?"

"No, no, no!" said Father Keon, speaking in a discreet, indulgent, velvety voice. "Don't let me disturb you now! I'm just looking for Mr. Fanning. . . ."

---

[1] The capturer of Robert Emmet.

"He's round at the *Black Eagle*," said Mr. Henchy. "But won't you come in and sit down a minute?"

"No, no, thank you. It was just a little business matter," said Father Keon. "Thank you, indeed."

He retreated from the doorway and Mr. Henchy, seizing one of the candlesticks, went to the door to light him downstairs.

"O, don't trouble, I beg!"

"No, but the stairs is so dark."

"No, no, I can see. . . . Thank you, indeed."

"Are you right now?"

"All right, thanks. . . . Thanks."

Mr. Henchy returned with the candlestick and put it on the table. He sat down again at the fire. There was silence for a few moments.

"Tell me, John," said Mr. O'Connor, lighting his cigarette with another pasteboard card.

"Hm?"

"What he is exactly?"

"Ask me an easier one," said Mr. Henchy.

"Fanning and himself seem to me very thick. They're often in Kavanagh's together. Is he a priest at all?"

" 'Mmmyes, I believe so. . . . I think he's what you call a black sheep. We haven't many of them, thank God! but we have a few. . . . He's an unfortunate man of some kind. . . ."

"And how does he knock it out?" asked Mr. O'Connor.

"That's another mystery."

"Is he attached to any chapel or church or institution or—"

"No," said Mr. Henchy, "I think he's travelling on his own account. . . . God forgive me," he added, "I thought he was the dozen of stout."

"Is there any chance of a drink itself?" asked Mr. O'Connor.

"I'm dry too," said the old man.

"I asked that little shoeboy three times," said Mr. Henchy, "would he send up a dozen of stout. I asked him again now, but he was leaning on the counter in his shirt-sleeves having a deep goster with Alderman Cowley."

"Why didn't you remind him?" said Mr. O'Connor.

"Well, I couldn't go over while he was talking to Alderman Cowley. I just waited till I caught his eye, and said: 'About that little matter I was speaking to you about. . . .' 'That'll be all right, Mr. H.,' he said. Yerra, sure the little hop-o'-my-thumb has forgotten all about it."

"There's some deal on in that quarter," said Mr. O'Connor thoughtfully. "I saw the three of them hard at it yesterday at Suffolk Street corner."

"I think I know the little game they're at," said Mr. Henchy. "You must owe the City Fathers money nowadays if you want to be made Lord Mayor. Then they'll make you Lord Mayor. By God! I'm thinking seriously of becoming a City Father myself. What do you think? Would I do for the job?"

Mr. O'Connor laughed.

"So far as owing money goes. . . ."

"Driving out of the Mansion House," said Mr. Henchy, "in all my vermin, with Jack here standing up behind me in a powdered wig—eh?"

"And make me your private secretary, John."

"Yes. And I'll make Father Keon my private chaplain. We'll have a family party."

"Faith, Mr. Henchy," said the old man, "you'd keep up better style then some of them. I was talking one day to old Keegan, the porter. 'And how do you like your new master, Pat?' says I to him. 'You haven't much entertaining now,' says I. 'Entertaining!' says he. 'He'd live on the smell of an oil-rag.' And do you know what he told me? Now, I declare to God, I didn't believe him."

"What?" said Mr. Henchy and Mr. O'Connor.

"He told me: 'What do you think of a Lord Mayor of Dublin sending out for a pound of chops for his dinner? How's that for high living?' says he. 'Wisha! wisha,' says I. 'A pound of chops,' says he, 'coming into the Mansion House.' 'Wisha!' says I, 'what kind of people is going at all now?' "

At this point there was a knock at the door, and a boy put in his head.

"What is it?" said the old man.

"From the *Black Eagle,*" said the boy, walking in sideways and depositing a basket on the floor with a noise of shaken bottles.

The old man helped the boy to transfer the bottles from the basket to the table and counted the full tally. After the transfer the boy put his basket on his arm and asked:

"Any bottles?"

"What bottles?" said the old man.

"Won't you let us drink them first?" said Mr. Henchy.

"I was told to ask for bottles."

"Come back to-morrow," said the old man.

"Here, boy!" said Mr. Henchy, "will you run over to O'Farrell's and ask him to lend us a corkscrew—for Mr. Henchy, say. Tell him we won't keep it a minute. Leave the basket there."

The boy went out and Mr. Henchy began to rub his hands cheerfully, saying:

"Ah, well, he's not so bad after all. He's as good as his word, anyhow."

"There's no tumblers," said the old man.

"O, don't let that trouble you, Jack," said Mr. Henchy. "Many's the good man before now drank out of the bottle."

"Anyway, it's better than nothing," said Mr. O'Connor.

"He's not a bad sort," said Mr. Henchy, "only Fanning has such a loan of him. He means well, you know, in his own tin-pot way."

The boy came back with the corkscrew. The old man opened three bottles and was handing back the corkscrew when Mr. Henchy said to the boy,

"Would you like a drink, boy?"

"If you please, sir," said the boy.

The old man opened another bottle grudgingly, and handed it to the boy.

"What age are you?" he asked.

"Seventeen," said the boy.

As the old man said nothing further, the boy took the bottle, said: "Here's my best respects, sir, to Mr. Henchy," drank the contents, put the bottle back on the table and wiped his mouth with his sleeve. Then he took up the corkscrew and went out of the door sideways, muttering some form of salutation.

"That's the way it begins," said the old man.

"The thin edge of the wedge," said Mr. Henchy.

The old man distributed the three bottles which he had opened and the men drank from them simultaneously. After having drank each placed his bottle on the mantlepiece within hand's reach and drew in a long breath of satisfaction.

"Well, I did a good day's work to-day," said Mr. Henchy, after a pause.

"That so, John?"

"Yes. I got him one or two sure things in Dawson Street, Crofton and myself. Between ourselves, you know, Crofton (he's a decent chap, of course), but he's not worth a damn as a canvasser. He hasn't a word to throw to a dog. He stands and looks at the people while I do the talking."

Here two men entered the room. One of them was a very fat man, whose blue serge clothes seemed to be in danger of falling from his sloping figure. He had a big face which resembled a young ox's face in expression, staring blue eyes and a grizzled moustache. The other man, who was much younger and frailer, had a thin, clean-shaven face. He wore a very high double collar and a wide-brimmed bowler hat.

"Hello, Crofton!" said Mr. Henchy to the fat man. "Talk of the devil . . ."

"Where did the boose come from?" asked the young man. "Did the cow calve?"

"O, of course, Lyons spots the drink first thing!" said Mr. O'Connor, laughing.

"Is that the way you chaps canvass," said Mr. Lyons, "and Crofton and I out in the cold and rain looking for votes?"

"Why, blast your soul," said Mr. Henchy, "I'd get more votes in five minutes than you two'd get in a week."

"Open two bottles of stout, Jack," said Mr. O'Connor.

"How can I?" said the old man, "when there's no corkscrew?"

"Wait now, wait now!" said Mr. Henchy, getting up quickly. "Did you ever see this little trick?"

He took two bottles from the table and, carrying them to the fire, put them on the hob. Then he sat down again by the fire and took another drink from his bottle. Mr. Lyons sat on the edge of the table, pushed his hat towards the nape of his neck and began to swing his legs.

"Which is my bottle?" he asked.

"This, lad," said Mr. Henchy.

Mr. Crofton sat down on a box and looked fixedly at the other bottle on the hob. He was silent for two reasons. The first reason, sufficient in itself, was that he had nothing to say; the second reason was that he considered his companions beneath him. He had been a canvasser for Wilkins, the Conservative, but when the Conservatives had withdrawn their man and, choosing the lesser of two evils, given their support to the Nationalist candidate, he had been engaged to work for Mr. Tierney.

In a few minutes an apologetic "Pok!" was heard as the cork flew out of Mr. Lyons' bottle. Mr. Lyons jumped off the table, went to the fire, took his bottle and carried it back to the table.

"I was just telling them, Crofton," said Mr. Henchy, "that we got a good few votes to-day."

"Who did you get?" asked Mr. Lyons.

"Well, I got Parkes for one, and I got Atkinson for two, and I got Ward of Dawson Street. Fine old chap he is, too—regular old toff, old Conservative! 'But isn't your candidate a Nationalist?' said he. 'He's a respectable man,' said I. 'He's in favour of whatever will benefit this country. He's a big ratepayer,' I said. 'He has extensive house property in the city and three places of business and isn't it to his own advantage to keep down the rates? He's a prominent and respected citizen,' said I, 'and a Poor Law Guardian, and he doesn't belong to any party, good, bad, or indifferent.' That's the way to talk to 'em."

"And what about the address to the King?" said Mr. Lyons, after drinking and smacking his lips.

"Listen to me," said Mr. Henchy. "What we want in this country, as I said to old Ward, is capital. The King's coming here will mean an influx of money into this country. The citizens of Dublin will benefit by it. Look at all the factories down by the quays there, idle! Look at all the money there is in the country if we only worked the old industries, the mills, the ship-building yards and factories. It's capital we want."

"But look here, John," said Mr. O'Connor. "Why should we welcome the King of England? Didn't Parnell himself . . ."

"Parnell," said Mr. Henchy, "is dead. Now, here's the way I look at it. Here's this chap come to the throne after his old mother keeping him out of it till the man was grey. He's a man of the world, and he means well by us. He's a jolly fine decent fellow, if you ask me, and no damn nonsense about him. He just says to himself: 'The old one never went to see these wild Irish. By Christ, I'll go myself and see what they're like.' And are we going to insult the man when he comes over here on a friendly visit? Eh? Isn't that right, Crofton?"

Mr. Crofton nodded his head.

"But after all now," said Mr. Lyons argumentatively, "King Edward's life, you know, is not the very . . ."

"Let bygones be bygones," said Mr. Henchy. "I admire the man personally. He's just an ordinary knockabout like you and me. He's fond of his glass of grog and he's a bit of a rake, perhaps, and he's a good sportsman. Damn it, can't we Irish play fair?"

"That's all very fine," said Mr. Lyons. "But look at the case of Parnell now."

"In the name of God," said Mr. Henchy, "where's the analogy between the two cases?"

"What I mean," said Mr. Lyons, "is we have our ideals. Why, now, would we welcome a man like that? Do you think now after what he did Parnell was a fit man to lead us? And why, then, would we do it for Edward the Seventh?"

"This is Parnell's anniversary," said Mr. O'Connor, "and don't let us stir up any bad blood. We all respect him now that he's dead and gone—even the Conservatives," he added, turning to Mr. Crofton.

Pok! The tardy cork flew out of Mr. Crofton's bottle. Mr. Crofton got up from his box and went to the fire. As he returned with his capture he said in a deep voice:

"Our side of the house respects him, because he was a gentleman."

"Right you are, Crofton!" said Mr. Henchy fiercely. "He was the only man that could keep that bag of cats in order. 'Down, ye dogs! Lie down, ye curs!' That's the way he treated them. Come in Joe! Come in!" he called out, catching sight of Mr. Hynes in the doorway.

Mr. Hynes came in slowly.

"Open another bottle of stout, Jack," said Mr. Henchy. "O, I forgot there's no corkscrew. Here, show me one here and I'll put it at the fire."

The old man handed him another bottle and he placed it on the hob.

"Sit down, Joe," said Mr. O'Connor, "we're just talking about the Chief."

"Ay, ay!" said Mr. Henchy.

Mr. Hynes sat on the side of the table near Mr. Lyons but said nothing.

"There's one of them, anyhow," said Mr. Henchy, "that didn't renege him. By God, I'll say for you, Joe! No, by God, you stuck to him like a man!"

"O, Joe," said Mr. O'Connor suddenly. "Give us that thing you wrote—do you remember? Have you got it on you?"

"O, ay!" said Mr. Henchy. "Give us that. Did you ever hear that, Crofton? Listen to this now: splendid thing."

"Go on," said Mr. O'Connor. "Fire away, Joe."

Mr. Hynes did not seem to remember at once the piece to which they were alluding, but, after reflecting a while, he said:

"O, that thing is it. . . . Sure, that's old now."

"Out with it, man!" said Mr. O'Connor.

" 'Sh, 'sh," said Mr. Henchy. "Now, Joe!"

Mr. Hynes hesitated a little longer. Then amid the silence he took off his hat, laid it on the table and stood up. He seemed to be rehearsing the piece in his mind. After a rather long pause he announced:

THE DEATH OF PARNELL

6th October, 1891

He cleared his throat once or twice and then began to recite:

He is dead. Our Uncrowned King is dead.
O, Erin, mourn with grief and woe
For he lies dead whom the fell gang
Of modern hypocrites laid low.

He lies slain by the coward hounds
He raised to glory from the mire;
And Erin's hopes and Erin's dreams
Perish upon her monarch's pyre.

In palace, cabin or in cot
The Irish heart where'er it be
Is bowed with woe—for he is gone
Who would have wrought her destiny.

He would have had his Erin famed,
The green flag gloriously unfurled,
Her statesmen, bards and warriors raised
Before the nations of the World.

He dreamed (alas, 'twas but a dream!)
Of Liberty: but as he strove
To clutch that idol, treachery
Sundered him from the thing he loved.

Shame on the coward, caitiff hands
  That smote their Lord or with a kiss
Betrayed him to the rabble-rout
  Of fawning priests—no friends of his.

May everlasting shame consume
  The memory of those who tried
To befoul and smear the exalted name
  Of one who spurned them in his pride.

He fell as fall the mighty ones,
  Nobly undaunted to the last,
And death has now united him
  With Erin's heroes of the past.

No sound of strife disturb his sleep!
  Calmly he rests: no human pain
Or high ambition spurs him now
  The peaks of glory to attain.

They had their way: they laid him low.
  But Erin, list, his spirit may
Rise, like the Phœnix from the flames,
  When breaks the dawning of the day,

The day that brings us Freedom's reign.
  And on that day may Erin well
Pledge in the cup she lifts to Joy
  One grief—the memory of Parnell.

Mr. Hynes sat down again on the table. When he had finished his recitation there was a silence and then a burst of clapping: even Mr. Lyons clapped. The applause continued for a little time. When it had ceased all the auditors drank from their bottles in silence.

Pok! The cork flew out of Mr. Hynes' bottle, but Mr. Hynes remained sitting flushed and bareheaded on the table. He did not seem to have heard the invitation.

"Good man, Joe!" said Mr. O'Connor, taking out his cigarette papers and pouch the better to hide his emotion.

"What do you think of that, Crofton?" cried Mr. Henchy. "Isn't that fine? What?"

Mr. Crofton said that it was a very fine piece of writing.

Austin Clarke (1896-)

Night And Morning

I know the injured pride of sleep,
The strippers at the mocking-post,
The insult in the house of Caesar
And every moment that can hold
In brief the miserable act
Of centuries. Thought can but share
Belief—and the tormented soul,
Changing confession to despair,
Must wear a borrowed robe.

Morning has moved the dreadful candle,
Appointed shadows cross the nave;
Unlocked by the secular hand,
The very elements remain
Appearances upon the altar.
Adoring priest has turned his back
Of gold upon the congregation.
All saints have had their day at last,
But thought still lives in pain.

How many councils and decrees
Have perished in the simple prayer
That gave obedience to the knee;
Trampling of rostrum, feathering
Of pens at cock-rise, sum of reason
To elevate a common soul:
Forgotten as the minds that bled
For us, the miracle that raised
A language from the dead.

O when all Europe was astir
With echo of learned controversy,
The voice of logic led the choir.
Such quality was in all being,
The forks of heaven and this earth
Had met, town-walled, in mortal view
And in the pride that we ignore,
The holy rage of argument,
God was made man once more.

Tenebrae

This is the hour that we must mourn
With tallows on the black triangle,
Night has a napkin deep in fold
To keep the cup; yet who dare pray
If all in reason should be lost,
The agony of man betrayed
At every station of the cross?

O when the forehead is too young,
Those centuries of mortal anguish,
Dabbed by a consecrated thumb
That crumbles into dust, will bring
Despair with all that we can know;
And there is nothing left to sing,
Remembering our innocence.

I hammer on that common door,
Too frantic in my superstition,
Transfix with nails that I have broken,
The angry notice of the mind.
Close as the thought that suffers him,
The habit every man in time
Must wear beneath his ironed shirt.

An open mind disturbs the soul,
And in disdain I turn my back
Upon the sun that makes a show
Of half the world, yet still deny
The pain that lives within the past,
The flame sinking upon the spike,
Darkness that man must dread at last.

The Straying Student

On a holy day when sails were blowing southward,
A bishop sang the Mass at Inishmore,
Men took one side, their wives were on the other
But I heard the woman coming from the shore:
And wild in despair my parents cried aloud
For they saw the vision draw me to the doorway.

Long had she lived in Rome when Popes were bad,
The wealth of every age she makes her own,
Yet smiled on me in eager admiration,
And for a summer taught me all I know,
Banishing shame with her great laugh that rang
As if a pillar caught it back alone.

I learned the prouder counsel of her throat,
My mind was growing bold as light in Greece;
And when in sleep her stirring limbs were shown,
I blessed the noonday rock that knew no tree:
And for an hour the mountain was her throne,
Although her eyes were bright with mockery.

They say I was sent back from Salamanca
And failed in logic, but I wrote her praise
Nine times upon a college wall in France.
She laid her hand at darkfall on my page
That I might read the heavens in a glance
And I knew every star the Moors have named.

Awake or in my sleep, I have no peace now,
Before the ball is struck, my breath has gone,
And yet I tremble lest she may deceive me
And leave me in this land, where every woman's son
Must carry his own coffin and believe
In dread, all that the clergy teach the young.

F. R. Higgins (1896-1941)

An Old Air

As I was walking I met a woman
And she side-saddled on a horse,
Most proudly riding the road to Moyrus
On a stallion worthy of a fine race-course.

The horse it sidled; I asked her kindly,
With a timid hand on the jolting rein,
"Now are you Niamh[1] or Grace O'Maille,[2]
Or a female grandee from the fields of Spain?"

She merely fondled those bridled fingers
And little fearing sweetly replied,
"Among my people you'd grow so noble
That none would know you did here abide:

"Then live with me, man, and I will give you
The run of twelve hills with a still in each."
Her eyes were craving that rainy evening
While a gentle air was in her speech.

"But O, my darling, who is your father?
Ah, would your mother take kindly to me?"
And then she told me, "My folk ride over
The silver flowering of a green-lit sea."

---

[1] See "Oisin in the Land of Youth," p. 105.

[2] Grania O'Malley was a chieftainess of the 16th century who made war on English armies and fleets along the Connaught seaboard. Celebrated in song and story, her name became a synonym of Ireland.

At those strange words then I did remember
    Her folk they were of no good sort,
So I bid good evening to that young woman
    And she took herself to the woods of Gort!

Song for the Clatter-Bones

God rest that Jewy woman,
Queen Jezebel, the bitch
Who peeled the clothes from her shoulder-bones
Down to her spent teats
As she stretched out of the window
Among the geraniums, where
She chaffed and laughed like one half daft
Titivating her painted hair—

King Jehu he drove to her,
She tipped him a fancy beck;
But he from his knacky side-car spoke,
"Who'll break that dewlapped neck?"
And so she was thrown from the window;
Like Lucifer she fell
Beneath the feet of the horses and they beat
The light out of Jezebel.

That corpse wasn't planted in clover;
Ah, nothing of her was found
Save those grey bones that Hare-foot Mike
Gave me for their lovely sound;
And as once her dancing body
Made star-lit princes sweat,
So I'll just clack: though her ghost lacks a back
There's music in the old bones yet.

The Wild Sow

BY Liam O'Flaherty (1896-)

OLD Neddy the fisherman, of Kilmillick, bought a sow pig one day in Kilmurrage. He put the pig in a bag, dropped it into one of his donkey's creels and brought it home to his cabin. It was just six weeks old, a little black pig, with a long back, and big ears that dropped over its eyes and a little tail curled up in a knot.

The neighbours were surprised when they heard that Neddy had bought the pig, for he was an old man and lived alone in his two-roomed cabin and he had no land except a little patch in front of his door that grew enough potatoes to last him the year round. He was, too, very fond of drink, and whenever he had any money he stayed in Kilmurrage until he had spent it. So that the neighbours wondered what possessed him to buy the pig. In fact Martin Conroy came into Neddy's cabin and said, "Brother, it's plain that they fooled you into buying that young pig, so if ye'll throw ten rockfish into the bargain with it, I'll give you a pound for it."

Neddy hitched up his belt, glanced at Conroy with his little grey eyes and told him to get out of his cabin. Then he shook his fist after Conroy and said, "I'll have money while I have that pig and that's why I bought it. So may the devil choke the lot of you."

He made a straw bed for the little pig in the corner of his kitchen and sawed off the lower part of a barrel in which he salted his fish to make a trough for it. For a while he looked after it carefully and gave it plenty of potatoes, dry fish and whatever sour milk he could get from the neighbours. So that the sow got big and fat until it was six months old and fit for sale. But when a jobber came to look at it and asked Neddy what price did he want, Neddy told him to get out of his cabin. "I have money," he said, "while I have that pig, so I'll keep it."

That was in the month of April and Neddy's stock of potatoes had been all eaten by the sow and most of his dried fish along with the potatoes, so he turned the sow loose on the roadside to eat grass, saying, "Now feed yerself and may the devil choke you." And he took his basket and his fishing lines and went away to fish.

The sow wandered about on the road all the forenoon, smelling at everything, snorting furiously and making little short runs that make her foot joints snap under her fat body like hard biscuits being cracked, when a horse or a peasant driving a cow went past. She rooted among the grass until her head was caked with earth up to her eyes. Then towards her feeding time at midday she trotted back to the cabin, but the door was locked. For a time she waited at the door grunting and with her ears cocked listening to every sound, sniffing the air with her twitching hairy snout and tossing her head now and again in vexation. Then, when nobody opened the door, she began to whine with the hunger. She stood there motionless and whining until Neddy came back at dusk and let her into the cabin. He only gave her fish guts and potato peelings for her supper. "From now on," he said, "you'll have to fend for yourself, and may the devil choke you."

That went on for a fortnight with Neddy away fishing every day, and then the sow got thinner and wild with hunger. She began to eat grass by the roadside and roamed over the crags picking nettles and everything she could get hold of. She no longer snorted when horses or cows passed her. Her bristles grew rough and strong and her ears lost their tender transparency. Her eyes were hardly visible through the caked dirt that gathered around them. She used to run out of the cabin in the morning and never come near it again until dusk.

At first she roamed about the village of Kilmillick, eating grass and nettles, tearing up the ground for roots, chewing everything she found in rubbish heaps, old fish bones, rags, boots and potato skins. Then, as the summer grew, the heat and the long days tempted her farther, down the beach and along the lanes and the road leading to Kilmurrage. Often she never came back to the cabin for two or three days at a stretch, but would spend the night among the sandhills about the beach where the wild grass was very sweet and there was always a dog-fish or a piece of mackerel cast up by the sea among the weeds. Her bristles were now as stiff and thick as needles, and her black skin beneath them was cracked by the sun and scarred in places where dogs bit her or boys struck her with stones and dried sea rods when they cornered her in narrow lanes. All her flesh had hardened into muscle. She was lean like a hound and nearly as tall as a year-old donkey.

Towards the end of summer a jobber came again to Neddy and asked him would he sell the sow. "She's not much good now," said the jobber, "so I'll give ye a pound for her. I might be able to soften her a bit and get a litter from her." "Get out of my cabin," said Neddy, "and may the devil choke you. I have money while I have that pig, so I'll keep the pig." But the fishing was bad that year and he had to sell his donkey in order to buy flour for the winter. Still he wouldn't sell the pig. "It's like having money in a bank," he would say, "a pig is always money. I often heard my father say so."

But when winter came on and the ocean winds swept the crags viciously and sea foam was falling like snow over the cabins, the sow could go out no more, but sat on her haunches on her straw litter in Neddy's kitchen grunting and whining with the hunger.

Then one stormy day Neddy went into Kilmurrage to sell his dried pollock. He turned the pig out of the cabin and locked the door. Then he went away. The sow roamed about for awhile shivering with the cold and weak with hunger. Her stomach was drawn up into her back so that she looked like a cat that is stretching itself. She could discover nothing to eat around the village so she came back to the cabin.

She got on her knees at the door and began to gnaw at the bottom until she made a hole for her snout; then she seemed to go mad and tore at the door with her teeth and battered it with her head until she burst it off its hinges and she pushed right under it into the cabin. The door hung on one hinge and the sow's right ear was gashed down the middle by a nail in the jamb.

She stood in the middle of the kitchen grunting, with her snout to the ground and with blood dripping from her ear in a steady stream. Then she tossed her head and rushed at Neddy's bedroom door. Sticking her snout at the bottom near the jamb, she pushed and burst the string with which the door was fastened and got into the bedroom. Neddy's potatoes were lying in the far corner with a little wall of stones around them. His sack of flour stood against the wall near the potatoes. His dried rockfish were stacked on pieces of paper under the wooden bedstead. The sow began to eat. Snorting and tossing her head she ran from the flour to the potatoes and then to the rockfish, swallowing huge mouthfuls without chewing, and making a noise like a horse pulling her hoof out of a bog, until her stomach swelled out to a point at each side.

Then a big potato stuck in her throat.

When Neddy came in that evening he found her lying on her side, stone dead.

A Difficult Question

BY Kate O'Brien (1898-)

ON Wednesdays the chaplain addressed the school for forty minutes on Christian doctrine. This lecture took place at half-past five in the *salle d'études*, his hearers sitting as for marks in a "hairpin," very orderly and with gloves on. It was an ordeal for a young man, when every mannerism was pounced upon and giggled at, week after week, by the school wags. Indeed, Reverend Mother thought it a questionable tradition that in this Irish house the chaplain was always so young. Elsewhere in the order's convents he was usually an old and experienced priest, hardened to folly and indifferent to giggles. But here in this rural parish the duties of chaplaincy fell ex officio on the second curate of the village, which meant a succession of nervous young men for budding feminine wits to lacerate.

The Wednesday lecture was made additionally painful for the chaplain by the ceremony which preceded it, of drinking tea in St Anthony's parlour, waited on by Reverend Mother. This custom held throughout the order and was based on the supposed need of chaplain and Mother Superior to discuss such problems of spirit or character as might have struck either in dealing with the school. But as week after week, year after year, Reverend Mother poured tea for and offered buttered toast to a succession of shy or truculent young Irishmen she smiled wryly to herself at the characteristically Latin idea which justified the stiff reflection. No Irish boy just out of college was going to be drawn into other than the most perfunctory generalisations on the character or spiritual difficulties of a pack of schoolgirls. Nor, indeed, did she blame the successive young chaplains for their negative resolution. Still, she had to obey custom and torture them with her half-hour of politeness. But as she really believed in discipline, for herself and all human creatures, she thought it no harm that the curates should have to sit for one half-hour each week and make conversation with her, when she knew they really feared and disliked it.

Father Conroy was the third chaplain she had known in her four years in Ireland and the one with whom she felt least sympathy.

The two were nervous and at sea with each other.

"Well, Reverend Mother—that's a nice hare your friend Joe Chamberlain is making of himself these days!"

"*My* friend, Father Conroy?"

"Oh well—he's English; that's all I meant."

"I come of a Liberal family, Father. I have never known any statesmen, but if you were to speak of Mr Chamberlain's opponent, Mr Asquith, as 'my friend,' I mightn't be so startled."

"Aha! So you think there is some good in Asquith, Reverend Mother? I am surprised to hear that. Six of one and half a dozen of the other, if you ask me."

"Nothing of the kind, if you ask me," said Reverend Mother amiably.

"Well, well—we must agree to differ there. But tariff reform, God help us!"

"You ought to be delighted with Mr Chamberlain's tariff reform, Father."

"I—delighted?"

"Because it is a pernicious, greedy conception which will very likely cost the present government its office. And then Home Rule will become a near possibility again, surely?"

"Yah, Home Rule. What good would that be to us, Reverend Mother?"

"It is difficult to say." She spoke with faint malice, but he did not see the mild joke. "In any case, what should a nun know of these matters?" she amended gently.

"Ah, that's the trouble," he said, and as he went on she conceded that there was real trouble and some diffidence in his voice and face. "Nuns shouldn't trouble themselves with these secular things, I suppose. And yet you know, Reverend Mother, a convent like this wields great influence—through its girls afterward—in the world."

"We are very conscious of that, Father Conroy."

She realised wearily that he was circling, as usual, round the Irish hierarchy's distrust of an independent religious order. It was a patent exasperation to the authoritarian bishop that, short of grave scandal, he had no power to counsel or direct the Compagnie de la Sainte Famille. And this exceptional privilege of the order increased the offence of its forgiveness; in fact, Reverend Mother knew very well that, as far as his lordship was to be reckoned with, the independence of this house was the sole safeguard of its peculiar tradition, which the bishop called "exotic" and *démodé* and which he would have overthrown without hesitation had he the power.

The bishop had some of the weapons of an intellectual to his hand, but Father Conroy had only an untutored, unbridled nationalism. He disliked the spirit of Sainte Famille, Reverend Mother suspected, solely because it was governed by an Englishwoman. And as such an emotional and bad ellipsis of argument was distasteful to her in anyone but incomprehensible in a consecrated priest, spiritual communication between the two was impossible.

"To be sure you are, Reverend Mother. And the young ladies of Sainte Famille are beautifully educated—we all know that. But times are changing here, and somehow——"

"Somehow what, Father Conroy?"

The cold English tone annoyed him.

"Somehow it's a bit of a pity, it seems to me, Reverend Mother, to be training Irish girls as suitable wives for English majors and colonial governors!"

He spoke angrily because he was afraid of his own audacity.

"We educate our children in the Christian virtues and graces. If these appeal to English majors, why, so much the better for those gentlemen!"

"Our young girls must be educated *nationally* now, Reverend Mother—to be the wives of *Irishmen* and to meet the changing times!"

"We do what we can about that, Father. But if the 'changing

times' you are so sure of are to have no place for Christian discipline and common politeness, I can only say I'm glad I shall not see very much of them."

She spoke very coldly and offered the young man some cakes.

"No, thank you, Reverend Mother," he said. "It's a terror the way you won't see what I mean at all."

"I do see what you mean, Father—and I find you are rude and officious. But you are, after all, very young."

He looked so startled and indignant that at once she was ashamed of herself and distressed in her turn at the cruel enmity she felt toward him. As she sought a way of apology there was a knock on the parlour door.

Anna Murphy came in.

"Yes, Anna, that's right—come along. I told her to come to the parlour to you this evening, Father, as she appears now to understand her catechism well, and you may wish—after you've talked with her—to arrange her instructions for first confession. She will be seven next month."

"On April fifth," said Anna.

"Will you now?" said Father Conroy. "You're a small girl for that—aren't you, Anna?"

Anna drew near.

"Still, I'd like to make my first confession, please," she said.

"Well, I expect we'll let you. On April fifth you will have reached the age of reason, Anna—and even now you sound reasonable enough, God bless you!"

Reverend Mother smiled.

"Reasonableness is her forte at present, Father."

"Would you like a biscuit, Anna? May I give her one, Reverend Mother? Which kind will you have?"

"The one that's like a piece of orange, please."

Father Conroy handed her the yellow-sugared biscuit shaped like a piece of orange.

"Thank you, Father Conroy."

"Now, Anna, we must prepare you for first confession, so that you can make it about April fifth. You know I come to hear the other girls' confessions every Saturday at half-past five. This Saturday I'll come at five—if I may, Reverend Mother?—and have a talk with you about Christian doctrine and what confession is. Then on this day week we could have another talk, I suppose, Reverend Mother? And when we have talked together about six times I think you will be able to receive the sacrament of penance. You know it is a sacrament, don't you?"

Anna nodded.

"I'm doing that chapter now in catechism. I had two questions about contrition to learn today."

"Oh, good girl. You're quite far on in your catechism. You've learned the Ten Commandments then and the explanations of them?"

"Well—yes."

The frowning uncertainty which entered her face made both nun and priest smile faintly.

"You mustn't worry if you don't completely understand them all," Father Conroy said. "You couldn't expect it yet. They cover a wide field."

"I can see that," said Anna. "Still——"

"Still—what?"

"Well, since they really are *commandments*, I think I should have a rough idea—and Mother Felicita too, I think she should. After all, she's *old*."

"And what's bothering yourself and Mother Felicita, may I ask?"

"We don't know what adultery is. Either of us. What is it?"

Reverend Mother sat very still, anxiety in her heart. The awkward, not to say loutish, young priest was in charge of this conversation. He was the spiritual director, and Anna had rightly put her query to him. He must answer as his wit directed, but the child who questioned him was not easy to hoodwink, and the questing ease of her mind was, in Reverend Mother's eyes, a very delicate and cherishable thing. As she waited alert for the sequence of dialogue one region of her heart was rapidly flooded with uneasy prayer. If this little child were told a lie or made to suspect already, by any clumsiness, the sordid hush-hush of sexual troubles—— The nun winced with anxiety as she searched, without any clue, the broad, unsubtle face of the young priest.

"Are you sure Mother Felicita doesn't know the meaning of adultery?" Father Conroy asked Anna.

"Oh yes. She didn't exactly say so, but anyone could tell it muddles her."

The priest nodded.

"Well, of course, being a nun, she wouldn't have to know, as it doesn't have anything to do with her, in her life. And until you are grown up it won't be any concern of yours."

"Still—it's in my catechism, after all——"

"Yes—and I'm going to tell you what it is. I was only explaining to you why Mother Felicita might happen not to understand about it. You see, it isn't everyone's business. But when you are grown up, left school, you will perhaps decide to be a nun and live entirely for the glory of God; or you may decide to live alone in the world, devoting yourself to work or study of some kind; or, very likely, you will feel that you do not want to live always alone, that you would like a husband and children. In that case you will choose some man who will also choose you; you'll choose each other by what is called 'falling ing love'—which means you will find that you love each other more than you love other people. And so you'll receive together the sacrament of marriage—you've learned about that? —and, having promised in that sacrament to love each other always, you live together and have children. Well—if afterward either of you should stop loving the other and begin to let yourself love another person more than the one you had promised to love best always—that is adultery."

"I think it might be very easy to commit," Anna said.

"Why do you think that?"

"Well—how could you be sure of loving anyone best always?"

"You couldn't be *sure*, I suppose—on our own steam we

can't be sure of anything. But marriage is a sacrament—which is, you know, a special way of receiving special grace from God. God helps us a very great deal in difficulties, as you'll discover when you grow up, young lady. Well, are you clear in your mind now about the sixth commandment?"

"Oh yes. Thank you very much. Do you mind if I explain it to Mother Felicita?"

"Not at all. But after all, it has nothing to do with her."

"But she's *teaching* catechism. I think it'd be better if she understood—for another time."

"Perhaps. Well, off with you now and eat your sugar biscuit. And remember, on Saturday at five I'll examine you on the first two chapters of the catechism."

"I'll remember. Good-bye, Father Conroy. Good-bye, Reverend Mother."

Anna shook hands with the priest and bowed to Reverend Mother, who smiled at her as she withdrew.

The bell for religious instruction rang, and Father Conroy rose from his chair.

As the nun ascended the broad staircase with him on the way to the *salle d'études* she pondered in bitter humility. This priest whom she judged crude and unwise had just shown himself gentle and wise and a good, honest teacher. He had shown perfect understanding of innocence and intelligence and had spoken to them out of peace and humour and without a shadow of evasiveness in word or implication. She was ashamed of her earlier extreme severity with him; she felt very grateful to him for the guarded sensibility with which he had impressed her as he replied to the good sense of childhood. She racked her brain for a way of expressing friendliness and repentance. She decided that the only just course was to apologise for having sought to humiliate him.

"I hope you will forgive me for having spoken unjustly a few moments ago, Father. But I fear I lose my sense of proportion and of justice when I think people want to make a political weapon of the education of children."

But he thought he saw a further thrust at himself in this piece of self-explanation—and he was still rankling with dislike of her.

"To be sure, Reverend Mother. But isn't that exactly what you English have done all the same, all over the globe?"

"I was only speaking for myself," she answered wearily.

Genevieve Ahern opened the swing door of the *salle d'études*, and as the chaplain and Reverend Mother entered the school stood up and bowed.

My Grander

BY Sean O'Faolain (1900-)

"HE was a vain man," somebody who knew him once said to me, "and ambitious; but very weak in the carnalities."

I must say all the "carnalities" I ever saw in him at that time was when he would be with his friend Arty Tinsley, and I after him with young Christy Tinsley, in and out of every pub in the city of Cork, and rain, hail, or snow, every third Sunday of the month galloping out the country in wagonettes, decorating the graves of the Fenian dead. Then we would be, the four of us with his friends, over a pub fire in Kilcrea or Ovens or Kilcroney, the talk floating up the chimney with the steam of our legs, while the rain hissed into the misty grass and the pokers hissed in the mulled stout, surrounded by a procession of names, hour by hour, corner to corner, Rossa and O'Neill-Crowley, Land and Labour, Davitt and the Tory "hoors"; a drink to Lomasney, who was found in his own clots of gore on the mud of the Isle of Dogs after floating down from London Bridge that he had tried to blow up—nothing less would appease his wild imagination, I suppose; and a drink to the men who swung for the agent they sunk in a bog near Tipperary; and a drink to His Lordship of Cashel who talked up to the Pope when he went to Rome *ad audiendum verbum* . . . all ending with the road thick with night and a singing born of liquor, and Christy Tinsley and myself wrapped into one another with cold and sleep.

Then came the day when old Arty Tinsley died. It was a wretched rain-down of a southern evening when my grander and myself set off to the cemetery on the Douglas Road, that was for some crazy reason called the Botanic Gardens, to fix about the burial. I was not sad but frightened, for this was the first real death I knew. But my grander took my dread for sorrow and as a reward he packed me with Shandon Mixtures and Peggy's Leg until I was sick in the stomach and sticky around the mouth as I stood under the yews of the graveyard. In the Gothic porch of the gate lodge—smelling of laurels and wood-smoke—my grander was discussing the details of the funeral with a long dreep of a caretaker who kept on remembering all the Tinsleys who ever came in the gate on the flat of their backs. Then we went into the lodge itself, very small with its red and black tiles and even more odorous of the fallen leaves and the damp wood-smoke; and I was looking at a photograph of a bishop, and at the framed photos of the sons in their red coats holding their arms very stiff to show the sergeant's stripes, when I suddenly felt a strange silence and saw my grander over the book, making slow circles with the pen in his hand.

"That's the way, sir," the foxy caretaker was saying, "that's grand, now, Mister Crone, religion now, sir, enter the religion of the deceased."

"He was born a Catholic," said my grander.

"Down with it, sir," said Foxer.

"But . . . I don't know what he might be, now."

The man looked at him in surprise, as if he was asking himself: "Does the ould lad think there's no religion in heaven?"

"Fill it in, sir," he said politely.

"Yes, grander," said I. "C—A—T—H——"

"Go out, boy, and wait outside," says he very shortly.

But I was soon sick of the misty hills and the swaying wet

yews around the marbles—ever since I have hated that white Carrara marble for outdoor monuments—and I returned to the porch. There, inside, was a terrible argument going on between the two of them, and my old grandfather shouting:

"What I say is, if an unfortunate Fenian isn't left in peace by the clergy when he's alive, then they should leave him in peace anyway when he's dead."

And the man crying out:

"For God's sake, now, Mister Crone, fill in the two words—R.C.—and be done with it—the Church is wise, Mister Crone—the Church has to look after us all, dead and alive—and for God's sake and God is the best judge of all those things and God will judge you and me . . ."

"What I say is, the Church wouldn't admit he was a Catholic when he was alive, so why should the Church want to say he's a Catholic because he's dead?" (I knew what he was at—the Church had banned Fenianism in Ireland.)

"My dear good sir," said the man, beyond all patience, "I'm not the Church and you're not the Church, and if the Church says he was a Catholic, then it's dogma, and a Catholic he is, and no wan can get behind that. Write it down—R.C."

"The Church never admitted he was a Catholic. It denied him the sacraments. It now wants to deny him Christian burial."

The foxy man held out his index finger as if he were balancing a pin on the ball of it. Solemnly he looked at it; solemnly he looked at my grander; then he tapped that finger with the tip of another, saying quietly but finally:

"Did the Church say he was a Protestant?"

"No."

He tapped his second finger. "Did the Church say he was excommunicated?"

"No!"

The man drew out a sail of a handkerchief and blew his nose.

"Write down R.C.," he ordered, like a Pope.

"NO!" said my grander, and he flung down the pen in a

fury. "The Church never said yiss or no to Arthur Tinsley. But you know and I know and everybody knows that no Fenian could get absolution in confession or the sacrament from the altar unless he retracted his oath to live and die for his country. And . . ."

"Mister Crone . . ."

"And . . ."

"Excuse me, one moment, mister. . . ."

"AND if Arthur Tinsley was asked here and now whether he would retract that oath . . ."

"There's nobody asking him. . . ."

". . . whether, to obtain burial in this bloody cemetery, he would bow the knee to the Church, and the first question they'd put to him would be, Do you admit that oath was a sin?—what would he say? What would he say?"

The man walked away to the door.

"What would he say?" roared my grander. "He'd say: 'I wo'NOT!' And what would they say?" he bellowed, with a great sweep of his hand through the air. "They'd say: 'Then we'll have nothing to do with yeh, and yeh can go to hell!' "

"This cemetery," said the caretaker loftily, "is a Catholic cemetery."

"Then," sobbed my grander, "where will I bury him?"

"Look here," said the man in a kindly voice, and he picked up the pen. "I'll sign it, R.C."

"NO!" cried ould Ten-to-Wan. "NO!"

"Very well," said the man. "You can put it to the Cemetery Committee. I won't have anything to do with it." And he walked out about his business.

"Come on, boy," said the old lad, and away we went, I with big eyes and beating heart, he muttering his rage:

"Damn the Committee! Damn the Committee!"

In the Train

BY Frank O'Connor (1903-)

I

"THERE!" said the sergeant's wife. "You would hurry me."

"I always like to be in time for a train," replied the sergeant with the equability of one who has many times before explained the guiding principle of his existence.

"I'd have had heaps of time to buy the hat," added his wife.

The sergeant sighed and opened his evening paper. His wife looked out on the dark platform, pitted with pale lights under which faces and faces passed, lit up and dimmed again. A uniformed lad strode up and down with a tray of periodicals and chocolates. Farther up the platform a drunken man was being seen off by his friends.

"I'm very fond of Michael O'Leary," he shouted. "He is the most sincere man I know."

"I have no life," sighed the sergeant's wife. "No life at all! There isn't a soul to speak to, nothing to look at all day but bogs and mountains and rain—always rain! And the people! Well, we've had a fine sample of them, haven't we?"

The sergeant continued to read.

"Just for the few days it's been like heaven. Such interesting people! Oh, I thought Mr Boyle had a glorious face! And his voice—it went through me."

The sergeant lowered his paper, took off his peaked cap, laid it on the seat beside him, and lit his pipe. He lit it in the old-fashioned way, ceremoniously, his eyes blinking pleasurably like a sleepy cat's in the match-flame. His wife scrutinised each face that passed, and it was plain that for her life meant faces and people and things and nothing more.

"Oh dear!" she said again. "I simply have no existence. I was educated in a convent and play the piano; my father was a literary man, and yet I am compelled to associate with the lowest types of humanity. If it was even a decent town, but a village!"

"Ah," said the sergeant, gapping his reply with anxious puffs, "maybe with God's help we'll get a shift one of these days." But he said it without conviction, and it was also plain that he was well pleased with himself, with the prospect of returning home, with his pipe and with his paper.

"Here are Magner and the others," said his wife as four other policemen passed the barrier. "I hope they'll have sense enough to let us alone. . . . How do you do? How do you do? Had a nice time, boys?" she called with sudden animation, and her pale, sullen face became warm and vivacious. The policemen smiled and touched their caps but did not halt.

"They might have stopped to say good evening," she added sharply, and her face sank into it old expression of boredom and dissatisfaction. "I don't think I'll ask Delancey to tea again. The others make an attempt, but really, Delancey is hopeless. When I smile and say 'Guard Delancey, wouldn't you like to use the butter-knife?' he just scowls at me from under his shaggy brows and says without a moment's hesitation 'I would not.'"

"Ah, Delancey is a poor slob," said the sergeant affectionately.

"Oh yes, but that's not enough, Jonathon. Slob or no slob, he should make an attempt. He's a young man; he should have a dinner-jacket at least. What sort of wife will he get if he won't even wear a dinner-jacket?"

"He's easy, I'd say. He's after a farm in Waterford!"

"Oh, a farm! A farm! The wife is only an incidental, I suppose?"

"Well, now from all I hear she's a damn nice little incidental."

"Yes, I suppose many a nice little incidental came from a farm," answered his wife, raising her pale brows. But the irony was lost on him.

"Indeed, yes; indeed, yes," he said fervently.

"And here," she added in biting tones, "come our charming neighbours."

Into the pale lamplight stepped a group of peasants. Not such as one sees in the environs of a capital but in the mountains and along the coasts. Gnarled, wild, with turbulent faces, their ill-cut clothes full of character, the women in pale brown shawls, the men wearing black sombreros and carrying big sticks, they swept in, ill at ease, laughing and shouting defiantly. And, so much part of their natural environment were they, that for a moment they seemed to create about themselves rocks and bushes, tarns, turf-ricks and sea.

With a prim smile the sergeant's wife bowed to them through the open window.

"How do you do? How do you do?" she called. "Had a nice time?"

At the same moment the train gave a jolt and there was a rush in which the excited peasants were carried away. Some minutes passed; the influx of passengers almost ceased, and a porter began to slam the doors. The drunken man's voice rose in a cry of exultation.

"You can't possibly beat O'Leary!" he declared. "I'd lay down my life for Michael O'Leary."

Then, just as the train was about to start, a young woman in a brown shawl rushed through the barrier. The shawl, which came low enough to hide her eyes, she held firmly across her mouth, leaving visible only a long thin nose with a hint of pale flesh at either side. Beneath the shawl she was carrying a large parcel.

She looked hastily around, a porter shouted to her and pushed her towards the nearest compartment which happened to be that occupied by the sergeant and his wife. He had actually seized the handle of the door when the sergeant's wife sat up and screamed.

"Quick! Quick!" she cried. "Look who it is! She's coming in! Jonathon! Jonathon!"

The sergeant rose with a look of alarm on his broad red face. The porter threw open the door, with his free hand grasping the woman's elbow. But when she laid eyes on the sergeant's startled countenance, she stepped back, tore herself free, and ran crazily up the platform. The engine shrieked, the porter slammed the door with a curse, somewhere another door opened and shut, and the row of watchers, frozen into effigies of farewell, now dark now bright, began to glide gently past the window, and the stale, smoky air was charged with the breath of open fields.

II

The four policemen spread themselves out in a separate compartment and lit cigarettes.

"Ah, poor old Delancey!" said Magner with his reckless laugh. "He's cracked on her all right."

"Cracked on her," agreed Fox. "Did ye see the eye he gave her?"

Delancey smiled sheepishly. He was a tall, handsome, black-haired young man with the thick eyebrows described by the sergeant's wife. He was new to the force and suffered from a mixture of natural gentleness and country awkwardness.

"I am," he said in his husky voice, "cracked on her. The devil admire me, I never hated anyone yet, but I think I hate the living sight of her."

"Oh, now! Oh, now!" protested Magner.

"I do. I think the Almighty God must have put that one in the world with the one main object of persecuting me."

"Well, indeed," said Foley, "I don't know how the sergeant puts up with the same damsel. If any woman up and called me by an outlandish name like Jonathon when all knew my name was plain John, I'd do fourteen days for her—by God, I would, and a calendar month!"

The four men were now launched on a favourite topic that held them for more than an hour. None of them liked the sergeant's wife, and all had stories to tell against her. From these there emerged the fact that she was an incurable scandal-monger and mischief-maker, who couldn't keep quiet about her own business, much less that of her neighbours. And while they talked the train dragged across a dark plain, the heart of Ireland, and in the moonless night tiny cottage windows blew past like sparks from a fire, and a pale simulacrum of the lighted carriages leaped and frolicked over hedges and fields. Magner shut the window, and the compartment began to fill with smoke.

"She'll never rest till she's out of Farranchreesht," he said.

"That she mightn't!" groaned Delancey.

"How would you like the city yourself, Dan?" asked Magner.

"Man, dear," exclaimed Delancey with sudden brightness, "I'd like it fine. There's great life in a city."

"You can have it and welcome," said Foley, folding his hands across his paunch.

"Why so?"

"I'm well content where I am."

"But the life!"

"Ah, life be damned! What sort of life is it when you're always under someone's eye? Look at the poor devils in court!"

"True enough, true enough," said Fox.

"Ah, yes, yes," said Delancey, "but the adventures they have!"

"What adventures!"

"Look now, there was a sergeant in court only yesterday telling me about a miser, an old maid without a soul in the world that died in an ould loft on the quays. Well, this sergeant I'm talking about put a new man on duty outside the door while he went back to report, and all this fellow had to do was to kick the door and frighten off the rats."

"That's enough, that's enough!" cried Foley.

"Yes, yes, but listen now, listen, can't you? He was there about ten minutes with a bit of candle in his hand and all at once the door at the foot of the stairs began to open. 'Who's there?' says he, giving a start. 'Who's there I say?' There was no answer and still the door kept opening quietly. Then he gave a laugh. What was it but a cat? 'Puss, puss,' says he, 'come on up, puss!' Thinking, you know, the ould cat would be company. Up comes the cat, pitter-patter on the stairs, and then whatever look he gave the door the hair stood up on his head. What was coming in but another cat? 'Coosh!' says he, stamping his foot and kicking the door to frighten them. 'Coosh away to hell out of that!' And then another cat came in and then another, and in his fright he dropped the candle and kicked out right and left. The cats began to hiss and bawl, and that robbed him of the last stitch of sense. He bolted down the stairs, and as he did he trod on one of the brutes, and before he knew where he was he slipped and fell head over heels, and when he put out his hand to grip something 'twas a cat he gripped, and he felt the claws tearing his hands and face. He had strength enough to pull himself up and run, but when he reached the barrack gate down he dropped in a fit. He was a raving lunatic for three weeks after."

"And that," said Foley with bitter restraint, "is what you call adventure!"

"Dear knows," added Magner, drawing himself up with a shiver, " 'tis a great consolation to be able to put on your cap and go out for a drink any hour of the night you like."

" 'Tis of course," drawled Foley scornfully. "And to know the worst case you'll have in ten years is a bit of a scrap about politics."

"I dunno," sighed Delancey dreamily. "I'm telling you there's great charm about the Criminal Courts."

"Damn the much charm they had for you when you were in the box," growled Foley.

"I know, sure, I know," admitted Delancey, crestfallen.

"Shutting his eyes," said Magner with a laugh, "like a kid afraid he was going to get a box across the ears."

"And still," said Delancey, "this sergeant fellow I'm talking about, he said, after a while you wouldn't mind it no more than if 'twas a card party, but talk up to the judge himself."

"I suppose you would," agreed Magner pensively.

There was silence in the smoky compartment that jolted and rocked on its way across Ireland, and the four occupants, each touched with that morning wit which afflicts no one so much as state witnesses, thought of how they would speak to the judge if only they had him before them now. They looked up to see a fat red face behind the door, and a moment later it was dragged back.

"Is thish my carriage, gentlemen?" asked a meek and boozy voice.

"No, 'tisn't. Go on with you!" snapped Magner.

"I had as nice a carriage as ever was put on a railway thrain," said the drunk, leaning in, "a handsome carriage, and 'tis losht."

"Try farther on," suggested Delancey.

"Excuse me interrupting yeer conversation, gentlemen."

"That's all right, that's all right."

"I'm very melancholic. Me besht friend, I parted him thish very night, and 'tish known to no wan, only the Almighty and Merciful God (here the drunk reverently raised his bowler hat and let it slide down the back of his neck to the floor), if I'll ever lay eyes on him agin in thish world. Good night, gentlemen, and thanks, thanks for all yeer kindness."

As the drunk slithered away up the corridor Delancey laughed. Fox resumed the conversation where it had left off.

"I'll admit," he said, "Delancey wasn't the only one."

"He was not," agreed Foley. "Even the sergeant was shook. When he caught up the mug he was trembling all over, and before he could let it down it danced a jig on the table."

"Ah, dear God! Dear God!" sighed Delancey, "what killed me most entirely was the bloody ould model of the house. I didn't mind anything else but the house. There it was, a living likeness, with the bit of grass in front and the shutter hanging loose, and every time I looked down I was in the back lane in Farranchreesht, hooshing the hens and smelling the turf, and then I'd look up and see the lean fellow in the wig pointing his finger at me."

"Well, thank God," said Foley with simple devotion, "this time to-morrow I'll be sitting in Ned Ivers' back with a pint in my fist."

Delancey shook his head, a dreamy smile playing upon his dark face.

"I dunno," he said. " 'Tis a small place, Farranchreesht, a small, mangy ould *fothrach*[1] of a place with no interest or advancement in it."

"There's something to be said on both sides," added Magner judicially. "I wouldn't say you're wrong, Foley, but I wouldn't say Delancey was wrong either."

"Here's the sergeant now," said Delancey, drawing himself up with a smile of welcome. "Ask him."

"He wasn't long getting tired of Julietta," whispered Magner maliciously.

The door was pushed back and the sergeant entered, loosening the collar of his tunic. He fell into a corner seat, crossed his legs and accepted the cigarette which Delancey proffered.

"Well, lads," he exclaimed. "What about a jorum!"

"By Gor," said Foley, "isn't it remarkable? I was only talking about it!"

"I have noted before now, Peter," said the sergeant, "that you and me have what might be called a simultaneous thirst."

III

The country folk were silent and exhausted. Kendillon drowsed now and again, but he suffered from blood-pressure, and after a while his breathing grew thicker and stronger until at last it exploded in a snort, and then he started up, broad awake and angry. In the silence rain spluttered and tapped along the roof, and the dark window-panes streamed with shining runnels of water that trickled on to the floor. Moll Mor scowled, her lower lip thrust out. She was a great flop of a woman with a big coarse powerful face. The other two women, who kept their eyes closed, had their brown shawls drawn tight about their heads, but Moll's was round her

[1] Ruin.

shoulders and the gap above her breasts was filled by a blaze of scarlet.

"Where are we?" asked Kendillon crossly, starting awake after one of his drowsing fits.

Moll Mor glowered at him.

"Aren't we home yet?" he asked again.

"No," she answered. "Nor won't be. What scour is on you?"

"Me little house," moaned Kendillon.

"Me little house," mimicked Moll. " 'Twasn't enough for you to board the windows and put barbed wire on the ould bit of a gate!"

" 'Tis all dom well for you," he snarled, "that have someone to mind yours for you."

One of the women laughed softly and turned a haggard virginal face within the cowl of her shawl.

" 'Tis that same have me laughing," she explained apologetically. "Tim Dwyer this week past at the stirabout pot!"

"And making the beds!" chimed in the third woman.

"And washing the children's faces! Glory be to God, he'll blast creation!"

"Ay," snorted Moll, "and his chickens running off with Thade Kendillon's roof."

"My roof, is it?"

"Ay, your roof."

" 'Tis a good roof. 'Tis a better roof than ever was seen over your head since the day you married."

"Oh, Mary Mother!" sighed Moll, " 'tis a great pity of me this three hours and I looking at the likes of you instead of me own fine bouncing man."

" 'Tis a new thing to hear you praising your man, then," said a woman.

"I wronged him," said Moll contritely. "I did so. I wronged him before the world."

At this moment the drunken man pulled back the door of the compartment and looked from face to face with an expression of deepening melancholy.

"She'sh not here," he said in disappointment.

"Who's not here, mister?" asked Moll with a wink at the others.

"I'm looking for me own carriage, ma'am," said the drunk with melancholy dignity, "and, whatever the bloody hell they done with it, 'tish losht. The railways in thish counthry are gone to hell."

"Wisha, if 'tis nothing else is worrying you wouldn't you sit here with me?" asked Moll.

"I would with very great pleasure," replied the drunk, "but 'tishn't on'y the carriage, 'tish me thravelling companion. . . . I'm a lonely man, I parted me besht friend this very night, I found wan to console me, and then when I turned me back—God took her!"

And with a dramatic gesture the drunk closed the door and continued on his way. The country folk sat up, blinking. The smoke of the men's pipes filled the compartment, and the heavy air was laden with the smell of homespun and turf smoke, the sweet pungent odour of which had penetrated every fibre of their garments.

"Listen to the rain, leave ye!" said one of the women. "We'll have a wet walk home."

" 'Twill be midnight before we're there," said another.

"Ah, sure, the whole country will be up."

" 'Twill be like daylight with collogueing."

"There'll be no sleep in Farranchreesht tonight."

"Oh, Farranchreesht! Farranchreesht!" cried the young woman with the haggard face, the ravished lineaments of which were suddenly transfigured. "Farranchreesht and the sky over you, I wouldn't change places with the Queen of England this night!"

And suddenly Farranchreesht, the bare boglands with the hump-backed mountain behind, the little white houses and the dark fortifications of turf that made it seem the flame-blackened ruin of some mighty city, all was lit up within their minds. An old man sitting in a corner, smoking a broken clay pipe, thumped his stick upon the floor.

"Well, now," said Kendillon darkly, "wasn't it great impudence to her to come back?"

"Wasn't it now?" answered a woman.

"She won't be there long," he added.

"You'll give her the hunt, I suppose?" asked Moll Mor politely, too politely.

"If no one else do, I'll give her the hunt myself."

"Oh, the hunt, the hunt," agreed a woman. "No one could ever darken her door again."

"And still, Thade Kendillon," pursued Moll with her teeth on edge to be at him, "you swore black was white to save her neck."

"I did of course. What else would I do?"

"What else? What else, indeed?" agreed the others.

"There was never an informer in my family."

"I'm surprised to hear it," replied Moll vindictively, but the old man thumped his stick three or four times on the floor requesting silence.

"We told our story, the lot of us," he said, "and we told it well."

"We did, indeed."

"And no one told it better than Moll Mor. You'd think to hear her she believed it herself."

"God knows," answered Moll with a wild laugh, "I nearly did."

"And still I seen great changes in my time, and maybe the day will come when Moll Mor or her likes will have a different story."

A silence followed his words. There was profound respect in all their eyes. The old man coughed and spat.

"Did any of ye ever think the day would come when a woman in our parish would do the like of that?"

"Never, never, ambasa!"

"But she might do it for land?"

"She might then."

"Or for money?"

"She might so."

"She might, indeed. When the hunger is money people kill for money, when the hunger is land people kill for land. There's a great change coming, a great change. In the ease of the world people are asking more. When I was a growing boy in the barony if you killed a beast you made six pieces of it, one for yourself and the rest for the neighbours. The same if you made a catch of fish, and that's how it was with us from the beginning of time. And now look at the change! The people aren't as poor as they were, nor as good as they were, nor as generous as they were, not as strong as they were."

"Nor as wild as they were," added Moll Mor with a vicious glare at Kendillon. "Oh, glory be to You, God, isn't the world a wonderful place!"

The door opened and Magner, Delancey and the sergeant entered. Magner was drunk.

"Moll," he said, "I was lonely without you. You're the biggest and brazenest and cleverest liar of the lot and you lost me my sergeant's stripes, but I'll forgive you everything if you'll give us one bar of the 'Colleen Dhas Roo.' "

IV

"I'm a lonely man," said the drunk. "And now I'm going back to my lonely habitation."

"Me besht friend," he continued, "I left behind me—Michael O'Leary. 'Tis a great pity you don't know Michael, and a great pity Michael don't know you. But look now at the misfortunate way a thing will happen. I was looking for someone to console me, and the moment I turned me back you were gone."

Solemnly he placed his hand under the woman's chin and raised her face to the light. Then with the other hand he stroked her cheeks.

"You have a beauful face," he said, "a beauful face. But whass more important, you have a beauful soul. I look into your eyes and I see the beauty of your nature. Allow me wan favour. Only wan favour before we part."

He bent and kissed her. Then he picked up his bowler which had fallen once more, put it on back to front, took his dispatch case and got out.

The woman sat on alone. Her shawl was thrown open and beneath it she wore a bright blue blouse. The carriage was cold, the night outside black and cheerless, and within her something had begun to contract that threatened to crush the very spark of life. She could no longer fight it off, even when for the hundredth time she went over the scenes of the previous day; the endless hours in the dock; the wearisome speeches and questions she couldn't understand and the long wait in the cells till the jury returned. She felt it again, the shiver of mortal anguish that went through her when the chief warder beckoned angrily from the stairs, and the wardress, glancing hastily into a hand-mirror, pushed her forward. She saw the jury with their expressionless faces. She was standing there alone, in nervous twitches jerking back the shawl from her face to give herself air. She was trying to say a prayer, but the words were being drowned within her mind by the thunder of nerves, crashing and bursting. She could feel one that had escaped dancing madly at the side of her mouth but she was powerless to recapture it.

"The verdict of the jury is that Helena Maguire is not guilty." Which was it? Death or life? She couldn't say. "Silence! Silence!" shouted the usher, though no one had tried to say anything. "Any other charge?" asked a weary voice. "Release the prisoner." "Silence!" shouted the crier again. The chief warder opened the door of the dock and she began to run. When she reached the steps she stopped and looked back to see if she were being followed. A policeman held open a door and she found herself in an ill-lit, draughty, stone corridor. She stood there, the old shawl about her face. The crowd began to emerge. The first was a tall girl with a rapt expression as though she were walking on air. When she saw the woman she halted suddenly, her hands went up in an instinctive gesture, as though she wished to feel her, to caress her. It was that look of hers, that gait as of a sleep-walker that brought the woman to her senses. . . .

But now the memory had no warmth in her mind, and the something within her continued to contract, smothering her with loneliness and shame and fear. She began to mutter crazily to herself. The train, now almost empty, was stopping at every little wayside station. Now and again a blast of wind from the Atlantic pushed at it as though trying to capsize it.

She looked up as the door was slammed open and Moll Mor came in, swinging her shawl behind her.

"They're all up the train. Wouldn't you come?"

"No, no, no, I couldn't."

"Why couldn't you? Who are you minding? Is it Thade Kendillon?"

"No, no, I'll stop as I am."

"Here! Take a sup of this and 'twill put new heart in you." Moll fumbled in her shawl and produced a bottle of liquor as pale as water. "Wait till I tell you what Magner said! That fellow's a limb of the divil. 'Have you e'er a drop, Moll?' says he. 'Maybe I have then,' says I. 'What is it?' says he. 'What do you think?' says I. 'For God's sake,' says he, 'baptize it quick and call it whiskey.' "

The woman took the bottle and put it to her lips. She shivered as she drank.

" 'Tis powerful stuff entirely," said Moll with respect.

Next moment there were loud voices in the corridor. Moll grabbed the bottle and hid it under her shawl. The door opened and in strode Magner, and behind him the sergeant and Delancey, looking rather foolish. After them again came the two country women, giggling. Magner held out his hand.

"Helena," he said, "accept my congratulations."

The woman took his hand, smiling awkwardly.

"We'll get you the next time though," he added.

"Musha, what are you saying, mister?" she asked.

"Not a word, not a word. You're a clever woman, a remarkable woman, and I give you full credit for it. You threw dust in all our eyes."

"Poison," said the sergeant by way of no harm, "is hard to come by and easy to trace, but it beat me to trace it."

"Well, well, there's things they're saying about me!"

The woman laughed nervously, looking first at Moll Mor and then at the sergeant.

"Oh, you're safe now," said Magner, "as safe as the judge on the bench. Last night when the jury came out with the verdict you could have stood there in the dock and said 'Ye're wrong, ye're wrong, I did it. I got the stuff in such and such a place. I gave it to him because he was old and dirty and cantankerous and a miser. I did it and I'm proud of it!' You could have said every word of that and no one would have dared to lay a finger on you."

"Indeed! What a thing I'd say!"

"Well, you could."

"The law is truly a remarkable phenomenon," said the sergeant, who was also rather squiffy. "Here you are, sitting at your ease at the expense of the State, and for one word, one simple word of a couple of letters, you could be lying in the body of the gaol, waiting for the rope and the morning jaunt."

The woman shuddered. The young woman with the ravished face looked up.

" 'Twas the holy will of God," she said simply.

" 'Twas all the bloody lies Moll Mor told," replied Magner.

" 'Twas the will of God," she repeated.

"There was many hanged in the wrong," said the sergeant.

"Even so, even so! 'Twas God's will."

"You have a new blouse," said the other woman in an envious tone.

"I seen it last night in a shop on the quay," replied the woman with sudden brightness. "A shop on the way down from the court. Is it nice?"

"How much did it cost you?"

"Honour of God!" exclaimed Magner, looking at them in stupefaction. "Is that all you were thinking of? You should have been on your bended knees before the altar."

"I was too," she answered indignantly.

"Women!" exclaimed Magner with a gesture of despair. He winked at Moll Mor and the pair of them retired to the next compartment. But the interior was reflected clearly in the corridor window and they could see the pale, quivering image of the policeman lift Moll Mor's bottle to his lips and blow a long silent blast on it as on a trumpet. Delancey laughed.

"There'll be one good day's work done on the head of the trial," said the young woman, laughing.

"How so?" asked the sergeant.

"Dan Canty will make a great brew of poteen while ye have yeer backs turned."

"I'll get Dan Canty yet," replied the sergeant stiffly.

"You will, as you got Helena."

"I'll get him yet."

He consulted his watch.

"We'll be in in another quarter of an hour," he said. " 'Tis time we were all getting back to our respective compartments."

Magner entered and the other policemen rose. The sergeant fastened his collar and buckled his belt. Magner swayed, holding the door frame, a mawkish smile on his thin, handsome, dissipated face.

"Well, good night to you now, ma'am," said the sergeant primly. "I'm as glad for all our sakes things ended up as they did."

"Good night, Helena," said Magner, bowing low and promptly tottering. "There'll be one happy man in Farranchreesht to-night."

"Come! Come, Joe!" protested the sergeant.

"One happy man," repeated Magner obstinately. " 'Tis his turn now."

"Come on back, man," said Delancey. "You're drunk."

"You wanted him," said Magner heavily. "Your people

wouldn't let you have him, but you have him at last in spite of them all."

"Do you mean Cady Driscoll?" hissed the woman with sudden anger, leaning towards Magner, the shawl drawn tight about her head.

"Never mind who I mean. You have him."

"He's no more to me now than the salt sea!"

The policeman went out first, the women followed, Moll Mor laughing boisterously. The woman was left alone. Through the window she could see little cottages stepping down through wet and naked rocks to the water's edge. The flame of life had narrowed in her to a pin-point, and she could only wonder at the force that had caught her up, mastered her and thrown her aside.

"No more to me," she repeated dully to her own image in the window, "no more to me than the salt sea!"

Patrick Kavanagh (1905-)

Father Mat

I

In a meadow
Beside the chapel three boys were playing football.
At the forge door an old man was leaning
Viewing a hunter-hoe. A man could hear
If he listened to the breeze the fall of wings—
How wistfully the sin-birds come home!

It was Confession Saturday, the first
Saturday in May; the May Devotions
Were spread like leaves to quieten
The excited armies of conscience.
The knife of penance fell so like a blade
Of grass that no one was afraid.

Father Mat came slowly walking, stopping to
Stare through gaps at ancient Ireland sweeping
In again with all its unbaptized beauty:
The calm evening,
The whitethorn blossoms,
The smell from ditches that were not Christian.
The dancer that dances in the hearts of men cried:
Look! I have shown this to you before—
The rags of living surprised
The joy in things you cannot forget.

His heavy hat was square upon his head,
Like a Christian Brother's;
His eyes were an old man's watery eyes,
Out of his flat nose grew spiky hairs.
He was a part of the place,
Natural as a round stone in a grass field;
He could walk through a cattle fair
And the people would only notice his odd spirit there.

His curate passed on a bicycle—
He had the haughty intellectual look
Of the man who never reads in brook or book;
A man designed
To wear a mitre,
To sit on committees—
For will grows strongest in the emptiest mind.

The old priest saw him pass
And, seeing, saw
Himself a mediaeval ghost.
Ahead of him went Power,
One who was not afraid when the sun opened a flower,
Who was never astonished
At a stick carried down a stream
Or at the undying difference in the corner of a field.

II

The Holy Ghost descends
At random like the muse
On wise man and fool,
And why should poet in the twilight choose?

Within the dim chapel was the grey
Mumble of prayer
To the Queen of May—
The Virgin Mary with the schoolgirl air.

Two guttering candles on a brass shrine
Raised upon the wall
Monsters of despair
To terrify deep into the soul.
Through the open door the hum of rosaries
Came out and blended with the homing bees.
                                        The trees
Heard nothing stranger than the rain or the wind
Or the birds—
But deep in their roots they knew a seed had sinned.

In the graveyard a goat was nibbling at a yew,
The cobbler's chickens with anxious looks
Were straggling home through nettles, over graves.
A young girl down a hill was driving cows
To a corner at the gable-end of a roofless house.

Cows were milked earlier,
The supper hurried,
Hens shut in,
Horses unyoked,
And three men shaving before the same mirror.

III

The trip of iron tips on tile
Hesitated up the middle aisle,
Heads that were bowed glanced up to see
Who could this last arrival be.

Murmur of women's voices from the porch,
Memories of relations in the graveyard.
On the stem
Of memory imaginations blossom.

In the dim
Corners in the side seats faces gather,
Lit up now and then by a guttering candle
And the ghost of day at the window.
A secret lover is saying
Three Hail Marys that she who knows
The ways of women will bring
Cathleen O'Hara (he names her) home to him.
Ironic fate! Cathleen herself is saying
Three Hail Marys to her who knows
The ways of men to bring
Somebody else home to her—
"O may he love me."
What is the Virgin Mary now to do?

IV

From a confessional
The voice of Father Mat's absolving
Rises and falls like a briar in the breeze.
As the sins pour in the old priest is thinking
His fields of fresh grass, his horses, his cows,
His earth into the fires of Purgatory.

It cools his mind.
"They confess to the fields," he mused,
"They confess to the fields and the air and the sky,"
And forgiveness was the soft grass of his meadow by the river;
His thoughts were walking through it now.

His human lips talked on:
"My son,
Only the poor in spirit shall wear the crown;
Those down
Can creep in the low door
On to Heaven's floor."

The Tempter had another answer ready:
"Ah lad, upon the road of life
'Tis best to dance with Chance's wife
And let the rains that come in time
Erase the footprints of the crime."
The dancer that dances in the hearts of men
Tempted him again:
"Look! I have shown you this before;
From this mountain-top I have tempted Christ
With what you see now
Of beauty—all that's music, poetry, art
In things you can touch every day.
I broke away
And rule all dominions that are rare;
I took with me all the answers to every prayer
That young men and girls pray for: love, happiness, riches—"
O Tempter! O Tempter!

V

As Father Mat walked home
Venus was in the western sky
And there were voices in the hedges:
"God the Gay is not the Wise."

"Take your choice, take your choice,"
Called the breeze through the bridge's eye.
"The domestic Virgin and Her Child
Or Venus with her ecstasy."

A Christmas Childhood

I

One side of the potato-pits was white with frost—
How wonderful that was, how wonderful!
And when we put our ears to the paling-post
The music that came out was magical.

The light between the ricks of hay and straw
Was a hole in Heaven's gable. An apple tree
With its December-glinting fruit we saw—
O you, Eve, were the world that tempted me

To eat the knowledge that grew in clay
And death the germ within it! Now and then
I can remember something of the gay
Garden that was childhood's. Again

The tracks of cattle to a drinking-place,
A green stone lying sideways in a ditch
Or any common sight the transfigured face
Of a beauty that the world did not touch.

II

My father played the melodion
Outside at our gate;
There were stars in the morning east
And they danced to his music.

Across the wild bogs his melodion called
To Lennons and Callans.
As I pulled on my trousers in a hurry
I knew some strange thing had happened.

Outside in the cow-house my mother
Made the music of milking;
The light of her stable-lamp was a star
And the frost of Bethlehem made it twinkle.

A water-hen screeched in the bog,
Mass-going feet
Crunched the wafer-ice on the pot-holes,
Somebody wistfully twisted the bellows wheel.

My child poet picked out the letters
On the grey stone,
In silver the wonder of a Christmas townland,
The winking glitter of a frosty dawn.

Cassiopeia was over
Cassidy's hanging hill,
I looked and three whin bushes rode across
The horizon—the Three Wise Kings.

An old man passing said:
"Can't he make it talk"—
The melodion. I hid in the doorway
And tightened the belt of my box-pleated coat.

I nicked six nicks on the door-post
With my penknife's big blade—
There was a little one for cutting tobacco.
And I was six Christmases of age.

My father played the melodion,
My mother milked the cows,
And I had a prayer like a white rose pinned
On the Virgin Mary's blouse.

If Ever You Go to Dublin Town

If ever you go to Dublin town
In a hundred years or so
Inquire for me in Baggot Street
And what I was like to know.
O he was a queer one
Fol dol the di do,
He was a queer one
I tell you.

My great grandmother knew him well,
He asked her to come and call
On him in his flat and she giggled at the thought
Of a young girl's lovely fall.
O he was dangerous,
Fol dol the di do
He was dangerous
I tell you.

On Pembroke Road look out for my ghost,
Dishevelled, with shoes untied,
Playing through the railings with little children
Whose children have long since died.
O he was a nice man
Fol dol the di do
We all enjoyed him
I tell you.

Go into a pub and listen well
If my voice still echoes there.
Ask the men what their grandsires thought
And tell them to answer fair.
O he was eccentric,
Fol dol the di do
He was eccentric
I tell you.

He had the knack of making men feel
As small as they really were—
Which meant as great as God had made them—
But as males they disliked his air
O he was a proud one,
Fol dol the di do
He was a proud one
I tell you.

If every you go to Dublin town
In a hundred years or so
Sniff for my personality,
Is it vanity's vapor now?
O he was a vain one,
Fol dol the di do
He was a vain one,
I tell you.

I saw his name with a hundred others
In a book in the library
It said he had never fully achieved
His potentiality.
  For he was slothful
  Fol dol the di do
  He was slothful
  I tell you.

He knew that posterity has no use
For anything but the soul
The lines that speak the passionate heart
The spirit that lives alone.
  O he was a lone one
  Fol dol the di do
  Yet he lived happily
  I tell you.

Louis MacNeice (1907-)

Valediction

Their verdure dare not show . . . their verdure dare not show . . .
Cant and randy—the seals' heads bobbing in the tide-flow
Between the islands, sleek and black and irrelevant
They cannot depose logically what they want:
Died by gunshot under borrowed pennons,
Sniped from the wet gorse and taken by the limp fins
And slung like a dead seal in a boghole, beaten up
By peasants with long lips and the whisky-drinker's cough.
Park your car in the city of Dublin, see Sackville Street
Without the sandbags in the old photos, meet
The statues of the patriots, history never dies,
At any rate in Ireland, arson and murder are legacies

Like old rings hollow-eyed without their stones
Dumb talismans.
See Belfast, devout and profane and hard,
Built on reclaimed mud, hammers playing in the shipyard;
Time punched with holes like a steel sheet, time
Hardening the faces, veneering with a grey and speckled rime
The faces under the shawls and caps:
This was my mother-city, these my paps.
Country of callous lava cooled to stone,
Of minute sodden haycocks, of ship-sirens' moan,
Of falling intonations—I would call you to book
I would say to you, Look;
I would say, This is what you have given me
Indifference and sentimentality
A metallic giggle, a fumbling hand
A heart that leaps to a fife band:
Set these against your water-shafted air
Of amethyst and moonstone, the horses' feet like bells of hair
Shambling beneath the orange-cart, the beer-brown spring
Guzzling between the heather, the green gush of Irish spring.
Cursèd be he that curses his mother. I cannot be
Anyone else than what this land engendered me:
In the back of my mind are snips of white, the sails
Of the Lough's fishing-boats, the bellropes lash their tails
When I would peal my thoughts, the bells pull free—
Memory in apostasy.
I would tot up my factors
But who can stand in the way of his soul's steam-tractors?
I can say Ireland is hooey, Ireland is
A gallery of fake tapestries,
But I cannot deny my past to which my self is wed,
The woven figure cannot undo its thread.
On a cardboard lid I saw when I was four
Was the trade-mark of a hound and a round tower,
And that was Irish glamour, and in the cemetery
Sham Celtic crosses claimed our individuality,

And my father talked about the West where years back
He played hurley on the sands with a stick of wrack.
Park your car in Killarney, buy a souvenir
Of green marble or black bog-oak, run up to Clare,
Climb the cliff in the postcard, visit Galway city,
Romanticise on our Spanish blood, leave ten per cent of pity
Under your plate for the emigrant,
Take credit for our sanctity, our heroism and our sterile want
Columba Kevin and briny Brandan the accepted names,
Wolfe Tone and Grattan and Michael Collins the accepted
names,
Admire the suavity with which the architect
Is rebuilding the burnt mansion, recollect
The palmy days of the Horse Show, swank your fill,
But take the Holyhead boat before you pay the bill;
Before you face the consequence
Of inbred soul and climatic maleficence
And pay for the trick beauty of a prism
In drug-dull fatalism.
I will exorcise my blood
And not to have my baby-clothes my shroud
I will acquire an attitude not yours
And become as one of your holiday visitors,
And however often I may come
Farewell, my country, and in perpetuum;
Whatever desire I catch when your wind scours my face
I will take home and put in a glass case
And merely look on
At each new fantasy of badge and gun.
Frost will not touch the hedge of fuchsias,
The land will remain as it was,
But no abiding content can grow out of these minds
Fuddled with blood, always caught by blinds;
The eels go up the Shannon over the great dam;
You cannot change a response by giving it a new name.
Fountain of green and blue curling in the wind

I must go east and stay, not looking behind,
Not knowing on which day the mist is blanket-thick
Nor when sun quilts the valley and quick
Winging shadows of white clouds pass
Over the long hills like a fiddle's phrase.
If I were a dog of sunlight I would bound
From Phoenix Park to Achill Sound,
Picking up the scent of a hundred fugitives
That have broken the mesh of ordinary lives,
But being ordinary too I must in course discuss
What we mean to Ireland or Ireland to us;
I have to observe milestone and curio
The beaten buried gold of an old king's bravado,
Falsetto antiquities, I have to gesture,
Take part in, or renounce, each imposture;
Therefore I resign, good-bye the chequered and the quiet hills
The gaudily-striped Atlantic, the linen-mills
That swallow the shawled file, the black moor where half
A turf-stack stands like a ruined cenotaph;
Good-bye your hens running in and out of the white house
Your absent-minded goats along the road, your black cows
Your greyhounds and your hunters beautifully bred
Your drums and your dolled-up Virgins and your ignorant
dead.

Carrickfergus

I was born in Belfast between the mountain and the gantries
  To the hooting of lost sirens and the clang of trams:
Thence to Smoky Carrick in County Antrim
  Where the bottle-neck harbour collects the mud which jams

The little boats beneath the Norman castle,
  The pier shining with lumps of crystal salt;
The Scotch Quarter was a line of residential houses
  But the Irish Quarter was a slum for the blind and halt.

The brook ran yellow from the factory stinking of chlorine,
  The yarn-mill called its funeral cry at noon;
Our lights looked over the lough to the lights of Bangor
  Under the peacock aura of a drowning moon.

The Norman walled this town against the country
  To stop his ears to the yelping of his slave
And built a church in the form of a cross but denoting
  The list of Christ on the cross, in the angle of the nave.

I was the rector's son, born to the anglican order,
  Banned for ever from the candles of the Irish poor;
The Chichesters knelt in marble at the end of a transept
  With ruffs about their necks, their portion sure.

The war came and a huge camp of soldiers
  Grew from the ground in sight of our house with long
Dummies hanging from gibbets for bayonet practice
  And the sentry's challenge echoing all day long;

A Yorkshire terrier ran in and out by the gate-lodge
  Barred to civilians, yapping as if taking affront:
Marching at east and singing "Who Killed Cock Robin?"
  The troops went out by the lodge and off to the Front.

The steamer was camouflaged that took me to England—
  Sweat and khaki in the Carlisle train;
I thought that the war would last for ever and sugar
  Be always rationed and that never again

Would the weekly papers not have photos of sandbags
  And my governess not make bandages from moss
And people not have maps above the fireplace
  With flags on pins moving across and across—

Across the hawthorn hedge the noise of bugles,
  Flares across the night,
Somewhere on the lough was a prison ship for Germans,
  A cage across their sight.

I went to school in Dorset, the world of parents
  Contracted into a puppet world of sons
Far from the mill girls, the smell of porter, the salt-mines
  And the soldiers with their guns.

From Autumn Journal

Nightmare leaves fatigue:
  We envy men of action
Who sleep and wake, murder and intrigue
  Without being doubtful, without being haunted.
And I envy the intransigence of my own
  Countrymen who shoot to kill and never
See the victim's face become their own
  Or find his motive sabotage their motives.
So reading the memoirs of Maud Gonne,
  Daughter of an English mother and a soldier father,
I note how a single purpose can be founded on
  A jumble of opposites:
Dublin Castle, the vice-regal ball,
  The embassies of Europe,
Hatred scribbled on a wall,
  Gaols and revolvers.
And I remember, when I was little, the fear
  Bandied among the servants
That Casement[1] would land at the pier
  With a sword and a horde of rebels;
And how we used to expect, at a later date,
  When the wind blew from the west, the noise of shooting
Starting in the evening at eight
  In Belfast in the York Street district;
And the voodoo of the Orange bands
  Drawing an iron net through darkest Ulster,
Flailing the limbo lands—
  The linen mills, the long wet grass, the ragged hawthorn.
And one read black where the other read white, his hope
  The other man's damnation:

[1] Sir Roger Casement, hanged in London on August 3, 1916 for his participation in the rebellion of 1916.

Up the Rebels, To Hell with the Pope,
  And God Save—as you prefer—the King or Ireland.
The land of scholars and saints:
  Scholars and saints my eye, the land of ambush,
Purblind manifestoes, never-ending complaints,
  The born martyr and the gallant ninny;
The grocer drunk with the drum,
  The land-owner shot in his bed, the angry voices
Piercing the broken fanlight in the slum,
  The shawled woman weeping at the garish altar.
Kathaleen ni Houlihan! Why
  Must a country, like a ship or a car, be always female,
Mother or sweetheart? A woman passing by,
  We did but see her passing.
Passing like a patch of sun on the rainy hill
  And yet we love her for ever and hate our neighbour
And each one in his will
  Binds his heirs to continuance of hatred.
Drums on the haycock, drums on the harvest, black
  Drums in the night shaking the windows:
King William is riding his white horse back
  To the Boyne on a banner.
Thousands of banners, thousands of white
  Horses, thousands of Williams
Waving thousands of swords and ready to fight
  Till the blue sea turns to orange.
Such was my country and I thought I was well
  Out of it, educated and domiciled in England,
Though yet her name keeps ringing like a bell
  In an under-water belfry.
Why do we like being Irish? Partly because
  It gives us an edge on the sentimental English
As members of a world that never was,
  Baptised with fairy water;
And partly because Ireland is small enough
  To be still thought of with a family feeling,

And because the waves are rough
  That split her from a more commercial culture;
And because one feels that here at least one can
  Do local work which is not at the world's mercy
And that on this tiny stage with luck a man
  Might see the end of one particular action.
It is self-deception of course;
  There is no immunity in this island either;
A cart that is drawn by somebody else's horse
  And carrying goods to somebody else's market.
The bombs in the turnip sack, the sniper from the roof,
  Griffith,[1] Connolly,[2] Collins,[3] where have they brought us?
Ourselves alone![4] Let the round tower stand aloof
  In a world of bursting mortar!
Let the school-children fumble their sums
  In a half-dead language;
Let the censor be busy on the books; pull down the Georgian
    slums;
  Let the games be played in Gaelic.
Let them grow beet-sugar; let them build
  A factory in every hamlet;
Let them pigeon-hole the souls of the killed
  Into sheep and goats, patriots and traitors.
And the North, where I was a boy,
  Is still the North, veneered with the grime of Glasgow,
Thousands of men whom nobody will employ
  Standing at the corners, coughing.
And the street-children play on the wet
  Pavement—hopscotch or marbles;

---

[1] Arthur Griffith, first president of the Irish Free State (1922).

[2] James Connolly, one of the leaders of the rebellion of 1916.

[3] Michael Collins, one of the leaders in the Anglo-Irish war (1918-1921).

[4] Sinn Fein, the name of a nationalist newspaper edited by Arthur Griffith and the name of a political movement started by Griffith and others in 1905, means in Gaelic *Ourselves alone.*

And each rich family boasts a sagging tennis-net
  On a spongy lawn beside a dripping shrubbery.
The smoking chimneys hint
  At prosperity round the corner
But they make their Ulster linen from foreign lint
  And the money that comes in goes out to make more money.
A city built upon mud;
  A culture built upon profit;
Free speech nipped in the bud,
  The minority always guilty.
Why should I want to go back
  To you, Ireland, my Ireland?
The blots on the page are so black
  That they cannot be covered with shamrock.
I hate your grandiose airs,
  Your sob-stuff, your laugh and your swagger,
Your assumption that everyone cares
  Who is the king of your castle.
Castles are out of date,
  The tide flows round the children's sandy fancy;
Put up what flag you like, it is too late
  To save your soul with bunting.
Odi atque amo:[1]
  Shall we cut this name on trees with a rusty dagger?
Her mountains are still blue, her rivers flow
  Bubbling over the boulders.
She is both a bore and a bitch;
  Better close the horizon,
Send her no more fantasy, no more longings which
  Are under a fatal tariff.
For common sense is the vogue
  And she gives her children neither sense nor money
Who slouch around the world with a gesture and a brogue
  And a faggot of useless memories.

---

[1] I hate and I love.

W. R. Rodgers (1909-)

The Raider

There, wrapped in his own roars, the lone airman
Swims like a mote through the thousands of eyes
That look up at him ironing out the skies,
Frocked and fanged by fire, by nagging fingers
Of guns jagged and jogged, with shell-bursts tasselled.

Does ever the airman's eye, speeding on
To grim conclusion, alight and loiter
Curiously on the country below?
Or does his gaze easily dissolve
Upon the moving surfaces, and flow
Evenly away like rain on rivers?

Or, roaring back over our armoured rims,
Does his mind take in only the bloom and boom
Of bomb beneath him, noting how neatly
It mopped up a map-point town or snouted out
This tip or else that tap-root of resistance?

Yet, pity him too, that navigator
Who now in archipelago of steel
Nears that place where, hooked upon barbed air, he'll
Halt, hang hump-backed, and look into his crater.

Lent

Mary Magdalene, that easy woman,
Saw, from the shore, the seas
Beat against the hard stone of Lent,
Crying, "Weep, seas, weep
For yourselves that cannot dent me more.

O more than all these, more crabbed than all stones,
And cold, make me, who once
Could leap like water, Lord. Take me
As one who owes
Nothing to what she was. Ah, naked.

My waves of scent, my petticoats of foam
Put from me and rebut;
Disown. And that salt lust stave off
That slavered me—O
Let it whiten in grief against the stones

And outer reefs of me. Utterly doff,
Nor leave the lightest veil
Of feeling to heave or soften.
Nothing cares this heart
What hardness crates it now or coffins.

Over the balconies of these curved breasts
I'll no more peep to see
The light procession of my loves
Surf-riding in to me
Who now have eyes and alcove, Lord, for Thee."

"Room, Mary," said He, "ah make room for me
Who am come so cold now
To my tomb." So, on Good Friday,
Under a frosty moon
They carried Him and laid Him in her womb.

A grave and icy mask her heart wore twice,
But on the third day it thawed,
And only a stone's-flow away
Mary saw her God.
Did you hear me? Mary saw her God!

Dance, Mary Magdalene, dance, dance and sing,
For unto you is born
This day a King. "Lady," said He,
"To you who relent
I bring back the petticoat and the bottle of scent."

Christ Walking on the Water

Slowly, O so slowly, longing rose up
In the forenoon of his face, till only
A ringlet of fog lingered round his loins.
And fast he went down beaches all weeping
With weed, and waded out. Twelve tall waves,
Sequent and equated, hollowed and followed.
O what a cock-eyed sea he walked on,
What poke-ends of foam, what elbowings
And lugubrious looks, what ebullient
And contumacious musics. Always there were
Hills and holes, pills and poles, a wavy wall
And bucking ribbon caterpillaring past
With glossy ease. And often, as he walked,
The slow curtains of swell swung open and showed,
Miles and smiles away, the bottle-boat
Flung on a wavering frond of froth that fell
Knee-deep and heaved thigh-high. In his forward face
No cave of afterthought opened; to his ear
No bottom clamour climbed up; nothing blinked.
For he was the horizon, he the hub,
Both bone and flesh, finger and ring of all
This clangourous sea. Docile, at his toe's touch
Each tottering dot stood roundaboutly calm
And jammed the following others fast as stone.
The ironical wave smoothed itself out

To meet him, and the mocking hollow
Hooped its back for his feet. A spine of light
Sniggered on the knobbly water, ahead.
But he like a lover, caught up,
Pushed past all wrigglings and remonstrances
And entered the rolling belly of the boat
That shuddered and lay still. And he lay there
Emptied of his errand, oozing still. Slowly
The misted mirror of his eyes grew clear
And cold, the bell of blood tolled lower,
And bright before his sight the ocean bared
And rolled its horrible bold eye-balls endlessly
In round rebuke. Looking over the edge
He shivered. Was this the way he had come?
Was that the one who came? The whole wieldy world
And all the welded welt that he had walked on
Burst like a plate into purposelessness.
All, all was gone, the fervour and the froth
Of confidence, and flat as water was
The sad and glassy round. Somewhere, then,
A tiny flute wriggled like a worm, O so lonely.
A ring of birds rose up and wound away
Into nothingness. Beyond himself he saw
The settled steeples, and breathing beaches
Running with people. But he,
He was custodian to nothing now,
And boneless as an empty sleeve hung down.
Down from crowned noon to cambered evening
He fell, fell, from white to amber, till night
Slid over him like an eyelid. And he,
His knees drawn up, his head dropped deep,
Curled like a question mark asleep.

The Net

Quick, woman, in your net
Catch the silver I fling!
O I am deep in your debt,
Draw tight, skin-tight, the string,
And rake the silver in.
No fisher ever yet
Drew such a cunning ring.

Ah, shifty as the fin
Of any fish this flesh
That, shaken to the shin,
Now shoals into your mesh,
Bursting to be held in;
Purse-proud and pebble-hard,
Its pence like shingle showered.

Open the haul, and shake
The fill of shillings free,
Let all the satchels break
And leap about the knee
In shoals of ecstasy.
Guineas and gills will flake
At each gull-plunge of me.

Though all the Angels, and
Saint Michael at their head,
Nightly contrive to stand
On guard about your bed,
Yet none dare take a hand,
But each can only spread
His eagle-eye instead.

But I, being man, can kiss
And bed-spread-eagle too;
All flesh shall come to this,
Being less than angel is,
Yet higher far in bliss
As it entwines with you.

Come, make no sound, my sweet;
Turn down the candid lamp
And draw the equal quilt
Over our naked guilt.

Spring

From my wind-blown book I look
Up and see the lazy rook
Rise and twist away,
And from every airy eave
The arrowy swallows wildly leave
And swoop as if in play.

Dark the daw with claw-wing sail
Swings at anchor in the gale,
And in the running grass
Daffodils nod and intervene
Like sud-flecks on a sea of green
Dissolving as they pass.

Mouldy and old the bouldered walls
Wake in the sun and warm their polls
And wag aubretia beards,
The snail-gaze of senility
Silvers each front, and backward they
Break wind and dree their weirds.

Bosoms of bloom that sob like moss
Beneath each jumpy breath, emboss
The bony orchard's breast;
And look, the leggy lilac canes
Are varicosed with ivy veins
Of envy coalesced.

There the hare, bound after bound,
Concertinas all the ground
As far as eye can spy it,
Like a fountain's dying spray
It falls in little frills away
Into a twitching quiet.

Still down the slow opposing slope
The intent ploughman draws his rope
Of parsimony fine,
Nor sees bold Icarus in his haste
Expend his spirit in a waste
Of aerobatic wine.

Icarus from his heady plane
Into depths of spinning brain
Bales out like a ball,
Pulls the ripcord, splits the sack
And lets the spilled silk splutter back
And speculative fall.

And hark, the lark sarcastic sings
To Icarus without his wings
Dawdling down the sky,
Indolent aeons have gone to make
Its gimlet bill, its song-gill's shake,
Its all-containing cry.

Part I

p. 3 *The Viking Terror*. Text in Whitley Stokes and John Strachan, *Thesaurus Palaeohibernicus* (Cambridge, 1903), II, 290.

4 *A Pet Crane*. Myles Dillon, *Early Irish Literature* (Chicago, 1948), p. 156.

4 *The Son of the King of Moy*. *Ibid.*, p. 155. Text in Kuno Meyer, "Bruchstücke der älteren Lyrik Irlands," *Preussische Akad. der Wissenschaften* (Berlin, 1919, no. 7), p. 69.

4 *The Wife of Aed Mac Ainmirech, King of Ireland, Laments Her Husband*. Myles Dillon, *op. cit.*, p. 155. Text in *Thesaurus Palaeohibernicus*, II, 295.

5 *A Love Song*. Myles Dillon, *op. cit.*, p. 155. Text in Kuno Meyer, "Bruchstücke der älteren Lyrik Irlands," p. 69.

5 *The Drowning of Conaing*. Sean O'Faolain, *The Silver Branch* (New York, 1938), p. 66. Text in Julius Porkorny, *A Historical Reader of Old Irish* (Halle, 1923), p. 4.

6 *The Deer's Cry*. Kuno Meyer, *Selections from Ancient Irish Poetry* (London, 1911), p. 25. Text in *Thesaurus Palaeohibernicus*, II, 354.

9 *In Praise of Aed*. Robin Flower, *The Irish Tradition* (London, 1947), p. 27. Text in *Thesaurus Palaeohibernicus*, II, 295.

10 *The Scribe*. Kuno Meyer, *Selections from Ancient Irish Poetry*, p. 99. Text in *Thesaurus Palaeohibernicus*, II, 290.

10 *A Miserly Patron*. Myles Dillon, *op. cit.*, p. 155. Text in Julius Pokorny, *A Historical Reader of Old Irish*, p. 20.

11 *Pangur Ban*. Robin Flower, *op. cit.*, p. 24. Text in *Thesaurus Palaeohibernicus*, II, 293.

13 *The Vision of Ita*. Text and translation in Whitley Stokes, *The Martyrology of Oengus the Culdee* (London, 1905), p. 44. I have made some slight alterations in the translation.

14 *He That Never Read a Line*. Robin Flower, *op. cit.*, p. 46. Text in *Zeitschrifte für celtische Philologie*, IX (1913), 470.

14 *On A Dead Scholar*. Robin Flower, *op. cit.*, p. 43. Text in Whitley Stokes, *The Martyrology of Oengus the Culdee*, p. 198.

15 *The Church Bell in the Night*. Kuno Meyer, *Selections from Ancient Irish Poetry*, p. 101. Text in Kuno Meyer, *A Primer of Irish Metrics* (Dublin, 1909), p. 21.

15 *Starry Sky*. Sean O'Faolain, *op. cit.*, p. 29. Text in *Zeitschrifte für celtische Philologie*, I (1897), 327, ed. Kuno Meyer.

16 *The Desire for Hermitage*. Sean O'Faolain, *op. cit.*, p. 34. Text in *Eriu*, II (1905), 55, ed. Kuno Meyer. O'Faolain has omitted nine quatrains. For a translation of the complete text see Ken-

[1] Unless it is otherwise indicated, the date of publication given for any item in the Bibliographical Notes is the date of first publication.

neth Jackson, *A Celtic Miscellany* (Cambridge, Mass., 1951), no. 34, p. 309.

p. 17 *The Wish of Manchín of Liath*. Kenneth Jackson, *A Celtic Miscellany*, no. 223, p. 308. Text in *Eriu*, I (1904), 39, ed. Kuno Meyer.

18 *The Pilgrim at Rome*. Kuno Meyer, *Selections from Ancient Irish Poetry*, p. 100. Text in *Thesaurus Palaeohibernicus*, II, 296.

18 *Winter Has Come*. Kenneth Jackson, *op. cit*., no. 87, p. 139. Text in Kuno Meyer, "Bruchstücke der älteren Lyrik Irlands," p. 67.

19 *The Ivy Crest*. Robin Flower, *op. cit*., p. 34. Text in *Thesaurus Palaeohibernicus*, II, 294.

20 *Summer Is Gone*. Sean O'Faolain, *op. cit*., p. 55. Text in Kuno Meyer, *Four Old-Irish Songs of Summer and Winter* (London, 1903), p. 14.

21 *May*. Frank O'Connor, *The Fountain of Magic* (London, 1939), p. 19. Text in Kuno Meyer, *Four Old-Irish Songs of Summer and Winter*, p. 28.

23 *A Song of Winter*, Kuno Meyer, *Selections from Ancient Irish Poetry*, p. 57. Text in Kuno Meyer, *Four Old-Irish Songs of Summer and Winter*, p. 16.

25 *To Crinog*. Kuno Meyer, *Selections from Ancient Irish Poetry*, p. 37. Text in *Zeitschrifte für celtische Philologie*, VI (1908), 266, ed. Kuno Meyer.

27 *The Old Woman of Beare*. Frank O'Connor, *op. cit*. p. 9. Text in *Otia Merseiana* (The Publication of the Arts Faculty of University College, Liverpool), I (1899), 119.

32 *I Should Like to Have a Great Pool of Ale*. Kenneth Jackson, *op. cit*., no. 227, p. 313. Text in *Celtica*, II (1952), 151, ed. David Greene.

33 *St. Columcille the Scribe*. Kuno Meyer, *Selections from Ancient Irish Poetry*, p. 87. Text in *The Gaelic Journal*, VIII (1897), 49.

34 *A Storm at Sea*. Robin Flower, *op. cit*., p. 51. Text in *Otia Merseiana*, II (1900-01), 76, ed. Kuno Meyer.

36 *The Praises of God*. Kenneth Jackson, *op. cit*., no. 119, p. 147. Text in *The Gaelic Journal*, IV (1889), 115, ed. Kuno Meyer.

36 *The Blackbird*. Kuno Meyer, *Selections from Ancient Irish Poetry*, p. 100. Text in Kuno Meyer, "Bruchstücke der älteren Lyrik Irlands," p. 66.

37 *St. Columcille's Island Hermitage*. Kenneth Jackson, *op. cit*., no. 222, p. 307. Text in T. F. O'Rahilly, *Measgra Danta* (Cork, 1927), II, 120.

Part II

39 *The Dream of Oenghus*. Kenneth Jackson, *A Celtic Miscellany*, no. 39, p. 99. Text in F. Shaw, *The Dream of Oenghus* (Dublin, 1934), p. 43.

p. 44 *The Boyhood Deeds of Cuchulain.* Tom Peete Cross and Clark Harris Slover, *Ancient Irish Tales* (New York, 1936), p. 137. Text in E. Windisch, *Tain Bo Cuailgne,* Leipzig, 1905.

61 *The Tragic Death of Connla.* Text and translation in Kuno Meyer, "The Death of Connla," *Eriu,* I (1904), 113.

65 *Fand Yields Cuchulain to Emer.* Sean O'Faolain, *The Silver Branch,* p. 86. Text in A. G. Van Hamel, *Compert Con Culainn,* Dublin, 1933.

66 *Cuchulain's Lament for Ferdiad.* George Sigerson, *Bards of the Gael and the Gall* (New York, 1907), p. 119. Text in E. Windisch, *Tain Bo Cuailgne,* p. 597.

68 *The Death of Cuchulain.* Tom Peete Cross and Clark Harris Slover, *op. cit.,* p. 333. Text in Kuno Meyer, *The Death-Tales of the Ulster Heroes,* Royal Irish Academy Todd Lecture Series, XIV, Dublin, 1906.

76 *The Story of Deirdre.* Kenneth Jackson, *op. cit.,* no. 7, p. 49. Text in Vernam Hull, *Longes Mac N-Uislenn,* New York, 1949. Jackson's translation omits some short passages. Hull translates the complete text.

81 *The Colloquy of the Old Men.* Standish Hayes O'Grady, *Silva Gadelica* (London, 1892), I, 94 (text); II, 101 (translation). I use the version of Tom Peete Gross and Clark Harris Slover (*op. cit.,* p. 457) in which modifications in O'Grady's translation are made for the sake of intelligibility and the text shortened by omissions.

95 *The Fianna,* Standish Hayes O'Grady, *Silva Gadelica,* I, 92 (text); II, 99 (translation).

96 *The Headless Phantoms.* Eoin MacNeill, *Duanaire Finn* (London, Irish Texts Society, VII, 1908), Part One, p. 28 (text), p. 127 (translation).

100 *The Bathing of Oisin's Head. Ibid.,* p. 14 (text), p. 111 (translation).

103 *Goll's Parting with His Wife. Ibid.,* p. 23 (text), p. 121 (translation).

105 *Oisin in the Land of Youth.* Michael Comyn, *The Lay of Oisin in the Land of Youth,* ed. Tomas O'Flannghaile (Thomas Flannery), London, 1896. Text and translation.

131 *The Voyage of Bran.* Text and translation in Kuno Meyer and Alfred Nutt, *The Voyage of Bran* (London, 1895), I, 3.

143 *Mad Sweeney.* Text and translation in J. G. O'Keefe, *Buile Suibhne Geilt, A Middle-Irish Romance* (London, Irish Texts Society, XII, 1913), p. 37ff., sections 26-41.

Part III

171 *Lamentation of Mac Liag for Kincora. Poems of James Clarence Mangan,* ed. D. J. O'Donoghue (Dublin, 1903), p. 49.

174 *At Saint Patrick's Purgatory.* Sean O'Faolain, *The Silver Branch,* p. 35. Text in *The Gaelic Journal,* IV (1889), 190.

p. 175 *The Dead at Clonmacnois.* T. W. Rolleston, *Sea Spray: Verses and Translations* (Dublin, 1909), p. 47. First published in *Poems and Ballads of Young Ireland*, ed. W. B. Yeats, Dublin, 1888.

176 *On the Breaking-Up of a School.* Osborn Bergin, *Studies*, XIII (1924), 85. Text and translation.

179 *The Student.* Frank O'Connor, *The Fountain of Magic*, p. 30. Text in T. F. O'Rahilly, *Measgra Danta*, I, 16.

180 *Hugh Maguire.* Frank O'Connor, *The Fountain of Magic*, p. 28.

182 *Civil Irish and Wild Irish.* Kenneth Jackson, *A Celtic Miscellany*, no. 182, p. 236. Text in *The Irish Review*, II (1912), p. 471, ed. Osborn Bergin.

184 *Maelmora MacSweeney.* Eleanor Knott, *The Bardic Poems of Tadhg Dall O'Huiginn* (London, Irish Texts Society, 1922), I, 180 (text); II, 120 (translation).

188 *The First Vision.* The Earl of Longford, *The Dove in the Castle. A Collection of Poems from the the Irish* (Dublin, 1946), p. 13. Text in Eleanor Knott, *The Bardic Poems of Tadhg Dall O'Huiginn*, I, 264.

192 *The Second Vision.* The Earl of Longford, *op. cit.*, p. 18. Text in Eleanor Knott, *op. cit.*, I, 268.

196 *The Good Tradition.* Robin Flower, *The Irish Tradition*, p. 165. The text is unpublished and survives in a manuscript in the British Museum. See Standish O'Grady and Robin Flower, *Catalogue of Irish Manuscripts in the British Museum*, London, II (1926), 6, no. 20.

197 *The Flight of the Earls.* Robin Flower, *The Irish Tradition*, p. 166. Text in *Eriu*, VIII (1916), 191, ed. Eleanor Knott.

200 *Were Not the Gael Fallen.* Robin Flower, *op. cit.*, p. 172. The text is unpublished and survives in a manuscript in the Royal Irish Academy.

201 *Who Will Buy a Poem?* Kenneth Jackson, *op. cit.*, no. 199, p. 265. Text in *The Irish Review*, III (1913), 82, ed. Osborn Bergin.

202 *How Emain Macha Got Its Name.* Text and translation in Patrick S. Dineen, *The History of Ireland by Geoffrey Keating D. D.* (London, Irish Texts Society), II (1908), p. 153.

204 *Loingseach's Horse Ears. Ibid.*, p. 173.

205 *The Death of Curaoi. Ibid.*, p. 221.

208 *Mochua's Riches. Ibid.*, III (1908), 71.

209 *St. Columkille. Ibid.*, p. 87.

214 *Brian Boru. Ibid.*, p. 267.

Part IV

219 *Against Blame of Women.* The Earl of Longford, *Poems from the Irish* (Dublin, 1944), p. 1. Text in T. F. O'Rahilly, *Danta Gradha* (Cork, 1926), p. 4.

p. 220 *Do Not Torment Me, Woman.* Kenneth Jackson, *A Celtic Miscellany*, no. 48, p. 111. Text in T. F. O'Rahilly, *Danta Gradha*, p. 60.

221 *Reconciliation.* Kenneth Jackson, *A Celtic Miscellany*, no. 46, p. 109. Text in T. F. O'Rahilly, *Danta Gradha*, p. 24.

222 *He Praises Her Hair.* The Earl of Longford, *op. cit.*, p. 9. Text in T. F. O'Rahilly, *Danta Gradha*, p. 17.

223 *No Sufferer for Her Love.* Robin Flower, *op. cit.*, p. 150. Text in T. F. O'Rahilly, *Danta Gradha*, p. 10.

225 *Of Women No More Evil.* Robin Flower, *op. cit.*, p. 149. Text in T. F. O'Rahilly, *Danta Gradha*, p. 3.

225 *He Praises His Wife When She Has Left Him.* Text and translation in Robin Flower, *op. cit.*, p. 156.

226 *Dark Rosaleen.* D. J. O'Donoghue, *Poems of James Clarence Mangan* (Dublin, 1903), p. 3. Mangan based his translation on a text published by Samuel Ferguson in the *Dublin University Magazine* in 1834 and attributed to Costello of Ballyhaunis.

230 *Death's Warning to Beauty.* Robin Flower, *op. cit.*, p. 140. Text in T. F. O'Rahilly, *Danta Gradha*, p. 138.

231 *He Charges Her to Lay Aside Her Weapons.* The Earl of Longford, *Poems from the Irish*, p. 3. Text in Patrick S. Dineen, *Danta Phiarais Feiriteir*, Dublin, 1903.

232 *The Harper.* Frank O'Connor, *The Fountain of Magic*, p. 33. Text in T. F. O'Rahilly, *Danta Measgra* (Cork, 1927), I, 7.

233 *The Woman of Three Cows.* D. J. O'Donoghue, *Poems of James Clarence Mangan*, p. 13.

235 *The Reverie.* Frank O'Connor, *op. cit.*, p. 58. Text in Patrick S. Dineen and Tadhg O'Donoghue, *The Poems of Egan O'Rahilly* (London, Irish Texts Society, revised edition, 1911), p. 22.

236 *The Geraldine's Daughter.* D. J. O'Donoghue, *Poems of James Clarence Mangan*, p. 74. Text in Patrick S. Dineen and Tadhg O'Donoghue, *op. cit.*, p. 168.

238 *A Sleepless Night.* Frank O'Connor, *op. cit.*, p. 60. Text in Patrick S. Dineen and Tadhg O'Donoghue, *op. cit.*, p. 26.

239 *A Grey Eye Weeping.* Frank O'Connor, *op. cit.*, p. 62. Text in Patrick S. Dineen and Tadhg O'Donoghue, *op. cit.*, p. 30. O'Connor has omitted three quatrains.

239 *Egan O'Rahilly and the Minister.* Kenneth Jackson, *op. cit.*, no. 187, p. 241. Text in Patrick S. Dineen and Tadhg O'Donoghue, *op. cit.*, p. 262.

241 *The Lament for Art O'Leary.* Frank O'Connor, *op. cit.*, p. 75. Text in Shan O'Cuiv, *Cuine Airt I Laere*, Dublin, 1908, and in *The Gaelic Journal*, VII (1896), 18-23, ed. Osborn Bergin. O'Connor has omitted some verses. For a translation of the full text see Kenneth Jackson, *A Celtic Miscellany*, no. 221, p. 294.

p. 251 *Tara Is Grass. Collected Works of Padraic H. Pearse. Songs of the Irish Rebels and Specimens from an Irish Anthology* (Dublin, n. d.), p. 35. Text in T. F. O'Rahilly, *Burduin Bheaga* (Dublin, 1925), p. 9.

251 *The Convict of Clonmel.* Geoffrey Taylor, *Irish Poets of the Nineteenth Century* (London, 1951), p. 69.

252 *The Midnight Court.* Frank O'Connor, *The Midnight Court*, London, 1945. Mr. O'Connor has altered the text of his translation for the present edition. Gaelic text in *Zeitschrifte für celtische Philologie*, V (1904), 205, ed. L. C. Stern. The poem has been translated also by Arland Ussher (*The Midnight Court and the Adventures of a Luckless Fellow*, New York, 1926).

282 *I Am Raftery.* James Stephens, *Reincarnations* (New York, 1918), p. 75. Text in Douglas Hyde, *Abhrain & Danta*, Dublin, 1933.

283 *The County Mayo.* James Stephens, *op. cit.*, p. 29. Text in Douglas Hyde, *op. cit.*

284 *The Brow of Nephin.* Text and translation in Douglas Hyde, *Love Songs of Connacht* (London, 1905), p. 9.

285 *My Grief on the Sea. Ibid.*, p. 29.

286 *Ringleted Youth of My Love. Ibid.*, p. 41.

287 *I Shall Not Die for Thee. Ibid.*, p. 139.

Part V

289 *The Irish Dancer.* St. John D. Seymour, *Anglo-Irish Literature 1200-1582* (Cambridge, 1929), p. 98. The text is preserved in a 14th century English manuscript and was first published by W. Heuser, "*Fragmente von unbekannten Spielmannsliedern des 14 Jahrhunderts*, aus MS Rawl. D. 913," *Anglia*, XXX (1907), 175.

290 *A Rhyme-beginning Fragment.* St. John D. Seymour, *op. cit.*, p. 92. This and the following selection are preserved in a manuscript in the British Museum (Harley 913) which appears to have been put together and written, in part at least, in Ireland. Of the fifty-two items in the manuscript, seventeen are in Middle English, the others in Latin or Norman-French. Thirteen of the Middle English poems are connected by similarities of dialect and probably are the earliest specimens of the English language as it was written in Ireland. Since one of these bears the name of its author, Friar Michael of Kildare, the whole group has been associated with the Franciscan monastery in Kildare. First published by W. Heuser, "*Die Kildare-Gedichte: die ältesten mittel-englischen Denkmäler in anglo-irischer Überlieferung*," *Bonner Beiträge zur Anglistik*, Heft XIV (Bonn), 1904.

p. 290 *Cokaygne.* Text and footnotes are from St. John Seymour, *op. cit.*, p. 104, and George Ellis, *Specimens of the Early English Poets* (London, 1811), I, 83. See preceding note.

298 *An Anglo-Irishman's Complaint.* St. John Seymour, *op. cit.*, p. 99. The poem is preserved in the Book of Howth, a 16th century manuscript, first published in *Calendar of the Carew MSS in the Archepiscopal Library at Lambeth,* ed. J. S. Brewer and William Bullen, London, 1867-73. Seymour explains "without lease," in the second line, as meaning *without lying, truly,* and construes it as qualifying the next line. But possibly the phrase qualifies the first line of the poem and means "charters of peace" granted *without period of time.*

299 *A Modest Proposal. The Prose Works of Jonathan Swift,* ed. Temple Scott (London, 1925), VII, 207. First published 1729.

308 *Adventure in Cork. The Works of Oliver Goldsmith,* ed. J. W. M. Gibbs (London, 1884), I, 413. Although the authenticity of this letter has been doubted, since the text is based on a manuscript copy of the original, most authorities accept it as genuine. It is undated, but Gibbs suggests 1751 as the most likely date of its composition.

316 *The Croppy Boy.* This version—from Thomas Mac Donagh's *Literature in Ireland* (Dublin, 1916), p. 204—differs slightly from that published by Padraic Colum in *Anthology of Irish Verse* (New York, 1922), p. 103. William B. McBurney's "The Croppy Boy" is an altogether different poem.

317 *Oh, Breathe Not His Name. Irish Melodies and Songs by Thomas Moore,* with an introduction by Stephen Gwynn (London, The Muses Library, n.d.), p. 18. The *Melodies* came out in ten separate parts or numbers, the first two in 1808, the others respectively in 1810, 1811, 1813, 1815, 1818, 1824 and 1834. "Oh, Breathe Not His Name" was first published in 1808.

318 *The Harp That Once Through Tara's Halls. Ibid.,* p. 21. First published 1808.

318 *The Meeting of the Waters. Ibid.,* p. 34. First published 1808.

319 *The Song of Fionnuala. Ibid.,* p. 52. First published 1808.

320 *She Is Far From the Land. Ibid.,* p. 104. First published 1811.

321 *The Minstrel Boy. Ibid.,* p. 129. First published 1813.

321 *Dear Harp of My Country. Ibid.,* p. 170. First published 1815.

322 *The Hedge School.* William Carleton, *Traits and Stories of the Irish Peasantry* (London, 1869), I, 277-280. First published 1830.

327 *A Vision of Connaught in the Thirteenth Century.* D. J. O'Donoghue, *Poems of James Clarence Mangan* (London and Dublin, 1903), p. 94. First published 1846.

p. 330 *To My Native Land*. D. J. O'Donoghue, *op. cit*., p. 107. O'Donoghue estimated the date of first publication as 1832.

332 *The Hunt*. Charles Lever, *Charles O'Malley, the Irish Dragoon* (Boston, 1894), I, 13-29. First published 1841.

348 *The Abdication of Fergus Mac Roy*. Samuel Ferguson, *Lays of the Western Gael and Other Poems* (London, 1888), p. 28. First published 1865.

354 *The Burial of King Cormac*. *Ibid*., p. 47. First published 1865.

358 *The Wedding of the Clans*. Aubrey De Vere, *The Sisters, Inisfail, and Other Poems* (London, 1861), p. 177.

360 *The Fairies*. William Allingham, *Poems* (London, 1850), p. 87.

362 *Aghadoe*. John Todhunter, *The Banshee and Other Poems* (London, 1888), p. 84. "Aghadoe" appeared first in *Poems and Ballads of Young Ireland*, ed. W. B. Yeats and others, which was published earlier in the same year.

366 *The Nameless Dun*. William Larminie, *Fand and Other Poems* (Dublin and London, 1892), p. 35.

367 *The Murrigan*. George Moore, *A Story-Teller's Holiday* (New York, 1929), p. 60. First published 1918 and revised for republication in 1929.

375 *The Rising of the Moon*. Lady Gregory, *Seven Short Plays* (New York, n.d.), p. 75-91. First produced at the Abbey Theatre, Dublin, March 9, 1907.

385 *The Grave of Rury*. T. W. Rolleston, *Sea Spray: Verses and Translations* (Dublin, 1909), p. 19.

386 *Poisson d'Avril*. E. Œ. Somerville and Martin Ross, *Some Experiences of an Irish R. M.* (London, Everyman's Library, 1944), p. 205. First published 1908.

398 From the Preface to *John Bull's Other Island*. *Selected Plays of Bernard Shaw* (New York, n.d.), p. 445-474. First published 1907.

428 *Cuchulain's Fight with the Sea*. *The Collected Poems of W. B. Yeats* (New York, 1951), p. 33. First published 1892 under the title "The Death of Cuchullin" and subsequently revised.

432 *The Folly of Being Comforted*. *Ibid*., p. 76. First published 1902.

432 *To a Shade*. *Ibid*., p. 108. First published 1913.

433 *In Memory of Major Robert Gregory*. *Ibid*., p. 130. First published 1918.

437 *Sailing to Byzantium*. *Ibid*., p. 191. First published 1927.

439 *Leda and the Swan*. *Ibid*., p. 211. First published 1924.

439 *Among School Children*. *Ibid*., p. 212. First published 1927.

442 *The Wild Old Wicked Man*, *Ibid*., p. 307. First published 1938.

444 *The Statues*. *Ibid*., p. 322. First published 1939.

p. 446 *Truth*. AE (George Russell), *Collected Poems* (London, 1920), p. 133.
446 *The Twilight of Earth*. *Ibid*., p. 183. First published 1904.
448 *On Behalf of Some Irishmen Not Followers of Tradition*. *Ibid*., p. 229.
450 *A Prisoner*. *Selected Poems* (London, 1935), p. 128. First published 1925.
450 *The King of Ireland's Son*. Nora Hopper, *Selected Poems*, London, 1906. The poem exists in three different versions. Although that which appeared in *Ballads in Prose*—it was inserted in a prose tale—was published first (1894), Yeats suspected that the longer and inferior version which appeared two years later in *Under Quicken Bows* actually represented an earlier draft of the poem. Still another version—the best of the three and the one which is most frequently quoted—appeared in *Selected Poems*, published the year of the poet's death.
451 *Deirdre of the Sorrows*, Act III. *The Complete Works of John M. Synge* (New York, 1935), p. 249-268. First produced at the Abbey Theatre, Dublin, January 13, 1910.
467 *The Crab Tree*. *The Collected Poems of* Oliver St. John Gogarty, (New York, 1954), p. 48. First published 1927.
468 *Ringsend*. *Ibid*., p. 37.
469 *Exorcism*. *Ibid*., p. 45.
470 *To the Liffey with the Swans*. *Ibid*., p. 49. First published 1923.
471 *Per Iter Tenebricosum*. *Ibid*., p. 191.
471 *Verse*. *Ibid*., p. 3.
472 *To the Maids Not to Walk In the Wind*. *Ibid*., p. 106. First published 1923.
472 *To W. B. Yeats, Who Says That His Castle of Ballylee Is His Monument*. *Ibid*., p. 25.
473 *Leda and the Swan*. *Ibid*., p. 144.
477 *The Old Age Pensioner*. Joseph Campbell, *Irishry* (Dublin, 1913), p. 31.
478 *The Unfrocked Priest*. *Ibid*., p. 44.
480 *I Am the Mountainy Singer*. Joseph Campbell, *The Mountainy Singer* (Boston, 1919), p. 11.
481 *I Am the Gilly of Christ*. *Ibid*., p. 30.
482 *As I Came Over the Grey, Grey Hills*. *Ibid*., p. 49.
483 *I Will Go With My Father A-Ploughing*. *Ibid*., p. 115.
484 *The Herb-Leech*. *Ibid*., p. 119.
485 *The Raid*. Sean O'Casey, *Inishfallen, Fare Thee Well* (London, 1949), p. 44-60.
503 *A Drover*. *The Collected Poems of Padraic Colum* (New York, 1953), p. 84. First published 1904.

p. 504 *A Poor Scholar of the 'Forties.* Ibid., p. 120. First published 1904.
505 *The Wind.* James Stephens, *Collected Poems* (London, 1926), p. 106.
506 *The College of Surgeons. Ibid.*, p. 118.
506 *Check. Ibid.*, p. 170.
507 *The Crest Jewel. Ibid.*, p. 252.
509 *Ivy Day in the Committee Room.* James Joyce, *Dubliners* (New York, The Modern Library, n.d.), p. 148. First published 1914.
526 *Night and Morning.* Austin Clarke, *Night and Morning*, Dublin, 1938.
527 *Tenebrae: Ibid.*
528 *The Straying Student. Ibid.*
530 *An Old Air.* F. R. Higgins, *The Dark Breed* (London, 1927), p. 34.
531 *Song for the Clatter-Bones.* F. R. Higgins, *The Gap of Brightness* (New York, 1940), p. 14.
532 *The Wild Sow.* Liam O'Flaherty, *The Short Stories of Liam O'Flaherty* (London, 1937, 1948), p. 102-106. First published 1924.
536 *A Difficult Question.* Kate O'Brien, *The Land of Spices* (New York, 1941), p. 100-108.
543 *My Grander.* Sean O'Faolain, *Bird Alone* (New York, 1936), p. 17-22.
547 *In the Train.* Frank O'Connor, *Bones of Contention* (London, 1936), p. 59.
563 *Father Mat.* Patrick Kavanagh, *A Soul for Sale. Poems* (London, 1947), p. 3.
568 *A Christmas Childhood. Ibid.*, p. 13.
570 *If Ever You Go to Dublin Town. The Irish Times*, March 21, 1953.
572 *Valediction.* Louis MacNeice, *Poems 1925-1940* (New York, 1940), p. 76. First published 1935.
576 *Carrickfergus. Ibid.*, p. 129.
578 from *Autumn Journal. Ibid.*, p. 212. First published 1939.
582 *The Raider.* W. R. Rodgers, *Awake and Other Poems* (London, 1941), p. 39.
582 *Lent.* W. R. Rodgers, *Europa and the Bull and Other Poems* (London, 1952), p. 34.
584 *Christ Walking on the Water. Ibid.*, p. 42.
586 *The Net. Ibid.*, p. 44.
587 *Spring. Ibid.*, p. 91.

INDEX OF AUTHORS, TRANSLATORS, AND TITLES